THE MAKING OF INDIAN DIPLOMACY

DEEP K. DATTA-RAY

The Making of Indian Diplomacy

A Critique of Eurocentrism

OXFORD

UNIVERSITY PRESS

Oxford University Press is a department of the
University of Oxford. It furthers the University's objective
of excellence in research, scholarship, and education
by publishing worldwide.

Oxford   New York

Auckland   Cape Town   Dar es Salaam   Hong Kong   Karachi
Kuala Lumpur   Madrid   Melbourne   Mexico City   Nairobi
New Delhi   Shanghai   Taipei   Toronto

With offices in

Argentina   Austria   Brazil   Chile   Czech Republic   France   Greece
Guatemala   Hungary   Italy   Japan   Poland   Portugal   Singapore
South Korea   Switzerland   Thailand   Turkey   Ukraine   Vietnam

Oxford is a registered trade mark of Oxford University Press
in the UK and certain other countries.

Published in the United States of America by
Oxford University Press
198 Madison Avenue, New York, NY 10016

Library of Congress Cataloging-in-Publication Data is available
Datta-Ray, Deep K.
The Making of Indian Diplomacy: A Critique of Eurocentrism

ISBN 978-0-19-020667-3

Printed in India on acid-free paper

CONTENTS

CONTENTS

A NOTE ON TRANSLITERATION, TENSE AND USAGE

The method for transliteration adopted in a work spanning Hindi, Sanskrit, Arabic, Persian and Urdu produces its own complexities. It is to avoid cluttering the text that the full set of diacritical marks has been omitted and considerable liberty has been taken with apostrophes. Spellings have not however been altered, hence Abu al-Fazl Allami rather than Abū al-Fazl 'Allāmī and Krsna rather than Kṛṣṇa. Exceptions occur when contemporary authors are quoted, in which case the original spelling has been left intact, as it has been with article and book titles. Similarly, the punctuation and spelling in quotations from English texts—be they translations or originals in antiquated English—have not been tampered with, except for the replacement of 'law' with *dharma*. It is to build on the sense of time that comes with such sources that I use the historic present for those authors I engage in discussion with. Thus 'David Hume and Gayatri Chakravarty Spivak write', but 'Mohandas K Gandhi wrote'. The historic present is however not used for oral data or archival records—including those not in the public domain which I encountered or sought out during the research—since those discussions and documents are presented as evidence. Intended for the benefit of general readers, it is expected that these conventions will not dissuade Indologists. As for usage, it is in keeping with the times and attitudes recorded in this text, and to avoid unnecessary semantic contortions, that terms like 'white' and 'natives'—artificial and derogatory though they are—will be found occasionally in the text. Finally, on occasion I have relied on my family and its archive, and in such cases there is full disclosure.

GLOSSARY OF INDIAN WORDS

-ji	an honorific added at the end of a name
acara	expected conduct (Sanskrit)
adharma	the opposite of *dharma* (Sanskrit)
ahimsa	non-violence (Sanskrit)
akhbarat	Indo-Mughal reports (Arabic)
akhbar nawis	Indo-Mughal intelligence gathering organization (Persian)
Allah-o-Akbar	God is Great or Akbar is God (Arabic)
anrasamsya	non-cruelty (Sanskrit)
antahkarana	individual truth (Sanskrit)
anustubh	a Sanskrit meter for composing epics
asakta karman	non-attached action (Sanskrit)
Asuras	Mythological beings opposed to the Gods
Ayurvedic	a native medicinal tradition
babudom	officialdom
bakshi	Indo-Mughal Paymaster General (Persian)
caste	Hereditary class system not limited to Hindus
casteism	judging on the basis of caste
chaprasi	orderly (Hindi)
crore	10,000,000 (Sanskrit)
dak	post (Hindi)
darogha	manager of an Indo-Mughal department (Mongol)
dastur-ul-amal	Indo-Mughal manuals of governance (Persian)
dharma	most succinctly translated as 'law' (Sanskrit)
Diwan/Duanny	Minister of Finance (Persian)
Diwani	right to tax directly (Persian)
diwan-i-khailisah/ Duan colsa	Minister of the Exchequer (Persian)

durbar	court or levee (Persian)
*dustuck*s	trading permits (Persian)
firman/phird	royal edict (including treaties granted to a supplicatory power) (Persian)
gora	white, a pejorative for Caucasians
gotra	clan (Sanskrit)
Hajj	Islamic pilgrimage to Mecca
*hicarrah*s	messengers (Sanskrit)
Hijri	dates in the Islamic lunar-based calendar, starts in 622 CE
husbul hoocum	letter of concurrence from a minor Indo-Mughal official (Arabic)
huw al-ghani	he is rich (Arabic)
ilchi	Indo-Mughal ambassador (Turkic)
Ingabanga	insider term for Anglo-Bengalis used by their descendants
itihasa	a rendition of the past (Sanskrit)
jahiliya	Islamic concept denoting the condition of ignorance and wrongfulness prior to Islam (Arabic)
jawhar fard	Islamic concept of the first human (Arabic)
jihad	Islamic concept of righteous war (Arabic)
jugar	making do (Hindi)
khil'at	Indo-Mughal robes of rank (Persian)
kufr	Islamic term for unbeliever (Arabic)
kya baat hai	what fantastic news (Hindi)
lakh	100,000 (Sanskrit)
lokasamgraha	holding together of worlds (Sanskrit)
Maharajah	Great King (Sanskrit)
mansab	Indo-Mughal bureaucratic rank of 'the holder of office or dignity' (Persian)
mansabdari	Indo-Mughal bureaucracy (Persian)
mansabdars	members of the *mansabdari* (Persian)
mofussil	provincial district/town (Persian)
mir bakshi	Indo-Mughal Chief Paymaster General (Persian)
mir munshi	Indo-Mughal Commander of the Secretaries (Persian)
mir saman	Indo-Mughal Minister in charge of the imperial household stores, the workshop for producing goods for the palaces and the arsenals (Persian)

moksadar	Indo-Mughal official holding revenue shares from villages (Persian)
mutsuddy	Indo-Mughal accountant (Persian)
moksha	liberation (Sanskrit)
munshi	secretary (Arabic)
Nabob/Nawab	honorific title of Governor bestowed by the Indo-Mughal emperor (Arabic)
Naqshbandis	Sufi group well known for their Sharia-inspired norms (Persian)
Naxal	militant Communist groups (Bengali)
nazr	symbolic tribute to the Indo-Mughal Emperor (Arabic)
Nizam	title for ruler of Hyderabad state (Arabic)
Padshah	emperor (Persian)
palki	Sedan chair carried by men (Bengali)
panch sheel	five virtues for peaceful coexistence (Sanskrit)
peon	office attendant (Portuguese)
prakrti	all existence (Sanskrit)
Puranas	post-Vedic texts typically containing a complete narrative of the universe from creation to destruction (Sanskrit)
raj	kingdom (Sanskrit)
raja	king (Sanskrit)
Rekha	a boundary (Sanskrit)
sadhu	holy man (Sanskrit)
sahib	used in Anglicized Indian locations and meaning 'sir' (originally 'companion') (Arabic)
sal	religiously significant tree of *Dipterocarpaceae* family (Sanskrit)
sarae	travellers' accommodation (Persian)
satyagraha	truth force to resist untruth in a truthful manner (Sanskrit)
satyagrahi	practitioner of *satyagraha* (Sanskrit)
sawanih nigar	Indo-Mughal reporter of events (Persian)
seaw	seal
Sharifs of Mecca	noble/steward of Mecca (Arabic)
sheikh	elder/leader (Arabic)
sudra	low caste grouping (Sanskrit)

sulh kul	Islamic concept of harmony and absolute peace (Arabic)
smrti	genre of remembered truth and hence secondary to *sruti* (Sanskrit)
sruti	genre of revealed truth whose divinity makes it paramount (Sanskrit)
swaraj	self rule (Sanskrit)
vasudhaiva kutumbakam	the world is one family (Sanskrit)
Vizier/Wazir	Indo-Mughal Chief Minister (Arabic)
wakil	Indo-Mughal diplomatic agent (Arabic)
waqi 'a nawis	Indo-Mughal writer of occurrences (Persian)

ABBREVIATIONS

123	Indo-US 123 Agreement
ACSA	Access and Cross-Servicing Agreement
AEA	Atomic Energy Act
APAR	Annual-Performance Assessment Report
BJP	Bharatiya Janata Party
CAT	Common Admission Test
CIA	Central Intelligence Agency
CISMOA	Communications Interoperability and Security Memo-randum of Agreement
DISA	Disarmament and International Security Affairs
DM	District Magistrate
DPS	Delhi Public School
EADS	European Aeronautic Defence and Space Company NV
EAM	External Affairs Minister
EIC	East India Company
FM	Foreign Minister
FS	Foreign Secretary
FSB	Foreign Service Board
FSI	Foreign Service Institute
IAEA	International Atomic Energy Agency
IAS	Indian Administrative Service
ICS	Indian Civil Service
IFS	Indian Foreign Service
IFS-R	Indian Foreign Service-Retired
IR	International Relations (academic discipline)
IIM	Indian Institute of Management
IIM(A)	Indian Institute of Management, Ahmedabad

IIT	Indian Institute of Technology
IPS	Indian Police Service
IRS	Indian Revenue Service
JS	Joint Secretary
LBSNAA	Lal Bahadur Shastri National Academy of Administration
LSA	Logistics Support Agreement
LSE	London School of Economics
MAD	Mutually Assured Destruction
Mb	*Mahabharata*
MBA	Masters in Business Administration
MBBS	First degree to qualify as a physician in India
MEA	Ministry of External Affairs
MFN	Most Favoured Nation
MMRCA	Medium Multi-Role Combat Aircraft
MOS	Minister of State
MOU	Memorandum of Understanding
NAM	Non-Aligned Movement
NFU	No First Use
NOC	No Objection Certificate
NPT	Non Proliferation Treaty
NSA	National Security Advisor
NSG	Nuclear Suppliers Group
PCR	Producer-Centred-Research
PM	Prime Minister
PMO	Prime Minister's Office
PP	Policy Planning
NSA	National Security Advisor
NSAB	National Security Advisory Board
NSSP	Next Steps in Strategic Partnership
PLA	People's Liberation Army
PWE	Protestant Work Ethic
R&D	Research and Development
RAW	Research and Analysis Wing
RIS	Research and Information System for Developing Countries
RPO	Regional Passport Office
RTO	Road Transport Office

ABBREVIATIONS

SAFTA	South Asia Free Trade Area
SB	South Block
SS	Schutzstaffel
UCD	Uneven and Combined Development
SNEP	Subterranean Nuclear Explosion Project
SOFA	Status of Forces Agreement
UPA	United Progressive Alliance
UPSC	Union Public Services Commission
US	United States
VIP	Very Important Person
WWII	World War II

INTRODUCTION

What I want to say here and now is that India is not heading towards catastrophe: India is a living catastrophe and its people, including its intellectuals, know it.

— Paul R. Brass[1]

India is a democracy, by far the best functioning and genuine free system of any of the nations achieving independence following the Second World War. Its ruling group speaks excellent English. The Indian civil service, though extremely bureaucratic and influenced by theories imbibed at the London School of Economics, is one of the most effective in the developing world. Almost all of its leaders have studied in Western universities. Yet Americans have great difficulty in coming to grips with the way Indian leaders approach foreign policy.

— Henry Kissinger[2]

In 2007 Indian diplomats negotiated a treaty that undid decades of what India—to United States (US) officials' surprise—called 'nuclear apartheid', and unravelled a nuclear regime crafted specifically to contain India.[3] This treaty, the 123 Agreement, generated a political crisis that threatened to topple the government—the first time an international negotiation had done so. India's Prime Minister (PM) Manmohan Singh, the arch proponent and principal architect of the deal, faced a triple challenge arising from domestic political opposition, elements of his bureaucracy, and the international community.[4] Singh confronted his challengers and was willing to sacrifice himself if his party did not support him.[5] Faced with Singh's intransigence, which was undoubtedly courageous, his party and Parliament did support him. The US Congress approved the treaty, as did the international Nuclear Suppliers Group (NSG). All

1

of this was possible only because US President George W. Bush was firmly behind the agreement.

A president universally derided for pre-emptive strikes resulting in the quagmires of Iraq and Afghanistan pushed through a deal with a prime minister regarded as spineless—a 'very civil servant' said the former Bharatiya Janata Party (BJP) cabinet minister Arun Shourie.[6] The 123 Agreement arose from a meeting of minds between Singh and Bush at their very first meeting.[7] Over the next few years Indian diplomats worked out how to bring India in from the cold to a nuclear powered fire. The move was opposed almost uniformly, and several Western nations were shepherded by China into opposing the deal. India persisted, and joined the international nuclear community. In return, the US expected payment, but India refused.[8] Moreover, always exceptional in the nuclear debate, India remained unique even upon joining the international nuclear community.[9]

Clearly, India's foreign policy can remake the international order. In two short years, India deconstructed the West's nuclear order diligently fashioned since World War II, broke a Western-led international cartel and secured exceptional privileges for itself. India seeks to reproduce these successes in other fields, to overcome international regimes in trade, the movement of people and the environment, crafted by Western Europe, North America and to the chagrin of China.[10] The reasons for doing this, and the manner in which it is being done, remain inexplicable not only to those India is engaging, but to many Indians themselves. This is evident from the responses to the 123 Agreement. Hostility without was not matched by jubilation within India at the treaty's realization. Rather, it was viewed as a capitulation, the shredding of ethics. Others saw in it the triumph of *Realpolitik*, the inevitable victory of a universal logic over the illogicality of Non-Alignment.

This variety in response is not new. What they reiterate is only that the facts of Indian diplomacy are polysemic and analysts ought to be commended for their diversity in interpretation. What is more interesting than analytical interpretations is however Indian diplomacy, and it, as the very diversity in analysis shows, remains beyond analysts. They remain fundamentally incapable of explaining Indian diplomacy in terms of the practitioners. The result of the rampant failure of analysts to do so is Indian strategic thought being understood as something derived from Europe. To note this makes for an axiomatic insight not found anywhere else: that

INTRODUCTION

Indian diplomacy may be sensible, that is rational, in terms of its practitioners rather than the language of existing analysis. To even contemplate this possibility is to approach the limits of the rationality guiding those who engage Indian diplomacy. It is precisely this threshold that the present work seeks to cross to become an exegesis, with the aid of a defining hermeneutic: producer-centred-research (PCR). That is, a style of searching devoid of the paternalistic sentimentalism that is Liberal (including Marxist, Realist and Global Historians) theorizing, the egocentric fantasia of the postcolonial and postmodern or mechanistic notions of the world being a self-organizing and regulating ecosystem.[11] The failures of all three are evident in their politics, including the politics of analysis. For work in the first camp, their analytic categories apply to all to make for a politics of trusteeship that is really the imposition of order by the powerful. Postcolonial and postmodern analysis swings to the other extreme to make for a politics of hopelessly individuated subjects constantly, at best, sparring with each other. The violence intrinsic to both camps is completely removed by 'Gaia' theories whose cure is to render us all apolitical. In short, the answer to power politics—defined as it is by violence—is no politics, seeing us as part of an automatically regulating ecosystem, cogs in a machine beyond our comprehension, let alone control. In contrast, PCR turns away from dominant models to assume that politics may be possible without violence. This enables, indeed necessitates the second and final feature of the hermeneutic: looking at hard practices of politics with the insight that they can only be made sensible in terms of their producers. Conducting such referencing entailed turning to Indian pasts, as Gayatri Chakravorty Spivak does in her most famous essay, because of 'the accident of birth and education' which makes for 'a *sense* of the historical canvas'.[12] Even if PCR is not familial, my family was instrumental. For instance, this PCR would have been impossible if I were anything but Indian: not because the Government of India (GoI) could care less about my speaking on its behalf, but because this PCR makes requisite mass exposure in a multiplicity of forms to the state, and that would have never have come to pass if I did not have a father whose friends were willing to be leveraged by me.

In the absence of PCR—defined as it is by being open to impossible possibilities and willing to seek them by conducting research on subject's terms—the rationality of Indian foreign policy continues to lie beyond foreign diplomats and the academy. Assuming their competence, they come away either mistaken that Indian practice is derived, or confounded because they never engaged the foreign policy community—the political elite and its base, the Ministry of External Affairs (MEA)—in terms of its rationality. The reason for this failure is reliance on the rationality that is modernity and used by people committed to European Enlightenment ways. Although it is deployed to make India sensible, what it actually makes for is a fluctuation between occluding (rather than revealing) practitioners and practices, and entrapping them within modernity. The corrective is the insight that makes for the PCR. It is essential to apply this hermeneutic to the international, for it is there, increasingly, that the most significant decisions of today are made.

As has already been indicated, PCR is contingent on access. The idea originally came to me while arguing with an MEA officer in South Block (SB), the sandstone edifice located in the heart of British-built New Delhi. He tried to help but failed. Next, at a function where the MEA minister was presiding, I was the first in the scrum trying to claim him once he got up from the podium and said, 'Minister, my name is … my father is Sunanda, and I want to do ….' Though this was our first meeting, Natwar Singh heard me out and said, 'Good. Do it. Speak to my man,' who turned out to be Vikas Swarup. He put me in touch with Syed Akbaruddin, at the time Joint Secretary (JS) Administration, and he told me how to apply and taught me to write in bureaucratese. I did, and simultaneously embarked on 'networking' with the Foreign Service Institute (FSI). However, nothing happened. Meanwhile I learnt from my sources in the MEA that my file had been sent to the Department of Personnel and Training (DOPT)—'a black hole from where nothing can be retrieved,' exploded an officer when he heard. At a loss, I met the PM at his house and again one Sunday evening. As his grandchildren milled about, I explained myself. He asked for 'a proposal', which he gave to his Foreign Secretary (FS). Still there was no progress. Finally, a missive to the PM resulted in his personal secretary and gatekeeper, B.V.R. Subrahmanyam writing that he would retrieve my file and process it because the PM was convinced by the project. It was Subrahmanyam who, in between theorizing about how he worked while demonstrating its practice because I was sitting in front of him, advised me, 'Why do you want to look at files? Files convey only process. Never intent. For that you need to speak to people.' A point repeated by the former National Security Adviser (NSA) M.K. Narayanan.[13] It is intent, that is rationality, that this project seeks to uncover.

Several people have helped refine the work. Apart from the anonymous readers arranged by Hurst and Oxford University Press, Faisal Devji read the script in its entirety while Simon Brodbeck, Gary Feldman, Michael Fisher and Douglas Peers read parts and John D. Smith helped with classical sources. Others advised on the many modern concepts this work engages. Michael Dwyer and his team are to be commended for arranging for co-publishing with Oxford University Press and editing. They worked with what began as a thesis in an inhospitable intellectual climate, ameliorated by my supervisor Fabio Petito. A motley crew of boon companions kept me company including Vegar Andersen, Gustaf Blomberg and Pierre Bartouilh de Taillac. Usman Sajjad Akhtar was ever hospitable. Anna Wojtania remains a living expression of free play. She was there when Sir Stephen Chan and Kees van der Pijl passed the thesis without any corrections.

In-depth exegesis propelled by the present is at the mercy of those being studied. Hence my gratitude to the officers and ministers, frequently amused, occasionally perplexed, who endured me and endeavoured to answer my questions. The majority of the probationers with whom I lived made work seem like pleasure. There would have been no project but for PM Manmohan Singh. Only his personal intervention overcame bureaucratic resistance. Underlying all this was a father's support for, in his words, a 'remittance man'.

Plan of the book

Chapter 1 introduces anarchy, alienation and civilization as the three categories ordering the rationality that is modernity, and used by it to contain Indian diplomacy within Eurocentric paradigms of evolutionary progress. The finitudes of modernity may be measured by its being limited to its own time at the expense of space. As for modernity's offer of a homogenized end free of violence driven by reflexivity, it is exposed as a delusive myth, for systemizers are incapable of transcending the violence produced by the power politics they practice in their own time. These moments of failure are used to create an analytical space to operationalize the hermeneutic that is PCR to explore non-Western ways of being on their terms.

Deploying the PCR in Chapter 2 renders translucent practices at the level of individual diplomats and Indian foreign policy that are inexplicable in modernity's terms. In keeping with the hermeneutic, this exegesis, rather than seeking to fit observed practices into liberal (including Marxist, Realist and Global History), postmodern or mechanistic notions, assumes the conduct of politics and makes its producers, diplomats, the source of theorizing the logic of those practices. This is made possible by the heuristic termed the structure-of-structures. Synonymous with a unified cosmos, it is required not to challenge modernity but, because of its analytical failures, to comprehend what actually happens. This ranges from an inability to manage conceptions of the self and the absence of the 'other' at the MEA to multifarious notions of progress, the manner of progressing. These include not moving towards a destination but transforming it to the origins and speaking in manners inexplicable to the audience. There is also the operation of a reflexivity unfathomable to moderns. Incapable, too, are modernity's pet theories including, amongst others, nationalism and the Protestant Work Ethic. The coherence of these multiple divergences from standard issue modernity is what necessitates the structure-of-structures. Its exegetic power lies in proposing that everything is a variation of the cosmos and making action dependent not on time, but on time-in-space (context). In combination, what is done away with are a host of modern malaises, for instance anomie. The heuristic also permits elaboration of why Indian diplomacy is not in awe of the past, and does not seek to offset desires to the future: rather, it achieves them resolutely by transforming the present. Nor is this achieved in modernity's manner, for what is also laid bare is that the violence endemic to any politics of progress is not the only possibility. Violence—which modernity can only manage by dehumanizing us, by making us cogs in a gigantic machine—is instead managed by the variationality inherent in the structure-of-structures. It is this ability to provide a consolidated explanation for the present without repressing it that converts the heuristic into a rationality.

Chapter 3 explores how this rationality could come to be in what is presumed to be a modern world. Ensuring that modernity did not overwhelm the exegesis is the reason why the answer was sought in practitioner's terms, and they inadvertently offered the *Mahabharata* (*Mb*), which is probed in its terms to uncover a metaphysic explaining the present: *dharma*. With no mention of descent from anarchy, *dharma* posits truthful action, that is, contextual action. Implicit too is another idea of truth as being something abiding: the truth that all contexts produce their own different truths or highest-*dharma*. In combination they make for a rationality alternative, because anterior to them is the interlinking notion of a totally enmeshed society, that is, a unified cosmos making for a fitting context to the structure-of-structures. That this contextualizing is done in terms of time also satisfies modernity, for it knows nothing else. The *Mb* however knows time and space and this is why, though avowedly anti-war, the text dwells upon war. It is understood as a moral impasse and the text is intent on providing a lesson on how to act peaceably. However, the teachings on how to preserve society, for all are expressive of the cosmos, and therefore the right to existence, is undermined by a central contradiction: the *Mb* sanctions the destruction of one seeking to destroy the cosmos, thereby patently undermining the lesson.

Chapter 4, in seeking to explain how today's Indians can possibly play fast-and-loose with modernity in the *Mb's* terms, finds a double inversion of modernity's dynamic. Investigating the till now overlooked diaries left behind by the British, self-proclaimed harbingers of modernity, makes evident that not only did they seek to efface themselves (rather than control and subsume what they encountered), but they also encountered a proto-modern rationality that had already been ameliorated by *dharma*. The result of the Indianization of the Mughals was the Indo-Mughal Empire. Contrary to the claims of modernity, its most successful early envoys sought to dissolve themselves into the pre-existing order. The process was made possible by their practical flexibility, though this was also fundamentally misguided because of their modern rationale. The British were flexibly adapting to something they completely misunderstood because they assumed it had to be not just different, but the polar opposite to themselves. That they were never able to transcend this notion is testimony to the emphasis their rationality placed on time, making their reflexivity incapable of analyzing context, that is learning from actual encounters.

Despite these beginnings, modernity's resounding hyperbole is that it captured and reordered the intellectual circuits of Indian diplomacy. This is why Chapter 5 explores the moment modernity is supposed to have taken root: the colonial period. What is found is that the descendants of the harbingers of modernity continued to display remarkable practical adaptability as they learned pre-existing diplomatic practices and appropriated wholesale Indo-Mughal diplomatic complexes. However, the British superimposed on this their rationality. In other words, what they found was put in service of modernity: diplomacy was converted from a tool to conduct politics now by minimizing violence into a function of the past, intended to achieve a futuristic utopia by an excess of violence in the present. It was the beginning of power politics and this very modern form of diplomacy is, we are told, how India conducts its diplomacy today. Yet, to reiterate, this contradicts the fieldwork, and so Chapter 6 engages the most significant relationship in India's history: that between Mohandas Gandhi and Jawaharlal Nehru. Gandhi's innovations within a tradition of *dharma* and his reconceptualization of violence are captured in the heuristic that is the art-of-politics. Founded on the unified cosmos, the art-of-politics was a means of conduct fundamentally removed from politics. This is because while it must be aggressive, Gandhi's invention made aggression logically impossible. The practical result was *satyagraha*, and it permitted preserving the cosmos while defending it, that is, without falling into the *Mb's* paradox. Though Gandhi was the most excellent practitioner of *satyagraha*, its cosmological basis inhibited him from dictating how to practice it. That had to be decided by the practitioner in context. These developments are traced because their practical significance lay in Gandhi's influence on Nehru, which led to the rebirth of diplomacy by its reconnecting with the cosmos. Having started as a modern, Nehru sought to move towards his mentor: Gandhi. However, modernity precluded Nehru from grasping the intellectual synthesis Gandhi achieved. Instead, Nehru became a principled-Gandhian. What this also meant is that what was the most mundane result of the logic of an alternative rationality was converted into an act of sheer courage, and Nehru was convinced that no one else was capable of the self-control required to practice the art-of-politics understood as principled action. That Nehru steadfastly managed what modernity calls the 'international' in terms of the art-of-politics is evident in the heuristic's ability to resolve analytic failures and inconsistencies in analyses of the most momentous diplomatic events in his time. Indian diplomacy, in short, is rendered explicable only if the integrity of the most significant relationship in India's recent past is restored.

It is to check whether the art-of-politics continued to be the hallmark of diplomacy in post-Nehruvian times that Chapter 7 turns to nuclear diplomacy. A playing field extending across the state, nuclear policy has also been uniquely subjected to both the analytical styles available to modernity, and its practically programmatic analytical-violence is what permits verification. Modern hermeneutics resorts to violence to paper over analytical failure. If, however, the criterion for success is the minimization of analytic-violence, then the art-of-politics non-violently renders post-Nehruvian diplomacy rational. Indeed, so resolutely cosmic is policy that post-Nehruvian strategists, curiously, mimicked not modernity, but Gandhi. In doing so they hollowed out the integrity of the art-of-politics, to convert it from a comprehensive rationale outlawing aggression to something quite dangerously pedestrian. The extent of the danger was exposed when India spoke with the 1998 nuclear tests. What this speech act also exposed was that though India was a subaltern because it was denied the 'lines of social mobility',[14] this did not prevent movement. Progress was possible by creating a liminal zone whereby India spoke in its language which India knew would be misunderstood. This was precisely the aim, because it delivered modernity's inventions arising out of its history of violence, but in terms of India's non-violent rationale. The Conclusion connects the assiduous maintenance of the art-of-politics at the level of the state with the frequency with which diplomats fail personally, to argue for the nationalization of the rationality underpinning practice by incorporating intellectuals on Gandhi's terms. To do so removes the tremendous will required in a modern world to conduct *satyagraha*, by revealing it to be what it is: no more than the logical outcome of a rationality that governs the everyday lives of the sort of people who become Indian diplomats.

Deep K. Datta-Ray   Singapore, June 2012

1

DELUSIVE UTOPIA

The Indian political theorist has a harder task than his Western counterpart. He first of all has to be a good deal more learned, for he is required to know the history of Western political thought as well as the history of Asian thought. He has to be able to reckon with the contributions of empirical political science in the West as well as with the findings of his more empirically minded colleagues in India. And in all this he has to possess an array of linguistic skills that are uncharacteristic nowadays of Western political theorists. Second, he has to sustain a relationship with his Western colleagues in which he takes their concerns with a seriousness they rarely, reciprocate. Thus, a genuine dialogue is for the most part lacking. It is we in the West who are impoverished by our failure to sustain our part in this dialogue.

— Alasdair MacIntyre[1]

Diplomacy is not just the 'engine room' of international relations,[2] it is understood to be the key to social life.[3] Despite this, the people professionally tasked with diplomacy, and diplomacy between the most significant social units in existence, have never been the subject of systematic analysis—much less on their terms.[4] This is particularly the case with works purporting to transgress theoretical models.[5] This lacuna arises from diplomacy being understood in relation to two debilitating assumptions:[6] 'anarchy' and binarism. Combined, they make for a world, anarchical at inception and brimming with irreconcilably alienated actors in opposition. This is 'anarchical-binarism' and it makes diplomacy's purpose the pursuit of unity. This utopian end is to be attained by assimilation, which is an act of violence. The process of first conceptualizing in such

11

terms and then practicing diplomacy within its bounds is the coming of modernity. Having originated in the West, modernity is the fruit of Western civilization. To be a diplomat, then, is to resonate to a tune set by Europe,[7] and the refrain is violence, produced by anarchy, organized binarily and waged both within modernity and by it as it assimilates non-moderns to realize a unified modern society. Moreover, for moderns the study of non-Western diplomacy only elucidates how the 'position on the map' shapes the inevitable battle between moderns and non-moderns.[8] As Iver Neumann concludes after studying and practicing Western diplomacy, diplomatic culture might change but 'it carries with it the memory of its history, and that history is a Western history.'[9]

The problem is not a tyranny of categories imposed on non-Western diplomacy, nor distortion of it by shaping into alien forms.[10] The problem is that the triad of anarchy, binarism and civilization negates the need for the hermeneutic that is 'producer-centred-research' (PCR). Delegitimized is the attempt to find out the non-West's practices, let alone on its terms. To exceed these strictures is to contemplate the unthinkable: verifying modernity's claims it contains Indian diplomacy. Doing so requires collecting data, and not only theorizing from them, but doing so in a manner that does not reproduce modernity while making what is discovered explicable to it. In short, communicating the results of PCR, which is enabled by modernity's civilizational component. This is why there are two contexts to this work: modernity, and—because this work seeks not to impose it on practices observed and theories encountered—a rationale theorized from the subjects themselves.[11]

Modern diplomacy

Modern diplomacy is sanctified by its claim to deliver us from violence. But what actually happens is that violence is rendered perennial, pernicious and acute. This is because moderns assume a state of 'anarchy'. The dominant trope for diplomacy,[12] anarchy remains 'the central fact of the international system and the starting place for theorizing about it,' writes Hedley Bull.[13] This makes for a peculiar understanding of causality: it begins with anarchy. The first to explicitly order his very being in terms of anarchy was Thomas Hobbes who wrote: 'Hereby it is manifest, that during the time that men live without a common Power to keep them all in awe, they are in that condition which is called Warre; and such a warre, as is of every man, against every man.'[14] Given modern's reliance on anarchy, it is not surprising that Bertrand Russell found Hobbes 'the first really modern writer on political theory', an opinion that remains dominant today.[15] Underscoring modern politics, then, is the denial of unity, the presumption of violence and the expectation that actors will be violent.

This deferral to violence is the first aspect of power politics and it is a characteristic of the Westerner, because modernity, which includes its assumptions, makes for a culture. As Bull writes: 'if contemporary international society does have any cultural basis, this is not any genuinely global culture, but rather the culture of 'modernity'. And if we ask what is modernity in culture, it is the culture of the dominant Western powers.'[16]

Modernity is violent and it is the West's culture. It is a 'rationality in the sense of action that is internally consistent with given goals [and] the modern diplomatic tradition embodies an attempt to sustain behaviour on this model.' The model is of course founded in anarchy. Its followers are valorized as an 'elite culture, comprising the common intellectual culture of modernity,' and the elite are elite for they are the ones who, as Bull and Martin Wight note, form a '*corpus Christianorum* bound by the laws of Christ'.[17]

The violence coded into modernity by anarchy is made pernicious by another presumption: binarism. It completes the heuristic of power politics by gearing modernity to seek an end diametrically opposite to the origin: a utopian terminal point, which is an end free of violence. This is 'progress-through-history' or a unilinear teleological way of understanding time. At one end is anarchy and at the other, utopia. This understanding of time too descends from Christianity. Progress, the word itself, derives from the Christian *profectus*, understood as the perfection of the soul, that is, unity with God.[18] The notion recurs throughout modernity, for progress is aspirational, one-way, and the beginning sets the aim. Once again, what actually happens is quite different from the claim. The original deferral to violence between actors is made malignant. The prime explicator of how this happens is James Der Derian. Drawing upon centuries of modernist thought, he replicates it succinctly in the certainty that the history of diplomacy is the history of the mediation of estrangement.[19] Gregory Feldman, upon reading Der Derian, comments: 'European diplomacy's logical frame of reference … is the notion that unity is the natural condition of social order, which should be restored through proper mediation among its divided parts.'[20] At the core of this faith is that unity is presumed non-existent, and Der Derian calls this alienation.

It is unremarkable that Europe assumes modern diplomacy to be a function of alienation, for it is lodged deep in modern society. At its core is the Old Testament which depicts the beginning of alienation with the Fall of man.[21] The New Testament universalized alienation to include the 'brotherhood of man', and mankind is expected to overcome the state of alienation from God through Christ.[22] He represents the binarism orchestrating Christianity, and the gospel of peace is another reminder that unity is the opposite of violence.[23] A mediating figure, Christ legitimized the Papacy in medieval Europe. The Papacy in turn unified medieval Europeans—not politically but intellectually—because they believed. However, the Reformation marked the beginning of the end of the miracle of faith and the growth of states, accompanying the Papacy's decline, necessitated the modern diplomatic system.[24] In this process, sealed by the Treaty of Westphalia, there was a form of intellectual unity because faith was replaced with an intellectual contract: accept modernity's assumptions in an effort to mitigate violence. Precluded, however, is the ultimate aim, that is unity, because diplomacy assumes a bordered world.[25] Diplomacy between states after the end of medieval Christian unity was therefore defined by an intellectual unity, accompanied however by the fragmenting of people into distinct states. Der Derian politely calls this 'second order mediation',[26] thereby cutting out a stupefying paradox: the miracle of faith's replacement by the self-delusion of proclaiming a unity founded on real borders.

The baleful result of these developments is the valorization of violence. David Lake explains this with reference to 'hierarchy'. In anarchy, the leading power, necessarily modern, formulates rules for other moderns.[27] They follow the hegemon because it is coercive. But why does the hegemon coerce? Because it, like all moderns, aspires to utopia and, by virtue of its unrivalled power, views itself as most capable of delivering all to utopia. In short, Christianity aimed at unity with God, and though God was dethroned, the urge to become Godlike remained. Modernity therefore kept to Christianity's aims, translating unity with God into a unified society. What this means is the hegemon's imposition of order through coercion. In short, within modernity, violence remains perennial because of its Christian ordering principles.

It is for the very same reason as the the hegemon's coercion within modernity that its encounter with non-Christian peoples becomes unimaginably violent, because they have to be shown the right way.[28] India provides a practical example of how. Exponents of modernity, like Georg Hegel, decisively grasped how the manufacturing of 'India' had been thought of, and explained: 'Each is for the other the middle term through which each mediates itself; and each is for himself, and for the other, an immediate being on its own accord, which at the same time is such only through this mediation. They recognise themselves as mutually recognising one another.'[29]

At the centre of this conception is the self which knows itself not simply in terms of itself or another, but the 'other'.[30] It is this that led to the 'othering' of India and Hegel was explicit about how it was done. He wrote that 'as soon as he [a European] crosses the Indus, he encounters the most repellent characteristics, pervading every single feature of society.'[31] This repulsion is built into modernity because underpinning the practice of 'othering' is anarchical-binarism, which also makes modernity believe it will deliver us to utopia. Hence, modernity is good and everything else is not. This repulsion from the 'other' also became a technique of the self, the European, to create the illusion of nobility by removing the depraved from within.[32]

It is this particular intellectual archive that leads Der Derian to two critical moments in the history of diplomacy: its birth and its spread. They are 'when the mutual estrangement of states from Western Christendom gives rise to an international diplomatic system; and when the Third World's revolt against Western 'Lordship' precipitates the transformation of diplomacy into a truly global system.'[33] In short, Der Derian believes that anarchical-binarism governs diplomacy today. Modern diplomacy, then, is violence, for there is hierarchical coercion within modernity and when it encounters non-moderns there is even more violence. In both cases the cause of violence is the singularity of anarchical-binarism: the binary understanding of an end free of violence being possible and compulsory because the world is anarchical at inception. What it amounts to is an international project of assimilation by modernity, for it designates itself the only possible route out of the wilderness. This accounts for the West's perennial fear of being unable to assimilate, or of being assimilated by the East. Such an eventuality would be disastrous, for it would terminate the possibility of salvation.[34]

At the core of modernity's assimilative project is time. It orders modernity, but also leaves it open to contestation. Hence, modernity fights a rearguard action by evacuating the possibilities of something alternative ever having existed. The multiple births of non-Western diplomacy are understood to be identical, because to presume they are cast from the same Western mould is also to reinforce the inevitability of the rationality that makes such claims. Modernity, in short, assumes what Orvar Löfgren calls an 'international cultural grammar of nationhood',[35] which delegitimizes all non-modern practices as irrelevant to the realization of utopia. But perhaps even more significant is how the future is conceptualized. The causality programmed by modernity is inserted into actors. Der Derian abandons the post-Christian search for unity with the binary opposite of moderns, the 'other'. Instead, he encourages moderns to reconcile themselves with the fact that they are the 'other'.[36] What this means is that the only way to stop aspiring to unity is to learn that people are irreconcilably alienated within themselves. It is the ultimate victory of modernity, for not only do we inhabit it, we are it![37]

With the past and the future sequestered, all that remains is the present. After assuming that diplomacy was born in Europe, is synonymous with Western civilization and then overcame its 'other', understood as both predecessors and non-Westerners,[38] the next step is to proclaim that nothing exists beyond modernity's time. That is why the seminal authors of diplomacy today are, from Machiavelli to Kissinger, all from Christian societies.[39] They have to be, because 'the modern world system … first came into being in the Italian peninsula and reached its full expression in Europe'. As for diplomatic theory, it 'appeared at the same time as diplomacy began to assume its distinctively modern form in the late fifteenth century'.[40] At any rate, what we have here is modernity, which along with its successor postmodernity[41] makes diplomacy no more than the means to conduct violence to free us from violence. Resistance is therefore futile, for modernity is logical, founded as it is on its own presumptions which privilege time, and its own time at that.[42] This is the 'essence of diplomacy [and it] is unchanged [because diplomacy is] always … promoting and justifying states' interests.'[43] Naturally, these interests are produced by Europe's rationality born to manage the consequences of Christianity's belief system, an analytical stream defined by anarchical-binarism.[44]

The doxology that is modernity encloses not just diplomacy. Indeed it contains entire populations in two ways. Modernity for Dilip Gaonkar is 'everywhere', having 'travelled from the West to the rest of the world not only in terms of cultural forms, social practices, and institutional arrangements, but also as a form of discourse that interrogates the present.'[45] In encountering non-Western cultures, modernity produces 'alternative modernities'. What is maintained is the causality engendered by anarchical-binarism. Its logic is the reason why 'political modernity', regardless of location, is 'impossible' to comprehend, so Dipesh Chakrabarty writes, without first taking on 'the burden of European thought and history', because to become modern requires internalizing Western concepts and categories.[46] Perhaps the vast amount of self-transformation required by Chakrabarty in taking on that 'burden' explains why he is limited to asking: 'How do we think about the global legacy of the European Enlightenment in lands far away from Europe in geography or history?' Although he claims that his purpose is to conceptualize 'forms of modernity that have deviated from all canonical understandings of the term',[47] all he can do is seek variations in the causality produced by anarchical-binarism. In other words Chakrabarty, having made himself a functionary of modernity, assumes that the rest of the non-West too is a carbon copy. Patently this personalistic-theism cannot do.

The pre-eminence of the West is destabilized by Charles Taylor's removal of Eastern deviancy. 'On this view, modernity is not specifically Western, even though it may have started in the West. Instead, it is that form of life toward which all cultures converge ….' The transitions required are inflected by earlier understandings, and so 'change [is] moving from one dense constellation of background understanding and imaginary to another.'[48] It makes modernity the product of the intermingling of two dense cultures. Peter van der Veer investigated this meeting, to assert that 'national culture in both India and Britain is developed in relation to a shared colonial experience' and the means of finding this is to adopt an 'interactional perspective.' Such a method permits 'an escape from the essentialisms of British modernity versus Indian anti-modernity by attempting to lay out fields of historical interaction and encounter, however fragmentary.'[49] Thus a story of modernity formed by mutuality is presented. Though local behaviour is not regarded as deviant and the role of violence is uncertain, such analysis, by its reliance on binary clashes, implicates modernity in the Indian present. Impossible, once again, is the possibility of a non-Western rationality governing the present.

But why is analysis of Indian diplomacy located within these paradigms of dependency? Significantly, many scholars of India are not

Indian, and Rukun Advani says that 'non-Indian scholars', meaning those based in the West, 'aren't really breathing in the air.'[50] But certainly those who migrated from India once did breathe it, and that makes their disconnectedness intriguing. For instance, Sumit Ganguly claims Indians possess a rationality at a minimum different from Pakistan's, but he contradicts himself by falling back on the totalizing rationality of 'realism' to explain not just India, but also Pakistan![51] In the absence of any work on why Indian migrant scholars enclose India in modernity, a hypothesis from a much earlier migrant scholar is offered to explain this confusing morass. Thornstein Veblen sensed via experience that to be an academic in the US is to assume the ways in which the tiny group that is modern academia views the world as universal, 'although it is evident to any outsider that it will take its character and its scope and method from the habits of life of the group, from the institutions with which it is bound in a web of give and take.'[52] In short, migrants give themselves to partake of the new homeland. In their attempt to socialize into the most modern society of all, they have to demonstrate their modernity, and what better way than to do this than to reproduce modernity in their work?[53] What the migrant academic does, then, is buy acceptance by containing the peoples left behind. In short, migrant academics' insecurities about their ability to mimic to assimilate into the host nation—modern as they are—feed nicely into the modernist project of assimilation. There are exceptions of course. They are Indians abroad, for instance, Amartya Sen.

The willingness of the bulk of migrant academics to subsume themselves is a practical example of the contention that the world was not made Western but chose to become so. Choice, however, does not delete modernity's reliance on violence. The argument is that the West, culturally and civilizationally exceptional thanks to its Christian roots,[54] became adept at discovering military technology and made that its diplomacy. The purpose was to assimilate, but the world Westernized itself since it was the only way to challenge domination. The result? 'Western political ambition and competitiveness became universal,' declares Theodore von Laue.[55] The diffusion of this modernity was facilitated by purely cognitive integrations through communications to create a 'world society'. However, Indian reality contests this reading, hence the invention of 'cultural diversity' or the problem of remnants of earlier civilizations, to be assimilated at a later date by the civilization of modernity.[56]

Reflexivity and civilization

Modernity parades reflexivity as its hallmark and as a sign of the utopia to come. It marks the 'threshold of modernity … precisely'[57] because it enables challenging the prevailing order by giving 'rise to an awareness of multiple visions that could be contested'.[58] Reflexivity is the ability to fold back within oneself, one's own tradition, to question and problematize foundational premises, and produce modernity at the expense of engaging with another observes Philip Salzman.[59] This is why tradition is earmarked for elimination,[60] for only that enables 'progress'.[61] But what is missed is that reflexivity produces a highly insular notion of progress as it is based exclusively in one's own evolution. Modern reflexivity, as Salzman demonstrates with finesse, is incapable of transcending one's own time by resorting to space. This inability debilitates progress from learning from others in their time and space. This is ruled out because there is no need for moderns to look beyond their own 'history', since it has led to what is desirable: modernity. This sense of destiny also stops modernity questioning itself, not in postmodernity's insular terms, but by looking at others. Instead, they are to be made modern because it is the road to salvation. Hence reflexivity is deployed in the non-West, where there is no tradition[62] (for modernity has not developed), to destroy and instil Europe's timeline. In short there is no escape from oppositional violence, only modifications of anarchical-binarism within modernity and its imposition elsewhere.

Sudipta Kaviraj's argument about the introduction of reflexivity to the non-modern inadvertently shows why it can be much more than what modernity makes of it. For him, even if the 'single principle' of modernity was introduced and created a 'modern way of doing things', the principle 'is not written on a "clean slate."' Finally, because 'modernity' is defined by reflexivity, it generates a constantly recursive consideration of options and consequently learns from its own and others' experience. Because of the existence of this kind of recursive rationality, it is unrealistic to expect later societies to repeat Western experiences.[63] Although Kaviraj is willing to accept that there was no 'clean slate', the presumption is that reflexivity was introduced. This raises a conundrum: if reflexivity is defined by the ability to take on board something else, then this is precisely what was being done by non-moderns. In short, there already was, at a minimum, a kind of reflexivity enabling the reinscription that moderns glorify, and that undermines this story of dissemination. In short, an Indian reflexivity existed anterior to modernity. Furthermore, modern reflexivity is insular, limited to looking back within itself, never capable of exceeding its own rationality. Yet, non-moderns by taking on another rationality were patently operating on the basis of a reflexivity capable of looking at others in their time and space and taking it on. It is precisely this that is described in Salzman's critique of modern reflexivity, for its very internality fatally undermines it. What is required instead is to look out in space to other times and not just back in one's own time.[64]

Divinely devious, moderns have already closed off this possibility. It is to compensate for the possibility of pre-existing reflexivity that Shmuel Eisenstadt describes modernity as 'a case of the spread of a new civilization of a new great tradition—not unlike the spread of Christianity or of Islam or the establishment of the Great Historical Empires.'[65] But modernity is also 'a mutation of the European legacy into a global pattern.'[66] Eisenstadt's pre-emptive closure, however, cannot silence the question: what is it that modernity encountered? In short, is it 'civilization' or 'civilizations'? Neither answer is satisfactory because the singular implies that all civilizations are heading towards one terminal civilization (which began in Europe) while the plural ignores change through intercivilizational contact.[67] The notion of many civilizations transforming into a modern civilization answers the question, but raises two other questions: does 'a single principle' originating in Europe animate all civilizations, and if not, how do civilizations intermingle?[68] The questions have to be posed to expose that both conceptions of modernity—as a self-contained, complete civilization, imposing its logics on other civilizations and thereby converting them, or as a set of innovations arising from civilizational intermingling, *à la* Taylor—presume that the entire globe is a function of modernity's causality. In short, today is impossible without the West's rationality.

To reiterate, the civilization of modernity presumes violence and the successful use of that violence is the reason why Indian diplomacy is seen as no more than simulacra. Impossible is the possibility of a non-anarchical, non-binary starting point for theorizing and hence ways of being, aspiring and progressing. As for reflexivity, modernity limits it to recursiveness within modernity because there is no need to look beyond that tradition, since despite being earmarked for elimination, it contains the future. To contemplate an alternative to all this is to renounce violence, for it orders modernity. This is not to undermine causality, but to neutralize anarchy and binarism; it is the rethinking of what Navnita Behera calls the, 'foundational knowledge of what constitutes IR'. Next, validating whether practices founded on this are indeed possible requires two acts: 'creating alternative sites of knowledge construction' and investigating them 'with an alternative set of tools and resources.'[69] There are many unexplored sites and the one selected is the Indian Foreign Service (IFS), partly because it is at the centre of a state that moderns insist is modern. Yet the IFS, at a minimum, perplexes moderns. This cognitive dissonance is taken as indicative of the existence of an alternate rationality, and to verify if this is indeed the case, is why PCR is called for, because it investigates the IFS with its tools and resources.[70] This is essential because despite Bull's *Diktat*, this exegesis maintains that rationality is no more Western than perception, thought or language.[71]

Civilized genealogy

Deploying the PCR in this unfamiliar terrain, then, aims to verify if India's diplomacy is contained by modernity structured as it is by the triad of anarchy, binarism and civilization. Verification requires a bridge and 'civilizational analysis' is selected because of its centrality to modernity. Ensuring that this category does not simply slot Indian practice into modernity's timeline is why 'civilization' is understood in the plural. Each civilization is understood to embody a particular culture, understood as what Maurice Bloch calls a 'loose and implicit practical-cum-theoretical pattern networks of knowledge, based on the experience of physical instances',[72] or 'an ideas toolkit'.[73] It is not only 'a phenomenon to be accounted for' but also 'one that accounts'.[74] Civilizational analysis therefore permits PCR's study of the present and explanation of what makes it possible to be presented in terms of the *longue durée*, for this is of overriding concern to modernity.[75]

It is to handle the tremendous durations involved in the study of the *longue durée* that this PCR is organized genealogically.[76] This also ensures PCR is animated not by the past, but by the present. And so, this work is propelled not by Max Weber's question, 'Why has only the West produced cultural developments of "universal significance and value"'[77] but by its reverse: What is India's present and is it Western?[78] If it is, in any way or form, then Weber and his ilk have indeed succeeded in reordering Indian society, but the question is unanswerable without first engaging Indians on their own terms. To anticipate this is to argue that political theory is not an intellectual craft exclusive to a handful of Western thinkers, but is also evident in the practice of Indians. This is why PCR's method entails using Indians as 'authoritative sources' instead of relying on Western intellectuals to interpret Indian practices, something that, as Murphy Halliburton notes, anthropologists refuse to do.[79] But they are only the worst offenders of something endemic. In diplomatic studies, Der Derian writes: 'when shit happens—events that defy conventional language, fit no familiar pattern, follow no conception of causality—I reach for Virilio's conceptual cosmology.'[80] Why not reach out for the people that throw Der Derian's world into chaos? To hypothesize: probably because they would turn his gurus and himself into shit. Therein lies the precise generation of 'alterity', and it fundamentally exposes the compelling and absolutely obvious nature of modernity as no more than pretence.[81]

To permit PCR to follow its own course might also have remarkable consequences for politics as conceived by moderns. To explain in modernity's language, this is an investigation of the 'other': the target for conversion. However, if Indians are not contained by modernity, the category of the 'other' need not exist for them. There might be nothing more than 'another'. To posit this is to a challenge one of modernity's most insidious political projects: cosmopolitanism. Prescribed as a societal ideal and category of analysis, cosmopolitanism epitomizes binarism. Cosmopolitanism promises universalism, but the aspiration is fundamentally debilitated by its 'willingness to become involved with the Other'.[82] Based on Immanuel Kant's proposition of a voluntary pacific federation or cosmopolis composed of many 'others',[83] cosmopolitanism first requires conjuring the 'other' and then making space for that creation. Never conceived was the notion of another rather than the 'other'.[84] The 'other' is implicitly part of cosmopolitanism, it is Der Derian's alienated future now, for we are not only in opposition to others, but wracked with violence within. There is no possibility of a neutral origin making for a variational world, where all are variations of the same and where diplomacy is the means not to assimilate, but to negotiate.

The consequences of a rationality that generates another rather than the 'other' are no less startling when it comes to the politics of modern analysis. Another undermines a field of modern categories used most compellingly by anthropologists and cultural historians. Central is the principle of the 'master'. It animates 'hybridity' or the coming together of 'masters', and was first used by anthropologists describing the 'mixture' of 'pure races' as mongrelized 'hybrids'.[85] A binary concept, hybridity is only possible when the non-modern is assumed to also understand the modern as the 'other'. But there is no need to assume it was so, which also negates 'cross-contamination'.[86] A subset of 'acculturation', it appeals to the notion of Westernization or the wilful destruction of non-Western metaphysics.[87] The very terms and the processes they describe disclose that what is at work here is binarism producing violence, and to analyze in its terms is not to explain but entrap to non-moderns. This is analytic-violence and avoiding it necessitates, at the first instance, ejecting the 'other'.

Doing so is similar to skirting another binary, the false choice between 'macro' and 'micro' analysis. The macros for modernity are 'categories of the human spirit'[88] which define views across time and space.[89] However, these categories are experienced, activated and debated by elites in real life micro situations. Rather than investigate everyone, this PCR studies only those powerful enough to have an impact on a civilizational scale. Hence this work focuses on the apex of India's diplomatic community: the politicians and their base, the IFS. The types of situations they encounter that are of especial interest are 'intercivilizational encounters',[90] not least because modernity claims that in such encounters non-modern intellects were erased and rewritten. It is for these reasons that only the most significant peoples can be the subjects of this PCR. To employ civilization and genealogy as communicative tools does not deter PCR from converting the present into an archive to find out 'in practical terms, what diplomacy is, or where it might be heading'. Significantly, this is possible without being distracted by the modernist obsession with 'how it came into being'.[91] The aspiration to what Michel Foucault calls 'the innermost secret of origin'[92] is a mania peculiar to modernity. Working on the assumption of unilinear progress, moderns seek out genesis as it is supposed to make obvious how everything was programmed. In other words, the world around us is investigated in terms of matters barely conceivable. Instead, causality is maintained in another manner, by studying the present which is after all the sum of all that has passed. Hence PCR.

In other words, the hermeneutic maintains the possibility of Indian diplomacy being not the 'indigenization of modernity', but animated by a metaphysic external to modernity. This could make for a reflexivity unlimited by modernity's timeline. Such a reflexivity may explain not just the incorporation of products, institutions and social forms (that is, the possibilities produced by modernity), but also an impossibility within that rationality: the assimilation of modern rationality itself. In other words, what is being done is that it is being recognised that Indians must have had a metaphysic that made them capable of absorbing modernity. To do so suggests that modernity is being put to an altogether different purpose: furthering not modernization's search for utopia, but a politics incalculable in modernity's lexicon, relying on a diplomacy uninterested in progress understood as assimilation and the violence it relies on.[93] Far from denying causality, the premise is that causality is not limited by modernity's singular focus on its own timeline but also involves extra-modern contexts.

Conclusions

Though liberals Marxists, Realists, Global Historians and postmoderns assert that they follow rival philosophical conceptions, all these presumptions exist on a unifying spectrum, and it is anarchical-binarism.[94] Driven by diplomacy, the aim is to coerce us from anarchy to a point that is its polar opposite: in short, from ourselves. The only alternative is the even more violent aim of making us believe anarchy is intransgressible. Either of these makes for progress-through-history. Some variety in the route is afforded by social constructivists who claim that anarchy is what a state makes of it, but seeking a terminal point remains inevitable.[95] To ignore this is to refute the law that is anarchical-binarism. It amounts to the height of irrationality, for it signifies a turning away from the story of progress that underpins modernity. This entire conceptualization is Western in inception and production. Hence modernity as Western civilization.

However, PCR makes it possible to assume that modern positions—including constructivist assumptions—may be contradicted[96] and also verified, because the state is made of people who may operate independently of modernity. Indeed analytic confusion and violence suggest so. Hence this work seeks 'knowledge of a kind that has never yet existed or even been desired',[97] for such knowledge is what modernity seeks to erase. Operating beyond modernity's monochrome certainties, the hermeneutic may make visible a diplomacy defined by India's technicolour complexities and crowded with untheorizable possibilities. In short the hermeneutic amounts to challenging what Behera calls the 'implicit yet ubiquitous usage of western standards to judge knowledge produced through non-western modes of thinking or at non-western sites of knowledge making.'[98] Such work may be conducted on its own terms, but to communicate it to moderns is to start to erase their misunderstandings and confusion. In short, it is to start the 'genuine dialogue' MacIntyre spoke of.

2

IRREPRESSIBLE PRESENT

There's very little on how today's world actually functions. Instead there is the official story of modernisation.

— Bruno Latour[1]

The East has seen *totality in a far more consistent and systematic way than the West; and India more so than any other civilisation in the East.*

— Christian Godin[2]

Materially, the Ministry of External Affairs (MEA) Headquarters is in South Block (SB) in the heart of British-built New Delhi.[3] Mere physicality however is not indicative of anarchical-binarism, for there is nothing modern about monumentalizing. It is an affliction of government as old as the state. What about organizationally? SB, officers' shorthand for South Block, is at the centre of what is presumed a 'modern nation-state'. However, even if this arrangement was transplanted from Europe, what specifically makes the MEA modern?[4] Modernists tell us it has to be the very rationality for action, which has to assume anarchy, operate binarily and demonstrate reflexivity. All three categories are bound by modernity's timeline, but it, and hence modernity itself, were challenged by an unforeseen insurgency early on in the fieldwork. Rather than dismissing this as symptomatic of the failures of a people aspiring to modernity, the violation is used to unearth the MEA's rationality via what is termed the structure-of-structures. A heuristic device, it is crafted because only it permits exegesis of the practices of the MEA without analytic failure. The structure-of-structures is cosmological because it is neither anarchical nor organized binarily and its origins lie in officers viewing themselves as embedded in a protocol unlimited by modern boundaries and made palpable by interconnecting relations. Deploying this heuristic developed from diplomats to study diplomacy reveals reflexivity, but free of modernist inconsistencies. Indian reflexivity, despite taking on board modernity rather than just its practices, manages to avoid the aspiration to a utopian terminal point. The results are practices beyond modern reflexivity's contradictory insularity. The comprehensiveness with which the structure-of-structures makes sense of Indian diplomats and diplomacy is what converts the heuristic into a rationality.[5]

All this does not deny causality, but makes it far more permissive than modernity, while actually mitigating violence. The structure-of-structures, rather than dismissing, explains by keeping to the contours of India's diplomats and diplomacy how practice manages the present by making it violence free now. In this process, a host of modern categories, most significantly nationalism, become inapplicable. Ubiquitous in its use to explain India, nationalism is understood as primordial or instrumental.[6] The former explains nationalism as stemming organically from an unchanging cultural identity. Indian nationalism is however most commonly understood as instrumentality, the product of elites manipulating the masses to propagate a national identity to suit their own selfish interests.[7] The practices of the Indian state—in terms of the private choices of its functionaries and the state itself—disprove both categories. Yet there is an affinity for the state. Hence there is something, which is reflected better by allegiance to a 'geobody' rather than nationalism for that word is beleaguered by its 'history'. The multiplicity of such errors, spawned by the reliance on base presumptions quite different from the subjects studied, prompts the question: Why does a religiously loaded framework continue to be applied to India?[8]

Managing the MEA

That query, though in urgent need of interrogation, is beyond this exegesis. The MEA, however, is not. Traditionally categorized in terms of modernity rather than the terms of those who compose it, the MEA obliges adoption of a heuristic that does not inadvertently reproduce alien categories. In keeping with the hermeneutic that is producer-centred-research (PCR), the aim is therefore to verify whether modernity contains the practices that make up the MEA, and if not to treat the MEA as an archive capable of providing the means of making rational its practices. The first hint of modernity's inability to handle the MEA is indicated by the multiple narratives of the MEA, by the MEA and for the MEA. Early in the career of an MEA probationer—after selection but before formal confirmation as an officer though this is a given—there is a lecture on the 'evolution' and 'organization' of the ministry. Probationers were told the MEA emerged from the 'creation of the "Secret and Political Department" in 1842'. From this parsimonious introduction, the lecture rapidly moves to outlining the current configuration of the MEA.[9] The MEA's website is similarly sparse, despite pushing the date of modernity's diplomatic birth further back:

The origin of the Indian Foreign Service can be traced to British rule when the Foreign Department was created to conduct business with the "Foreign European Powers". [O]n September 13, 1783, the Board of Directors of the East India Company passed a resolution at Fort William, Calcutta (now Kolkata), to create a department, which could help "relieve the pressure" on the Warren Hastings administration in conducting its "secret and political business". Subsequently known as the "Indian Foreign Department", it went ahead with the expansion of diplomatic representation, wherever necessary, to protect British interests.[10]

To resolve this difference in explanation of origin, I approached the MEA's Historical Division, which provided me with a set of documents, an amalgam of 18th century papers. To my question 'What is this?' came the reply: 'What we give to someone who wants to know our past.'[11] The documents—comprising a thin folder—push the MEA's origins even further back to 1756 when a 'Secret Committee' comprising four members was formed and entrusted with conducting the political and military affairs of the British East India Company (EIC) in Bengal.

Despite some confusion about the origins of the MEA—only to be expected of a people aspiring to modernity's teleology—the three sources locate the institution firmly within the colonial narrative. Indicative of the acceptance of this modern story is a probationer who remarked indifferently, 'the institution was probably set up by them [the British]. Most of these things come from them.'[12] Probationers, like the institution, do not find origins worth talking about. However, intriguingly one probationer, upon prodding, unscrambled these narratives in terms of a purpose inexplicable to modernity: 'You see, we are secular. So a secular history cannot create a timeline going back further. We are so riven with all kinds of things but we are here. This kind of story then becomes the best way of ... you know ... maybe of not causing any problems. In any case you cannot connect institutionally the MEA to older institutions, can you? So for the purposes of an introduction it worked.'[13]

To view the past as the probationer does therefore makes the institutional story a balm that soothes the multitude of differences within the MEA, including those of caste, religion and social status, via the modernist principle of secularism.[14] Entranced by the future, modernity seeks to eliminate the past, but the MEA does not revel in this orgy of violence[15] and so there is no museumification in the MEA. The pre-modern is very much a part of the MEA because it seeks not to construct some homogenized utopian ideal.[16] Instead the purpose of secularism is transformed from a coercive mechanism to create a type of politics, patently not *power politics*, because it is capable of managing difference without seeking to destroy it. This process is highly significant for it requires an appropriation from modernity: secularism. Critically, this is not designed to spur on modernity. Rather, the appropriation refashions secularism to make for a non-modern rather than a homogenized new modern society. In other words, secularism is borrowed to manage a present that continues in terms of a variety of categories from the past. Pre-modern categories do not just persist, they are perpetuated and proliferate at the very centre of the state. And this is because secularism is shorn of its violence. Progress, then, is the maintenance of primordial differences by reducing the scope for violence through the category of secularism. In short, progress is not taming what time produces, but reducing the scope for violence in space. This managing undermines claims of India being motivated by primordial nationalism, for the MEA does not project an artificial cultural unity onto the past, present or future. The very use of secularism is to recognize the diversity of the past that continues to define—and threaten—society today. In short, the pre-modern thrives by borrowing from modernity.

Hence Indians utilize modernity, but it would be an error to read this as the wilful furthering of the modern project. Undoubtedly, secularism in the MEA is reminiscent of the Westphalian system whereby actors contracted (no matter how self-delusively) to coexist, a phenomena known more generally as cosmopolitanism. But further probing unambiguously shows that the MEA's practices of secularism make for the antithesis of modernity. Indeed, in modernity's terms, these are practices of what George Orwell with acuity called 'doublethink',[17] for every time they are enacted they indicate a failure of modernity's reason, since the aim is not to realize a future ideal but to make the present liveable. At play is a shift from acting in time to using time to make the present violence free. To designate the use of time alongside space unreasonable is to view the practice within modernity's rationality: anarchical-binarism. If the exegesis is to avoid considering Indian practice unreasonable, then an altogether different metric for rationality is required, because it is entirely reasonable for Indians to maintain the past in its multihued diversity, rather than create a monotone present. Nor is it unreasonable for them to focus not on the future, but on making the present liveable in technicolour. None of this denies the past, or causality, because no reading by the MEA misrepresented any of the 'facts' of its 'history'. The incalculable in diplomats is that modernity's linear causality is not taken to its inevitable conclusion. Rather, 'progress-through-history' is transformed into a tool of the present by the smuggling in of secularism, from the inventory of another intellectual order altogether.[18]

This appropriation and refashioning are suggestive of the contention that the MEA lies in a zone unavailable to moderns, for what is at work here is not just time, but time-in-space. This can only be recognized if indigenous practices are viewed for what they are rather than through the plethora of domineering notions valorized by moderns. Wilhelm Halbfass, for instance, writes: 'Modern Indian thought finds itself in a historical context created by Europe, and it has difficulties speaking for itself. Even in its self-representation and self-assertion, it speaks to a large extent in the European idiom.'[19] Halbfass is wrong because the idiom is a veneer appropriated by an alternate rationality that, in turn, is actually inexplicable in the appropriated idiom.

Of a different qualitative order, indigenous time management presents a threshold for modernist thought. Extending beyond it is the MEA's rationality and a reflexivity that by being cognisant of the past (expressed in space) meets the modernist criteria for reflexivity. However, the MEA's reflexivity seeks to maintain the past in the present but also to alter it. Hence there is another refutation of modernity's itinerary. Seeking to explain such alternate habits, analysts have turned their gaze to the 'subaltern', to locate the moments when they were silenced. But recognizing how alterity was snuffed out is a painstaking manner of recovering those moments. Furthermore, such exertions are rendered superfluous by the insight that non-moderns may exist today. This is why the emphasis is being shifted back to the present. At the very least this exposes the extent of modernity's grip on Indians. But the prize on offer is far greater. It is the tantalizing possibility of conversing with alterity, as has just been done with the 'secular' probationer.

Ever present, though, is the spectre of being entrapped by modernity's analytical limits, a causality limited to modernity's time. This danger was exposed in the clash between 'postcolonial studies' and the 'Cambridge School' represented by Gyan Prakash, Rosalind O'Hanlon and David Washbrook.[20] For Prakash, India is known through the reference points of modernity: objectivity and progress.[21] Modernity in India is insidious and pervasive, even today anthropologists search for it and are incredulous at encountering 'hyper-examples' of it. But this is because anthropological approaches reproduce disciplinary understandings of what progress is, which in turn arise from modernist premises, and these are then foisted on subjects.[22] Prakash's solution is to eliminate this teleology by conceptually discounting 'progress', never defining the subject and retreating into known archives to reread them for silences.[23] O'Hanlon, Prakash's perfect 'other', counters that categorization—based on known categories—is imperative to conduct analysis. The purpose is not to constrict the subject, but to free it from known forms of oppression such as capitalism and social ills: in short, to induce progress. Neither the postcolonial nor the liberal-Marxist-Realist approach is satisfactory. Prakash refutes the possibility of subalterns possessing self-defined concepts of 'progress',[24] while O'Hanlon imposes a totalizing understanding of 'progress'. One denies the subaltern progress while the other enmeshes the subaltern in the narrow teleology that is progress-through-history.

Paradoxically, Prakash's postcolonial nihilism and O'Hanlon's distorting liberal contribution meet in the realm of method. It unifies the two and analogically provides the means of handling the MEA.[25] After all, Prakash invites the Cambridge School's wrath because he proceeds in such a logical manner.[26] He reads sources to conclude that changes in the presentation of India over time mean that Indians cannot be fixed.[27] This insight is used to argue for the overturning of modernity's objectivity, which attempts to ossify Indians in a particular way, and for a method of writing (mythography) that seeks to represent alterity by not claiming permanence.[28] However, Prakash then commits the same category error as O'Hanlon, but in reverse. He denies his subjects the possibility of alternate notions of progress and permanence within the zones delineated by the subject.[29] In short, Prakash seeks to break out of modernity's causality, but ends up denying causality altogether. Yet causality is capable, but it can only be understood in terms that emerge from the self-delineated milieus of the people being studied.

These are precisely what the PCR uses as the optic of depiction, because representation is stable within self-delineated zones. Since this PCR adopts them from the MEA, this exegesis does not impose an alien causality. Nor does such an optic predicate against generalization about the Indian state, because the micro-macro 'conjuncture'[30] is individual-state—since the subjects of this work, unlike any other when it comes to studying the Indian state, are those who are animating it now. The combination of the subject matter with the optic is what ensures that this work is not petrified by 'incredulity towards meta-narratives', for if the data are messy or contradictory, it is not because of any failure of the MEA's reason but because of the misapplication of reason due to an imposition of alien categories:[31] in short, my inability to limit contamination of observed practices by modernity. This is also why the work on occasion reflects on myself via the subjects.

To access the centre of what is presumed by modernists to be modernity, I had to secure an unprecedented attachment for fourteen months with the MEA in New Delhi.[32] During the attachment nearly seventy civil servants, mainly diplomats, were interviewed at all levels, and there were conversations with the National Security Adviser (NSA) and the Foreign Secretary (FS). The number takes on significance because the IFS remains a small organization—at the time approximately 600 strong (and now around 760).[33] There were also extensive conversations with several cabinet ministers including the External Affairs Minister (EAM), that is, the Foreign Minister (FM), and the Prime Minister (PM).[34] This was done while living with diplomats, accompanying them on their training, teaching them, socializing with them and investigating what few MEA archives were opened to me. There was also a short visit to the Lal Bahadur Shastri National Academy of Administration (LBSNAA, or La-bas-naa as probationers, despite being told not to, called it) where all civil servants are trained and where members of the Indian Administrative Service (IAS), Indian Police Service (IPS) and Indian Revenue Service

(IRS), including Customs and Excise, were interviewed. All conversations and interviews require 'supplementary evidence about their provenance and purpose'.[35] This called for triangulating the information presented, with other renditions and where possible against documents and on occasion by travelling with diplomats and other officers both within and beyond New Delhi, to homes and weddings. The officers and others who spoke to me must however remain anonymous because, while they were perfectly frank, revealing them in any manner might compromise their engagements with the Weberian foreign ministries of the West who insist on deleting the personal from their officers—or at any rate claim to do so.[36]

In contrast, Indian diplomats view the world in terms of themselves and mediate within themselves a (civilizational) complex called 'many Indias', reflective of a past thriving in the present. Though disparate and contradictory, these 'Indias' are all located by diplomats within the sociopolitical unit, the geobody that is India, because that too is quite real for them.[37] Hence this work is sometimes guilty of what modernists call 'methodological nationalism' because one of the contexts for the people in this study is the state, indeed they are the state, but as will become quickly apparent, this is a state unlike anything conceptualized by the inventors of 'nationalism'.[38] Guilt about 'nationalism' is of course a by-product of the way it has been conceptualized by modernists, hence the turn to geobody. However, as the exegesis will demonstrate, taking a modicum of note of the people who compose the Indian state eliminates the logic of nationalism. In other words, this exegesis seeks to operate within the MEA's contexts. In doing so, this is also a space outside modernity, not because of uniquely Indian specificities, but because this exegesis is construed in the categories of the practitioners and these are intolerable to anarchical-binarism.[39] One context is time management, which is indicative of something broader and already known to International Relations (IR), making modernity's refusal to acknowledge it all the more astounding.

The structure-of-structures

Evidently, Indian time management presents a horizon for modernity. The 'secular' probationer's transgression is therefore taken as the key to developing a structural reading capable of handling the MEA. This is the structure-of-structures. It is a unified cosmos and is not altogether unknown to modernity as a heuristic device. Arlene Tickner writes:

Contrary to the Western model of universality which is premised upon a self-other binary in which the other's agency and identity must necessarily be negated, Hindu culture's universality does not require the suppression of difference, given that each of the particularistic identities that comprise it are viewed as legitimate and equal parts of a unified whole.[40]

The unified whole is the cosmos to which everything belongs, so that everything is a variation of a theme: the cosmos. As everything is an expression of the cosmos, existence itself is the virtue legitimizing each constituent part.[41] Nothing can be produced just by time or just by space. Nothing *a priori* has *a priori* significance within the cosmos, and that applies to time and space, because they are a part of the cosmos. Time and space exist within the cosmos and may combine to produce elements willing to overrule time, space or even the cosmos, to further some imperative arising from either, or the intersection of time and space. However, overcoming or eliminating elements is self-destructive since everything is a manifestation of the cosmos and so everything is like one. Or to put it inversely, one is like everyone else—and identical if two elements were produced in the same time and space. Of course nothing is. The most fundamental implication is the delegitimation of violence by the realization that everything is a variation of the theme, and that is the cosmos. In short, there is no 'other' in the cosmos, only another.

The introduction of space as an equal to time has other implications. Causality is generated in a far more complex manner than than is possible within modernity. It emphasizes the past and the future but never the present, which is only instrumental. In the cosmos, however, the present becomes the site for politics because of the dual operation of time and space, which makes for context. The cosmos also enables a far broader repertoire of practices than in modernity. In it all practices are geared to a unilinear highway from the state of nature to utopia, whereas in the cosmos origins and ends may very well overlap because the origin is simply the cosmos. This means that practices may have a destination but they are a part of the cosmos and thus not in any sense attempting to move beyond the cosmos. In other words, all action is in keeping with the cosmos. Causality is therefore a function of the origin but makes itself apparent in space, since all spaces are expressive of the sum total of the cosmos. This is why the emphasis for action shifts to context, for it is here that the origin is made apparent. There is thus no need to secure origins, for instead of the past dictating the future, the context, that is the present, provides the terrain where past and future are laid bare, thereby making it the preeminent site for all action.

Mohandas Gandhi expressed all of this far more succinctly in saying: 'The winking of the eyelids does not need to be willed, there must be some disease if it is otherwise.'[42] The body as cosmos is perfect, and all is in consonance with it. The very neutrality of the origin ensures this. However, it is quite wrong to think there is no right way of acting. The very notion of the cosmos makes it inevitable that violence should be abjured. Hence the need for a politics neither indebted to the past nor in hope of a future, for all that results in is progress-through-history or the sanctioning of violence now on the basis of some past authority to realize a future goal: in short, *power politics* What the cosmos sanctions instead is a politics informed by the realization that causality does not entrap because it is the cosmos in operation. It is both time and space made evident now, hence the focus of action is not only the present, but the emphasis lies on it being non-violent to maintain everything in the cosmos and therefore the cosmos itself.

Such a politics also makes for a form of exegesis that may be delineated by the dilemma of why the cosmological can explain modernity, but it cannot. What is an impasse for moderns is resolved by cosmological exegesis because of time and space. In conjunction, they affected a part of the cosmos to produce a variation in the cosmos, the socio-religious experience of the West which, having encountered Christianity, concluded that man was once unified with God but is now alienated, so that man for ever aspires to unity.[43] Indeed this was the birth of modernity, which 'arose in Europe out of a debate over the question of the place of God and the sacred axiology in the world-view and the life-world of man'.[44] In a cosmological view, Christianity automated a group within the cosmos to see themselves as alienated from God and each other, and hence always seeking unity. This process is a binary one that repeats itself within the modernist process, which is also why modernity cannot. For moderns, there is only seeking programmed by the origin and it makes space a function of time. Evidently this is exceeded by the cosmos where there is more than time; there is also space. The key is the duality of time and space and it is precisely the missing of space that leaves moderns incapable of grasping the cosmos.

This supersession of the cosmos beyond modernity offers a way of operating untheorized by, and frankly inexplicable to, modernist analysis. The reason is that within a cosmos, the parameters for operation are not limited to the purely modern (anarchical-binarism or self/other, in other words, limited to the flow of time between anarchy to its binary opposite), or the purely unified (variational, contextual, that is time-in-space), or a mix, that is, operating within modernity in a unified manner, which is what Homi Bhabha's notion of hybrid (equivocal, 'not white/not quite') describes.[45] In practice, Bhabha's notion requires accepting the binarism of modernity and somehow operate within those parameters in a variational manner, which is of course impossible.

Instead there is an impossible possibility and since it is unquantifiable by modernity, it is called the 'fourth-possibility': operating within a unified cosmos but in a modern manner. This makes for an Indian reflexivity, identifiably so in modern terms, but simultaneously exceeding its parameters.[46] What makes this reflexivity different is its folding back on itself in context. This makes it possible to access another rationality rather than simply its practices. Unlike modernity, the moment of manoeuvre is not just time, but time-in-space. This dual use permits looking beyond one's own timeline to others and permits taking on board a rationality that views itself as the only possible rationality, the only product of time.

Nor is there any need to maintain the fiction that reflexivity completely overrules the past. This is, of course, logically impossible, yet modernity persists in claiming this absurdity. Instead, Indian reflexivity due to space may acknowledge different pasts to produce a range of opportunities bewildering to modernity because it is limited to its own past. Hence what is impossible for modernity is mundane and everyday for Indians. There may be both rebellion against and agreement with the past, which may even be altogether repudiated in certain spaces. Nor do these moves predicate against maintaining and harnessing the past in other spaces, or even simultaneously. Change therefore may be total, but also selective, omnidirectional or ever changing, depending on the contextual requirements of actors. These possibilities rely on a particular rationality—just as modernity produces a limited set of practices—but the point is that the cosmos may also contain the modern, whereas the reverse is impossible. Finally, since all of this is by default done to further the cosmos, actions are geared to eschewing of violence.

The cosmos also has exegetical implications. Because the relationality of a unified cosmos predicates against the self/other divide, it is imperative to knowing oneself on one's own terms rather than in opposition to an 'other'.[47] One may know oneself on one's own terms (conjunctures and spaces), and in another's (even modernity's, because despite its pro-testations, it is no more than a variation within the cosmos), and this may be done on one's own terms and another's. This is possible because, unlike modernity's binarism, one's own terms are a unified cosmos where every-thing is a variation of a theme: the cosmos. Hence there is only another, not an 'other'. If one wants to, then one may also reflect on the relation-ality between knower and known. To effectively delineate relations pro-duces a zone within which knowledge is not equivocal, but certain—a certainty borne out by the definition of the life changing decisions dip-lomats make, which contradicts postcolonials.[48] Such a way is then not a 'postcolonial rearticulation that attempts to intervene in and interrupt the Western discourses on modernity'; rather, it replaces that entire dis-course because as the practices of time management at the MEA sug-gest, modernity never totalized India's indigenous—unified cosmos—matrix.[49] In other words, Gayatri Chakravorty Spivak's analyt-ical purpose of making interventions 'in the structure of which you are a part' to try 'to change something that one is obliged to inhabit'[50] is irrel-evant because there is no obligation to inhabit. One exists certainly, but not within modernity, but in a neutral cosmos, and thereby free of a host of debilitating notions, of which one of the most pernicious is the notion of having to exceed the cosmos to be free.

The impact of the cosmos on diplomacy is its being invested with an instrument unavailable elsewhere: empathy. This relieves the burden of assimilation (unrequired since there are no others) and diplomacy becomes synonymous with negotiations with another to realize contextual aims: the amelioration of violence. In other words empathy is possible because all is relational—rather than alienated and that too in an oppositional manner—because the underlying premise is variation within a unified whole. All are expressions of the cosmos. Thus one may, or may not, nego-tiate with another, dependent on time and space and of course on what one makes of oneself, which arises from the interaction of time and space. However, the cosmos predisposes actors towards the amelioration of vio-lence via negotiation, in contrast to the West where the purpose of diplo-macy is to overcome because its uniquely Christian past instilled in it a modern culture. In any case, empathy is impossible within diplomatic modernity, for how can one empathize with one's 'other'? This modern-ist limitation also produces the malaise of *anomie*,[51] which cannot exist in a unified cosmos because although meaning is constructed in modernity and the cosmos through relations, in the latter relations are not ordered along the self/other divide. And so, while anarchical-binarism discounts empathy, it is the only means for conducting any diplomacy worth its name within the unified cosmos.

This structural reading animates policy[52] and is the *leitmotif* of the civilization, unlike in the West where it is a recent discovery.[53] One of the earliest manifestations of the cosmos is the phrase *vasudhaiva kutumbakam*, 'the cosmos is one family'.[54] Its articulation around 350 BC in a fable is testimony to the concept's antiquity, for it must have already been established to make its way into storytelling. The point is made simply because time is so important to modernity. For the cosmological what is of significance is something else: the framing of the phrase. It is located in the verse, 'the narrow minded like to ask, "Is this person one of us, or is he a stranger?" But to those of noble character the whole world is one family.' What appears to be a prescription is however destabilized by the verse in which it is located. The verse is spoken by a jackal (devious as jackals are) to a deer and a crow who are great friends.[55] The jackal uses a noble idea but for dastardly ends—he wants to befriend the deer to eat it. A valuable and sophisticated lesson on the operation of time and space, the story however does not negate the core phrase, but confirms that even guiding principles ought to be understood in terms of time and space. The medium is the message and it is the ultimate lesson of a philosophy confident of unity rather than consumed by fostering it.

The diplomatic present

Nonetheless, modernity insists on ignoring the intellectual premises of what may be called Indian civilization's diplomatic present. Viewing it as composed of a series of micro-sociological processes permits substantiating which of the two heuristics—anarchical-binarism or the unified cosmos—better accounts for practice. In short, the discussion is investigating in terms of both modernity and a unified cosmos, because the former is how it should be whereas the latter has been developed from early contact with diplomats themselves—to account for how the quotidian becomes an insurgency for modernity. The discussion is oscillating between individuals and state because the two are not viewed as oppositional. Rather the boundaries between them are blended not only because the subjects of this study activate the state, but because the context may be a unified cosmos where the state and people are a variation of a theme: the cosmos.[56]

Such a possibility is proscribed by modernity, and given its hegemonic status, to argue that it plays no role in Indian diplomacy is a violation in need of more than simply positing the cosmos as an alternative measure for rationalization. This is why the section that follows, 'Status Anxiety', builds on the alterity of the MEA's time management to demonstrate why only a cosmological understanding can explain Indian practice. The evidence is the relationality of Indian diplomats, and it indicates that for them everything is unified at inception. One type of relations is selected because diplomats (and analysts) use it: status. It is social capital, existing not only 'in the relations among persons'[57] but also in oneself (pride, for example). A matter of evaluation, not objective difference,[58] studying diplomats and diplomacy through status lays bare how it interlinks everything to also expose how diplomats and the state locate themselves to negotiate the cosmos.[59] These negotiations overthrow that unimaginative category used to explain India: nationalism. Contra modernity, the people of the state are very much their own custodians of their self-manufactured desires. Nor does the impetus for their practice arise from some mythical cultural unity. Yet they successfully engage in a plethora of practices to achieve goals centred on the state. What this means is that there is a something akin to nationalism, but so removed from modern understandings as to make its definitions superfluous. This is why a new term is required to communicate and explain what is practical-pragmatic allegiance to the geobody. This makes for a reflexivity geared not to the future but arising from the present and to changing it now.

Assessments of location and evaluation conducted in terms of status are detailed in the second section, 'How on earth did you get out?' to clarify how people actually traffic in a unified cosmos and if they are moving towards modernity. To know this is to make sense of a host of moves that violate the sanctity of modernity, because whereas modernity predetermines movement, the unified cosmos is permissive. All modernity can do is deem diplomats and diplomacy as illogical. However, to grant them their logic, what is disclosed is that the destination is patently not modernity. The contention is reinforced by the fact that though there is violence, there is no pleasure in it, rather there is only reluctant violence. Having demonstrated that movements are taking practitioners to modernity, the third section, 'The *jugar* of negotiating the cosmos', turns to verifying if there is any purpose in movement. Is movement itself modern? The manner of Indian movement is termed *jugar*. The art of making do, *jugar*, is the way of the weak, tactics rather than strategy, produced in context and for the present rather than the future. The virtue of *jugar* lies in that though it is the way of the weak, those who effect it choose to respond reflexively to violence without violence. That *jugar* is not modern is revealed by setting it alongside modernity's Protestant Work Ethic (PWE). The product of Christianity, the PWE orchestrates a multitude of moves via the origin to coagulate them into a juggernaut: modernist progress. These are operations of dominance, expressions of inevitability arising from an origin deterministic at conception. Besides, in transposing work with virtue, there is also a dangerous lack of concern about violent work (for a diplomat this could for instance be a declaration of war).

The final three sections engage reflexivity and expose its workings in terms of progress, since that is what modernity claims to deliver. The fourth section, 'Mobility's aim: progress', deals with unilineal progress. The simplest kind, it is the only type understood by modernity, which calls it progress-through-history. Although it exists in the MEA, unilineal progress is used by the MEA to forward not anarchical-binarism but a unified cosmos in the manner of the fourth-possibility. The result is that modern violence is dealt with but without violence, as are treacherously modernist tendencies within the MEA. These processes are demonstrated via the method whereby the MEA deploys personnel. In setting it out, what is also illustrated is that although the MEA is a bureaucracy, it does not keep to any modern bureaucratic theory. In short, the MEA cannot be contained by modernist disciplines—including every formulation of the state—which draws upon bureaucratic theory. The fifth section, 'Unspectacular suffering', moves on to more complex, multidimensional types of progress. These cannot be a modernist denomination because they are nonsensical if not seditious within that rationality. However, such progress makes perfect sense if the notion of Christian predestination and its entwinement in violence are discarded. How this is possible in practice is demonstrated by setting the 123 Agreement (123) negotiations its proper context: US pronouncements and the unguarded Wikileaks cables dating back to 2005. What is revealed is that although there was an agreement, it was between two completely different rationalities: one intent on dividing the cosmos violently, the other committed to responding without violence to maintain the cosmos. Even more challenging to modernity's premises are practices of progress that are neither rebellion against the past nor a transforming of the self. Instead progress may arise from transforming the very destination, which is crucial to gauging progress[60]—an actor progresses, paradoxically for modernity, by folding back to the origin. Progress for the MEA therefore implies mobility, but warps the modernist weft of time and space and with it certainty. This occurs because unlike modernity, there is no master narrative about what progress should be. In other words, diplomacy may be conducted in ways unimagined but with empathy and the eschewal of violence. The final section, "Nothing makes sense in this country", shows the extent to which modernity is defied. Indian diplomats and the state do not simply reformulate the destination and themselves, but negate modernity altogether. They do so with noted erasures of the past upon which modernity—reliant as it is on a timeline—rests. However, such moves do not discount progress. How this and the other theoretical conundrums outlined—if only in terms of modernity—actually play out in the everyday life of the Indian state is what the remainder of this chapter charts in terms of actual practice, to reveal the workings of a reflexivity that is alternate because it is founded on a rationality altogether different.

Status anxiety

Every post-2000 IFS officer interviewed said 'status' was central to their joining, indicating the significance of status, a lack of it and the fact that it is obtainable. Status is also an interlinking concept, permitting the argument that diplomats inhabit not modernity but a unified cosmos. To use status to navigate the cosmos is therefore to do so in their terms and ensures that a space suggestively alien to modernity is not contaminated by it. To navigate this space, the waypoints are highly localized microsociological processes. The specific types of process investigated are decisions. Not only do they undermine modernity's claims on the present, they also destabilize nationalistic explanations of India's past, present and future. Indians, as shall be shown, do seek out the state, but not because they are coerced or for primordial reasons. Rather, nationalism is meaningless because they inhabit a relationally unified world that makes for an allegiance of practical-pragmatism to a geobody. Decision-making also outlines a non-modern reflexivity since actors aim to realize possibilities barely conceivable in terms of their past but arising from their context, which also means that there is no hypocritical claim of totally repudiating the past. Since this work is about the state, the micro-sociological decisions of interest are those between individual and state. What entwines the two is status. At LBSNAA an IAS officer dryly recited what sounded like a set-piece honed over years of teaching: 'You do not have a contract with the government. At the moment you are confirmed into the service you are ruled by the Constitution. You have no terms and conditions because there was no bargaining in negotiating the terms of contract. Hence it is a status that you are conferred.'[61]

Desirous of status, people join the state. It is easily recognized as a crucible of status. To my question about why, an officer exclaimed: 'I saw they [officers of state] were respected, had power, had a good life from when I was a boy, the boys knew who the respected were. The District Collector would come to the school for prize day. The Superintendent of Police would come for sports day.' Unambivalent is the officer locating himself within a cosmos, as is his sliding from the singular to the plural indicating that his immediate society shared his awareness.[62] These events were not the outcome of a 'banal nationalism' of superficial baubles. In fact they were highly significant in diplomat's pre-official lives.[63] The exposure to society activated self-requirements for status and people lacking security desired it. But most seek economic security rather than status. An officer remarked: 'Out of my year at IIT (Indian Institute of Technology), I think three people out of hundreds applied for the government. Everyone else went into the private sector. They want money. ... That did not do it for me. So I persevered, I took the exam three times.'[64]

On occasion some, despite not wanting the state's status, acquired it: 'Why have I joined the service? Because I come from a typical middle class family. I was a management trainee with a multinational, [implying that it was a lucrative job in the modern economy] but my father said: 'Forget about the neighbours, even I don't know what you are doing!' So I wrote the exam and when I got in, forget about the neighbours, the entire *mohalla* [area] knew what I was doing!'[65]

Whether status is sought or unsought, officers obviously locate themselves variationally and then operate to acquire what they desire, even if it is indirectly. These processes cannot be explained by alienation, let alone be organized binarily. Rather, these practices inextricably intertwine everyone and everything to make for a cosmos unified by relations.

In achieving status, one source increasingly valued is the state. So in demand is the state's imprimatur that it trumps some of the highest paying professions internationally. A Goldman Sachs banker recently gave up banking for the state,[66] but modern explanations for such behaviour, most commonly nationalism, are wrong, because they impose alien categories in the absence of even any analysis attempting to explain why the people who join the state do so, by quite simply asking them! To do so, one cannot but not note that the reasons for becoming officers are neither coercion nor some primeval instinct. Rather, people seek the state for immediate, local and personal reasons. These are produced by negotiations within the immediate context, most commonly family and teachers. In short, these actions again undercut modernity's premises to ineluctably show bureaucrats as legible only as interdependent social agents coordinating their actions and cognition through interaction. Even if the result is discordancy, it is a function of interactive choice.[67] As a probationer reminisced: 'I gave up medicine to try the exams. Medicine did not suit me. The blood, the …. When I changed my mind everyone thought I was mad. When I finally got in, I didn't have five minutes to myself. The very same aunties and uncles who thought I was mad now kept pushing sweets into my mouth.'[68]

Though devoid of some primeval impulse, was he coerced? The change in attitude amongst relatives, along with the probationer's joy, might suggest, especially to the psychoanalytically minded, an underlying magnetism of the state unconsciously motivating actors. To assume this is to once again ignore the subject who quite clearly said his choice to engage the state was opposed. But this psychoanalytic hypothesis is but a shadow of the real analytic confusion that is consistently manufactured by modernity using itself to explain Indians.

For instance, even when trying to take Indians sincerely, modernists are confounded. Christopher Fuller and Haripriya Narasimhan mistake sentiments similar to those expressed by the relatives who opposed the probationer's choice as 'disdain' for the state amongst Information Technology (IT) workers. But of course, Fuller and Narasimhan never sought to engage those who turn away from IT. They therefore do not know that if possible, some of the most enterprising beneficiaries of globalization rebuff it in the infinitesimally microscopic hope of becoming the state. In doing so these (overwhelmingly) men demonstrate evaluations of the cosmos that stupefy modernists because they, convinced of the superiority of their ways, insist that everyone is moving towards 'globalization'. Never more than the violence of modern politics or the erasure of all politics as we are all reduced to an ecosystem,[69] Indian diplomats contradict these postures at every turn because they refute the logic of power politics. An officer who quit an IT major made the point succinctly: 'Do you know what IT work is? It's sitting at a computer writing lines of code *man*. Where is the life in that? This work is about life. It's about people, lives … creating something real. It offers so much: excitement, social interaction with many India's. … and anyway, do you really want to work for a bunch of *goras*? Their racism is mind-boggling … they don't even know they're racist.'[70]

It is therefore not some grand modernist aim and certainly not nationalism or even postcolonial angst that animates officers. Rather, they are driven by immediate concerns understood in a multitude of ways including, of course, status. Acquiring it requires not only negotiation within one's immediate locality but it also on occasion entails compromise. With evident regret a probationer recounted that he 'had a place at IIM(A) [Indian Institute of Management—Ahmedabad]. But my father insisted I write the exam. I wrote it. My father then insisted I put down the IAS as my first choice but I drew the line there. My choice was the IFS.'[71]

But while diplomats are made necessary by the entanglement of everything, they are not the best examples of how deeply enmeshed everything is. 'Who are our best diplomats(?),' asked a very senior officer rhetorically: 'Our politicians of course. Look at what they have to manage to decide, to make a decision.' In schematic terms, what was expressed is the mutually inextricable operation of cosmos and individual in the form of a range of constituencies demanding a variety of actions and also offering a number of routes that are then mediated through an individual's personal calculus, itself manufactured within an individual in relation with society. The officer added, 'their [politicians'] management involves concerns from everywhere.'[72] It is in such an intellectual landscape devoid of either anarchy or binarism that the modern academic's claim on the mind of the Indian bureaucrat unravels.

But are Indian diplomats loath to think nationalistically because they inhabit a self-regulating ecosystem which tempers that excessive sentiment? Older members of the IFS, who joined up to the late 1980s, have evaluations similar to their younger compatriots. Even when nationalism does seep in, it is actually a geobodic commitment for it lies somewhere in the background far removed from the primacy of decision making. Nationalism is reduced to practical-pragmatism, because the state helps fulfil individuated desires and duties. 'I was a scientist. My father wanted me to take the exams, so I did. And I have to say I've no regrets,' said a Joint Secretary (JS).[73] Mani Shankar Aiyar, a former IFS officer, who spoke to me while a minister, explained his choice economically: 'What opportunities did I have? There were the covenanted services, and the state. Today there are many more [choices] so people have choices I did not.'[74] A Muslim officer joined for love: 'As a young man I was in love with a girl, a Hindu girl, and there was all sorts of opposition. That's when I realized I needed to be self-supporting.' Almost as an afterthought he added: 'I'm a committed Nehruvian. Those ideas are my ideas.'[75] Another explained, 'it's the family profession.'[76] And finally, a retired officer who comes from a family that served in a pre-independence princely court offered with quiet pride, 'seva [service] … my family's profession was seva.'[77] While older officers on occasion overtly attribute their intellectual orientation to the first PM Jawaharlal Nehru— as embodying the nation-state—even then personal factors dominate. References to Nehru remain secondary and are totally absent amongst post-2000 candidates' renderings of themselves. What is obvious then is the all-encompassing notion of meeting responsibilities, of duty to oneself and others.

It is to meet those obligations—rather than to feed nationalism—that relations are sought with the state and through it to hitherto untapped, and even unknown, parts of the cosmos, thereby relegating binarism to no more than a figment of the imagination. Aiyar said:

the IFS is shaped by the people who come into it. It's an escalator to social status … economic certainty. You come from a village and you end up in Delhi. Your children will be born abroad and they will settle abroad because they are as much a product of wherever they have grown up as they are of India. Look at me, I'm from the South, but I grew up in the North, and I've stayed here ever since. … In my batch not a single officer's child is in India. It's the way of the world.[78]

Implicit in Aiyar's 'way of the world' is the notion of a cosmos, which although in the first instance is the family, rapidly expands to include India and the world. Crucially, this idea of an interlinked world, or a cosmos, is not produced by diplomacy, but by conjunctures from diplomats' pre-diplomatic lives (as Aiyar demonstrated using himself). Notions of differing locations offering differing opportunities cannot be premised on modernity but make requisite a cosmos which in turn permits these practices of practicality.

What all of this makes for is the inappropriateness of nationalism as a heuristic for exegesis, and it entwines Aiyar with today's probationers. One said his father was a manual labourer before stating with absolutely no hesitation that might indicate shame that: 'I would have emigrated if I didn't get into the services.' Where lies the possibility of nationalism if the second choice is migration? However, even America is trumped by a job in the IAS, not because of nationalism but because of context: the status an IAS officer enjoys in a highly localized space. That is why 'the IFS will just have to do because too much effort is again required to emigrate … I'm at least in the government,' says another officer who put the IFS down as his second choice in the entrance exams.'[79] Explicit is a variational view that converts modernity's limits into a cosmos replete with possibilities waiting to be tapped, and not necessarily through violence or to result in some utopian end, but certainly to transform the self now by making oneself capable of discharging one's duties. The reason for engaging others is therefore neither to overcome nor to realize utopia, but to realize possibilities to improve the personal and the present. This is a family affair for another diplomat: 'I'd never left my state before I went for the interview to Delhi. … My brother's an engineer in the US. Maybe he'll get a green card. … It's a good means to secure a livelihood. But not for me. … See you have to understand … a kind of person wants to stay home.'[80]

It would be a miscalculation to posit that this kind of person stays home for nationalistic reasons. Rather he stays home because of the geobody he is enmeshed in makes practical-pragmatism possible. This phrase is used to maintain the conversation with modernity. What the phrase implies may be approached via George Mead's conception of the 'social act' (including non-performative acts) being a temporally emergent and transactionally based (including within the self) expression of social agency.[81] The individual-in-society choosing to do something is a product of the cosmos, hence the decision-making process itself is not alienated, but binds together everything making for the cosmos. The decision is produced by the origin, but made apparent in space. That all decisions are tolerated is evident from a probationer noting his minority choice, without dismissing or claiming to understand the majority. Out of 'fifty people in my class … twenty-two went abroad immediately after graduate school, later seventeen followed.' He rationalized the motivation behind the numbers, unsurprisingly for the intellectual world he inhabits, in his terms:

People think going abroad is good. I don't understand it. I was in the Middle East [he had been sent as part of his training] with 1.7 million Indians and I asked them, "why do you come?" They give the same answer as my university people: money. Some lie to their homes about their hardship, it encourages others. I can't understand it. I really don't understand how you can put up with that life for money.[82]

Notable is the way this probationer characterizes his choice as just like any choice, a product of the cosmos. Since the cosmos is not deterministic, no choice is regarded as beyond the pale. His choice is representative of why people choose to join the state. It is to choose not money but status, which is something that only the cosmos (ironically, usually experienced as the village or district similar like the place one comes from) can provide. Status is also the reason why people stay not just within India, but within their own state, because within that corner of the cosmos, a state employee has status because his context—as civil servant—is understood. This highly localized understanding is a product of constituting oneself over time and locating oneself within spatial frames. These are local, national and international to use modernity's terms. In contrast to modernity, the indigenous conception operates in time-in-space, which makes primordial nationalism inapplicable. Meanwhile coercive nationalism is discounted by practical pragmatism, that is a politics to transmute one's context, via decisions in context.

These practices are also redolent of a reflexivity evident if modernity's totalizing and contradictory understanding of that concept is eschewed. Doing so also shows how the violence endemic to modernity may finally be handled. Once again the route to excavating reflexivity will be status. It is sought not as an end in itself, but because it permits people to reconstitute themselves to escape from the tyranny of everyday violence that is corruption which scars ordinary Indian life.[83] That diplomats persist in freeing themselves by following society's rules should not diminish the magnitude of their task. They first have to conceptualize a life free of violence, and this is done not by an insular reflexivity focused on their past and future but rather by a reflexivity that reaches out in space through observations to craft alternatives to the present now. There is virtue in this because it authorizes people to respond to the violence that is corruption in a non-violent way. In short, reflexivity is not a rebellion against tradition but a means to escape the present by first manufacturing in individual terms an alternative, and then moving to realize it without replicating the very phenomena they are attempting to escape.

How this reflexivity is receptive to the world in practical terms became apparent when an officer outlined how the nearly unimaginable violence-free future was realized. The goal was 'that red-light on the white Ambassador … everyone wants imported cars, but a white Ambassador with the light. The power that comes with it …. That is status. People treat you differently.'[84]

An innocuous enough example, yet it is the tangible outcome of the intellectual process being sketched. The significance of the symbolic red light may be appreciated by noting that though an officer is resplendent with status, it is quite likely he was born at the bottom of society both economically and socially. This is why the envisioned alternative—*babu-dom*—is so radically different to the present most aspirants exist in, because the alternative is one free of violence, which is no less taxing by being routine. Most significantly, this alternative is realized by looking not in but out, and the outcomes are blatant. A probationer elucidates how this intellectual process transforms lives in practical terms: 'I wanted to move my motorcycle from my home-place to here. I asked a friend to get the NOC [No Objection Certificate] permit for me and he went to the RTO [Road and Transport Office] and was asked for a bribe. He told me. I phoned the office and told them who I was and was issued the NOC. That's status in operation.'[85]

That officers choose to respond to such violence on a different register is what makes practice virtuous. How this happens, in practical terms, is once again explained by an officer: 'At medical school I was failed for the practical because I couldn't afford to pay the bribe … so it took me another six months to pass. I know I must have done fine in the practical because in the theory exams I did very well.' In an earlier career as a state doctor he describes his first posting as 'doctoring in a totally Naxal infested district. I was sent there because the Deputy Director said if you want a good place, give me money. I had none, and so!'[86]

This mention of Naxals by a member of a 'small ethnic' group who seeks the state destabilizes the assumption that localized, remote peoples by their very nature oppose the entry of the state.[87] In this case, petty corruption and the want of a few thousand rupees meant that this man wound up in a district that was shunned. Within the district he was sent to the worst part—not only unsafe but with 'no electricity, roads or telephone.' The outfit he was placed in had a sanctioned strength of twenty-five: 'including auxiliary staff. … Nurse, sweeper, lab technician, male health worker, pharmacist and an MBBS … all sanctioned, but there were only five people including me, a chaprasi, driver, technician and a male health worker who never showed up.'[88]

In short, this life was repeatedly undermined by the violence that is corruption. Yet the probationer persisted in realizing a future that must have seemed nearly inaccessible—because it is, for the vast majority—and did so without reproducing the practices of violence that he had suffered. It is in this sense that the probationer dealt with violence in a non-violent manner and therefore became virtuous. He did not pay the bribes and he persisted in following society's rules.

In doing so, the probationer not only reinforced the contention of society, above and beyond experience, but was also indicating a reflexivity operating in terms of both time and space. His reflexivity was contextual for it was organised in terms of space, that is external stimuli—it was not solely introspective self-reflection. Simultaneously, he was bound by time because the purpose was to surmount his present, which is the sum total of the past. In contrast to anarchical-binarism, bureaucrats understand themselves according to relations leading to tangible moves in the world, produced by time and space to change the present. Whether these moves are organized towards modernity is what we explore next.

'How on earth did you get out?'

'How on earth did you get out(?!),' exploded the irrepressible Aiyar upon hearing where a probationer originated from.[89] The probationer was born in a district where 50,000 out of a population of 1,200,000 live in state controlled camps; the area is overrun by Naxals (left-wing insurgents in central and eastern India), or 'simply robbers and bandits devoid of any ideology,' he said with evident disgust. Now that he was at the centre of the state, his moves were social in that they were contextual, and were significant for providing a means of gauging the nature, direction and ultimately the rationality of movement.

To start, New Delhi was not where he wanted to be, abroad still less. His ambition was to join the IAS and to return to a district. Having failed, he aspired to politics. His grandparents were forest dwellers who saw their first road in the 1920s; it did not come to them, but 'passed by their forest'. By his father's time there was a village. 'The English used to come to our area for hunting. Villagers were used for labour to cut *sal* and teak trees.' The disgust evident in his tone denoted a theme of unequal imperial extraction. Interconnected is a theme of remoteness. His 'place is remote … no newspapers … I first watched television in class 11,' when he was living in a town, at the age of 18. The 'nearest railhead' to his village is 'about 80 kilometres from the nearest town which in turn is 300 kilometres away.' The railway is 'still narrow gauge', which means that the connection with the Indian railway network is indirect. A road was finally built to the village, 'but till the 1980s it was impossible during the monsoons to get to the town.' His moves were also linguistic: 'We speak our tribal language at home. Now it's becoming extinct because it's of no use to the outside world. Hindi was the medium of instruction at the next level of schooling after the village school. That language requirement creates a high dropout rate from education.'

Not more than '10 or 20 per cent' make the transition, but this probationer persevered, learned new skills and continued to educate himself. In continuing to pursue education, he knew what he wanted, and that was not to transition from 'tradition' to 'modernity' but to secure what he considered essential for 'decent' human life, 'only possible via the state education system.'[90] It is a bevy of such quotidian aims that motivate Indian diplomats, rather than some greater sense of doing some theoretical good for a theoretical construct, be it nation or humanity, in the unimaginable future.

In keeping to the everyday, what is on display is however a remarkable rate of mobility rarely replicated in the West, where most modern analysis originates. As the examples above and to come illustrate, the speed at which large sections of the MEA are transitioning in terms of lived lives and experience is difficult to come by within modernity which claims to be transforming all of us, and this raises a question: Does the very pace of such lives indicate Indian diplomats are modern? Paul Virilio sees speed as a violent tool deployed by the modern state to constrict freedom.[91] It certainly is, because as John Torpey notes, the modern state has monopolized the movement of peoples around the globe,[92] but this is to sequester the non-modern world, as the modern world permits relatively unfettered travel within itself. In an earlier era, the colonial state used speed in similar ways, to segregate people—for example the ancestors of this probationer—but today he puts speed to a very different purpose, and one encouraged by the state, not only to access it but to become it. This reversal in the use of speed is not irrational, and Virilio made a mistake: William Connolly observes, 'that Virilio allows the military paradigm to overwhelm all other modalities and experiences of speed.'[93] Connolly then suggests that speed is instead an ambiguous term. However, ambiguity is removed if the analytic is changed. To adopt a cosmic method is to realize that speed ought to be understood in the contexts of those using it. While for modernity speed might be violence, for the probationer speed is therapeutic. Connolly also argues that speed is a solvent of 'thick universals' that enhances cosmopolitanism by exposing peoples to each other.[94] In this Connolly is completely at odds with the tribal diplomat, for he made clear his use of speed was to not lose himself but to make the state aware of people like himself. Speed was used not to transform oneself to create a new 'cosmopolitan' person, but to transform society to suit the individual.

However, the probationer's actions do suggest a paradox. Modernity in his thinking was the engendering of remoteness, but inexplicably he sought not just to close the gap but to use the modern nation-state to do so. People appear to be moving towards what is thought of as an outpost of modernity in India, mainly because it brought modernity prior to independence and at great cost to tribal people. This raises the question: Why would someone who has suffered from the onset of the modern nation-state seek to move towards it? Answering this requires viewing the world in terms of where the diplomat comes from, to understand how movement is actually comprehended. Regardless of whether this probationer is a subaltern or not, his moves arise from a political desire realized through the acquisition of status, and its purpose is to not play power politics, but to even out power imbalances between his locality and the state.[95] Implicit are processes of self-location (spatially, his remoteness, and in time, his reference being the English-built road). The moves are therefore redolent of a cosmos unified by time and space. Nor does the probationer seek to leave this rationality behind, as the aim is to not to radically reinvent the self, but to realize certain relationally calculated requirements, stemming from earlier conjunctures made evident in the present. Hence, the moves towards the state are not motivated by modernity, nor by searches for it. It is nevertheless the state that the probationer seeks, but the manner of the search is not modern, and what is sought is not understood to be any more than an enabler, powerful yes, but no more than a means for people to further integrate into society to realize contextual goals. What the probationer's actions demonstrate is therefore not a paradox, for the state is devoid of the modern. Instead, the state is a variational element that permits a variational person succeed. That he did demolishes Ronald Inden's contention that the Indian 'nation-state remains ontologically and politically inaccessible to its own citizens.'[96] In actuality Inden totally misunderstands today's state as a colonial state, as do all moderns.

At the core of the probationer's understanding of the post-independent state and his using it (and the state itself providing him the means to do so) is the idea of violence. It is what decides whether actors, including the state, correlate with the cosmos. Charting this in practice requires recognizing that the engagement between individual and state is two-way: it is not just the state that confers status, individuals also imbue the state with status.[97] Penetrating this complicity is possible via the complex of decisions made by entrants. A significant decision is made after clearing the prelims, the first step in the common entrance exams held by the Union Public Services Commission (UPSC),[98] when candidates have to decide which service they want. This decision makes apparent that a unified cosmos does not delete violence, but provides a means of curtailing it by directing it away from the modernist purpose of division and assimilation. IFS officers during the fieldwork reported overwhelmingly that they had opted to put the IFS as their second choice after the IAS. 'Officers entering the IFS in this millennium do not want to be diplomats,' said a member of the UPSC interview committee.[99] Of those who do put down the IFS, there are two sub-categories. One opts for the IAS, followed by the IFS (or vice versa). Another puts down the IAS, followed by the IPS and IRS and then the IFS. These two sets of choices disclose visions of oneself, conceptions of status and elucidate the distinctiveness of one's entanglement in the cosmos. 'There are two types of officers. The first is of a more intellectual bent, less interested in raw power and in a different idea of status,' reported a probationer who put down the IFS as his first choice. He explained the operation of status in terms of himself, saying: 'I had seen IFS people, liked the aura of their lives ... they are part of a gentry.[100] People grudgingly respect the IAS and IPS because they have power but about the IFS, of whom people know nothing, but they say "ah, that is something".'[101]

The second vision is shaped by violence and seeks to be violent. It was revealed by an IRS probationer: '… we want power. Earlier this country used to be run by a stick. So you put down IAS and the IPS. Now this country is run by a chequebook. Anyone who earns more than a lakh has to come to me for tax. If that is not power then what is?'[102]

Hence there are at least two visions of self, one violent because it seeks to escape violence by joining the state but also undermine it violently, while the other is content with being a part of the state and upholding it. Both however are entrenched in a causality that does not differentiate between time and space, but uses both to act contextually and hence in the present unlike moderns who act only in terms of the past. In short, both the reasons for joining the state are produced cosmically, but one seeks to uphold it and the other to undermine it.[103]

However, if the cosmological rationality generates violence, is it really any different from modernity? The difference from anarchical-binarism lies in it regarding violence as part of the course, whereas in the unified cosmos a non-violent response is not only possible but encouraged and violence is therefore an oddity, inimical to the cosmos that is irenic by definition. It makes for an instinctive repulsion for violence, which is why one probationer, upon telling me in the most cosmological terms why he was going to be corrupt, then added: 'What do you think of me Deep?' and before I could reply he said, 'Doesn't matter, I can tell from your face what you think of me.'[104] He knew he was being disobedient for he was intending to contravene the cosmos. Hence his extended justification and then his question to check if I had been convinced. So pressing was the need to convince that even the look on my face did not deter him from asking me, and this is testimony to the magnitude of instinctive repulsion towards violence fostered by the cosmos.

Although the cosmological rationality subsumes violence, it was not always what defined the state. There existed alongside the watershed that was independence a very different understanding of the state and the IFS in particular: it was a vehicle for violence. This may be portrayed in terms of movements. For instance, the probationer who sought to acclimatize himself to the state to further engage society did not always exist. At independence when the MEA was established, those seeking to join it were motivated by the violence endemic to modernity: entry into the MEA was an act of anarchical-binarism because early entrants sought to reinvent themselves as members of modernity—much as migrant academics do today. The difference is that whereas state seeking today is a means to become at one with society rather than divide it, those seeking to become Indian diplomats around independence wanted to extricate themselves from their society to become modern.

In Nehruvian India, the IFS was held in high status. At independence, royalty—the very pinnacle of the old regime—sought out the IFS because it invested that service with the capacity to replace their lost royal status. Having internalized Western ideas of alienation, in which the European self was viewed in opposition to the native other, royals attempted to efface their selves by Europeanizing themselves to become 'hybrids'. This is of course only possible within a modern conception, because the presumption is a binary divide.[105] Hence one may be a hybrid between two originary selves, 'masters'.[106] The violence involved in this process of self-deletion and rebirth may be apprehended by the practices of hybridity. One was to join the IFS, the 'last bastion of the brown sahib' where the natives were 'despised and kept at a distance to avoid offending the prime responsibilities of their masters.'[107] In short, Indians aspiring to modernity, in keeping with modernity's teleology, used violence both to reinvent themselves and to distance themselves from the nonmodern in an attempt to make themselves modern and display how developed the process was in themselves.

Nehru knew this and slotted royals into the IFS to provide 'psychological and political rehabilitation for erstwhile rulers,' wrote V.P. Menon, who was intimately involved in the dissolution of the imperial order.[108] Royals were given important assignments,[109] and as the agents of hybridization they may have mimicked to mock, just as colonial administrators indulged in mimesis to control, but as diplomats they failed because of the cognitive dissonance caused by attempting the impossible task of entering anarchical-binarism from a unified cosmos (which contains the former, but the former cannot contain the latter).[110] It was in recognition of this that in 1955 Nehru said despairingly: 'I do not think one can entrust them [royals] with diplomatic work. They have not been a success at it. Of course it might be useful to send them to some out of the way place if they are prepared to go, or someplace where no political flair is necessary.'[111]

This spelled the gradual removal of royals from diplomatic life. Some continued, but the days of the likes of the Maharajah of Alirajpur, High Commissioner to Singapore, dashing around in a red Mustang, acquiring a reputation for fast living and 'messing things up', were numbered.[112]

The 'decline' in the IFS's status from the heights of royalty meant that other mimic-men (the English-educated metropolitan elite) began eschewing the service. It was no longer a suitable vector for them to differentiate themselves, to make evident their 'master' status. The corollary was the decline of the MEA as a site for the violence implicit in anarchical-binarism. Both may be measured by the decline in numbers of 'toppers' opting for it. From 2000 to 2009, the IFS received just one topper. Before him, the last topper to opt for the IFS was in 1976. That year is indicative of the decline of the elite in opting for the IFS: 1976 was the last year when nearly half of the 25 officers recruited came from the leading liberal arts college, St. Stephen's.[113] Calling it 'venerable', Prasenjit Duara recalls that history graduates from St. Stephen's were 'simply expected to join the civil service.'[114] The lack of toppers opting for the IFS meant that the organization had to proceed further and further down the merit list to fill vacancies. This marked the end of its status for the modernized Indian, the type permitted to access St. Stephen's. This may be illustrated by how rapidly and how far down the UPSC merit list the state had to go to fill the IFS's ranks, for lower down the list were the unmodernized products of the hinterland. In 1959, three persons joined the IFS from the top 15 of the merit list. In 1970, 11 persons joined from the top 72. The next year, ranks 1, 2, 4, 6, 7, 10, 12 and 13 joined the IFS. In 1972, 20 of the top 26 chose the IFS. But by 1988 ten IFS vacancies could be filled only by reaching down to the 480th position and a decade later, filling IFS vacancies required going down to the 709th candidate. In 1993 15 positions were filled by going to the 641st candidate.[115] From 2005 to 2008, almost no one from the top 20 joined the IFS. In 2007, of the first 50, only two joined the IFS and in 2008, only four out of the top 50.[116]

The decline in the IFS's status is made palpable in the transient figure of Jivat Thadani who, though he had come top in the exam, inexplicably chose the IAS. The singularity of the choice was made material by his proximity to the old order. Thadani is the husband of Jaya—who is a relative, but what makes her a member of the old order is that she is also of the Kapurthala royal family and had been lady in waiting to the last Viceroy's wife. Thadani's choice was therefore a double turning away from both modernity and the old order, and so extraordinary was it at the time that Jawaharlal Nehru himself questioned it. 'He wanted to know why on earth I hadn't joined the IFS and offered me the option of changing my mind,'[117] recounted Thadani. His not choosing the IFS marked the moment when even members of the old order began to cast off the accretions of unbridgeable difference reinforced under the colonial regime. Instead they began to opt for a rationality uncontainable by modernity, thereby marking the beginning of the transition from entering the bureaucracy to split the cosmos to becoming at one with society.

Evidently, the IFS's devaluation in terms of modernity is decades old and began amongst the metropolitan elite closest to the royals. The decline, from modernity's viewpoint, may be most instructively measured by tracing the rapid diversification in the type of people taking the UPSC exams. The state began to encourage heterogeneity in socio-economic terms by a complex social and economic formula[118] which lowered entry requirements for poor and low caste candidates.[119] The weighting of the exams vis-à-vis the interview also makes a difference. 'The interview is given less weight nowadays. That was a way of checking the social abilities of aspirants,' disclosed a UPSC interview board member.[120] Implicit are conceptions of behaviour cloaked in the innocuous phrase 'social abilities'. The exams involve the prelims designed to sort the wheat from the chaff.[121] Those who pass take the mains: qualifying papers in English and an Indian language, an essay paper (200 marks), six additional papers (300 marks each) and finally an interview (300 marks). Officers are ranked on the civil list in terms of overall marks where the interview makes up only a small percentage. In practice it means a strong exam candidate has a better chance of success than a candidate resplendent with 'social abilities' but lacking in exam marks. The situation is complicated by the reduction of humanities graduates entering the service because 'it's much easier to score marks in a mathematical test than in an English exam,' said a LBSNAA instructor.[122] What it means is that rural, underprivileged people who 'don't know what the IFS is,' said a probationer from such a background, have a far greater chance of getting in. He continued with some bewilderment: 'Where we come from we have never seen anything like this. Some of my batch grew up in totally lawless areas. I myself had never heard of the IFS before the prelims. With the Collector or the Superintendent in the district, we have grown up with them. They've been there at the top of our worlds. But the IFS?'[123]

The effect of positive discrimination has been to transform the IFS from an arena of modernist violence deployed to create and then heighten difference, into a society that reinforces unity in its permissiveness of contextual diversity. In other words, whereas the unified cosmos understands difference as variation, those seeking modernity sought to remake variation as binary and oppositional and hence unbridgeable. In practice this was a hangover from a discrepancy founded on the laughable exceptionalism of the divine, royal birth and blood. Moves towards 'a representational' IFS saw the replacement of royals by city elites and now, increasingly, by people from regions from which it was inconceivable until recently that diplomats might come.[124] Whereas once the IFS was an English-speaking elite, a symbol of modernity in India amongst the old elite, today Indian diplomats are just as likely to have been educated in vernacular languages and be unable to speak English. Six out of the 19 officers who entered the IFS in 2008 took the exam in Hindi, prompting an old-timer to carp: 'Imagine getting recruits who cannot even speak English!'[125] What the policy makes for are diplomats more attuned to the majority dynamic of Indian life than ever before. It also therefore mitigates the violence generated by modernity's utopia seeking, because people now join the IFS to become a part of society rather than to differentiate themselves from it.

But what of the old-timer's implied charge that the change in intake would dilute or has diluted operational competence? Actual practice reveals that as candidates are drawn so far down the merit list, the policy of positive discrimination has been in effect for much longer than officially sanctioned policy suggests. An officer concluded in 1994 that the earlier quota of 22.5% reservations had been in force for the last 30 years 'without causing any notable disasters', and he went on to argue that 'some reserved category recruits may well have been substandard or worse. But so have some from the general category. Both categories have produced officers of proven competence, which shows that everyone can do well if given the opportunity.'[126]

This is an opinion supported by serving ambassadors today.[127] With nearly 50% of seats reserved, the IFS is no longer a playground for royals but a repository for reluctant members of the masses, and just how advanced this process is can be seen from the fact that in November 2006, out of a total strength of 599, 175 officers came from the positive discrimination categories.[128] By August 2011 the total strength had expanded to 677, of whom 228 came from the reserved categories. In 2014, of a total strength of 483, the reserved categories were 277 strong.[129] This increase of around one percent per year[130] makes evident that the ratio of general to other categories will gradually decrease to reflect the realities of Indian society as conceptualized by Indians themselves.

In short, while at the MEA's inception diplomats joined it to move towards modernity, that is not the case today. Early entrants were frequently of the royal elite who joined the service to differentiate themselves, to affirm their new 'elite' selves in a democracy shorn of the imperial; in fact this was of course no more than the old imperial iniquities repackaged in modernist garb. Today the moves into the MEA are made within a variational cosmos where everything is open to evaluation along a multiplicity of vectors, as distinct from the narrow limits imposed by anarchical-binarism. These evaluations are relational, rather than oppositional as they were at the IFS's inception. This change explains why today's moves, despite their speed, are not towards modernity, but are intended to remain entrenched within a unified cosmos. The contention is reinforced by officers seeking not to differentiate themselves from society, but to become a part of it, a goal which only the state can help make reality. The implication for violence is not that it has been eliminated altogether, but that a particular type of violence has been. Modernist violence was ended by the officers of today seeking unity with society and making that decision on the basis of a unified cosmological rationale, rather than acting in tune with modernity to binarily differentiate themselves from their society.

Officers now create each other and the state through evaluative processes. For instance, at the start of a career probationers inevitably seek French as their language, not because Paris or Geneva epitomizes modern nation-states, but because they make for a pleasant posting (as opposed to, say, Pyongyang).[131] It is precisely the same evaluative process that ensures that as careers progress, careerist officers choose postings not in Western Europe but in the neighbourhood. The decision was explained by an officer asking rhetorically, 'What else is more important than our region? Our neighbourhood ....'[132] Geography therefore reveals a shift not only towards but also away from modernity, and both are possible through the application of contextualism. Its workings are evident in the processes of the MEA itself. Until Shyam Saran, every FS had served in a senior post at a Western capital, for modernity was imbued with significance.[132] Now the emphasis is not Berlin or London, but Kathmandu or Islamabad. Testimony to the weight attached to contextual, rather than originary, causality. The result is a practice that discloses a politics unquantifiable in modern terms, for what Indians do is theo-retically constrained from degenerating into violence.

The jugar *of negotiating the cosmos*

'They are very hard working. They have to be to get in. Once in, they get very lazy, very fast,'[134] said Natwar Singh without any prompting, upon hearing what my research was. With decades in the MEA as an officer and then its minister, it is not surprising that his concern was echoed at LBSNAA:

You have all worked very hard to get here. But how much longer will you work? The problem is in the Constitution. You are appointed by the President and you cannot be removed by someone junior to who has appointed you. It provides protection. It also erodes the incentive to work. Add to this that, barring a few exceptional cases, you cannot be promoted out of turn, will you work at the opti-mal level? … The government has contractual employees. They can be dismissed for not performing or if the office is abolished. I wish that were the case for all of us.[135]

JS and higher rank officers often grumbled about the 'lack of work-ethic and reading' and 'a great sense of entitlement'.[136] It is produced by success, say several ambassadors. One complained: 'I've got a probationer who has no interest in learning anything. And he's got a real bitch of a wife. Constantly making demands for this, that and the other. That's all that occupies them.'[137]

Natwar Singh's and the IAS officer's complaint signals a type of vio-lence, and exploring the nature of that violence exposes that the very manner in which diplomats operate is uncontainable by modernity. To start with, dereliction of duty due to an obsession with self-aggrandise-ment, though distinct from violence done to the state by perverting it through misuse of power, is nevertheless violence to the state and those who compose it. Both types of violence are however different qualita-tively from the kind inflicted by modernity as it marches inevitably for-ward. The violence of diplomats—and bureaucrats in general—in contrast to modernity's violence of inevitability, is the violence of the weak, for the people who inflict it are those earmarked for deletion by moderni-ty's progress.

An experience during fieldwork elucidates how the weak are violent. Probationers and officers had flats. Some probationers wanted a second flat, and they got them, which resulted in a shortage of flats, and so they moved into larger flats to which senior officers were entitled. One probationer moved into a larger flat he was not entitled to (but with permission) and I was promised the flat he vacated. Weeks went by but he refused to hand over the keys. Ultimately it took a JS to retrieve the keys. He went to the officer's flat, rang the bell for 'what seemed like an eternity' and finally was able to speak to the probationer. 'A JS at his door created the necessary alarm and alacrity in him, you see,' said the JS.[138] A probationer later chastised my asking for the keys as being outrageous. When I tried to explain she screamed: 'We are not animals you know. Only animals need rules. Not us.'[139] Explicit was the violence in her outburst, but implicit is the calculation of the IRS probationer above: that societal norms do not apply to those who have gained status via exams. This is in stark contrast to the probationer who was a doctor. While he persevered within the rules, this female IFS probationer sought the service to break the rules, in short, to violently undermine the very system she was supposed to uphold. Curiously, she did this to maintain what little status she had managed to accrue thanks to a tremendous investment of time—some categories of candidates may continue taking the exam till the age of 35.[140] Average life expectancy in India in 2011 was 64.5 years, which means that just under 54% of one's life may be spent in preparation for life![141] The screaming probationer continued: 'You have come here for some other reasons, but we think only people who have won right to this [banging the wall with her hand to show she meant the flats] should get this.'[142] In other words, she was violent twice over, but it was defensive, the thrashing of a minnow in a bowl with a crack rather than the overwhelming violence instigated by modernists and waged with a fanaticism that only comes to those convinced that they are the future.

The violence of the weak as experienced by me was pathetic. One probationer informed me that the probationer who kept on bumping me in the swimming pool did so because he did not like my being in their circle (this is likely since he did not speak to me either). Although the field-work is long over, another uses Facebook as a vector to lash out every so often. And then there is self-promotion by the incorporation of 'IFS' or 'Diplomat' into their names on Facebook. Yet by no means is this violence of the feeble expressive of all the IFS. Many in talking amongst themselves censured some of their number's use of their newfound status to boost themselves economically and socially. This in itself reinforces the contention that their violence is that of the weak. Their violence was necessary because they perceived themselves as originating from a very low position. Secondly, this sensibility became a sensitivity exacerbated by their encountering Indians of a type that had been, until they joined the service, beyond their horizon. Naturally, none of this was voiced explicitly. However, it may be apprehended through assumptions. One probationer in a conversation with me about remuneration said that his pay was insignificant because as an officer he would have to 'maintain a particular style'. It was said in a manner that made it quite apparent that I was unaware of what this style was, because I was not an officer.

Many months later, when he came to my home I was surprised at the astonishment he expressed at the *décor*. In between commenting and asking, his surprise was evident: 'This is pretty swanky, did you rent the flat furnished?' Obviously he was impressed by the 'style' of my house; his pellucid question indicated his assumptions that I had rented a flat, and that it was a flat rather than a house—even though he had entered what was quite obviously a three-storey house; also that it could not be owned by me (the house is actually a family property) and finally, that the furnishings, the Tagores and Jamini Roys on the walls, could just be there rather than be accoutrements installed by a designer to convey what he called 'style'.[143] In short, I met and surpassed his notions of 'style'. The point of relating this incident is that he had originally assumed that since I was so much like him, up to the point when he joined the hallowed portals of the IFS, I was unaware of 'style'. He was viewing me in terms of himself rather than an 'other'. I could not know what 'style' was because he had not known it as a civilian; he had learnt 'style' only after becoming an officer. The implication for this officer, because of his experience, was that civilians live at a level, at a maximum, lower than officers. This idea explains why he experienced cognitive dissonance upon entering my home. His assumption about civilians—certainly those with whom he was on equal terms—living at a level lower than officers had been thrown into turmoil. And the cause of the turmoil was the dramatic change in this officer's status upon getting the job. Yet, he was also locating himself variationally, not least by thinking I was like him, and thereby reinforcing the cosmos. He was not operating on the basis of some 'other' as moderns do. Furthermore, he was also locating himself variationally, and in these two moves he reinforced the cosmos by making evident an entirely non-modern way of rationalizing his encounter with me.

As for officers who were violent, the impulse undoubtedly overruled the very rationality that generates their will to rise, but that is not the entire story. Violence is generated by their low self-calculated origins. Marriage is often the means for men who are the overwhelming majority. One probationer, I was told, carried four mobile phones because he put advertisements in four newspapers for a wife—but ultimately married someone he already knew. Others required an extra flat after marriage, 'Why? Because of all the stuff they got ... dowry!'[144] The requirements went beyond economics. An officer explained: 'Some marry for class. You can tell if the girl is from a better background, just listen to her English ... if she's fluent and he's not, that's all you need to know.'[145]

It would appear that while the original mimic men have vanished from the IFS, some lower caste and 'class' officers continue to seek to differentiate themselves from whence they come. Some do this as blatantly as the original mimic men, which explains the outraged letters by IFS 'A' officers, the category that is destined to become ambassadors, wrote at the appointment of someone who was not even of the IFS 'B'—that is the support staff who may be promoted to the IFS 'A'—but a stenographer as Ambassador to North Korea. They were outraged even though no one from the two superior services wanted to go to North Korea! Furthermore, the IFS 'B' in 2009 forced the MEA to pass a rule barring stenos from being elevated to the IFS 'A'.[146] However, frequently this differentiation does not make them modern. What is at stake is not that they are acting against the cosmos (by being violent and differentiating), but that their decision-making processes make them act with full cognizance of the cosmos and they know they are refuting it. This is what made for embarrassing silences when I put this thesis to some officers. I knew it would, but it needed testing. What is key, then, is that the violence is generated from their relationally self-defined low origins clashing with their new social environment. In short, they seek to integrate into a new world and in doing so they are violent. However, this does not necessarily imply disconnection from the old world: marriages, after all, are overwhelming governed by language, caste, and *gotra*. The girl might be higher class, but she is in a multitude of categories of precisely the same background as the officer.

Patently the rationale behind initiating these moves is cosmological, but so too is the manner in which moves are conducted. What is required is a superabundance of work so taxing that it is more appropriate to designate it a struggle. From joining the MEA to fighting for 'stuff', diplomats struggle, and this way of working is termed *jugar*. Found in both reserved and general category officers, *jugar* makes for practices of mobility neither anarchical nor modern. Nor is *jugar* the overwhelming use of violence along a single trajectory, it is the way of the feeble. Most often, *jugar* is not an expression of violence at all, because people seek to operate within society by keeping to established relations—rather than undermining them—or else to respond, violently indeed, but knowing full well that it will have no impact. In other words, what is violence for the weak is often no more than an expression of frustration at the possibility of what has been secured slipping away. Such responses, but in particularly non-violent ones, are what makes for virtue, and they animate the MEA as a unit because it is an expression of *jugar*.

The difference from modernity is clarified if *jugar* is set against the PWE. The rationale for work in modernity, the PWE is understood as 'people who work hard succeed', and those who are presumed not to do so become the target of prejudice. This is unsurprising for Christianity, and hence anarchical-binarism animates the PWE. Weber developed the PWE out of Christianity, translating the concept of religious calling into a secular world. Work became a means of gaining salvation and workers were expected to act selflessly for a greater good. According to this ideology, work and employment were defined as positive actions for the glory of God and the preservation of the soul.[147] In short, the PWE denies distinctions within the work it spawns. The result is that there is no differentiation in types of work or the violence that all work engenders in some form or another. Indeed, the violence of work is dignified by the subsuming of all work to the glory of God.

This means that the PWE cannot contain the violence of the weak, because it does not result from the realization of destiny, but simply from the contextual desire to improve one's contextual position. Moreover, the very idea of work is different. Arrived at relationally, the requirement to work is understood variationally. That is, while the PWE is totalitarian in judging itself superior, those operating with *jugar* find no prior reason to deem any particular type of work superior. A probationer stated matter-of-factly: 'We always had to work, my grandparents were illiterate and they worked as farmers … I worked to educate myself … it's all work.'[148]

Low social and economic opportunities inculcated *jugar*, a work-ethos intending to solve real and particular problems encountered contextually rather than satisfy some greater good generated by some inconceivable originary point and to be realized at some equally implausible terminal point. This is what makes *jugar* sensitive to context and the practitioner anticipatory, for the weak have to seize opportunities to make ends meet, unlike the strong who are convinced their use of force guarantees victory. In short, *jugar* is not destiny but chance and circumstance. *Jugar* in terms of modernity is no more than an assortment of fragmentary moves.

While work is work for the probationer, some work is more rewarding in improving the present, and it is this aim that reveals the practice of *jugar*. For this reserved category probationer, his route to managing his context was education, but to get it required *jugar*: an itinerant life from the age of eight bursting with anticipation and made possible by rewards from the state.[149] His parents, who are first generation literate and teachers, helped him anticipate. His mother was 'very special' in having had an education which was explained by her coming from 'a better family, a plains family where there were schools.' She married his father and in coming to his village, brought education. 'Before she came the school was just on paper because my village had no roads.' This probationer's *jugar* was individual as much as familial. Out of a population of 90,000 in his 'home-place', he was 'the sixth person to pass class twelve.' He did it from his third school. All of the schools were state-run: 'There were no teachers for the science subjects ... the district headquarters is far away and we were out of sight. ... My area was a punishment post. ... There was violence. When I was in class seven about 10 to 30 policemen died.' It was a 'small' school and by class eight, he was teaching himself.[150]

Jugar, then, is not just an ethic for work, but also a style of working, a politics of the present. *Jugar* makes for seeking out opportunities or innovating.[151] It is the survival of the weakest and produced by immediate lived reality, and seeks to change it, in contrast to the PWE, which is produced by the past and seeks something in the future. And so, to transform his present, the probationer attended his third school, living as a 'paying guest in a friend's friend's house.' He passed his exams and wanted to become an engineer. It was a living, but 'to get into the Engineering College there was a test. I asked the bus driver (which ran once a day from my village to the nearest town) to get the form for me. But the driver keeps on changing and I never got the form. It was a 12 hour ride. We used to get books like that as well.'

Travel was avoided because of the cost. His parents earned a combined salary of 'around Rs. 5,500 in the 1990s.' Though his state schools were inadequate, he also received scholarships. The 'first was in class eight. It was the Jawaharlal Nehru Talent Search Scholarship for class nine to twelve for Rs. 1,000 per year,' and though he did not need the money then, he 'saved it because I knew I would need every penny later.' An endless run of exams was no reason for him to stop aspiring. His next scholarship was 'Rs. 3,600 per annum and included a Rs. 1,500 book grant.' It enabled him to go to university, not in the nearest town but in the state capital. 'Lots of people said why not go to the local town, but this was the best to my knowledge.' It was the combined operation of individual and state aid and infrastructure—no matter how basic—in deepest darkest India that enabled him to realize desires manufactured in context.

With help from the state, the probationer attended university. Here his *jugar* came into its own to make him intent on overcoming suffering. However, escape from his context was in itself a matter of suffering. This is not to suggest that he was acting for the future. The very fact that he was educated was a reward, for him it was better than tilling the land. But the suffering persisted. At university he felt the lack of a 'supportive atmosphere. No seniors from my place to protect me, show me the way. I was the first one from my place to go to the state university.' He recalled the physical ragging which forced him out of his hostel. The work-ethos, transferred to seeking out educational opportunities, now manifested itself as a fully developed expression of *jugar*, a will to make do, seize opportunities and finally pay the cost. 'I decided to take it as a challenge.' But there was a price: 'I was alone most of the time, started losing self-esteem. People would form groups along their regional lines. The group from my area was the worst because they knew my background.'

After university he applied for a job at a large national manufacturing concern. Getting the job was another round of applications, and at the same time he also applied to the Indian Institute of Technology (IIT). 'Their criterion was those who had not failed anything. This was 15 days after I finished my degree.' He went to a major town, 'to take the Graduate Aptitude Test for Engineers for IIT.' He qualified, with the help of his quota status, and attended one of the newer IITs. Here language was once again a barrier: 'In IIT the medium of instruction was English and so I began learning it on my own. The teachers were competent. ... I was offered a job which required moving to Western Europe, but did not want to leave India ... I took the CAT for IIM and got into IIM(A) which is the best.' Education by now was 'just a step,' but not to going abroad. With admission secured, he had to find the money to pay for it: 'I could not arrange money in time ... I needed a loan and had to apply from my home-place. That meant taking leave from my work-place. So I went to my village and was told that to apply for the loan I had to go to the district HQ, there they didn't know anything. But having exceeded my leave, I lost my job.'[152]

Patently this probationer's work ethic—founded on a relationally self-defined weakness and seeking to change it—comes from a rationality different from the one that produced the PWE. This is why the PWE cannot identify the virtue in his ethic, for he, like most others, seeks to move without violence and for contextual reasons. This is fundamentally incomprehensible to the PWE, for it rides on violence to realize a utopia programmed by 'history'. The virtue that *jugar* fosters is not limited to those who come from the lowest rungs of society, but also enwraps general category probationers. What interlinks the two categories of entrants, as will become obvious below, is the violence inflicted on them and their nonviolent response. The difference is only one of degree. For clarity's sake, it ought to be noted that the cosmological is implicit in the general category probationer's self-understandings because he contextualizes himself, and not in oppositional terms. He is from a state regarded within India as 'backward' and 'a very small town' in that state, and he repeatedly noted that 'there are many Indias' and that his words were clearly defined as emanating from what he calls 'my India', indicating a self-conscious locating within a cosmos understood as encompassing variety and organized in ways that proper nouns—founded on false binarism of elite/masses—fail to comprehend.[153]

Though both probationers have mothers who are teachers, this general category probationer's grandparents were minor state employees. He locates himself within the 'middle class'. A term reminiscent of 'many Indias', it may be tied down monetarily: the 'combined salary of my parents ... some Rs. 15,000 per month in today's [2007] money.' His mother taught him at home. As with the reserved category probationer, this man's first language is a dialect, but he had access to vernacular newspapers. He also learned 'English, because you need it to get ahead.' His parents chose an English-medium school—and he got the grades to get in. Later, he went to Delhi to find out about a reputed school, 'but the fees then were

Rs. 45,000 per year ... my father would have supported me ... but it was too much to ask.' This failure at innovation did not stop him from attending one of the best local schools. It taught in English and he was a boarder. It was his inauguration to talent, the first time he met 'high-achievers from around my district. That was very important because there were strikes, which meant that the teaching was not continuous. We had to teach ourselves and living with people who were motivated meant that we worked together.' They also came from 'better backgrounds and spoke English.' It was here that he began to read the *Times of India*, which, 'came two days late. ... I read ... papers to pass the time ... for the short stories they published'.[154] Nothing in his childhood inculcated nationalism, rather these experiences helped him hone the *jugar* required to overcome the everyday failures of ordinary life in his geobody.

Jugar is evident in every decision he took to realize contextual desires. He studied science, 'because everyone does it. It secures your future,' and took the entrance exams for the IITs and other colleges. Unlike the reserved probationer, he went to a local college and after graduation took a series of tests for the local engineering university. After graduation, he had to approach companies 'because campus recruitment didn't really exist then.' He applied to an internationally known IT firm, travelled for tests, then had the interview and got the job. 'It was a cakewalk.' Having applied for MBA programmes, he took the entrance exams and did not succeed and so took the IT job which 'paid more than both my parents earned ... but I soon realised what the New Economy was [as opposed to the core heavy industries set up by Nehru].' The old economy had made 'us into what we were in the 1990s, laid the bedrock of industry, schools, colleges and hospitals. They might be bad, but there was nothing before!' His dissatisfaction with IT was not only intellectual, he disliked the lifestyle that accompanied it. The first day

itself I realised what this was going to be. I started living with three friends in a flat. The day began at eight ... and finished ... at nine p.m. ... quite often I would stay on longer. I was doing well, I mean I was doing what everyone else was doing. ... What kind of a life is that? You become a machine, just doing what you are told to do. But you make money. ... I lacked interest in the work. It was dull. Boring. Sometimes I had to miss dinner and make do only with pizza or burger ... that's not even real food.

He then did what can only be astounding for modernity, for he turned away from the globalized economy by starting the process of applying for a job in the long established Nehruvian economy, and heavy industry in particular. He needed books, which his father mailed him, 'but this was my life, I could not even collect them because I had no time.' An application for leave was refused. So he skipped work to go and collect the books and study. 'For this I needed my parent's moral support.' Later at his UPSC interview there was bewilderment at his leaving the private sector. He explained to the panel: 'There is a sense of achievement. If you are working on a hydroelectric project you know that ten years down the line it will provide water and energy to farmers in *mofussil* [provincial] towns like the one you come from. In an IT firm you are just doing some work for foreigners.' There is nothing wrong with any of that, but 'in my case this [government service] was better for me.' Searching for tangible qualities to explain a frame of mind he added 'the public sector has job security.' He got the state job and joined a massive hydroelectric plant for training—the first step towards realizing a duty to people like himself by contributing something concrete.

While he was undergoing training, with time on his hands, the idea of the IAS came to him, 'I can't explain why … maybe it is because we had always known of and seen IAS officers, maybe ambition?' The very inability to explain indicates that he was pursuing the practically unachievable. But undeterred by the odds, he began to pursue it. The first step was to get some more books and study for two or three hours every day. A few months later he was transferred and 'suddenly had responsibility. I began to enjoy the job and studies took a backseat. Facilities were good … good working environment … work was stimulating. But the UPSC was in the back of my mind and I filled in the forms that November. I took the prelims in May.'

Over a series of questions what became apparent was that the subjects he chose to prepare for were the ones that required the least effort. This was important as he was working eight-hour shifts daily. Within months he had taught himself as much as he could and 'had to make a choice. Either I stay on or move to Delhi for a coaching class to prepare for the Mains. I decided to leave and went to stay with some friends in Delhi and joined Sri Rams IAS [a crammer] for a twelve-day crash course. It was pointless (people study for months to prepare for the exams) but I had no option [because] I was working to earn some money and then spending it on studying for the exams.' He got in the first time around, testimony to his skills in making do, to *jugar*.

Neither of the probationers introduced above mentions nationalism, though they emphasize a particular manner of cultivating development—understood as broadening opportunities by being sensitive to their contexts and also dispensing with obligations to people like themselves. The purpose is to produce the type of changes that they themselves benefited from, reminiscent of a geobody that permits practical-pragmatism or a type of politics at odds with modernity's power politics. Both probationers progressed through the cosmos via *jugar* or hard work, seeking advantages, making sacrifices, ignoring setbacks, paying the price for failure and yet doggedly persevering. In short, making the best out of the tiny repertoire of abilities their situation provided them. In doing so, they exceeded the conventional understanding of citizen as participant (voting), by seeking not just to hold a stake in governance, but to become governance.[155] This exceptionalism of the weak is also, and unlike modernity, geared to the present, indeed it is only possible in a rationality fixated upon the present. In other words, the present is not instrumental to a future. In choosing to respond to acts of violence towards themselves in a non-violent manner they also became virtuous, something that modernity cannot recognize because modernity is violence.

The virtue of *jugar*, which motivates the individuals who perform diplomacy, not surprisingly personifies the MEA and characterizes Indian diplomacy. In a meeting in the office of a member of the Research and Information System for Developing Countries (RIS),[156] the MEA's back office, we were interrupted by a telephone call. It was an Indian ambassador calling from abroad to ask what the PM had said India ought to do in a public speech the last time he had visited that country—less than five years ago. The ambassador's lack of knowledge is astounding, but explained by the demands placed on ambassadors. During the India-Africa Forum Summit in 2008, one of the three top Secretaries in the MEA was—so I gathered from overheard conversations—overseeing minute matters of protocol, to the point of ensuring guests were seated correctly at state dinners. This might come as a surprise, for a senior diplomat might be expected to be mulling matters of state. In India it is just as well that they instead attend to table plans nowadays, given what has occurred. For instance, in 1970 Singapore's PM Lee Kuan Yew hosted a dinner in New Delhi for PM Indira Gandhi. He was not supposed to see the seating plan, but by mistake he was given a copy. He took one look and asked why Mrs Gandhi was seated on his left. Lee's staff discovered that the Indian printer had made a 'ghost printing error' (placing the typeset the wrong way around). It was left to Lee's staff to sort out the mess and personally escort the 60 guests to their new places.[157]

If properly internalized, *jugar* offers the ability to recover with aplomb even in the most telling of negotiations. S. Jaishankar, one of India's negotiators in the 123 talks, recalled walking into a negotiating room with his two aides to be met by 'fifty-five American lawyers'. With a smile slowly spreading across his face, his explanation for how he managed was: 'We are Indian you know, we can make do.'[158] Jaishankar's comment becomes a studied understatement when contextualized in National Security Advisor (NSA) M.K. Narayanan's reading of the entire negotiating process. He said the 'difficult part' of the negotiations was the asymmetric drafting process between three MEA officials and dozens of US lawyers. The lack of Indian lawyers, in Narayanan's understanding, was due to cultural difference. Indians are not litigious. As he put it, 'We don't have prenuptial agreements before one gets married here.'[159] The analogy of marriage is once again suggestive, because taken for granted is universality making for a unified, not alienated, cosmos. The analogy also highlights that within the unity that is the cosmos, there is variation.

If making do is how a Secretary and JS operate, it was even more obvious at lower levels in the MEA. When I met a Director at SB he offered me tea. In between numerous phone calls he talked about his work on that day which was as diverse as 'having to make photocopies of the passports of visiting US Senators, taking it to North Block to make passes for them' and 'collecting the information for a paper for his superiors.' He had 'very little time at Headquarters to finish [his] work and with no help ... we have to make do.' An hour later, as I was preparing to leave he said, 'but you can't go, you've not had your tea.' It had not arrived. Finally, after he had plaintively cajoled an employee ('Do you have something against me?', 'Why won't you do what I ask, please'), the tea came, and as I drank it the officer said, 'Write about this. About our working conditions, about how I can't even get a cup of tea for you.'[160]

Jugar defines the MEA's work style because like its members, it too is weak. As the FS lamented to parliament in 2007, 'the IFS is really less than 700 people today; and when we look at comparable countries, for every Indian diplomat, there are four Brazilian diplomats; for every Indian diplomat, there are seven Chinese diplomats. Now, we might be wonderful and very efficient, but we are not that efficient or that good. I mean, it is really a problem.'The figures take on an absolute significance because, 'in the last 10 years,' said the FS:

our work has increased manifold. Our foreign trade has grown 7 times in the last 10 years, passports issued have doubled to 44 lakhs last year and visas granted have tripled to over 57 lakhs. If you look at just high level state visits—the visits by Heads of States and Governments and official visits of Foreign Ministers—these have increased by about 165 per cent. India has joined 13 new multi-lateral organization or groupings in this period. To cope with this increased workload and apart from our increased political workload, our budget has tripled in these ten years. But the number of personnel has actually shrunk. We have gone down from 4,866 to 4,746 [including chauffeurs and sweepers]. I must speak frankly that the strain is telling on us.[161]

Shortages affect every aspect of Indian diplomacy, making *jugar* essential to the practice of diplomacy. The FM has a staff of 'essentially two, making it smaller than Algeria's,' said an officer who served in the minister's office and in Algeria.[162] Officers do not respond to foreign embassies because 'there is a lot of work ... usually we don't have anything to say ... they want us to change something, and if we are going to, we don't need them to tell us.'[163] Simultaneously, working conditions at Headquarters are poor. Some officers work in rooms without air-conditioners in the summer heat. A formal application for an air-conditioner was made by an officer in November, but when I met him in the following June—when temperatures in New Delhi hit 40 degrees centigrade—there was still no sign of it.[164] Bathrooms attached to offices are often stacked with rotting files[165] and Indian heads of mission complain that Headquarters never replies to notes and memos, leaving heads of mission to their own devices to get things done.[166] An Indian High Commissioner told me to call him on his wife's mobile phone in New Delhi because 'getting a phone from the Ministry is impossible' when he visits Headquarters.[167] During the India-Africa Forum Summit, it took a Minister of State to get mobile phones for liaison officers.[168] Given the paucity of resources, even the most successful officers spend their time on routine procedures that do not befit the expense of maintaining a high-ranking civil servant, for much of their time is consumed in doing what would be expected of a clerk. It is this weakness that makes for *jugar*, for only it can enable someone to work in such conditions.

The need for *jugar* is unlikely to be reduced by the MEA's 'cadre expansion plan' put into effect in 2008. The plan is to add around 50 posts throughout the service (including support staff) annually, and it will continue till 2018.[169] Whether that will be enough in the future is an unknown. What is known is that between 2011 and 2014 the MEA grew by just 83 when its size should have increased by 150. Furthermore, in 2008 there were not enough people to fill the sanctioned intake. In other words, of the tens of thousands of people who took the exams for the IFS 'A', there were not 20 who wanted to be diplomats! In the meantime, the technical inability of staff and their lack of knowledge about what their role entails and how to perform it (see above and chapter 3) means that it is not simply a question of numbers. But even materially, there are very real shortages which have made for a particular kind of entrant, and this problem continues after they join. This is tangible enough to be apparent to foreigners. During the Indo-Africa Summit two junior MEA officers attached to visiting African dignitaries spoke of a type of incident that had occurred to them and, they claimed, to others. The incident happened as they were seeing off a dignitary. The visitor slipped some US dollars into the MEA officer's palm while shaking hands to say good-bye. The MEA men were put out, but admitted that it probably had something to do with 'even Africans having more money than us'.[170] Experiences such as these are not however the main irritant for officers. Nor is the lack of facilities—which is the norm for most. The main irritant, for post-2000 entrants, is that they find expectations dashed and the work demeaning, though this is in part a product of an inflated opinion of what they are capable of. The error is to mistake the amount of status they have secured by becoming the state with capacity.[171] As a senior officer says: 'Can you expect a science graduate or a doctor of Ayurvedic medicine to enter the IFS and the next day to be making policy decisions? It requires developing a sense of politics, of understanding Nehruvian policy. At least 20 years [of education] are required.'[172]

This is why only a tiny minority ever makes policy or negotiates. 'If the government wants to spend one crore [rupees—the annual cost of keeping him in service] on a taxi service then that's the government's choice,' says a Deputy High Commissioner.[173] The majority perform the routine tasks of 'coordination, arranging delegations,' says another officer. Nor are they necessarily capable of doing much more. An IAS officer and trade negotiator commented that during negotiations on a ground-breaking treaty for India (not so important for the other country), the IFS's responsibilities were limited. To my question of what the

IFS did, the officer, barely able to contain his chuckling, said: 'Arranged hotels. Picked us up from the airport!' Regaining his composure he added: 'How many people do you need to make policy? Two, three? And that's done by the PM. Its enacting that is the difficulty, most cannot enact … a negotiation nowadays is a complicated technical affair, you know!'[174] Most remain 'glorified *peons* but this is essential to simply maintaining basic relations,' and the ones who do it best do so because they most fully exploit the idea of *jugar*.[175]

Modernity obviously cannot account for the plethora of Indian practices sketched above. Nor can modernity identify the MEA's ethic and locate its virtue. Unlike the PWE, *jugar* is not modern, because it is not motivated by an overwhelming sense of purpose: to realize utopia. *Jugar* is not a politics of the future. Rather *jugar* is the way of the weak, to secure immediate goals arising out of context. This rationale for *jugar* evidently requires the notion of a cosmos, for operating in such a manner is impossible within modernity. Finally, since *jugar* is the way of the weak, it also seeks to shy away from violence in favour of using what little opportunities are available to innovate, to overcome the numerous acts of violence inflicted upon the weak. None of this is to say that violence is eliminated, only that given the material background of diplomats it is remarkable that they do not resort to violence with greater frequency. Finally, when violence is resorted to, it is not modernity's assimilative violence, but is of a defensive type, seeking to protect what little has been secured. Naturally, there is the greatest virtue when *jugar* is operationalized without recourse to any violence at all. In addition, that *jugar* is the work ethic of at least one branch of the Indian state raises the question: What of the other branches of the state? If the MEA's work-style cannot be contained by modernity, can the state?

Mobility's aim: progress

The next three sections use the concept of progress, which is reflexivity's aim, to show why the concept needs to be freed from the deadening hand of modernity, which at its touch turns to black and white the technicolour possibilities of Indian diplomacy. Progress lends itself to evaluating the operation of reflexivity in the MEA because it is measureable. To start with, the simplest variant of progress—for as will become evident, there are several types—is to engage the only type modernity comprehends: unilinear progress. Within the MEA such progress may be measured in terms of promotions and postings. Yet even this simplistic type of progress devastates attempts to explain the bureaucracy that is the MEA in terms of modern bureaucratic theory.

Quite how this is so is made tangible in the reflexivity generating progress which begins with someone seeking out the state, for to become the state is to progress. A representative explanation for why people seek out the state is a retort I received to what must have seemed a terribly naïve question: 'At least the government came. Who else will come? J.P. Morgan? No one is going to help anyone in the rural areas apart from the government.'[176]

In India, Michel Foucault's and Gilles Deleuze's *dispositif*[177] heuristic just does not suffice, because the state is not part of a 'constellation of institutions, practices, and beliefs that create conditions of possibility within a particular field,' but is the only entity.[178] And it requires prodding. The only 'way to ensure the government will do something is if we do something,'[179] said a probationer—a contextual response, rather than the product of nationalism however defined. The mantle of provisioning rests squarely on the state and in seeking the burden, these lives signal their dissatisfaction with everyday life not through Michael Adas's concept of 'avoidance', that is running away, but through fearlessly engaging the state by aspiring to the impossible.[180] The aspiration arises from a wider sensibility recorded by Neera Chandhoke on the basis of a questionnaire-based survey. She wrote: 'policy-makers and advocates of civil society would establish a parallel system, which can substitute for the state. And yet one significant factor inhibits this plan, the fact that people repose little hope in the ability of civil society agents to negotiate their problems. They would rather fix responsibility on the government, which has presented itself as the guardian of the collective interest.'[181]

The state is not to be resisted, nor do people comply with it quietly. Instead people proactively engage the state to secure their interests, and in doing so exceed anthropological expectations of what politics is by modifying the state 'quietly' to suit themselves, and, remarkably, in overwhelmingly violence-free forms.[182] As for what the government is supposed to do, why people want to become a part of it, the answer was elliptical but no less sharply put for that: 'You live on the pavement … in the jungle.'[183] It was conveyed quite plainly that one purpose was to move out of what is, if anything, a *dispositif* of everyday violence produced by the lack of the infrastructure that Foucault critiques in Europe. Despite the dismal failure of the Indian state to provide education, health and basic infrastructure, this type of conversation was repeated—in varying forms and tones—with several diplomats.[184] The weakest assertion of the state's centrality is, 'everyone expects the state to do everything, build roads, schools … What for? … why cannot the private sector do this? … Government should enable, not do the work.'[185] Yet, as the preceding discussion has shown, economic betterment is not the sole aim for diplomats—for many could secure far better paying jobs in the private sector. Instead they crave status. In doing so they are in keeping with Amartya Sen's prescient and holistic argument that development exceeds the economic, and should be the delivery of substantive freedoms. This is incomplete without political, economic and social freedoms along with transparency and protective security. It would appear that the denizens of the MEA would concur, for their practices are not limited to economic betterment but seek to reduce the violence that inhibits their freedom in a multiplicity of ways.[186] This is progress, and though unilinear it spreads out to include the entire political life of the diplomat.

In viewing the state as the primary agent of unilinear progress, officers are unselfconsciously reproducing Nehruvianism. It may have been modified and adapted, but nevertheless remains Nehruvian because not only is it progress, but the Nehruvian state is also the primary agent for change.[187] That Nehruvianism has become unselfconscious and therefore quite different from an ideology—let alone one of nationalism—is not really surprising if viewed from diplomats' contexts. For them, it is the state that has provided them with what little freedoms they have attained. Furthermore, Nehruvianism today is not an ideology because it provides what Martin Wight calls the 'common frame of reference' in terms of lived experience both positive and negative, for MEA officers.[188] Although the IFS is becoming heterogeneous (in terms of every social benchmark) the common experience of the Nehruvian state ensures that India is not becoming a 'heterogeneous state'.[189] There is no break between the unity of the state and its administrative operations, because unselfconscious Nehruvianism fuses the two. It is unselfconscious Nehruvianism that propels people towards the state, making it their status destination.[190] This movement is all too often interpreted in terms of modernity (rebellion against tradition, transforming the self, to arrive at a prescribed destination),[191] to entrap locals within unilineal progress.[192] However, although the type of progress being outlined here is unilineal, it is not motivated by modernity, for it cannot explain the combined growth of differentiation along one vector (type of person entering the IFS) and homogenization of the experience along another vector (Nehruvianism). Underpinning both is mobility of the individual and the state, but this is not to say that India is unique in its mobility, Pharaonic Egypt's records show that a number of leading figures rose from humble origins.[193] But in the case of India, the attempts to ensnare the country in modernity are unceasing.

The MEA remains blithely unconcerned with these attempts, for it continues in terms made explicable by the unified cosmos. In doing so it not only replicates the cosmos, but also demonstrates the operation of the fourth-possibility.[194] This is to adopt modern processes, but not to further modernity, because the adopting rationality remains doggedly cosmological. These processes undoubtedly involve sequencing, but it is done in a variational rather than oppositional manner. One such practice occurs once people have progressed into the MEA, and it is the organization's means to progress its officers: 'total-evaluation'.

The operation of 'total evaluation' is what makes the practices of managing the MEA's human resources contradict every tenet of modernist bureaucratic theory. Yet this makes for unilinear progress. A modern bureaucracy, it is decreed, must be hierarchically *straff* (taut) through *Akten* (written records).[195] Bureaucracy is supposed to be enwrapped in writing, and modern analysts aspire to documents. In this the MEA does not disappoint naïve researchers. Written records do exist within the MEA. There is the confidential Annual-Performance Assessment Report (APAR) for each officer. But what if these documents are meaningless? An ambassador says, 'You never know, the fellow might just accuse you of caste-ism! So everyone gets either a "good" or "outstanding" report.'[196] Yet there is evidently progress, which refutes Jack Goody's notion that writing is critical to the development of bureaucratic states. Instead the bureaucracy relies on assigning responsibilities on the basis of judgements that eschew framing through reports, exams or tests. This is not contradictory. Judgement requires framing, as it must. The problem is that all modernist assessment programmes are an approximation based on an analysis of particularization, facets of the subject. The MEA, however— in keeping with the cosmological approach—judges officers totally, from the moment of joining and in the spread of jobs available to them at their grade (a modernist category). The assessments are personal, conducted by the immediate superior and through observations and interactions, and activated by the Foreign Secretary Board (FSB).[197] The drawback of a total-evaluation is that 'nothing is certain unless it is put on paper. I've asked for a letter confirming what was said to me [about a posting],' says a high commissioner who adds, 'the closed nature of decision making leads to talk, unsubstantiated but damaging about people getting assignments because their father is something.'[198] As it happens he did not get the job he had been verbally promised.

Arguably, the benefits outweigh this uncertainty, which is produced by the very fluidity and responsiveness of the assessing process. Benefits lie in the very totality of the procedure and accounting for relations between judge and judged to make for a comprehensiveness that binary analysis of humans can only aspire to. This is not 'socio-ideological control' because an ideology is not being reproduced selectively.[199] Rather, total-evaluation channels and tailors unselfconscious Nehruvianism towards the orthodox Nehruvian foreign policy, which is the MEA's forte, just as in capitalism innate enterprise is tailored to profit.[200] Total-evaluation may also work remarkably well. For instance, how can a test check for the qualities required to handle a pivotal diplomatic incident in Tiananmen Square? It was 1970 and at the time relations with China were 'exceedingly bad'. Greeting a line of diplomats, Mao Zedong asked Brajesh Mishra, the Indian Chargé d'affaires, 'Indu(?)' and without waiting for a response said: 'How long are we going to keep quarrelling like this? Let us be friends again.' The Indian diplomat decided Mao was not just being pleasant and resolved to pursue the matter, made an appointment with the Chinese Foreign Office, which told him the ball was in his court. Then, despite Delhi—as usual—not taking a decision, the Chargé d'affaires forced the matter on the PM, as he was able to do given his privileged birth, paving the way for the normalization of relations.[201] The ability to place an officer capable of managing such a unique opportunity is repeatedly possible through comprehensive evaluations of personality, ability and approach. In short, a cosmological evaluation rather than one based on narrow technical analysis of a person.[202] Even if such a test were formulated, it would necessarily be extremely complicated and time consuming—because that is what a 'total evaluation' is. The reason why it does not distract staff from their everyday duties is because it continues alongside, as indeed it must, the more obvious and everyday diplomatic functions diplomats are tasked with.

Total-evaluation however does not consign the MEA into the realms of post-bureaucratic organizations (which are a 'frameshift' from the Weberian ideal type, but nevertheless an accretion from modernity) because the MEA simultaneously uses modernist principles,[203] but to forward another rationality. In practice what this means may be apprehended through the modernist notion of hierarchy. It makes for rank and is dependent purely on years in service and a few general criteria, all of which was recently modified and set out in a letter by the FS to his staff.[204] What this standard modern system makes for is an escalator-like quality, and it also means that there are many more officers than positions available commensurate to their rank. At Headquarters (SB) there are five openings at the highest level (Secretary) which anyone with around thirty years in service qualifies for, but since there are more secretaries than openings, the MEA has invented the category of Special Secretary. The holder of this title has passed the modernist seniority test (years in service), but in most cases he has not been selected for the significant jobs at SB because of relatively negative total-evaluations. It was a Special Secretary, for instance, who blundered in putting up an unqualified man for an ambassadorship.[205] Total-evaluations might appear arbitrary because they are predicated on something as fleeting as being known. A JS in charge of a territorial division and on the verge of becoming a Secretary exclaimed: 'I got this job because I used to be in Moscow! There I had to fetch VIPs from the airport which was a long way away. It meant that I would sometimes be in the car for a long time with people like the FS. Since everyone visits Moscow, everyone got to know me. Being known meant that I was on their minds. That's how I got this job.' An officer must be known, but being known to be ineffective would not have secured him his job. He was in an important embassy because he had passed a series of preceding total-evaluations.[206]

A total-evaluation therefore starts with hierarchy, because that makes the officer eligible for a range of postings at a particular rank. This co-opting of hierarchy provides the means for an alternative rationality to function. Progress within the MEA may therefore be categorized as a fourth-possibility operation—modernist ways are deployed and to bring about simple unilineal progress. However, the final selection of who does what is not done via uniform and pre-set promotions criteria applied to one and all, but via a total-evaluation. It is cosmological because it maintains causality, but it makes analysis dependent on relations rather than

THE MAKING OF INDIAN DIPLOMACY

origins, on time and space rather than only time. This is because a total-evaluation is founded on relations, for the officer is judged by his immediate superiors and the Ministry, rather than through some limited tests. This is what makes a total-evaluation comprehensive, something enhanced by each total-evaluation building on several earlier and ongoing appraisals. That it is the final arbiter for postings is why unilineal progress in the MEA is a function of the fourth-possibility.

A recent controversy about progress within the MEA at its very pinnacle demonstrates the effectiveness of the MEA's recalcitrant ways. The controversy centred on the speed with which Shivshankar Menon was appointed FS, bypassing sixteen officers.[207] A mere 48 hours was required for the PM to look through 20 officers' (meaningless) 'service profiles' and appoint India's top diplomat, who remained in office far longer than most of his predecessors.[208] One of the officers passed over suspected that the speed of the decision was due to the 'Malayali mafia', a much touted and unverifiable clique pushing their own kind, and made a request under the Right to Information Act. She was correct in her reading that 'a mere 48 hours' is not enough to appoint the FS, but incorrect in thinking that the Government of India could be co-opted by a tiny group of civil servants. What is overlooked in these alarmist assessments is the possibility that the PM was not relying on modernist criteria or subterfuge, but on a long running total-evaluation programme. Apprehending how it resolves decisions of great magnitude, effectively and with great speed, is possible in the first instance via modernist hierarchy.

It was definitely placed in service of total-evaluation because, although Menon was incontrovertibly a Secretary at the time of appointment and therefore senior enough for the job, the job was not given to him because of his seniority. This is clear from the controversy that ensued upon his appointment. The appointing authority for the position of FS is the PM and he screened 20 officers for the job.[209] The choice made resulted in a furore and at least three officers (who in terms of seniority should have got the job) took voluntary retirement. The reason why some officers objected is indicated by the objections raised by one bypassed officer, Rajiv Sikri, in print. But first, a caveat: it cannot be claimed that these officers were self-serving, that is, they lusted after the top job, for to do so is to walk into the vestibule leading to exegesis without an archive. That is what limits this section to available and excavated records.

Sikri objected because for him the seniority system was sufficient for progress to the top of the MEA. In effect the officers who objected to

Menon's appointment thought time served was enough to progress.[210] It was a replaying of the difference between modernity and the cosmological, about where the focus of investigation ought to lie. The objecting officer, in modernist style, thought originary causality enough. In this case one's position in the entrance exams decades ago was sufficient for promotion to the top job. However, 'total evaluation' shifts the emphasis from time served to include what was done in that time, that is, context. In this shift originary causality is not contradicted. What is challenged is the subsumation of space to time, by restoring the former.

The inability to do this is modernity's failing, and it makes for a divide within the MEA that is not only debilitating but also dangerously close to decision makers. So obvious is the divide that even the US Embassy in New Delhi—not particularly sensitive to what takes place in India—was aware of it.[211] The nature of the divide arises from Sikri's time-bound view, making for an understanding of diplomacy decidedly at cross-purposes with the cosmic rationale. How it shapes Sikri's understandings may be gleaned from his self-conceptualization. This was in keeping with his modernist entrusting of all to time. As he put it, 'A diplomat is an honest man sent abroad to lie for his country.'[212] In other words the ends justify the means, which is counter to the cosmos (where origins and ends may overlap and hence means ought to be in keeping with ends). Unsurprisingly Sikri's view is endorsed by the US Army War College,[213] but not by the man who got the job. A Secretary level officer introducing Menon to probationers said, '… today we have the Foreign Secretary who will tell you all young people how to lie for your country.' Menon's response was: 'That might be what Western diplomats do, but Indian diplomats don't lie,' before explaining that an agreement based on a lie was fundamentally unstable.[214] Furthermore, Sikri in his monograph—an extension of a paper—lays out international policies required to achieve great power status, without explaining why India ought to be a great power.[215] It is almost as if Sikri, having read modern IR theory, has learned that the international produces 'great powers' and since India inhabits the international, India too ought to strive to become a 'great power'. In short, his mimesis displays a reflexivity that is insular because he looks within modernity's timeline (the international) to find the reason for India to act. But of course this is a rather shallow basis for policy, and is also time-bound, by being in awe of the past in a very limited way: everyone must follow the path modern nations took, as if it is the only way.[216] If he was cosmic, then he would have arrived at a far more convincing, ethical reason for changing India's situation, rather than parroting the aspiration to become a 'great power'. The reason could have been to end abject poverty, to change India's status now, rather than to strut brute power in the international. In pursuing such an aim he would also have kept to the everyday logic of today's diplomats. However, Sikri never touches upon poverty, nor upon how these internal complexities might detain India.[217] In thinking so, Sikri was fundamentally out of touch with how his masters thought. That is exposed succinctly with US Secretary of State Condoleeza Rice's magnanimous offer to make India a 'great power'. FM Natwar Singh replied: 'We are not in the game of becoming a great power. Our job is to eradicate poverty.'[218] In short, modernity plays to win itself titles, but India plays to fulfil duties. Implicit is an understanding of the cosmos. Sikri missed this, to view the world in standard modernist ways: there is in his writings no concentrated attention to policy by contextual analysis, rather just a modish evolutionary understanding of the international.

What such an approach meant in practice were finite policy suggestions at odds with the established ways of Indian diplomats and diplomacy. An example is Sikri's objecting to the PM's decision to vote against Iran at the IAEA in 2005.[219] Sikri's reasoning was that the US coerced India into voting against Iran not because it made any material difference to Tehran, but because Washington wanted a sign that New Delhi would in the future pay for the 123 by becoming pliable. The nub of Sikri's argument was that in agreeing, India played the US's game and lost. New Delhi should have stood by Iran, just because it would showcase Indian power and spite the superpower. His reading is therefore a perfect replication of diplomacy as laid out by the arch-modernist Kenneth Waltz, who understands power as coercion and diplomacy as limited to alliances.[220] This patently contradicts a rationality that refuses to countenance violence and which opposes the notion of further sub-dividing the cosmos. That such a rationality could have been at work is indicated by Sikri detailing how India's response was irrational in Watzian terms, thereby himself opening the fissures in his argument. In other words, by the rules of power politics, it was illogical for India to agree with the US. After all, as Sikri correctly notes, Iran was a steady source of oil, whereas the US had an uneasy relationship with India at best. Hopes of a future grand alliance with the US were highly implausible given Pakistan's historical position as both opposed to India and ally of

Washington. Furthermore, there were US interests in Afghanistan. In short, as Sikri volubly demonstrates, Indian actions were not based on a modern reading of international politics.

But why then did the PM strike out in ways inadvisable within modernity's canon? The answer only becomes apparent with the rejection of the modernist charge of irrationality. This reveals that the PM's choosing to engage the US was an exemplar of the fourth-possibility: using the pre-eminent bastions of the modernist intellectual project but in ways quite impossible within modernist thought. In short, by delivering the vote on Iran, an empty sign, India managed an external pressure, while contradicting power politics. Sikri's advice would have instead led India straight into the trap of power politics in three ways. Firstly, in replying to coercion in the same language, India would have further divided the cosmos. India would have reinforced the notion of alienation. This patently could not be done for it would contradict the cosmos, and so India voted to undermine alienation twice: Iran was not alienated by the vote and India was able to continue establishing relations with the US. Secondly, the decision was not based on anarchy, because it arose from the context of decision makers and broadened India's relations, which reinforced the notion of society. Thirdly, there was therefore no instrumental use of the present, rather everything was geared to the maintenance of the cosmos. That the PM acted as he did, despite his Oxbridge educational background, suggests that formal educational training has very little to do in shaping a person's conceptual apparatus.

The societal aspect of how the PM contradicted power politics also reveals the working of an alternative reflexivity. Before outlining its workings, and in the PM's terms, it should be made explicit that the decision to engage the US was the PM's alone, because policy level decisions are the PM's.[221] Centralization meant that the MEA's Policy Planning (PP) division 'was a dead duck from the start. To begin with we wrote dozens of papers … which were never read,' said Jagat Mehta who established it. Today the PP division is a parking site for officers who simply want to survive while enjoying the perks of a government job or are deeply ambivalent about their job (but not enough to resign) and have, owing to the seniority system, risen to the requisite rank to even head the PP.[222]

To detail the working of reflexivity in the key decision-maker is to assume he is rational, which is to discard modernity and instead adopt his rationale. This was clearly cosmological, which is why it becomes unintelligible within modernity's framework. Like his diplomats who express their contextual approach in the mechanisms of the state, the PM too kept to that model. Conversations between him, me and my parents—on occasion others such as Montek Singh Ahluwalia and his wife were also present—made apparent his thinking.[223] However, there is no need to refer to those conversations because what he said in private matched his public pronouncements.[224] As he told parliament, his decision to engage the US was based on time and space, that is context, and it was his life. By harking back to his past in parliament he was not reminiscing but laying out an alternate rationality founded on the contextual. And so the PM described how he had risen from poverty and was the first in his family to be educated. The overlap with Nehruvianism was implicit, which is why he quoted Nehru to locate himself: 'foreign policies are not just empty struggles on a chessboard. … Ultimately, foreign policy is the outcome of economic policy.'[225] As the PM made clear, policy is honed in the unselfconscious suffering of individual lives, which is largely a matter of economics. Intertwined is status: decades-old 'nuclear apartheid' arising from racial prejudice was expressly mentioned by the MEA and the PM as the other reason for overcoming what was understood as an economic barrier.[226] This approach is also what makes the MEA not what Sharon Traweek called a 'culture of no culture', but one of contextual enmeshment.[227] In short, arising from and engaged with, society.

Understanding society as more than time made for a cosmological rationality, and it is what permitted the PM to be reflexive in time and space and arrive at an impossible possibility for moderns: reaching out to another timeline to forward the cosmos. This is why the PM could imagine managing the particular social constraints imposed upon India's economics by engaging and then changing the 'international'. At work were not micro-concerns limited to steady oil supplies or securing nuclear energy. The ultimate purpose of engaging the US politically was to further India's enmeshment in the globe by breaking a Western-controlled international cartel that kept hidden thousands of US 'Entity List' technologies. These had long been denied to India because their inventors class them as 'dual use'.[228] The aim was to give birth to a 'knowledge economy' founded on India accessing technologies hitherto denied to it. The purpose was to become a Research and Development (R&D) hub. India's immediate aim remains replicating China's example in manufacturing, but in R&D.[229] With cheaper labour costs the expectation is that India will be able to undercut the West. 'That's how our economist PM views it,' said K. Subrahmanyam, the formulator of India's nuclear doctrine and father of a 123 negotiator (not to mention an established Western academic and another civil servant).[230] The basis of the plan was that while demand for manufactured goods is susceptible to economic considerations, technology is far more resistant to market fluctuations. Breaking out of the Western quarantine was therefore essential to India because on it hinged the fate of hundreds of millions escaping poverty. Secondly, it was also an emotive issue, resonating with the injustice arising simply from India's exclusion. In short, what was at work was a reflexivity without insularity or an urge to repudiate the past to establish modernity, but rather seeking it out from another angle, to realize another project.

The first step to securing all of this was the 123, and it required a FS who matched the PM's assessments since he remains the ultimate decision maker. Menon was selected because he passed his total-evaluation. It is therefore dependent on the person conducting it, but this is not the arbitrary forwarding of a personal agenda. Suggesting this does not take account of the reasoning of practitioners, and so the dynamic governing progress and foreign policy making in India are missed. Such reasoning falls back on viewing the world in terms of classical IR devolving, as it must to keep with the notion of originary causality propounded by moderns, from a few 'great' European minds focused on not just power, but 'great power'.[231] This patently was not the way in which policy was formulated by either the PM or Menon, because if it were, then Sikri—the simulacrum of Anglo-Saxon IR theory—would have been selected. Indeed, in not selecting him, the PM's total-evaluation safeguarded the state's rationality by weeding out the invasive rationality that is modernity and thereby undermined yet again the very notion of arbitrariness or what is called 'ad hocism.'

This point is confirmed by a speech Menon gave soon after he got the job, which inadvertently illustrated the gulf between his approach and Sikri's and in doing so yet again reinforced the integrity of political thought at the most significant level: PM, FM and FS.[232] Menon, like the PM, is insular not in the sense of looking into the evolution of the 'international' to find policy options, but because both look at themselves in a contextual manner. In doing so neither is in awe of the past as presented by modernity; they are able to view it and use it to further themselves. What Menon did in his speech was remarkably similar to what the PM did. Menon located himself relationally in a poor country where lives were wracked by everyday suffering. He compounded his uncontainability within modernity by then demonstrating his *jugar* in explaining that his aim was to find ways to end the tyranny of suffering that pervades India. Finally, he demonstrated a reflexively that was contextual and also aimed at arriving at a solution quite impossible in the context in which it was formulated, and it was not modernity's timeline, but time in his space. It was on the basis of this highly inward looking, localized rationale that he argued for seizing new opportunities (engaging the US) while managing the setbacks such a course might entail. Such a rationalizing process does not replicate the teleology of violence produced by modernity, but rather activates a course arising out of the dual operation of time and space, and so seeks to minimize violence. The use of violence in standing up to violence is crucially what Sikri leaves out in his analysis, as do those who see India descending to alliance diplomacy in the coercion of 2005.

Looking back, the practical benefits of Menon's reflexivity are evident today in a manner that would have been impossible at the time: India continues its good relations with Iran and negotiated a path-breaking nuclear agreement with the US.[233] This did not involve deception, for that would be a form of violence and in any case the empathy provoked by the cosmos predicates against it. Hence, India was highly sensitive to US objections to engaging Iran. The MEA empathized with the US and managed US concerns by keeping the US informed, but continued to do what India decided, from its relational calculus, was right for itself, a path the US opposed.[234] The US for its part continued on its unilinear path by imposing sanctions on Iran. India responded not by falling in line, but by continuing to deal with Iran by negotiating innovative solutions to circumvent US sanctions.[235] This makes for an altogether different brand of diplomacy that seeks to continue play, rather than modernity, which seeks to win. In setting it out Menon also noted:

Some of you might see a great omission in this listing of challenges. What about balance of power issues … and issues of conventional security? Speaking personally, I believe that there is a good realist or balance of power argument to be made for choosing precisely these issues as our major foreign policy challenges. But sadly the language of strategic discourse in India is not yet developed enough to describe what we empirically know and face as reality around us. We need to develop our own strategic concepts and vocabulary. I am repeatedly struck by the use of concepts, ideas and methods of analysis that come from other situations and interests, (such as deterrence, parity, or reciprocity), and bear little relationship to our unique circumstance. That is something that needs serious examination on its own. It is probably best left to thinkers like you.[236]

Evidently, Menon believes modernity could arrive at his conclusions. Anarchical-binarism might posit itself as alienated from variational thought, but the latter never alienates, for that is impossible within a unified cosmos. The implication for modern disciplines is that they have to develop—as Menon suggests—an altogether new set of categories suited to Indian reality as understood by those who compose India, rather than rely on those developed by and for some distant place. To do so requires more than sidestepping the hubristic sense of inevitability undergirding modernity. It is to adopt the methods and ways of the weak. Only by doing so can anthropologists, IR scholars and others make some contribution to knowledge beyond what amounts to no more than containment.[237]

Menon, in short, reiterated the PM, in operating in a non-anarchical and non-dualistic manner which arose from personal lived, localized experiences of India, and his method of acting on those decisions was to strike out to engage modernity, not on its terms, but on his. The purpose was therefore not to realize some later totality, but the here and now, while managing secondary concerns. This is Indian reflexivity for it operates not in time but in context. That this reflexivity is operationalized through *jugar* means that the thresholds to be crossed are not only intellectual but physical. The operation of this type of reflexivity was evident immediately after the Mumbai attacks. Even though the attacks were 'on a whole new level', Menon told the US Ambassador, 'We must make opportunity out of crisis'.[238] The person-state conjuncture explains why this reflexivity is the rationale of the state, and it uses modernity's protocols without becoming a function of them. What the practices within the MEA and its interactions with other states—especially in the light of Sikri's readings—demonstrate, then, is that the state's practices and policy may only be made sense of in terms of a unified cosmos.

Unspectacular suffering

Quite how inapplicable modernity is as an exegetic framework becomes apparent from the very multidimensionality of progress by both diplomats and the state. Not only does progress at the MEA surpass modernist calculations, it is completely confounded. This is because progress is not simply unilineal and therefore oppositional. While progress always involves a destination, progress in the MEA can mean folding back or changing the very texture of the destination. The abiding consistency in these multifarious moves, however, is that, unlike modernity, they do not rely on violence but indeed are predicated against it. It is for such an assorted set of reasons that these procedures cannot be the product of modern reflexivity, for it is unilinear and fixed. Nor does progress in the MEA need to claim that it is questioning the very rationality that produced it. This is of course a counterfeit claim, for the rationality that makes it, anarchical-binarism, reproduces the Christian ordering principles that spawned it. Yet Indian diplomacy's reflexivity is similar to modern reflexivity because it imagines the barely imaginable but realizes it in the present. The question then is how does this reflexivity generate a politics composed of movements to destinations scarcely imaginable, which contradicts modernity's timeline and is free of its deleterious effects?

At the core of the apparent contradiction in reflexivity contradicting progress-through-history and still delivering progress lies modernity's limited comprehension of progress. Geography explains this succinctly. Modernists narrowly understand progress as linear movement, for instance, from rural to urban. This is binarism, and progress-through-history is understood, by anthropologists amongst others, as movement towards 'the global political economy'.[239] An outgrowth of a commonplace understanding in modern societies, the equating of progress with the accumulation of capital, this idea is uncritically applied to all and sundry.[240] Yet individual officers mainly want 'the IAS because they are sent to a district after a year in service, spend at least seven years there, rising to Magistrate (DM). That is the pinnacle for many because a DM has immense power, controls vast funds. You are mother and father to hundreds of thousands of people.'[241]

Commenting on this, a High Commissioner said disapprovingly: 'They are the ones who want to go back to their areas to show what a big man they've become.'[242] Hence mobility is not to move away, but the means of return to origins in a new guise: as a civil servant. Nor is this mobility necessarily motivated by power or wealth; this indicates the multiple purposes of status acquisition. A JS briefing probationers spoke frankly when he advised:

a lot of you will come from India, I mean real India not Delhi, and you will want to go back because you will be wondering what all this Foreign Service is. A lot of the work you will do will be very remote and … we are all friends here … quite pointless. But becoming a Regional Passport Officer (RPO) can give you something real. You don't have to go abroad. You can be posted in your part of India. You can actually help people from your place![243]

The variety in the uses and understandings of mobility expresses itself fluidly both spatially (return to the village) and in time (turning away from the dynamic of progress-through-history), but it does not discount progress. Rather, what is demonstrated is a vibrancy of possibilities made possible by the incorporation of the global economy but not determined by it as modernity is. As the briefing made clear, the officer's return and turning away from the global economy helps others access it, and it is only by providing this succour that the officer maintains status and obtains virtue. What happens every day in the MEA is that modernity's unilineal progress is converted into a process of self-inflicted exposure to new repertoires not limited to economic progress, but certainly delivering it. The exposure is self-inflicted because of the exertion required to enter and master it and the limited means available to do so. This is why *jugar* is essential because diplomats do not enjoy modernity's certainty, Indian's routes are not ordained by 'history'.

The lack of predestination also means that progress need not be realized in a unilineal path ending with the successful transformation of the self. Instead, to put it in modernity's terms, progress may end with some parts of the self moving towards the terminal point—something of course inexplicable to anarchical-binarism, which is intent on complete overhauls. For the diplomat, then, the aim is not a transformation, but realizing a variation of the cosmos. Such a conceptualization is also therapeutic in a way impossible in modernity. What for modernity is a perilous journey is for the cosmological a familiar route, for ends and origins are no more than variations of each other and expressive of the cosmos. In other words, transformational change within the totalizing project that is modernity is no more than a regulating of an aspect of the self by recourse to another.

A probationer explained the point. His family has been secure for generations—ancestors were landlords, grandfather went to university; his maternal grandmother worked in a scientific department; his father holds a senior post in a district; mother went to one of the leading women's

colleges in India; his younger brother is a professional in the private sector—and he answered the question 'did you need the leg-up of the quota?'
with 'Look boss, if you can take advantage of something won't you? I
have followed the rules, after all.'[244] Caste is therefore evoked when useful,[245] when the context requires it, but this does not define him. It is why
it is possible to speak of 'India's national culture' without mentioning
caste.[246] He changed schools five times before securing a place in one of
the leading Delhi Public Schools (DPS)—known for both producing
good results and its brash *nouveau riche* clientele.[247] About DPS he said
with clarity:

Obviously I wanted to be a part of that society. I differentiated between preten-
sions and what I thought were valuable and took that. I knew where I came from
and saw no reason to forget. People made fun of my accent. I changed that. One
has to change, otherwise you get left behind. Hindi is my language at home but
I learnt English. I changed because I realised there was something deficient in
me. And anyone who thinks I've lost something of myself because I speak English
needs to have their head checked!

He has progressed, but only if that term is understood in the contexts
of his self-understanding developed relationally: his time operating in a
space with other times. To view this as the product of modernist reflexivity is to distort him into non-existing 'projects of transformation' by
obliterating his continuing and defining enmeshment in the 'start' group:
caste.[248] Nevertheless he has progressed in terms of micro-aspects in himself (language for instance) by transforming them through self-selection
from those he encountered to make for a unified and relational dynamic
of self-management.

Thus the need to reject modernity and replace it with the cosmological is made immediate by the notion of progress as regression. For
instance, one probationer spends nearly one-third of his salary on educating two girls in the village he worked so hard to leave. He has also set
up a 'library', adding modestly, 'it's just a room in the community centre
with books useful for study.'[249] The probationer's movements are best
understood not as moving through a series of stages in 'history', discard-
ing what has been done with, but rather as accessing in Menon's way new
possibilities through relations and creatively blending them. These acqui-
sitions are not intended to be transformative or progressive in a unilineal sense. Rather, reflexivity only delivers progress by looking at oneself
in terms of relations. Such a manner of progressing negates the need to

eradicate one's past. This is why Indian diplomats do not operate on the basis of the terminal group being alienated binarily from the start group. Rather they are entrenched in a start group, which is simply a variation of the terminal group, and what appears contradictory is only so within modernity's finitudes.

The reflexivity that generated these uncontainable practices of progress is also the tempering of violence. Such an understanding permeates bureaucratic life. One evening, after a party, an IFS probationer asked my opinion of another guest, a Customs officer, who had been volubly expounding about getting a position in Bombay. I presumed that man was eager and keen to perform well in an important port for international trade. Bemused by my (modern?) naivety, the IFS probationer gently chastised me: 'You think he wants to go to Bombay to further his career? He wants to further himself … there is nothing wrong with that, but he should also do something for the country too.'

Not only is the officer locating himself physically within the cosmos, but he is also orienting himself morally in terms of the cosmos: one must help oneself, but that does not necessitate a dereliction of duty.[250] This is impermissible within modernity, for progress—as escape from violence—is simultaneously accompanied by violence. The episode is indicative of a common refrain amongst junior civil servants. For instance, an IRS probationer says: 'See … what does the government pay me? I'll let 99.9999 per cent of people go through without any problem [when it comes to tax]. Once a year someone who is making 70, 80 crores, I'll fuck him another hole.'[251]

Once again, status is a multidimensional category understood in a variety of ways. In these examples, probationers posit themselves relationally as victims of what Akhil Gupta calls the 'unspectacular suffering [which] slips beneath the radar of politicians, academics, journalists, and concerned citizens.'[252] This day-to-day subjection to small acts of violence is considered reason for a cynical view of their job.[253] They aspire to change their status to free themselves of the violence of corruption. Hence they progress. Furthermore, this is to imagine an alternative future, barely achievable. At the same time, however, they are violent. Yet their violence is contained, and how this is done is stated explicitly by the IFS probationer and implicit in the four decimal points the IRS probationer used. In other words, the latter will target not the bulk of the population, to which he belongs, but the ultra-rich who are presumed to be corrupt.

Hence there is violence, but it is directed against the already violent, thereby saving people like himself who were poor and incapable of fostering corruption. For these civil servants, rampant corruption is being contained because it is being directed towards the already corrupt. Indeed, their actions might even be regarded as virtuous. In this manner reflexivity need not ride on violence, but may mitigate it.

If violence without is diminished, violence within is eliminated. It is precisely because they operate in undetermined climes that Indian diplomats avoid the phenomenal amounts of self-harm modernity generates. So ubiquitous is this violence in modernity that it has a name: anomie.[254] A major disciplinary device, anomie is theorized by both Emile Durkheim and Robert Merton as 'normlessness'. Anomie is a lack of cohesiveness producing feelings of powerlessness and alienation.[255] This state is unavoidable within modernity because it is a function of progress. For Durkheim, anomie is endemic to societies that are transitioning, and for Merton anomie is rampant in democratic societies because they offer the most possibilities to progress.[256]

It is startling therefore that Ruohui Zhao and Liqun Cao find, on the basis of comparative research, that the most modern nation of them all, the US, has the lowest incidence of anomie. But as Zhao and Cao explain, this is only due to incredible and ongoing self-inflicted violence. Its name is the 'American dream' and this comes into play because progress for Americans is most overwhelmingly understood as economic betterment. Improving one's economic situation should generate anomie, but this is negated by US society having removed the cultural barrier to economic movement through the 'American dream'. Although it has multiple meanings, this futuristic mechanism suggests that self-generated progress is not only possible but requisite to economic progress.[257] The reason why this pro-progress mechanism, which should generate anomie, but does not, is that practically all Americans subscribe to this norm. Hence the anomie-producing norm, by virtue of being ubiquitous, counters anomie.

The cost, however, is self-deception, because structural barriers to improving one's economic self continue despite—and in contradiction to—the culture of economic permissiveness.[258] In short, the 'American dream' manages anomie by making everyone aspire to economic betterment but, by making the self wholly responsible and deflecting the result of the self's work into the future, ensures that the present continues in its iniquities.[259] Statistics show that there is therefore much less movement than would be expected given the prevalence of the norm.[260] In New York, the capital of world capitalism, 25% of all children and 50% of African-American children live below the official poverty line. As Cardinal Paulo Everisto Arns put it, 'there are 20 million abandoned and undernourished children in a country that not only has the means to feed all its own children, but also hundreds of millions in other countries.'[261] And as Ashish Nandy has argued, US-style democracy reduces poverty to a level where it is democratically insignificant—around 11%.[262] The cost of being anomie-free, then, is vanishing mobility. In other words, the unifying norm of the 'American dream' is an incredible example of violence: the violence of entrancement.

Zhao and Cao also find that the second lowest incidence of anomie occurs in India. Why? That cannot be answered by modernist paradigms or the US example. The industrialization and democratization that dominate India obviously do not generate anomie. And quite clearly there is movement in the MEA at rates and of types incomprehensible to modernity. Yet there is no anomie, despite any culture of entrancement such as the 'American dream' being encountered during the fieldwork. It is proposed, then, that the lack of anomie is due to the very rationality that produces movement. 'Identity,' writes William Connolly, 'requires difference in order to be and it converts difference into otherness in order to secure its own self-certainty.'[263] The MEA renders the second part of the statement impossible and superfluous since no 'othering' was encountered. Instead, officers drew certainty from themselves in relation to their contexts rather than in opposition. It is therefore posited that anomie is not necessarily the function of mobility—as Durkehim and Merton argue—but simply another manifestation of the originary causality that motors modernity.

In other words, anomie is already there given the intellectual assumptions modern society makes. Anomie is not the result of movement, but creates it in modern society and in doing so reproduces anomie. This is why in modernity unity is sought, because it is assumed to be absent. Moves are thus made to realize unity—which US society understands as narrowly economic, to become participants in the 'American dream'. In contrast, in India unity is not required, but this of course does not mean that economic progress is not required. It is, but an entirely different rationale motivates it: lived poverty understood as a form of violence requiring eradication by tapping the unified cosmos. Embedded in this is certainty in the self because it belongs to the cosmos. Anomie is therefore not a function of movement, but of the spirit in which the movement is entered into. And the spirit of modern society is anomie because of its rationality. That this is not the case in India is why an officer said: 'Put someone—no matter where they are from—in my shoes, I'm sure they would make my choices if they had my life, experiences.'[264] Free of anarchical-binarism, officers do not appear to suffer any of the psychological wounds oppositional life inflicts on the Western self.[265] Hybridity cannot rationalize the absolute lack on anomie because it requires, at a minimum, recognizing binarism and hence transitioning oneself into the binary world of modernity. Evidently, officers do not do that. Despite moving, they remain firmly grounded in where they came from, and this is evident, if only in their fear (overcome by *jugar*) of having to realize status by joining the MEA and being sent abroad.

Given the applicability of cosmological reflexivity to diplomats, it is hardly surprising that it defines India's negotiation style. As Gary Fine argues, negotiating styles are contingent on the internal structure of an organization,[266] which in the MEA's case makes for a type of reflexivity inaccessible to modernity.[267] In keeping with their cultural kit, Indian diplomats do not negotiate with an 'other' but with another much like oneself. Diplomacy ideally is a 'mixed-motive decision making enterprise', involving both cooperation and competition.[268] Operationalizing this in a unified cosmos shifts the emphasis not to violence towards the 'other' but to cooperation with another. This is because the underlying assumption is of unity. The negotiating partner is a variation of oneself. This makes for empathy, which predicates against violence.[269] As an Indian 123 negotiator advised: 'In a negotiation you have to always remember there is someone else. You have to think of them. If you do not think of them and … say … you are able to force your view upon them then your agreement won't last. A successful negotiation is when both parties are satisfied. There is give and take. So remember. Think of the other party.[270]

In the Indian view, it is not only possible to entertain the other party's ideas and adopt their position, but absolutely essential. Self-evidently, different players have differing positions, but what is key is that these are understood not as oppositional, but variational, therefore negating the chances of differences coalescing into what Sigmund Freud calls a 'narcissism of small differences', because in a unified cosmos the starting point is not alienation.[271] Hence, reflexivity does not work to exaggerate differences between selves to distinguish oneself from the 'other' but fosters understanding, since both parties are just variations of the cosmos. In short, the present is the product of time in space; all are variations; and the result is that a player aware of this may look back in his time, to access the results of another's time.

The versatility of such diplomacy was amply in evidence in 2007 during the final stages of the 123 negotiations. It involved a process of give-and-take and India was able to give in without any sense of anomie because the contextual reflexivity of the MEA permitted diplomats to empathize with the Americans and take seriously their concerns. One such requirement was an explicit Indian commitment to maintain its self-imposed nuclear moratorium on testing. This could have undone negotiations because India understood the requirement as surrendering a sovereign right.[272] Responding empathetically to US anxieties—by taking them seriously—the Indians sought to creatively manage them. The result was the formulation of Article 14.[273] It allows India to test because the test will not automatically terminate the Agreement. Instead, a test will trigger a round of negotiations to ascertain whether the broader political and security situation justified the test. If India can convince the US that this is the case, then the US will not terminate the agreement or ask for the return of equipment and fuel. As India's prosperity hinges on this equipment, there is a vested interest in not testing.[274] This solution is not a hybrid solution, arising from the interstices of two national cultures. That is a decidedly specular perspective. Instead, the solution is the restructuring of the international nuclear order to suit India because, 'We live in a dangerous part of the world ... everything is fluid ... countries are changing their political systems, borders are in flux ... This is not Europe ... fixed .... We are not some minor player like Norway.'[275]

In short, the difference from modernity was that India achieved its goals not by losing itself or seeking to overwhelm another, but by empathizing with another very much like oneself to transform the present, thereby managing concerns about itself arising from its own past.

A related concern with maintaining the self makes the state, like its diplomats, seek not to move to a destination but to convert it to the origin. Just as individual diplomats have changed the very organization that is their destination, India sought to change its destination. In other words, not content with maintaining themselves, Indian diplomats sought to change the very zone they were aiming to enter, the terminal group that is the 'international' itself. There was movement, but it was not the modish movement that takes the self from one historic stage to another.[276] Nevertheless, this was progress for India. How this was so may be explained via an Indian infrangible: some reactors had to be beyond IAEA inspections. This may be appreciated via an Indian infrangible: some reactors had to be beyond IAEA inspections. This amounted to Indian exceptionalism—because no other state enjoys this privilege— and it was to be achieved without violence.[277] In setting out this boundary, India did not over-detail the requirement by spelling out which reactors or even how many.[278] That was decided during negotiations.[279] In arriving at the negotiating table with a broad framework and expecting to negotiate the details India avoided the inflexibility and defensiveness which once plagued Japan as it tried to become modern. In doing so, Japan's negotiating stance was mimicry: outdoing the moderns at their own game in an attempt to fit in.[280] Indian negotiators, however, kept to their position and also secured the right to build new military reactors as and when deemed necessary. As for inspection, IAEA officials have access only to civilian reactors.[281] The right to reprocess spent fuel under India-specific IAEA safeguards addressed another dual concern: India benefits from the additional energy potential in spent fuel while managing international concerns about material being siphoned off for military applications. In short, India progressed but it was only possible by the international community itself readjusting itself rather than India transitioning into it.

Punctuating this reading is the inescapable question arising from the fact that negotiation is a dual process and India was only able to secure these impossible possibilities because the US agreed. This prompts the question: is it possible for states propelled by modernity to also be empathetic and practice a diplomacy of the type being outlined for India? A munificent answer is needed, for it must compare India's diplomacy with the US's and do so without dislodging it from its intellectual moorings. To do so is to very quickly gather that US diplomacy was not a contextually driven process of securing variations, rather it was the full venting of diplomatic modernity. While the 123 for India was to secure certain variations to itself and the cosmos, the treaty for the US was intended to totally transform India by revoking its rationality. In practice this was the political conversion of India into a function of US policy and all that it entailed: the splitting of the cosmos (alliance politics) and the reliance on violence as the only tool for progress (converting all remaining 'others'). In short, anarchical-binarism and US diplomacy sought to make India play by its rules by incorporation. The US failed to do so because India's rationale is neither anarchical nor binary. The US remains for India an important expression of the cosmos but categorically no different. The US may therefore be tapped usefully to improve India's here and now. That this fundamental idea eludes the US may perhaps be excused since it also evades some within the MEA itself.

In practice the preeminent modernist power gave ground on the 123 not because it empathized, but because it was intent on totalizing India. This becomes apparent by presenting the US's engagement in the most appropriate expression available: comments of US officials and the secret cables they sent to each other. Located thus, the 123 is revealed as not an end in itself but as instrumental, the means to ensnare India and then reel it into the modern camp. But the ultimate purpose was not that, but to make India a tool in that archetypical modernist game the US excels at: containment. The difference between the two negotiators was that the US negotiated to contain India and use New Delhi instrumentally in an attempt to contain China,[282] whereas for India the aim was mundane: to secure its present now. In other words, the US operated in terms of its time and sought to make both India and China like itself, whereas India was able to divert that time to serve completely different aims: strengthen India's enmeshment with the cosmos to improve the present. The contrast was evident when Condoleezza Rice took the treaty as indicating the state of Indo-US relations as a whole, misunderstood India's rationales[283] and explicitly told India to ditch Nehruvian Non-Alignment for an alliance with the US.[284] In short, US diplomacy's modernist assumptions could only lead to one way of acting: the conversion of the 'other'. For Rice, it was incomprehensible for India to persist in its non-modern ways, for to do so was illogical since it meant turning away from progress-through-history. Most harmful to modernity is the very persistence of non-modern ways. They undermine modernity's terminal point and hence the process that is modernity. US expectations thus reveal that its diplomacy is the product of anarchical-binarism and is intent on ripping apart the cosmic whole by establishing massive alliances founded on violence.

Cables from the US Embassy in Delhi to Washington between 2005 and 2009 make for the most appropriate context to the 123 negotiations and also divulge how the US's unceasingly violent diplomacy, activated by modernist goals, was met on a different, non-aggressive register in SB. What transpired was that Indian negotiators were able to successfully manage the US's bipolar approach of overcoming the 'other', so as to secure the treaty.[285] In contrast, the US establishment over changing administrations expected that India would respond in a sensible way, that is, in a modern way. Ever recalcitrant, India disappointed repeatedly. Trapped in its own time, the US was incapable of learning in the space that was the Indo-US engagement. On the one hand was modernity's hubristic belief in itself but on the other was Indian obduracy. The result was US 'self-deception'[286] or the belief that India would change, and it became the identifying characteristic of US negotiations. As it happens the belief is also administration-resistant, engulfing Barack Obama's presidency just as it did his predecessor's.[287] The cables establish that the US aimed to transform India in 'foundational' terms.[288] In seeking to realize the total transformation of India, US diplomats repeatedly demonstrated a total lack of empathy, to the point of missing what they themselves were being told and noting and passing to Washington. It meant that no matter what India said or did, there was no dissuading the US from the practice of its juggernaut diplomacy. Trapped in its own time, the US aimed to bring India into its time, for it was justified by the past and sought to deliver whatever one desired in the future.

The only problem was that all of this was contingent on violence in the present, because India inexplicably (for modernity) refused despite a concerted effort at assimilation from at least 2005. To achieve the aim of a strategic partnership, the main techniques were military. What was to be fostered was the interoperability of military systems.[289] The conjunction between military cooperation and strategic partnerships was made baldly in a cable: 'deepening our mil-mil relationship … will help our strategic partnership realise its potential.'[290] The US held on to this notion at least until 2009. Another cable stated: 'Military Sales will provide opportunities for a sustained relationship far more robust than exercises and exchanges. If we can continue our trend of major military sales, we will cement a relationship for the next several decades with the most stable country in South Asia.'[291]

The US's persistence however had nothing to do with the reality of Indian diplomatic communications. Indeed India had to manage American diplomacy assimilative onslaught without replicating it. The most significant pointer in this was the signing in June 2005 of the New Framework for the U.S.-India Defence Relationship. However, this was no capitulation to US objectives, rather it was the managing of US assertiveness from an alternative register. Rather than meet US coercion with coercion and thereby sacrifice means for ends, or imperil India's further enmeshment in the cosmos, the New Framework deflected the grand military alliance the US wanted into the uncertain future, to secure the present.[292]

The US ought to have been aware of this from what Indian officials and ministers were saying, and ought never have pushed for the New Framework. As US cables testify, a military alliance was the last thing on the minds of Indian politicians. One cable, for instance, sent before FM Pranab Mukherjee went to the US to sign the New Framework, recorded that India's objective was to secure technology, which alone would guarantee a 'long-term sturdy relationship.'[293] This is verified explicitly by another cable sent just after Mukherjee returned to New Delhi. Mukherjee 'underscored what the UPA views as the hallmark achievement of his visit: US acceptance of India's desire for co-production and technology transfer.'[294] In other words, precisely what the PM had already said. Furthermore, in early August Mukherjee told parliament that the Framework 'contains only enabling provisions. It does not contain any commitments or obligations.'[295] Despite this coming on the back of earlier comments, the US, which operated to an altogether different tune, was incapable of comprehending India's limited requirements, produced by another rationality. Within days of Mukherjee's parliamentary speech, a cable set out how the US had proposed a Status of Forces Agreement (SOFA) which would grant immunity to all US military personnel in India for mutually agreed activities. An identical US request had been turned down earlier, but US officials thought it would fare better after the New Framework, thereby completely missing the point that this was no more than a deflective measure. Unsurprisingly, the MEA turned down the proposal, but the US chose to persist.[296]

The US, despite understanding what India wanted or at least noting it,[297] persisted in trying to enmesh India in a series of foundational agreements with the purpose of converting New Delhi into an alliance nation. What this would mean in practice would be the deployment of Indian troops under US command. This is because Andrew Bacevich infers from the history of US military deployments, 'there would be much resistance to [US soldiers] serving under Indian command, in large part for racial reasons that few Americans would actually be willing to acknowledge.'[298] The process was to first get signed agreements enabling the sale of US military platforms to India. That in turn was expected to result in a military and then a strategic realignment. These agreements included the Access and Cross-Servicing Agreement (ACSA), the Logistics Support Agreement (LSA) and the Communications Interoperability and Security Memorandum of Agreement (CISMOA). India was shy of such agreements because, according to US officials, there was apprehension that they would impose unwanted commitments.[299] Another cable noted Indian opposition stemmed from the view that such agreements implied basing rights.[300]

Founded on self-deception, US assessments were necessarily wrong. India began to rent out bases in 2007 to Singapore, and so the difficulty is not particular issues such as basing rights,[301] but what those rights will mean to the partner seeking them. It is here that the difference in rationality comes into play. The US's ultimate aim was to found an alliance that would fundamentally undermine the MEA's unified cosmos rationale. It is only a difference in rationale that explains the uneasy fact of the same issue generating resistance with one partner only to dissolve into eager compliance with another. A Singaporean diplomat put it like this: 'Our relationship with you is asymmetrical, but we come with no ideology. Senior Indians tell me that you come under all kinds of political pressure from the US. … I mean they want an alliance. We don't ask for anything like that, which is why we are your number one investor— and that includes renting airfields, testing ranges ….'[302] In short, India's diplomacy seeks out variations and is comfortable with those who do not challenge this. The US's diplomacy however aims at reinvention to divide the cosmos. It is this basic and underlying difference that made India resist the US's diplomacy of coercion.

The MEA continues to manage US pressure without replying in kind. Testimony to this is the fact that the US continues to court India despite its having made no response at all to repeated calls to convert the New Framework into an alliance.[303] In contrast, the repercussions on US diplomacy have been significant because while India can get away with resistance, the US is fulfilling 'history'. In the immediate aftermath of the failure of another US bid to entangle India, to fulfil India's Medium Multi-Role Combat Aircraft (MMRCA) requirement,[304] the US Ambassador in New Delhi resigned. About who was to get the contract, a senior Indian Ministry of Defence official said with prescience in late 2011, 'It should go to EADS. We've a cyclical approach to buying platforms and the purpose is to have everyone onside. But it will go to Dassault because the French have been aiding us with nuclear and other matters.'[305] Indian diplomacy therefore continues its course by shying away from military alliances and seeking variational change. Rather than follow Pakistan's example and play the courted virgin to eventually become the dependent housewife,[306] India developed a clear position arising from its self-delineated context and sought out the US. India was successful in its engagement, not only because it secured what it wanted but because this was achieved in a manner that did not replicate Washington's coercive strategies of subsumation and conversion.[307] Yet, as a variety of US officials continue to state, Washington continues in its attempts at conversion. It must, because modernity's linearity means that the US must convert an India enticingly modern and ripe for the plucking. At stake are not only US conceptions of its security but the rationality that is modernity itself. After all, a modern nation believes that only it can deliver us all to utopia.

Indians patently did not believe this, which is why the entire negotiation process was yet another example of the fourth possibility: The US's lexicon of bipolarity was used by India because the geobody kept to its own reflexivity. India calculated impossible possibilities based on self-reflection in its own time, but they were only deliverable by reaching across in space to another's time. This was fraught with difficulties as the US is a modern power, and so India relied on *jugar*.[308] The distinctiveness of this approach lies in the fact that though the US used reflexivity, it was incapable of operating in time and space. The US therefore sought to flatten space to its time, whereas India sought to transcend its space by using another's time. It is this difference in ambitions and processes that makes for a diplomacy conducted on a register impossible within modernity, and necessitates resorting to a rationality and reflexivity alternative.

'Nothing makes sense in this country'

Indian ways not only escape the future ordained by modernity, they revoke modernity completely, and the frequency with which this occurs is an incitement to knowledge of another kind. For instance, progress is a piecemeal affair for Indian diplomats since some elements are not required to change or resist change. Resistance does not however imply that these elements are unmanageable, for the means of management are noted obliterations of the past. This is altogether unprecedented for modernity, making for a surplus to modernity's justification for itself: progress-through-history. Individuals do this all the time and it is re-enacted at the level of the state. In terms of diplomats one facet of personality is caste, and this social construct quite literally shapes the Indian state, since caste helps officers secure their objectives. While caste is usefully invoked in certain spheres (such as the UPSC exam) it is erased in other inter-actions within the cosmos because of its significance (low status)—something resistant to job status. A probationer stiffened visibly when, as I took down his cell phone number, I asked his surname. Only later did he divulge that he had dropped his surname because it betrayed his caste. Caste is an everyday reality for many, but that does not make it any less confounding. As an officer put it: 'My father was travelling by train and every time the ticket collector came his status changed. Once his name was thought of as high caste so he got a top berth, another time he was a low caste so was on the floor. What kind of a country is this! I tell you nothing makes sense in this country!'[309]

This diplomat later accused me of 'being inherently "castist", you can't help it,' because of my own higher caste (which was apparent to him for the same reason for which Spivak turns to India for her empirical work). It was only after I showed him an article I had written in the *South China Morning Post* that he somewhat reconsidered his opinion of me.[310] Of course, the probationer was being ironic, for he knew full well that his society is not straitjacketed by impermeable concepts.

The reinvention of the self may not involve deleting aspects of one-self, but rather mimicry. However, both means and purpose ensure that this is not hybridity at work. While hybridity approaches in terms of polar opposites and then seeks to close that gap, what Indians do is con-tinue in an enmeshed cosmos to seek out variations. Vitally, these are intended to further integrate into society, and are therefore categorically different from the type of mimicry performed to demonstrate difference, as was the case with the original inhabitants of the MEA. An observed form of reinventive mimicry was performed by a General Category pro-bationer who did not smoke in front of his parents but insisted on doing so in front of mine. The probationer's action was not necessarily a case of smoking because the cigarette is 'fashionable and modern', as Frank Dikötter writes that it is in China.[311] In fact this probationer's father used to come to my room to smoke (hence avoiding the gaze of wife and son)! For the father smoking was a pleasure frowned upon by his context, hence he sought mine.[312] For the son, cigarettes were a means of mimicking the cultural forms he expected me, in the timeline of my family, to follow. Whether these were understood as superior is a moot point. Since the probationer would not smoke in front of his parents but insisted on doing so in front of mine, it is taken as a symbol of his seeking to fit into what he presumed were my familial conventions. His reasoning, for smoking and not smoking, was of course fatally flawed because he left out the reality of his father's smoking,[313] and for that matter my reformed parents' objections. Significant, too, is that he avoided answering my questions about why he did not smoke in front of his parents. In short, he sought to reinvent himself, but in doing so his calculations were fatally flawed: he discounted his father and assumed that my family were somehow remarkably different.

At the level of MEA policy making, too, there are obliterations and reinventions, but conducted with far more thought than the smoking probationer was capable of and without the irony of the officer whose father was shuffled around. The result is not the consumption of time, but its generation to make for not a finite game, but infinite play. In all of this however, Indian policy never discounts the past but invests it with possibilities impossible within progress-through-history. In other words, just as the past is not denied, nor is it limited to entrapping the present. Rather the past is seen as provoking possibilities that may liberate the present. This is possible by revoking sequencing, by managing the present, that is, in context and in the present. To explain, diplomatic engagements are viewed as composed of many times in the space of the engagement. Hence, engagement can be envisioned as multidimensional, because the multifaceted nature of relations is acknowledged. An example is India's call to downplay the border issue with China to ensure that other areas of the Sino-Indian relationship thrive.[314] The initiative has borne little result, for reasons that elude the Indian establishment—mainly the opacity of decision-making in Beijing.[315] Nor has there been much success in applying such a policy to Pakistan. Practically, such a policy would end the primary concentration on the real but painful issue of Kashmir, to reveal areas of cooperation beneficial to both states. This technique was used to present the multiple histories of the MEA, but it takes on an unprecedented urgency when the security and prosperity of millions are at stake. The aim, for a very senior officer, is to 'make Pakistan an investor in India. Let them have a stake. That way they will think twice about attacking us. ... The benefit is in shifting the focus from the pain of partition ... it gives us something positive to talk about rather than terror all the time [and the means is] ... economics.'[316]

In doing so the diplomat recognises the past, chooses to ignore it and is unafraid to acknowledge this. 'The past is the past, let it remain there,' said another officer.[317] Such behaviour relieves diplomacy from the trauma of Partition which has set the tone for Indo-Pakistani relations for too long. But none of this makes for forgetting, that is self-indulgent 'amnesia', because it is the highly charged—so much so that it is practically tangible—nature of the past that has led the officer to revoke it.[318]

Of course such approaches may only be explained in concordance with the cosmos for modernity can only build on the past. The denial and it animates a proposal that could change the socio-economic landscape of the subcontinent. The proposal is the South Asia Free Trade Agreement (SAFTA) which came into effect in 2006.[319] The possibilities it offers were recorded in the MEA's Fifteenth Report as 'a small but significant beginning on a long path towards economic integration within the region.'[320] However, unable to match the MEA's abilities to cease giving priority to a pain-focused sequencing of the past, Pakistan, despite ratifying the SAFTA, singled India out for 'special treatment'.[321] India granted Most Favoured Nation (MFN) status to Pakistan in keeping with the letter and spirit of SAFTA; Islamabad, however, 'refused to extend the negotiated tariff concessions to items outside the positive list.'[322] The MEA's Annual Report drily concluded in 2009: 'Incremental expansion to the Positive List is the preferred policy in Pakistan as the means to expand bilateral trade rather than address issue of MFN status frontally.'[323] In fact, the list was not even incrementally expanded. In February 2012, six years after the proposal came into effect, the list was practically unchanged, restricted to a paltry 1,900 items.[324] In refusing to broaden the engagement with India—proposed by the latter to overrule the pain of the past to create new opportunities—the Pakistanis choose to wallow in a particular sequencing of the past,[325] demonstrating yet again that economic decisions are never neutral but always embedded in the social.[326] That Pakistan refuses to broaden the engagement indicates a self/other binary approach. Trapped in the system's teleological history, Pakistanis lose practically. Their exports to India are growing faster than imports from India and so there is no threat of being overwhelmed by Indian exports. However, demand for Indian products remains high, and so there is a thriving black market for smuggled Indian products. Naturally, prices are vastly inflated. In other words, the costs of refusing to take Partition away from the centre of India-Pakistan relations continue to be borne by ordinary Pakistanis.[327]

It is not just Pakistan that is trapped by modernity. Teleological sequencing circumscribes many Indians, leaving them in awe of the past and thus incapable of focusing on the present. In 2009 in Sharm el-Sheikh, the Indian and Pakistani PMs issued a joint statement, which was attacked violently in parliament by the BJP's Yashwant Sinha. He accused the PM of having 'walked all the way to the Pakistani camp.'[328] The offending line in the statement was: 'Both Prime Ministers recognized that dialogue is the only way forward. Action on terrorism should not be linked to the Composite Dialogue process and these should not be bracketed.'[329] The Composite Dialogue proposes to 'carry the process of normalisation forward,' and intends to 'lead to the peaceful settlement of all bilateral issues, including Jammu and Kashmir ....'[330] In this context, the only appropriate context, the Sharm el-Shaikh statement was no capitulation to Pakistan, but a reiteration that normalization is a virtue which cannot be predicated on the history of terrorism.[331] Of course, normalization in itself implies the ending of terrorism. The PM therefore changed the approach from 'so long as Pakistan uses terror, India will not aspire to normalizing relations' to 'India will aspire to normalisation despite what Pakistan does'.[332] This is not idealism. Nor does it imply that Pakistan can get away with using terror, because the context which produced this policy arose from the reality of Pakistan's government being frequently unaware of what goes on within its borders and, specifically, incapable of stopping all attacks against India, since they are on occasion committed without the knowledge of the state.[333] In short, the statement recognized the reality that much Pakistani soil lies beyond governmentality, and assumed that the best way to achieve normalization is to de-centre the sequencing that dominates current relations, that is, remove in a manner the 'history' of terrorism. This is not to forget the past, but to use it in a manner that liberates the present from 'history' and in doing so elevates policy into a time unavailable to modernity, which is time-in-space. But such diplomacy is impossible within the order of modernity. What is therefore required is the exegetical means of reconciling rationality as known with the intent to note and ignore the past and never be indebted to the future to improve the present. And the means is the unified cosmos. How diplomacy on such a footing is logically and practically possible is what this chapter has been establishing.

Conclusions

This chapter has made some bold claims about the state on the basis of hardly any official records, not only because paper is quite often meaningless in the MEA, but because the reliance on records is in itself a reproduction of an imperialist mind-set. S.R. Nathan, Singapore's sixth President, reacted with shocked surprise to my mentioning that the Indian government, to make a decision, created a file on the subject which was then read and commented on by various departments. Terming this the 'file system', Nathan then proceeded to roundly condemn it as a vestige of imperialism that Singapore had disposed of *post haste* to make for outstanding efficiency. Ironically, by insisting on revealing files, moderns reaffirm the need to create them and thereby reproduce the mentality of imperialism, something that India's governmentality, mercifully, casts aside when it comes to the most significant of decisions. Never trapped by the past, a diplomat, upon reading an article by an righteously indignant trainee historian,[334] paraphrased an ironic comment made by Lalloo Prasad Yadav in a speech at the FSI: 'Build buildings for pieces of paper? Remember what Lalloo said: "What kind of a country is this, where we make air conditioned shops for slippers, but our food rots on pavements." Man, I tell you, when Indians go to US universities, they forget ground realities.'[335] When it comes to choosing preserving paper or people, mercifully bureaucrats choose people, and they can because the structure-of-structures sensitizes them in a very particular manner.

But does the culture of an organization indicate the cultural organization of Indian society, the very nature of its politics?[336] Obviously practices uncontainable within modernity exist, possessing a logic discernable only in terms of the structure-of-structures because the instrumentality of power politics is absent. But where does this alterity come from? To ask the question is not to seek origins. Rather, it is to understand the present, which includes the contradiction between practice and modernity's claim that no non-Western logics survived the ordering finger of the West. To verify how an alternative rationality then continues in the heart of what is considered a bastion of modernity is aided by Michel de Certeau. He conceptualizes modernity's arrival as a European male encountering a native naked female whose body will be used as if it were a 'blank, "savage" page on which Western desire will be written.'[337] Of course, this gendered portrayal betrays de Certeau's modernism, but intriguingly it offers a potentiality: a European woman might have reacted differently. This is delusional, given that the native continues to be written, just as de Certeau described it, by modernists, regardless of sex. Nevertheless, he offers a possibility preceding modernity: *metis*.[338]

Understood as an 'array of practical skills and acquired intelligence in responding to a constantly changing natural and human environment,'[339] *metis* is theorized, at best, to have been transformed by modernity, never that it might govern modernity. Nor is *metis* ever understood as anything more than tactics, *jugar*. To allow for the impossible possibility that *metis* governs, because it is a rationality rather than a response to rationality, is to turn away from the 'rationality of proper meaning'.[340] Doing so negates modernity's timeline because the assumption is that the past is in the present. This makes the search contextual but also capable of satisfying modernity's obsession with the past, and it is to one such context that we now turn.

3

THEORIZING THE UNCONTAINABLE

… whatever is here, that is found elsewhere. But what is not here is nowhere else.

— *Mahabharata*[1]

It would not be an exaggeration to say that the people of India have learnt to think and act in terms of the Mahabharata.

— R.N. Dandekar[2]

To provide a civilizational answer for how the structure-of-structures is possible today is not to replay modernity's obsession with 'origin'. Instead the purpose is to identify what, in the current circumstances of the Ministry of External Affairs (MEA), makes its insurgent practices possible. This is why the 'authoritative sources' must once again be Indian diplomats, but Maurice Bloch cautions that asking them to explain their logics generates purpose-specific *post hoc* rationalizations. Answers such as 'this is why we do that' obfuscate because they are removed from what they purport to describe under normal circumstances.[3] Nor do these explanations account for the efficiency with which people perform tasks. Understanding everyday circumstances requires abstracting culture as a tool-kit.[4] For instance, a chess player constructs apparatuses for the efficient handling and packing of specific domains of knowledge and practice. Once fabricated, perhaps through instruction, the operations connected with these domains are not only non-linguistic, they must be to become efficient. The methodological inference is greater reliance on the realm of bodily experience, internalization of this culture by the researcher and then through introspection, describing what has been internalized.

Once again, anthropology assumes that non-Westerners are unaware of why they do what they do. Obviously, verbalizing rationales are distortions,[5] but Bloch's cure—to present the entire observed culture through modern anthropologists, with all their preconceptions—is worse than the disease. Instead of people being silenced, the subject's words should be the guide to sources deemed relevant by themselves for themselves, because the point is to not elucidate my individuated cognitive workings during the encounter with the MEA, but its took-kit and its use. Undoubtedly a multitude of such kits exist, but the 'highest level cultural productions common over long historical periods'[6] are the most significant for they persist over time. One such kit is introduced because diplomats use it. Given that the kit suffuses Indian society[7] and is used by diplomats to orient themselves, the hermeneutic of producer-centred-research is once again applied to the kit to reveal a *metis* alternative to modernity. Contained in this alternative rationality is also a theory of diplomacy predating the entry of modernity. In combination then, what this tool-kit does is obliterate the notion that Indians learned diplomacy and explain—in providing the proper intellectual context, in time and space, for practice—why moderns are either confounded or completely misled by India's diplomacy.

Today's kit: the Mahabharata

Foreign Secretary (FS) Shivshankar Menon—since appointed National Security Adviser—began a lecture on diplomacy to probationers by referring to a pillar of Anglo-Saxon modernity before rapidly switching to a text never investigated as a repository of diplomatic practice, much less rationality.[8] Menon began with Harold Nicolson,[9] selecting seven practices the ideal diplomat is expected to possess from the famous (if only amongst Western diplomats) 'Nicholson test':[10] truthfulness, precision, calm, patience, good temper, modesty and loyalty.[11] For India's arch-diplomat, these practices were 'what your mother told you anyway' which is astounding because they are regarded as the unique fruit of Western civilization: Graeco-Roman ethics, the moral injunctions of the Enlightenment and the ways of the English gentleman.[12] Menon also ascribed to them an import absent in Nicolson: 'These [Nicholson's seven practices] are qualities which enhance your credibility as a diplomat. ... Even if you are threatening the use of force ... you are credible not because of the capability to use force, but because what you say is credible. There is no point in making the ultimate threat if you yourself are not credible.[13] In addition to 'credibility', Menon added 'the ability to think for the other', and repeatedly reminded his audience that they were 'dealing with people'. In short, he spoke of empathy or the identifying characteristic of India's negotiating style.

Menon's virtues were drawn from the *Mahabharata* (*Mb*), a text which provides other qualities he noted—'high personal reputation' and 'knowing everyone'—and deemed irrelevant to diplomacy as conceptualized within anarchical-binarism, because it is insular and privileges the modern self, which is pre-programmed to move along the dynamic of modernity. Menon's qualities introduced space, thereby correcting modernity's emphasis on time to make for an actor in time-in-space. The diplomat must negotiate relationally in a particular context, which makes for not modernity, but a cosmos. Nor was this the only overlap between the *Mb* and the MEA. Menon's speech is highly suggestive and requires quoting at length:

… when as an Indian diplomat you look back, our first earliest ideal diplomat was Krsna in the *Mb*. For six months before the Great War there was this intense period of diplomacy and tremendous negotiation and mediation between all the mini-states, tribes and dynasties. Krsna was involved in most of them and the *Mb* goes into this in great detail. It actually goes through the qualities that made Krsna a good diplomat. How did he manage to achieve his goals? And this is interesting. They come to the same list of seven virtues. It is almost identical. They used slightly different words but basically, it is the same seven things that they think a diplomat should be doing. He had two added advantages, if you read the *Mb*. One of them was high personal reputation. It helps, if people think you are God or think that you are special. More so, he personally knew everybody in every single royal family that he was dealing with—in those days, it was royal families. But for me, the interesting thing is that here are two people separated over time by thousands of years. Nicholson, early 20th century, classical European diplomat; he was at Versailles. Krsna in the *Mb*, 2,500 years ago at least, in what is still a semi-tribal society and yet they both say the same thing; both describe the same set of virtues for a diplomat. Which means that there is a remarkable continuity over time, over space; that the qualities required of a diplomat over vastly different cultures and over a very long period of historical time are much the same.[14]

Unlike moderns, who jealously assert that Europe invented and dis-seminated diplomacy, Menon assumed everyone understood his trade. In switching to the *Mb*, the arch-practitioner of Indian diplomacy returned home—because it was the only way he could make himself explicable to his audience.[15] Retired diplomats echoed the point, with a difference: they spoke in derogatory tones.[16] Indeed, after the talk a Joint Secretary (JS)—educated at St. Stephen's—exploded, 'of course Cookie [the FS's nickname] has to speak like that … they [the new diplomats] don't know anything else.'[17]

Diplomacy as invented and practiced in the West is unknown to Indians because, as Kwame Appiah writes of Africa, 'the experience of the vast majority of these citizens of Europe's colonies was one of essen-tially shallow penetration by the colonizer.'[18] Similarly, after investigat-ing the 'Bengali intelligentsia, the first Asian social group whose mental world was transformed through its interactions with the West,' Tapan Raychaudhuri concludes that 'the culture of the dominant race did not uniformly dominate colonial elite consciousness.'[19] Today's diplomats, by positive discrimination, cannot be of the Bengali colonial elite, or the most radically Anglicized amongst them, those who call themselves—that is the handful that remain—the *Ingabanga*.[20] In short, a '"better class" of Indians'[21] or Homi Bhabha's mimic men have been replaced and will increasingly be replaced by people from a social milieu which, though totally removed from Europe, is not a vacuum. The *Mb* suffuses it, which is why Menon did not need to introduce the text. He was confident of his audience's knowledge of the kit because Indians, unlike Europeans, do not suffer from having to master the anxiety of loss. Loss in European culture has created an identity problem, has made European culture less capable of transferring memory, and more obsessed by it.[22] In contrast, as teacher to two batches of MEA probationers I noticed everyone knew the ins-and-outs of the *Mb*. A probationer was symptomatic when she said early one morning—while exchanging Mughal couplets with another probationer—in a freezing train in Rajasthan: 'No matter how English speaking we are, this [the *Mb*] remains our basic.'[23] Furthermore, in con-versation with thirty-eight diplomats not a single officer contradicted Menon's view. Essentially, Menon retrieved a piece of intellectual kit already known so that new diplomats could make sense of their job. The efficiency of the task may be gauged by viewing it in European terms. Seven (or eight) times as long as the *Iliad* and *Odyssey* combined,[24] the

Mb is estimated to be around 2,500 years old, yet Indians deploy it instantaneously.[25]

It is a modernist ruse to think that in the case of the *Mb*, Indians means Hindus. To do so is to resort to 'religion' and hence to implicate the text in modernity. Even if 'religion' is maintained, Muslims have long been familiar with the text. They have used it from at least the 11th century for not religious, but philosophical and political purposes.[26] The *Mb* intrigued the Mughals and Carl Ernst argues that it is highly anachronistic to suggest modern Enlightenment principles governed their use of the text. The *Mb* was translated under Akbar as the *Razmnamah* or *Book of War*, and that denotes the text's non-religious reception, at least by Akbar. The translation has a foreword by the great courtier and *mir munshi* Sheikh Abu al-Fazl; of the translation project, Ernst comments:

Abu al-Fazl was interested in the philosophical and religious content of the epic, from the perspective of an enlightened intellectual. But I think it is fair to say that this intellectual project was thoroughly subordinated to the political aim of making Akbar's authority supreme over all possible rivals in India, including all religious authorities. The translation of the Sanskrit epics was … part of an imperial effort to bring both Indic and Persianate culture into the service of Akbar.[27]

The project's effects were dramatic for it succeeded in permitting the interweaving of two narratives. Indo-Persian dynastic records were radically rewritten to place the later Mughals in a series of 'the kings of India' beginning with the *Mb*'s Yudhisthira and other mythic heroes.[28] That the project was the meeting of two rationalities is evidenced by Akbar's fascination with the absence of a terminal point in the *Mb*,[29] which possesses no Judgement Day like Abrahamic religion does. But while Akbar sought to imbibe the text's rationality, others recoiled from its infinitudes and sought to subordinate it. The translator Abdul Qadir Badauni patently would have preferred not to be part of such a project and carped, 'such is my lot to be employed in works like this'.[30] He has also left behind a telling account of how he was told off by Akbar for subsuming the text's rationality to Islam.[31]

While only a handful of officers in the MEA are Muslim and only two were encountered, it is highly incendiary to suggest that they were quarantined from Muslim people's long engagement with the text. In part this is due to the way the two diplomats spoke of religion as identity. One officer, who was instrumental in helping me formulate the note asking for access, fobbed off the request to interview him. I wanted to interview him because he was a Muslim, amongst other reasons, but he demolished my modernist idiosyncrasy with the answer: 'What does that [being Muslim] matter?'[32] The other officer, despite speaking extensively and freely over coffee and lunch in London, responded to the question of religion by neatly sidestepping it. He called himself a Nehruvian.[33] Both were patently uncomfortable with the term 'Muslim' because it is symbolic of the modern category of 'religion', and rather sought to expose themselves in the lexis of a rationality alternate. However, with neither was the *Mb*'s role in that rationality discussed. Yet, indisputably the text continues to motivate Muslims.

The most famous Indian painter in recent times, who happens to be Muslim, was so moved by the text that it inspired him to produce 19 paintings.[34] M.F. Husain said that it was the 'conflicts' that he was working with in his *Mb* series, which is reminiscent of what Akbar's court saw in the text and provided the reason for its translation.[35] A deeper explanation of how Husain was shaped by the *Mb* in a non-religious and hence on a non-modern itinerary is given by the former MEA Minister of State Shashi Tharoor, who as it happens also used the text.[36] He writes:

the *Mahabharata* is an ideal vehicle for a creative artist's efforts to affirm and enhance an Indian cultural identity, not as a closed or self-limiting construct, but as a reflection of the pluralism, diversity and openness of India's kaleidoscopic culture. ... What Husain did was to recall, through images starkly familiar to *Mahabharata*-conscious Indians, the kinds of stories Indian society tells about itself. ... In reiterating the epic, the artist and his audience both reaffirm the shaping of their own cultural identity. This is an important statement for Husain to make as a Muslim and an Indian: he is staking his claim to a heritage that some chauvinist Hindus have sought to deny to those not of their own persuasion.[37]

That this comment appeared in the socialist national daily *The Hindu* yet again attests to the relevance of the *Mb* to Indians today as not a religious, but rather an intellectual text.

Moreover, the *Mb* has been—at the very least—a referential text not just for Indians, but specifically for Indian diplomats throughout the duration of what is presumed to be a modern nation-state. Jawaharlal Nehru recognized the *Mb* as 'a rich storehouse in which we can discover all sorts of precious things,'[38] and K.P.S. Menon, India's first FS, wrote:

... long before European diplomacy, and Europe itself, assumed shape, the art of diplomacy had been developed in India ... Take Krishna's mission as an envoy of the Pandavas to the Court of the Kauravas. [To a question] Krishna replies 'I shall go to the Court of the Kauravas to present your case in the best light and try and get them to accept your demands, but if my efforts fail and war becomes inevitable we shall show the world that we are right and they are wrong, so that the world may not misjudge between us.' Here, in a nutshell, is the essence of diplomacy, which may be defined as the art of negotiation. Its primary purpose is to avoid war, but if war should become inevitable the world should know who was responsible for it. Even in Sri Krishna's days, public opinion was a factor to be taken into account.[39]

Evidently, from independence to today, the *Mb* has been a trope for Indian diplomats. The presence of the text at the core of what is presumed a modern nation-state is jarring, for the text does not just orient Indian diplomats to the technicalities of diplomacy but may also be treated, following Bloch and Nehru, as a tool-kit to explain the structure-of-structures animating the practices of diplomats and diplomacy today. This has long been recognized. The *Mb* plays a major role in educating Indians, not Hindus or Muslims, in structuring and informing their imagination and sensibilities in fundamental ways.[40] For James Fitzgerald the *Mb* not only gives Indians grand heroes and villains, thrilling stories, and profound crises; it schooled them in cosmology, philosophy, theology, and ethics, and through it all, legitimized and inculcated ethical and political patterns fundamentally important to what is called 'Hindu' civilization.[41] The opinion is not new and may be traced to Joseph Dahlman.[42] The very metre of composition, the *anustubh*, was associated with the lower, and hence numerically much larger *sudra* caste, explaining the text's persistence in the cultural circuits of Indian society and diplomacy.[43] In short, the *Mb* does not lay down any rules to be followed, nor did it—to take Daud Ali's and Anand Pandian's phrase—'put into circulation resources with which to develop a particular mode of existence.'[44] The *Mb* is the rule and the resource. But this is not the only reason why the *Mb* is used as an entree into what is all-important for modernists, the development over time of the decision-making matrices in the spheres of opinion and action.[45] The *Mb* is used because of space: diplomats use it today. In doing so, they provide a tangible and, as will become obvious, the only possible route to contextualizing the structure-of-structures within the symbolic economy of the civilization while maintaining it.

The alternative is to choose the violence that is the imposition of modernist categories[46] which denigrate or confound rather than uncloak. Indicative of modern theorists is Benjamin Nelson who concludes that:

'the immense variety of languages, social groups and prescriptive rituals in India stood in the way of a full ventilation of the principal structures and a full rationalization of intelligence. The moves to neutralization, generalization, universalization, rationalization were checked at every turn.'[47]

In modern terms, Indian society was disabled, stationary until, presumably, contact with dynamic Europe. But what if this very variety—in modernity's terms Hindus, Muslims and innumerable others inexplicably intermixed—is constitutive of an alternate rationality as stated by Tharoor? This option is discounted by modernity for it converted pre-colonial systems of knowledge into the raw data for European progress-through-history.[48] What is therefore required is what has never been even been thought of: to study today in the lexicon of today's users. That this reading is of a text long present in the cultural circuits of the civilization is incidental to this exegesis, but is of course highly significant to modernity, which privileges time. It is to ensure those prejudices do not overwhelm this exegesis that a textured reading is developed because it deals not in modernity's finitudes, but keeps to rules of, and from, the text itself. The presumption is not that today's users use the text as it is intended for itself to be used (although this is highly likely) but to outline, at a minimum, the significant differences the text generates between Western and Indian intellectual thought and how the text is a suitable context for the present in terms of what is all important for modernity: time.

It however does not take a textured reading of the *Mb* to unravel the modernist fiction that the West bequeathed diplomacy as practiced today. A textured reading is required to ascertain the rationality of those practices. That it is alternative is indicated by a High Commissioner on the cusp of retirement, reflecting on himself and his kind:

> Our ancient heritage has not been institutionalized but it is there in our own lives, in our family lives, in the lives of our societies. MEA is not institutionally something ancient. I know we've had colonialism, but, regardless of our heritage not being institutionalized, it is in the sinews of our society. We acted and reacted to colonial rule, to situations and people that colonialism brought to us, in our way. That's our heritage, it's what shapes our official behaviour because we are the officials. We animate this bureaucracy even though it might once have been alien.[49]

Managing the text

The proposal is that there are two tools: genres and *texture*. Contesting the belief that pre-colonial Indians wrote ahistorical myths, it is contended that the past was written about in terms of dominant genres and that these change. They may come to be seen as 'literature'.[50] What is at stake between the past and myth is not what is true and false, but what is factual and fictive. The reader could arbitrate between fact and fiction through internal clues. This is texture or what Velcheru Rao et al. call 'subgeneric markers ... shorthand for the diagnostic elements that enable the reader to make distinctions within a genre ... the clues left for the reader to find, deliberately created as part of textual (and perhaps individual authorial) intention [and] comprehensible to its intended audience.'[51] The ideal reader therefore is part-and-parcel in constructing the text. But 'how do we know,' asks Rama Mantena, 'what makes up the cognitive world of the reader? Surely, by employing the same criteria/categories (such as verifiability) to identify that which is history, we attribute to readers the cognitive make-up of modern historians.'[52]

Mantena reiterates the challenge myth faced in ancient Greece from history and philosophy. History assumes myths contained a kernel of truth, while for philosophy myths contained a kind of truth.[53] Early historians constituted a realm of 'truth' over which they claimed authority: history.[54] The consequence was the devaluation of myth to a 'lie'.[55] Philosophers, on the other hand, while rationalizing myths concluded that they encoded a kind of truth. They began as sceptics but the process of studying myths made them 'hold a more thoughtful view of them',[56] and this provides the means to manage Mantena's critique. While philosophers created a dogma of interpretation by divorcing the facts in a myth from the stories of history and did so via a particular 'program of truth',[57] they did not reject myth because philosophers do not require verifiability. They may talk about the past and from their position but without having to subsume the past into their programme of truth.[58] The emphasis is not on verifiable fact, but on codes.[59] And one such code is to reconceptualize the pre-rupture past in the categories of a post-rupture present. This is not new. It is, Jonardon Ganeri finds, 'among the most characteristic hallmarks of Indian intellectual practice.'[60]

To search for codes, then, makes for a textured reading of the *Mb*. These codes, or *metis*, are not a lesser 'truth'. They may be more consequential because ethical and therapeutic benefits denied by 'history' are on offer.[61] Furthermore modernity, predicated on progress-through-history, is convinced that all pasts are the same. Even alternative conceptions of the past cannot escape; they are rendered the same through an 'imperialism of categories'.[62] The imposition of these categories, not the past, is Ashis Nandy's target, because for him the past is a balm against the malaise of progress-through-history. Nandy shows the clash between secularists and Hindu nationalists reveals both to be the same, for they are locked in a '"historical" battle [and so] understand each other perfectly' because the battleground is empirical, verifiable history.[63] But of course the facts are impossibly contested and Nandy's cure to this 'historical' battle is to negate empiricism by returning to the 'point of view' articulated by Swami Vivekananda in managing the pain of verifiable empirical 'fact'—the destruction of a temple by Muslim rulers—through a 'moral': principled forgetfulness. This 'moral' is, of course, 'ahistorical'.[64] Within Vivekananda, this particular manner of pain-management to survive the present affirms the power of the moral in managing 'fact', and in doing so affirms the concept of 'timeless truths'. However, such a way is an abomination to history's purpose of laying bare the past as a frame of reference.[65] In modernity's *lingua franca*, Vivekananda is either insane or a practitioner of doublethink.[66] But neither category can explain the processes propelling him which are identical to the practices of both Indian diplomats and foreign policy, without rendering them irrational or imposing some alien category on them.

But how can such categories be evaded to create a textured method? Nandy's work indicates a way. He presents Girindrasekhar Bose and after contextualizing him in the appropriate manner—that is, in a society looking for its own empirical verifiable history—states that Bose concluded the *puranas* were a type of truth beyond history's comprehension. In short, Bose's conclusions were that myths are important not because they abound with empirical facts but because they are suffused with theories expressed in stories of being and action. These are relevant, if only because they guide action, as Nandy shows they do, through concrete, contextualized examples.[67] Now, in using this method of analysis and presentation, Nandy sanctifies logic. He uses sources to both order and present his narrative by keeping to the boundaries of his sources.[68] Moreover, that Nandy uses logic (as Prakash did when he invited the wrath of the Cambridge School) to mount his attack on history is testimony to the independent value of logic. It may be used, as Nandy does, to craft a textured method, which seeks not 'facts' but 'morals' which are rational because they are logical.

Next, how should the search for a rationale be conducted? Nandy's work indicates what should not be done. Like Bose, Nandy logically searches for a rationality where 'all times exist only in present times and can be decoded only in terms of the contemporaneous. There is no past independent of us; there is no future that is not present here and now.'[69] The problem however is that he targets the psyche and in doing so makes use of a totally alien tool-kit: psychoanalysis.[70] In doing so he imposes something alien to his subjects (thereby reproducing the very same error he found historians to be making) and compounds the error by retreating into the cognitive.[71] But why use logic in a manner alien to Indians, and why ignore the verifiable material realm? Finally, self-evidently Nandy's uneducated masses are ahistorical,[72] but what of the powerful? Is it not more productive to target the powerful in any society for exegesis? The need is amplified by modernity's view of 'policy' as an unproblematic given, socioculturally abstracted, devoid of institutional complexity, and its framing of policy dichotomously ('state' versus 'private').[73] This makes for the confusion Kissinger noted and the analytical error exemplified by Brass.[74] It is because of such failures that the objects of exegesis are the powerful and their self-selected tool-kits are read in a textured manner, that is, in terms of the objects and their usage. It is to this that we now can proceed.

Application: the Mahabharata's dharma

The context for the MEA's rationality is sought in what is a vast and totally novel text to modernity. Hence an introduction is needed. To make dialogue possible this is done analogically, through a single word: 'sincerity'. For Europe it means authenticity, revealing the secrets of one's heart. In the *Mb* sincerity takes no less than thirteen forms depending on context.[75] This very quality led to the *Mb* being declared by Europe a 'literary unthing', a 'monstrous chaos'.[76] Yet it was in demand, and a textured reader gathers that it is an education in *dharma* for Yudhisthira, a prince, which is appropriate since the *Mb* has educated many others, on their 'mother's lap' says an Indian diplomat.[77] 'Whether we realise it or not,' writes Vishnu Sukthankar, 'it remains a fact that we in India still stand under the spell of the *Mb*.'[78] The text is how Indian society thinks of itself.[79] But what has it educated the people of the MEA to think and how?

To start with, a textured reader views the *Mb* very differently from how modernity does, which in turn provides an inkling of how and what the *Mb* teaches and why it is the most suitable context for the practices of the present.[80] The local term for the *Mb* is *itihasa*, which broadly means 'chronicle'. This Sanskrit word—part of the modern lexicon—is ironical. A literal translation of *itihasa* is: 'Thus (*iti*), indeed (*ha*), it was (*asa*)': implying that it could have been many other things. *Itihasa* then is an irony containing a contingency unfound in 'history'. That the term for 'history' in the modern sense in some of India's vernacular languages has been derived from this word is ironic because *itihasa* in the sense Indians use it clearly means the 'Once upon a time' of European story telling.[81] By not being a philosopher's stone but a construction of the present related to the past, *itihasa* undermines the English word it signifies and continues to do so with every usage. The very designation of the *Mb* then suggests a complexity unfound in modernity. Like it, the *Mb's* genre does not deny causality, but discounts the need to look back to discover causality. Indeed it is fruitless to do so. Much more instructive is to look at the present, which is the summation of all that has passed and that is precisely why the text is being looked at as it is now.

To turn to the text as has just been done would not surprise it. The *Mb* is generally accepted as the longest poem in the world, and a textured reading cannot miss its claim that all knowledge is contained within it. At some point a single written 'text' existed.[82] Cast as a narrative discourse, nearly three quarters of it is didactic or descriptive, and this texture interlinks the *Mb* with today because narrative, writes Hayden White, is a solution to the 'problem of how to translate knowing into telling, the problem of fashioning human experience into a form assimilable to structures of meaning that are generally human rather than culture specific.'[83]

Narrativization, therefore, is moralizing, but the *Mb's* moral is not anarchical-binarism, rather it is how to act in a totality, which necessitates the assumption of a unified cosmos and all that it entails. This is articulated in the story and the manner of the narration's deportment. The clue is in the contextual meaning for the word 'sincerity', and that itself is the moral: contextuality. The very manner of presenting the moral is in keeping with the moral of contextuality, for example after example is made to demonstrate the point. This is highly significant and, following the text, is termed *dharma* or context dependent action.[84] There is an interrelated category within the text: highest-*dharma* or the super-moral. Alfred Hiltebeitel notes that, for instance, *ahimsa* and *anrasamsya* (nonviolence and non-cruelty) are both amongst the highest-*dharma* in the

Mb, which means that context dependent action cannot be the moral. Naturally this confuses the man being educated in *dharma*, Yudhisthira, and seeking a way out of his quandary, he makes the highest-*dharma* of the king his first and most enduring question to Bhisma.[85] Of the fifty-four instances Hiltebeitel finds in the *Mb*, the tally of the different excellences said to be the highest-*dharma* includes more than 25 categories and numerous sub-categories, including individual *dharma*s.

This is not, for a textured reader, a quagmire of contradiction. If *dharma* is context dependent action, then highest-*dharma* is knowing that that is the way to act in whatever situation one is in, and recognizing that situation within an ontology that admits virtually endless variation and deferral in matters of formulating and approaching 'the highest'.[86] In other words, the *Mb's* moral—that is, the highest-truth—is that all contexts generate their own truth. In short, *dharma* is a metaphysic that enables highest-*dharma*. In putting them forward in combination what is constructed is the *dharma*-complex, and it makes for a rationality with no room for anarchy or binarism. Rather, the presumption is relations between actors produced in time and space, making for a unified cosmos.

The presence of this text within the MEA's lived reality then provides an extra-modern context for, and explains the prevalence of, seditious practices. In other words, 'the medium itself is the message,'[87] but modernist frames descended from Abrahamic religions delete this because they subsume space to time. Duncan Derret warned against this in 1978 with little, if any, avail:

[H]istorians and anthropologists ... understanding of them [Indians] is not so immediately relevant. Their conception of themselves is all important. Herein tradition is made and remade, and the dramatic events in India stress the vital importance of discovering what is DUTY. ... the innate sense of propriety (not 'fairness') which is called dharma! ... India's dharma owes nothing to freedom movements or Independence.'[88]

Dharma, the basis of the *Mb's* moral, is taken as the context for the structure-of-structures not because Indians use the word assuredly in regular speech,[89] or because *dharma* plays a role in international diplomacy. The former Foreign Minister Jaswant Singh, the man who initiated the negotiations with the US that resulted in the 123 Agreement, keeps a note on *dharma* on his desk.[90] *Dharma* is taken as the context because of a crucial overlap: the assumption of a unified cosmos underpins both the structure-of-structures and *dharma* making for a rationality distinct from anarchical-binarism and exegetically capable while eschewing analytic violence.

Not only is the notion of a unified cosmos implicit in the logic of the text, but stories within the text, about itself and the characters, refute anarchy being the originary state of man and go much further.[91] The *Mb* set forth, '… in the beginning … There was no government and no king; no rod of force, and no one to wield the rod. All creatures guarded each other in accordance with dharma.' In the *Mb* creation is the moral and so need not be any different from the end. In other words, if there is an end, then it is the beginning, and this is a momentous difference with modernity. The negation of binarism however does not delegitimize action, but proliferates an excess of actions impermissible within modernity. The overlapping of origins and ends means there is no teleology and so man may act against *dharma*. Viewed from modernity's canon, this is astounding, for it is to turn away from progress-through-history.

The conversation between a Seer and a barbarian illuminates the point. After a twelve-year drought that dried up the earth and killed most of its people, a Seer abandoned his hermitage and ran hither and thither in search of food. His wanderings brought him to a repulsive hamlet of a dog-eating barbarian, and hanging inside was the carcass of a dog. He resolved to steal it, reasoning that breaking the rules he was expected to follow was permitted in a time of crisis. However, in stealing it he disturbed the barbarian, and they had a conversation where, ironically, it is the barbarian who recites the rules of society to the Seer who insists life takes precedence over traditions. The Seer then ate the dog and at that moment it rained, restoring life, but the Seer through asceticism burned up his sin and entered heaven.[93] The point is that in the *Mb*, given the circumstances, what would normally be a mistake is in fact not a mistake.[94] Time is not what controls everything; space too comes into play.

The turn away from progress-through-history complicates 'religious' finitudes. For instance, whereas in Christianity it is the fear-of-God that keeps man in line, in the *Mb* the gods quiver with the fear-of-man. Weakened by man's lack of offerings, the gods fled to Brahma for help and he devised government and produced a king to ensure everyone did their duty.[95] But the system is not perfect and keeps on breaking down, requiring the gods to intervene. But why not make a perfect world? Because it is not God who has created man in His likeness, it is man who fashions his God, making Him reflect man's ideals at any given moment. Just as beginnings are not anarchical or oppositional, nor is the end, that is if it comes. This overlap of man and God, of origins and ends, is astounding for modernity because at the core of the *Mb* is the assumption of a cosmos, unified and neutral at inception.

This does not, however, engender chaos. The cosmos is regulated, by the axes for everything which are time and space. This dual use makes for another fitting frame for the MEA's practices and further reifies the text's distinctiveness from modernity. For instance, it cannot tolerate the idea contained in the following sentence: '*Adharma* becomes *dharma*, and, *dharma* becomes *adharma*, both on the basis of place and time. Place and time are like that.'[96]

Practices are then not simply a function of time, the inevitable march of 'history', but are also subject to space. This additional vector once again complicates modernity. How the two vectors operate in conjunction, and how space may overrule time, are evident in the conversation between the Bird Adorable and King Brahmadatta. In the story, Adorable lived for many years in the King's palace. She gave birth to a son when the Queen did. One day the boy and the bird were playing, and Adorable gave them each a piece of fruit that made the prince aggressive, and he killed Adorable's child. Adorable then put out the child's eyes and, expecting the King to take revenge, resolved to leave. The King said they were even and asked her to stay. In the debate as to whether they were now even the King argued that Time, not personal agents, determined what happens:

By time is done what will be done. Likewise, do all the different actions occur through Time. One is made to act by Time, one is alive because of it. Time burns all things up, like a fire that has gotten fuel; some are captured all at once, but not others, who are taken one by one. Good lady, I am not the one who measures, nor are you, in what one of us does to the other. Time is always the one who sets the pleasure and pain of beings. So live here with affection, unharmed, in accordance with Time. Whatever you have done to me is forgiven.

Adorable rebuts the assigning of responsibility to Time, but in believing that the King would never forgive her, she cannot escape from time. In short, she too maintains causality, but she arrives at a very different conclusion to the King. This is evident in her detailed counteracting of what the King said. For her, the King will not forgive her because—and she outlines all the reasons from the past—he has been wronged (and she knows she has wronged him). Two results are then possible, and they are both correct because both maintain causality. The results are different not because causality is overruled, for action is not possible outside time (that is why both rely on time to explain themselves). The difference is possible because a new space for causality is opened up: time-in-space. It complicates causality as understood by modernity, by making time open to space. Finally, that the bird resolves to, move out of the kingdom, and does so, is not to say that space overrules time. Rather, it demonstrates that beyond the space of the King, the bird may be free from his time, his causality, but that does not negate his causality.[97]

This story's underlying premise—of a neutral origin—has a significance shown by the fact that it is the subject of one of Yudhisthira's central questions. He asks it because unlike anarchical-binarism, where time is the sole generator of causality, the *Mb* includes space, thereby confounding him. He finally realizes that the sanctity of time is not overruled by space, but the *Mb* does not colour the origin in a particular way to make for a unilineal flow of time; instead, by making the origin neutral, what is restored is space. Hence, time and space are the guides to action, which via another angle demonstrates why the *Mb* is a fitting context for the structure-of-structures.

Following Yudhisthira's learning curve takes us to the story of the prince who is advised by a sage to use 'base dishonesty' and 'fraud' to regain a kingdom. The prince rejects the advice because it does not suit him, it is unbecoming of the princely self. At this the sage rejoices, because he has actually been leading the prince on, to test his knowledge of his self. Knowing oneself in time is central to the operation of *dharma*. It therefore does not deny time, indeed time is present in context, which is only so because it includes space. By not ascribing any particular character to origin, time is permitted to operate alongside space within any context. That there is no programming of time is why the opposite is true for Karna. When it is revealed to him that he is a prince by birth, he chooses, even so, to continue to live as he has been raised—as a commoner.[98] Both examples demonstrate time-in-space, and it is made apparent practically by Bhisma who elucidated the centrality of following one's father, mother and teacher, who represent the three worlds, and then said: 'All of this has been issued as a "super-teaching" of what a person must do here in this world. This is the best thing to do; there is nothing more excellent than it. It has been declared after perusing all the *dharmas*.'[99] In short, *dharma* requires knowing one's place in time. But Yudhisthira was also told:

The instruction I give you in *dharma* does not come simply from pure tradition. It is a grand passage to wisdom, it is honey collected from different sources by wise seers. The king must make use of many wise insights from here and there. The world's onward movement does not occur with a *dharma* which has just one branch. Victory belongs to the kings who always act according to *dharmas* derived by means of intelligent insights. Victory-seeking kings who hold intelligent insight to be best of all are the ones who are victorious. Using intelligent insight, the king should make use of *dharma* that comes from here and there. The *dharma* of kings was not ordained as a *dharma* made up of just one branch.[100]

Dharma, then, is to know causality, but a textured reading clarifies that the origin does not limit practice as it does in modernity, because the origin is the cosmos and it is all encompassing and neutral. Hence space is given a significance unfound in modernity, because it is in context that causality is re-expressed or re-modulated. Hence a cosmological analysis need not replicate modernity's obsession with origin, for it is managed with an equivalent emphasis on the present.

The very alterity of this conceptualization is the reason why practice is not an endless iteration of modernity's dynamic: assimilation to arrive at a binarily opposite perfect end. Rather, what is created is a space in the present to conduct a politics unbound by modern laws of time. There is the story of the Brahmin who is the very soul of *dharma*. He had taken a vow of silence. One day robbers hid in his house and he refused to tell anyone about it. They were found and since the Brahman had not told anyone, the King ordered him put to death. However, he willed life, was released and went to the god Dharma himself to ask why he had suffered. Dharma replied that it was because he had stuck blades of grass into butterflies as a child. The Brahmin said: 'For a small offence you have given me an enormous punishment. Because of that, Dharma, you will be born as a man, in the womb of a *sudra*. And I will establish a boundary for the fruition of *dharma* in the world: no sin will be counted against anyone until the age of fourteen.'[101] The ideal is realized in context, which requires rewriting the rules, and a man does it! Unlike modernity, which owing to its Christian roots views authority in binary terms, in the *Mb* authority is everyone's because it arises out of context, making for the only form of politics that may be regarded as genuine because it is not a function of the past and does not seek to deflect to the future.

Such a politics possesses real virtue because it is predicated against violence and therefore provides yet another context to the structure-of-structures. In contrast, anarchical-binarism makes the present, like the past and the future, not a realm for politics but for power politics, a bat-tleground between the forces of progress-through-history and its 'oth-ers'. While anarchical-binarism seeks to homogenize everything through violence, the *Mb* permits the proliferation of variations of the cosmos. Not only may all exist, but they must, for they are expressions of the cos-mos. As the sage Brihaspati noted:

Some recommend quiet calm, others vigorous exercise; some recommend nei-ther the one nor the other, and others recommend both. Some recommend sac-rifice, and others recommend renunciation. Some recommend giving, and others recommend receiving. Some others renounce everything and sit still in silent meditation. Some recommend kingship, the protecting of all creatures by slaying, shattering, and cleaving enemies and wrongdoers; and others live a solitary life.

Again, there are some guides: 'This is the definitive conclusion of the wise, after considering all this: "The *dharma* that is esteemed by the pious is the one that does no harm to beings ...."'[102]

For a modernist, for instance Kant, this is an objective rule because he views the world in a binary way. He writes, 'duty and obligation are ... two mutually opposing rules [which] cannot be necessary at the same time, then if it is duty to act according to one of them, it is not only not a duty but contrary to duty to act according to the other.'[103] However, the very texture of the *Mb* refutes such a reading. What the *Mb* does is complicate this simple rule because life is never theoretical and what matters is not rules, but the way rules are played out in context.[104]

This is precisely why the text is rampant with violence despite the injunction being peace. Undoubtedly violence is wrong but the *Mb* is about a great war. The *Mb's* violence is the product of a moral dilemma—roughly, when one is committed to two actions where one contradicts the other—rather than neat intellectual systems. The text is riven with such dilemmas because the assumption is a neutral origin, which gives space its due. Space combines with time to make for a cosmos teeming with interests, ideas, elements, all bound together relationally and hence burdening the practitioner navigation the cosmos. This is why the *Mb* dwells on these situations: to illustrate by the operation of causality in space not as ideal types, but as everyday occurrences. They include declar-ing the vow sacrosanct while undermining it; upholding life while coun-tenancing death; and encouraging social order while undoing it, or the wilful forgetting of everything society holds dear. While these themes of paradox suggest that the *Mb* is beyond modernity, they are precisely what encapsulates the *Mb*'s message: the maintenance of order is dependent not on the nature of that order but on the multitude of contexts we find ourselves in. This is because contexts are expressive of the origin and therefore the cosmos, and are also the only way we can comprehend it, for the origin is undoubtedly beyond even modern science's grasp. This makes the individual not just a product of the past, but continually in dialogue with it.

An inverse case demonstrates dialogue by showing how the vow need not be in keeping with *dharma*, and that upholding life is not necessarily good. The story is the killing of a blind beast by the hunter Balaka who is nonetheless transported to heaven because the beast had vowed to kill all creatures. But here there is a paradox. Underlying the destruction of the beast is a resistance to *dharma*, including the universalizing concept of *ahimsa* upon which the epic rests, and the goodness of the vow. In other words, the laws of the cosmos—that everything deserves to exist by virtue of existing—are re-expressed in space. However, how does the text reconcile the notion of what is usually wrong becoming right in a particular context with the notion that nothing in a cosmos ought to be harmed for all is expressive of the cosmos? It is not something that is left resolved in the *Mb*.

As startling as time-in-space is for modernity, the reason for it being possible is the assumption of a unified cosmos containing both time and space. The unified cosmos makes for another unexpected difference, alluded to already. The *Mb* possesses intertextuality to make for the type of reflexivity seen in the MEA. This is not found in anarchical-binarism because it lacks the foundational basis the MEA has. In its absence, modernity only came to realize this possibility in the mid-1940s and coined the term *intertextualité* in 1966.[105] But this realization is fundamentally a production of violence because *intertextualité* is not preceded by a unified cosmos but by a binary—author-reader—and hence replicates once again the Christian divide between man and God. In yet another replaying of Christian binarism, the author held the authentic meaning of a text, and the reader sought to understand it. *Intertextualité* signified the move from this hierarchy in interpretation (an inevitability in meaning) to the production of meaning by the interplay of readers. The process began with violence—indeed nothing else is possible given the binary positioning of author and reader—and is evident in the language of *intertextualité*. For instance, Roland Barthes' seminal essay on *intertextualité* is entitled 'Death of the Author'. The author, of course, is killed by the 'other', the reader.[106] Nor is there any way of checking this originary violence. It is replicated with every new reader who engages the text because each reader becomes an author, generating meanings, and hence increasing the competition for authenticity. The problem is that *intertextualité* might repudiate the author's authority to generate the only meaning, but what persists is the notion of alienated authority. All that has changed is that there are now many more centres aspiring to authority. Correspondingly, there are many more possibilities for violent clashes. The *Mb's* intertextuality is very different because a neutral origin permits omnidirectional reflexivity. The *Mb*, therefore, never posits authority in binary terms; this is not to deny authority, which is the cosmos itself. It invests authority in intertextuality itself. This is in the text's lexis, between man and God rather than the sole prerogative of either. In other words, authority is generated by many different times in space. What is also engendered is looking into space, rather than only one's own time.

The textured reader cannot miss the phenomenal practices this reflexivity spawns. For instance, the last story, the closing lesson of the *Mb*, is one of wilful forgetting of societal norms, customs and rules or the overriding of 'history' in modernity's terms by time-in-space, that is, context. This is not an act of violence, the assimilation or eradication of anything, but a demonstration of the allied operation of both time and space. The lesson is that the individual self-reflexively located spatially and in time (society's accrued meanings) must decide whether to uphold society or not, by calculating whether it is in consonance with the cosmos. The *Mb* finishes with Yudhishthira, accompanied by a stray dog, walking into heaven. The king of the gods bars his way, since caste law regards dogs as unclean. Yudhishthira refuses to enter unless the dog is permitted. The very act of insistence is significant. The man who has been learning *dharma* chooses to forget all society reveres and holds dear. He is praised for his persistence since the dog faithfully accompanied him during his wanderings, and in a dramatic reversal, the dog turns out to be a disguised form of the god Dharma, *dharma* incarnate. Doniger translates the momentous significance of this story into Christianity's lexis, thereby enabling communication with modernity. In the Western canon the incarnation is astounding, the equivalent of the God of the Hebrew Bible taking the form of a pig. But the king's willingness to include the dog among those 'who are devoted to one,' as he puts it, is equally astounding and quite 'wonderful. ... When we realise by the epic's end that he departs this world through his noncruelty toward a dog, we see that it has been a long and painful lesson', and that the lesson is that even the highest rules of society are subject to space, and the actor who knows *dharma* operates within both vectors rather than only time as does the modern.[107]

None of the above, however deals, with the question of 'which rationality is better', the question is central to modernists from at least the time of O'Hanlon/Washbrook, to anthropologists and inversely to post-colonialists such as Prakash. Unfortunately modernity, having taken its cue from Plato, poses this question unfairly. What Plato did in his *Republic* was to demonstrate the possibility of space and time interacting in an unpleasant way, in the clash with Thrasymachus right at the start of that book. Then Plato let Socrates proceed in a nice, that is calm and collected, way (the hallmark of civilization), to set out practices based simply on time. In doing so he stacked the cards against the sort of politics that are occurring in the MEA.[108] The *Mb* keeps to Plato's injunction to learn the lessons of time, but also permits actors the ability to conduct politics. In other words, the *Republic* creates the notion of free will and then erases it by educating everyone into a particular way, but the *Mb* teaches how time and space may be understood expeditiously.

This is possible through the use of reason, which is essential to a cosmic actor. The type of reason being outlined is not one of rote learning, but requires great thought and judging knowledge within the coordinates of time and space. All of this is naturally only possible within a unified cosmos—where time and space (at a minimum) interlink everything. This does not however make for an oppressive network, nor a self-regulating ecosystem, the former trapping individuals into a singular course and the latter absolving them from politics. As Adorable demonstrated, individuals arrive at different conclusions (themselves dependent on time and space). This is in line with the complex that is *dharma* and highest-*dharma* only if reason is not used capriciously.[109] Those who do, well .... This is not the place to judge whether it is better to live in a Platonic world, where one's reason is disciplined from before birth, or a world of reasoned action. It will suffice to note that the difference is a question of politics. In the *Mb*, one is encouraged to be political. Founded on empathy, it makes for a purpose completely different from modernity's. It seeks to assimilate, while a politics of empathy seeks to navigate. The difference is not of degree, but of rationality.

The practice of diplomacy in the Mahabharata

Menon used the *Mb* because it instantaneously made the world sensible for Indian diplomats. That instance of referencing proves not only that the practice of diplomacy exists in the text, but that it is compelling. But these practices are also located in a text whose rationality is quite alternative to modernity's. This makes the *Mb's* diplomatic practices recognizable to modernity, but only at the level of the mundane. This segment lays out the practices of diplomacy, purely for form's sake given modernity's conceit. What is of far greater interest is why diplomacy is practiced and how, in terms of alterity. What is presented below, then, is not just practice, but the practical exposition of the conduct of diplomacy on another register.

The actual functioning of alterity, and therefore the context for today's practices, may be gathered by noting that the *Mb* ascribes a central role to diplomacy. It is the leading god—Krsna—who is the arch-diplomat, and his mission in the *Book of the Effort* is to maintain peace.[110] Krsna's mandate, given to him by Yudhisthira, was: 'Whatever sound advice is consistent with *dharma*, you can give them that, Kesava, whether it be for peace, or war.'[111] Krsna's *raison d'être* could be programmatic for any existing diplomatic service. He said: 'Bharata! May there be peace between the Kurus and Pandavas without any war on the part of the heroes—this is what I have come to accomplish. Sire, I have no other statement to make to you that could more redound to your benefit, for you yourself, enemy-tamer, know all there is to know.'[112]

What everyone knew is that two branches of a family, symbolic of a unified cosmos—the Pandavas and Kurus—are in conflict. They have a choice between Krsna and his armies.[113] The Pandavas are 'good', their virtue means they know that a man of quality is superior to vast armies and choose Krsna. With the choice made, relations between the factions disintegrate. Krsna makes a final attempt at peace by planning an embassy to the Kuru court. The mission discloses modernity's hubris in claiming diplomatic theory as modern. For instance, the Kuru leader Duryodhana tells his father that he will imprison the diplomat and therefore deny the Pandavas their main asset.[114] The father reproaches his son because 'This is not the sempiternal *dharma*! Krsna is an envoy and our dear friend.'[115] This example of diplomatic immunity demonstrates a remarkable continuity between Indian practice over millennia and European modernity. In fact, these practices predate the *Mb* and are there in the *Dharmasastra* and the *Arthasastra*, the latter better known in the West, as India's answer to Niccolò Machiavelli, than to Indians themselves.[116] This is mainly because, in contrast to the continuity of the Mb, the *Arthasastra* was rediscovered only in 1905.[117] At any rate, that the *Mb's* practices were already known is certain. The *Dharmasastra* for instance details the categories of ambassador. They are:[118]

Ambassador Plenipotentiary: who has the power to declare war.

Ambassador: has authority at his own responsibility to adapt his words to circumstances.

Ambassador-messenger: a mouthpiece.

This is the context for the *Mb's* diplomacy, and in keeping with it, Krsna is Ambassador Plenipotentiary and used four well established negotiating strategies: peaceful negotiations; bribery; subversion of the enemy's allies; and if these tactics fail, then war.[119] Krsna therefore pays courtesy visits during which he also gathers intelligence. Later he resorts to friendly persuasion.[120] Realizing he is not progressing, Krsna changes tactics. He tries to subvert Duryodhana's allies by warning of the coming danger.[121] A councillor, aware of Duryodhana's *dharma*, is convinced by Krsna's speech but fails to adequately debate the issue with his king, who storms out. This failure of Duryodhana's courtiers to adequately engage their king is for Krsna 'the grave fault of all the elders that they do not forcibly restrain this addlebrained king in his abuse of power'.[122] It is the duty of strategic advisers to advise according to their *dharma*, and if the king will not listen, then the adviser must have the courage to sacrifice either himself or the king.

Krsna continues negotiations by proposing to bribe the Kurus—giving up a kingdom for five villages—and since all fails, he departs.[123] As he leaves he tries dissension as well. He divulges to a Kuru called Karna that he, not Duryodhana, is the rightful heir to the Kuru throne.[124] Krsna offers to help make Karna king of the Kurus and so avert the war that Duryodhana is set upon. If Karna accepts, Krsna knows, peace will be concluded. But Karna, having been raised not to be a king, though by birth he is one, refuses Krsna and this final attempt at peace fails. Having done what theory prescribed, Krsna notes: 'Now I see no other course open but the fourth—punishment. The kings are marching to their doom!'[125] What is obvious is that there is nothing modern about the practices of diplomacy. As Mackenzie Brown writes, 'Ancient Hindu political wisdom is still a good key to the political thinking of Asiatic peoples', because in that ancient system, 'a precise code of international relations and power diplomacy was worked out.'[126]

What is far more interesting is how the complex of *dharma* and highest-*dharma* shapes diplomacy. A first glimpse is offered by Krsna's *raison d'être*, which is only apparent to a few. This is because what everyone does not know is that the Kuruksetra war is not what it seems, and the manner in which the text is framed reveals how time functions in space, that is, the working of context. To take the meta-frame first is to keep with the text's texture and Simon Brodbeck encapsulates it in observing that the war is the:

> result of a divine mission to rescue the earth. Asuras had been born in human form, and there was a need to exterminate them in order to re-establish dharma and renew the cosmos. Krsna was the leader of the divine rescue party. Krsna's principal aim is to make sure that the Kuruksetra war happens and that the cosmic miscreants all die. So what is he up to on that 'peace mission'? He is certainly not attempting to ensure a peaceful solution. He knows that Duryodhana is bent on war and not to be deterred.[127]

And Krsna admits that he is merely going through the motions of attempting to find a diplomatic solution, in order not to be held responsible for the war: 'May those who do not know *dharma*, the ignorant and the unfriendly, not say of me, "Krsna, though able to, did not restrain the angry Kurus and Pandavas". I have come to bring about the good of both: having taken pains in this, may I be irreproachable by the people.'[128]

As with *vasudhaiva kutumbakam*,[129] the frame changes meaning, but without diluting the core idea that is *dharma*. The actors do not know the divine plan (the workings of the cosmos), yet they seek to act in concordance with *dharma* for it is the sensible way to act. Secondly, the framing in the text is also a lesson. It is impossible to know all, for to know all is to be divine. There is thus no way of returning to the origin, yet this does not disable the notion of either *dharma* or highest-*dharma*. The Pandavas resort to war entirely on the basis of contextual action—they are driven to the battlefield by a series of iniquities inflicted on themselves. From this the reader learns highest-*dharma*, as does Yudhisthira. And finally, none of this contradicts causality, for all that has passed, all the *dharma* actions, are in consonance with the cosmos, because it is neutral. Not knowing all, people therefore still act in accordance with the principle of causality as expressed in context, as indeed they must, to maintain the cosmos. And this they of course do, because unknown to them they are saving the cosmos from Asuras.

In the *Mb*, then, politics does not require justification in origins; rather, what is called for is to make oneself aware of and reflect on the present in terms of time and space, for it is the summation of all that has passed. What is required is contextual exegesis. This difference from modernity is also why the *Mb* provides a fitting context for the structure-of-structures emphasis on actors engaging in politics through the judicious use of reason.

The conduct of this type of politics further differentiates the *Mb* because it follows the logic of the cosmos to posit an altogether new (for modernity) understanding of ownership and freedom quite inexplicable in terms of power politics. This is exposed, at the micro-level, through what Brodbeck calls a 'comprehensive deconstructive philosophy of deliberate behaviours'.[130] Krsna is the originator and most excellent practitioner of this philosophy. It is *asakta Karman* or action without attachment. Krsna's attitude to action is: 'For me there is nothing to be done, nothing in the three worlds to be obtained; even so I move in *karman* … Actions do not stain me. I do not delight in the fruit of actions. Whoever perceives me in this way is not bound by *karmans*.'[131] The attachment to be shed is to the fruits of one's actions, not activity itself (becoming an ascetic),[132] because Krsna is enmeshed in the cosmos, which enables him. What makes him different is that he can escape because he is also a god.[133] It is only by behaving as a god that Krsna realizes unattached action. Significantly, as a human, Krsna is unable to do so.[134]

But what does this mean for Krsna as man, for our politics? Rather than dwell upon Krsna's internal cognition, the *Mb* posits behaviour from which S.S. More constructs the answer of anti-imperialism.[135] However, there is more than a hint of anachronistic re-creation in this (though it does fit with the flux of society at the time of the *Mb*'s creation). Rather than limit analysis to 'history', Brodbeck decodes Krsna's famous dialogue with Arjuna in the *Bhagavadgita* in terms of *asakta Karman*, but for people rather than gods.[136] That both More and Brodbeck are capable of doing this, especially the latter, from a text which is resolutely empirical and—contra Nandy—unconcerned with psychology is indicative of texture.

Central to Krsna's philosophy is the idea of *lokasamgraha* or the holding together of worlds. Actions hold the world together because they bind.

However, the 'cause of action is never an independent human being, but is always *prakrti*, the material world as a whole, of which any individual person is an arbitrary subsection. The teleological view of actions as initiated and owned by individuals is, quite simply, a mistake.'[137] *Lokasamgraha* is not a goal. It just is. To put it in the vocabulary of the structure-of-structures, we act, but not in a particular way, because the origin is neutral. The determinant for action is therefore time and space. But those two vectors are of the cosmos and also shape our actions, hence we do not own our actions, they are products of a neutral unified cosmos.

The implication for politics is that the practitioner of *asakta Karman* can act without the delusive notion of moving towards freedom. This generates in the modern self a range of debilitating neuroses, including anomie. These arise from what Michael Smith calls 'a dogma in [Western] philosophical psychology'[138] or the mistake of assuming *prakrti* is negative, binding. It has to be so for modernity, because the origin is anarchy, resulting in the delusive search for utopia. This is why for David Hume liberty is the 'power of acting or not acting, according to the determinations of the will', which belongs to anyone 'who is not a prisoner in chains.'[139] The Humean view then reproduces the binarism endemic to modernity, but more significantly, rests on a belief: the very idea of 'chains'. In other words, Hume converts *prakrti* into a restrictive environment. Such a conceptualization produces the desire to be free of *prakrti*, which is of course impossible, and thereby opens moderns to psychoanalysis.

This opening never occurs in the *Mb* because the freedom offered by modernity is a phantasm. The cosmological actor acts in consonance with the cosmos. This does not of course negate politics, indeed it permits focusing on the real perversion of the cosmos, which is power politics. As Brodbeck writes, 'the non-attached actor's behaviour is motivated in the same sense as blinking, sleepwalking or digestive processes are motivated. We do not say of someone, when they blink, that their psychology is obscure. There simply is no psychology of blinking.'[140] But blinking contains a process, which maintains the organism. The implication for politics is that *prakrti* does not bind, rather it motivates to act politically in a very particular way: to conserve *prakrti*.

Conclusions

Hedley Bull is right: Indians are underexposed to European ways, but modernity need not fear this, because the *Mb* permeates Indian diplomatic society. Precisely why this means that there is no threat becomes apparent despite the fact that the text cannot be totally demythologized, for that is irrelevant.[141] What is relevant is that it contains a rationality alternative. This is possible because, as Ganeri reminds us, rationality is no more the unique property of any culture than is language.[142] Yet modernity makes the preposterous claim of being the be-all and end-all, and in doing so reproduces the tenets of Western religiosity. The result has been 'an underestimation of the reach of public reasoning' and the 'long tradition of rational assessment' in texts such as the *Mb*, notes Amartya Sen.[143] In its fatal hubris modernity has missed out on a rationality that does not need to bring order, but expounds the means of navigating a crowded cosmos without damaging it. This is the *Mb*'s rationale, and ensconced in it is the practice of diplomacy that Europe claims to have invented. What is striking is not the overlap in mundane practice, but how the *Mb*'s rationality makes for a practice impossible within modernity. This is not limited to diplomacy but shapes all politics for the cosmological actor. As a spiritualist wrote:

Indian spirituality is based upon a strong foundation of realism. It sees no conflict between spirituality and the ordinary values of life. Hinduism is by no means otherworldly or anti-social in the usual sense of these words. Indian thinkers have come to grips with reality, whose meaning, however, changes at different stages in the development of the soul. They have reflected upon and faced man's real problems of life, from his first wandering into the realm of phenomena to his final liberation, and have exhorted him first to idealize the real and then to realize the ideal.[144]

Such a politics, founded on practices of idealizing the real and realizing the ideal, is possible because underlying the *Mb* is a unified cosmos that must be negotiated without harming. This is mandatory, for all belong to the cosmos. In the *Mb*'s terms the modern obsession with uncovering origins dissipates, because navigating the cosmos is not dependent on simply time. Cosmological actors, by not being shaped by some ungraspable and unverifiable origin, do not seek to uncover causality, while knowing full well they are bound by it. Being therefore free of time in a manner impossible for moderns, the cosmological is open to the vagaries of space. It is here that time is made manifest, to make for context. It must be known intimately for one might be called to act against it to maintain the cosmos—as India did when it negotiated the nuclear treaty with the United States.

4

INVERTED 'HISTORY'

There is a need to understand the past in a more redemptive way.

— Foreign Secretary Nirupama Rao[1]

The period that saw the rationality central to the self-constitution of Indian society being altered, erased or incorporated by modernity upon contact with Europe was the colonial era. So those operating within the confines of modern thought tell us.[2] In Europe, theorizes James Der Derian, the uneasy intellectual contract of Westphalia regularized physical alienation. This assemblage was allegedly introduced into pre-colonial India, erasing its rationale. Yet, despite the *Mahabharata* (*Mb*) being articulated earlier, its lesson demonstrably orders the Indian present. Explaining this discrepancy requires turning to what European modernity encountered.

The context it found itself in was Mughal India. That this was an era of extended intercivilizational contact is shown by the intellectual ferment of the time and the result: the Indo-Mughal state. Islamic in theory, it was in practice dependent on including the non-Muslim majority, who over the period of contact transformed the Mughals themselves.[3] This is why K. Shankar Bajpai is both wrong and right when he pronounced, 'You see we do not know power' and went on to lament that 'we have not held power for a long time. We knew it and how to handle it … but we've been out of practice for … what … a thousand years?'[4] Bajpai was right in that the non-Muslims of the subcontinent were not supreme, but their rationality persisted. This is evident in the Indo-Mughal state whose defining intellectual characteristic was an uneasy move towards the complex that is *dharma* and highest-*dharma* (the *dharma*-complex) from a rationality categorically different: Islam. It is categorically different because Islam by being an Abrahamic religion, is motivated by a rationality nearly identical to the one that produced modernity: Christianity. However, Islamic theory was modified by *dharma*. Its absorption was due to a silence in Islam, which permitted the Mughals to open themselves to the *Mb's* rationality. It gave the Mughals succour by ameliorating their modern rationality and converted them into Indo-Mughals. The process was aided by the nature of the international society the Indo-Mughal state was implicated in. That society comprised, mainly, the Indo-Mughal's kith and kin in West Asia who were also Muslim. They engaged each other diplomatically, and since it was blood and religion that strung together a substantial portion of the world prior to Europe's arrival,[5] the setting was not dissimilar to pre-Westphalian Europe. However, because the 'othering' tendencies of Islam were checked and even reversed in the subcontinent by the *dharma*-complex, diplomacy had not degenerated into the means of overcoming the 'other' at the time of the British arrival. It meant that diplomacy was conducted not to assimilate but to negotiate a crowded world populated with another rather than the 'other'. This was the intellectual context that modernity met,[6] and there was no need to transform the texture of what was found because modernity could tessellate into it, and did so enthusiastically.[7]

In other words, what actually occurred was an inversion of the modern myth retailed by liberals, Marxists, postcolonials and others. In terms of practice, the harbingers of modern diplomacy gave up their ways, socialized themselves by learning local customs and manners and placed themselves in the care of Indo-Mughals. In doing so, they enthusiastically transformed themselves, though much of this effort was misguided as they were never able to discard their incipient propensity for 'othering' what they encountered, because they were incapable of a reflexivity that could cross the threshold of time and take note of space. Yet, it is more than ironic that the archives these dynamic individuals left behind—in fascinating detail—are discounted by the descendants of the very civilization that claims them as the torchbearers of modernity.[8] To avoid this analytical violence is to undermine modernity's dynamic. Recovering the harbingers' legacy is to remove the violence descendants inflict. Doing so is contingent on retrieving experiences and expressions,[9] to present in all their complexity a handful of people who have been converted over the course of modernity into automata. They were not, perhaps because they were themselves negotiating their own transformation into moderns. But that process lies beyond this work, for the concern is with what they encountered.

The coming of modernity, however, does necessitate a caveat. The practices presented are those of British ambassadors, but they were not the first Europeans to negotiate with the Indo-Mughals. Why then focus on the British? Because, modernity tells us, it is they who invented modernity, the modern state and international system.[10] It is therefore they who must have been the carriers of authentic modernity, a contention reinforced by the British being the first to negotiate—successfully—with the Mughal emperor.[11]

The rationale for diplomacy in the Indo-Mughal Empire

Identifying the dominant rationale for diplomacy at the moment the British entered the sub-continent is to delineate the Indo-Mughal state's rationality. It is laid bare in the *Ain-I Akbari*, or the mode of Akbar's governance,[12] volume three of the *Akbarnama*—'by far the greatest work in the whole series of Muhammedan histories of India,' wrote its translator Heinrich Blochman.[13] Written by the *mir munshi* Sheikh Abu al-Fazl Allami,[14] his discussion provides an economic notion of the world. He set out the reasons for state by stating that:

the meaning of the word Padshah shows; pad signifies stability and possession, and shah means origin, lord. A king is therefore, the origin of stability and possession. If royalty did not exist. The storm of strife would never subside, nor selfish ambitions disappear. Mankind, being under the burden of lawlessness and lust, would sink into the pit of destruction; the world, this great market place, would lose its prosperity, and the whole earth become a barren waste. But by the light of imperial justice, some follow with cheerfulness the road of obedience, whilst others abstain from violence through fear of punishment; and out of necessity make choice of the path of rectitude. Shah is also a name given to one who surpasses his fellows; it is also a term applied to a bridegroom—the world, as the bride, bethroes herself to the King, and becomes his worshipper.

Central to Mughal statecraft is 'stability and possession', so that 'the world, this great market place' did not 'lose its prosperity'. Maintaining this economic order required a king worthy of his title:

Silly and short-sighted men cannot distinguish a true king from a selfish ruler. In the case of the former [a large treasury, a numerous army, clever servants, obedient subjects, an abundance of wise men, a multitude of skilful workmen, and a superfluity of means of enjoyment] are lasting; but in that of the latter, of short duration. The former does not attach himself to these things, as his object is to remove oppression and provide for everything which is good.

This programme, noteworthy for its contextual practicality, is however only superficially similar to *dharma*, because it is founded in a radically alternative conception.

The difference from *dharma* lies in that the basis of Indo-Mughal theory was Islam, and it is like Christianity because both are teleological, binary and anarchical. Islam emphasizes time over space by making the origin divine, in contradistinction to the *Mb's* neutrality. Undoubtedly the Mughals melded the human with the divine in the body of the emperor. However this did not make man a partner and equal to God. On the contrary, this arrangement made temporal success divine because the belief was that the divine acted through the emperor. In practice, the Mughal emperor worshipped the sun as the visible representative of God and as the immediate source of life. 'Royalty is a light emanating from God, and a ray from the sun, the illuminator of the universe, the argument of the book of perfection, the receptacle of all virtues,' writes Abu al-Fazl in his 'Preface'. He also sets out in detail what is required of the emperor, who is clearly understood as the ordering finger of God and nothing more. Although the emperor was the instrument of God, Abu al-Fazl continually intersperses this general law with the notion that in the temporal world the emperor was expected to perform his duties in concert with his courtiers or his office.[15]

In theory, then, the Mughal state was radically different from what the *Mb* teaches, because the former did not base itself on the relations of equality between man and God. These are inherent to the *Mb* and oblige a unified cosmos where the origin is taken as neutral rather than pregnant with divine meaning. In contradistinction, Islam, like Christianity, privileged originary causality and hence time at the expense of space, ruling out intertextuality capable of learning in space. These features make Islam modern, identified by a linear binary view, in contrast with the *Mb's* intertextuality expressed in context or the dual operation of time and space. In short, and in the lexicon of Mughal state theory, its systemic base made for a hierarchy with God at the top.

The contention that the Mughal state was theoretically modern is concluded by the implicit use of anarchy in Islam. However, the Mughals sought to break out of their modernist mind-set, which is why they became Indo-Mughals. To map the transition in Indo-Mughal terms requires noting that Islam posits itself as revolutionary. The 'age of *jahiliya*, ignorance, savagery'[16] is what predates the moment before the epiphany that is Islam, notes Harbans Mukhia; *jahiliya* lies before 'history' and though it is not a state of being alienated, it is disordered and repugnant. Order is only established with the coming of Islam. In short, Islam dispels originary anarchy and, just like Christianity, has to spread to bring order. This is why, traditionally, Islamic historians present 'history' as would be expected of modernists: Islam engaged in combat with *kufr* (unbelief). Abu al-Fazl attempted to distance himself from this religious linearity that views the world as composed of polar opposites and therefore driven by violence. He sought to do so not by ejecting 'history', but by presenting Akbar not as a Muslim ruler, but as a ruler of all. The traditional dichotomy of Islam against its 'others', engaged in combat, was replaced by Abu al-Fazl's *sulh kul* or 'harmony' and 'absolute peace'. This was done by highlighting Akbar's common humanity as well as his Islamic faith. In doing so Abu al-Fazl 'inverts the received notion of historical time: for him it has an uncertain beginning but a definite goal.'[17] This was only possible by repudiating the very uniqueness Islam ascribes to itself, the notion of exclusivist divinity. This is precisely what Abu al-Fazl did. However, he did not do so by rejecting the divine, but by making everything divine. In doing so he came remarkably close to the *Mb*, a text he was familiar with. But how was such a move possible?

It was due to a silence within the baseline rationality: Islam. Gerhard Böwering illuminates the silence by differentiating between Islam's metaphysics or 'the vertical dimension of Islamic thought. It made for the overpowering dependence on the Creator.'[18] In accepting this limit, the Indo-Mughals did not reproduce modernity's hubris that it can overcome its origins. The 'vertical dimension' of Islamic thought is what makes it modern. The difference with the cosmic is evident in understandings of causality. Both Christianity and Islam are complicit in sharing a time bound by a particular type of origin, which makes them believe in progress-through-history. This is distinct from the *Mb* which, though not denying progress, opens it to space. Hence progress is a function of context. This is contra Christianity as it is contra Islam, because such an understanding permits the *Mb* to endorse a politics of the present quite unimaginable and quite likely repugnant to Christianity and Islam. The very notion of time explains this best. The Qur'an in verse 7.54 states: 'God created the heavens and the earth in six days and then He mounted [on Saturday in time] the Throne.' On day six, a Single Monad (*jawhar fard*), or a complete human being emerges. All of this is the product of the divine will. As Böwering explains:

God's personal command, "Be!" and it is …. God gave His command when He formed the first human being and made the heavens and the earth. He determines the beginning of a person's life and calls each individual to a final account after death. There is no place in the Qur'ān for impersonal time; each person's destiny is in the hands of the God. … From the "Be!" of creation to the time of death, existence falls under the decree of God: Allāh is the Lord of each instant; what He has determined happens.[19]

The entire process also comes to an end with the Day of Final Judgment—making for a direct binary relationship between origins and ends. Furthermore, unlike the *Mb*, Islam like Christianity makes the origin divine. In colouring the origin in a particular way time is made sacrosanct because it is divine. This is why 'a self-consistent world in space and time, working harmoniously, is only an appearance. The one true actor is God alone. The link of causality that appears to rule the world and human life becomes subordinate to Allāh, and natural causes give way to divine will.'[20]

In short, Islam organizes time within a divinely sanctioned plan terminating with Judgment Day, thereby sacrificing space. However, no modernist theory can contain its believers, quite simply because of the reality that is space. Böwering engages this inability by calling it Islam's horizontal dimension. Necessarily diverse, what is noteworthy is that the metaphysic that is Islam is silent on the ever-present question of space. In doing so, this silence permitted a plethora of non-Islamic practices to be absorbed into the metaphysic. It is what permitted the *mir munshi* and his Emperor to absorb the lesson of the *Mb*.

That it happened is why the British encountered an Indo-Mughal rather than a Mughal state. The Mughals became Indo-Mughals because in India they encountered the *dharma*-complex via the *Mb* (and undoubtedly other sources) whose very moral contradicted the metaphysics that governed the moderns. What put the 'Indo' into Indo-Mughal was Akbar's complicating the Islamic modern. Regardless of the reasons for his doing so,[21] it is clear that he moved very close to the *Mb's* notions of a neutral originary causality and a non-linear understanding of time. Furthermore, the move towards space was in itself contextual. Munis Faruqui makes the novel argument that it was sibling rivalry that persuaded Akbar to do this.[22] The role of temporal politics in this process is overlooked, notes Faruqui, because the chronicles of the day give short shrift to Akbar's half-brother Mirza Hakim, since he 'neither lived in Hindustan nor feigned any interest in fostering his political appeal among Hindustanis.'[23] However Akbar did this and had to do it. To start with, Akbar's context made him move towards a rationality of contextual action. In this the Qur'an's silence no doubt aided him, but he was also exposed to an explicit corpus that forwarded the altogether different rationality motivated by the *dharma*-complex. This was the *Mb* which he had had translated. Hence he continued his father Humayun's policy and sidelined West Asians in favour of Indian Muslims and Rajputs in the nobility.[24] The purpose was contextual—to negotiate the space he found himself in by modifying his conception of time—rather than time-bound or ideological: exterminating the 'other'. Mirza instead chose ideology, perhaps because of his geographical context which was West Asia, and fell back on an orthodox reading of Islam. He therefore formed an alliance with 'the dour Naqshbandis [which] helped him burnish his orthopractic, orthodox, and Sunni-Muslim religious credentials at a time when Akbar's own faith in normative Islam was wavering. Broadly perceived to oppose most expressions of ecstatism in Islamic faith and practice, the Naqshbandis were especially well known for their forceful advocacy of sharia-inspired norms and bitter opposition to Shiism.'[25]

Allied with the Naqshbandis, Mirza's challenge was real. He invaded India twice and harboured refugees from the Indo-Mughal state. In response, Akbar sought to further distance himself from Mirza. An expression of this was their father's tomb. Its 'innovative architecture reflects an imperial vision increasingly accommodative of the Indian environment.'[26] It was only with the death of Mirza that Akbar threw 'all caution to the wind, abandoning even the slightest pretence of being an orthodox-minded Sunni-Muslim ruler or even someone who was mindful of Islamic religious opinion.'[27] This was most potently expressed in Akbar equating himself with God. Akbar replaced the legend *Huw al-Ghani* (He is Rich) at the top of imperial documents with *Allah-o-Akbar*. This was, however, not entirely in line with Abu al-Fazl's rendering all divine. Akbar was making a deliberate play on his name. The term could mean either 'God is Great' or, as is more likely, 'Akbar is God'. That he was never able to equate all men with God was ultimately an intellectual limitation imposed upon him by Islam's time-bound hierarchy, and it persisted despite Abu al-Fazl's inversion. For Akbar only a royal person could become God, and perhaps of all royals only he—certainly not all and sundry, as in the *Mb*. Akbar travelled a great intellectual distance. His journey was as much a product of Islam's silence as it was due to the traditions he—unlike his brother—was exposed to.

This curious intermix, with varying emphasis on the *dharma*-complex and Islam, came to dominate the Indo-Mughal state for the next 150 years.[28] The notion of Indo-Mughal, or the uneasy balancing of a cosmo-logical view with a modern approach, continued after Akbar. Sovereignty, according to Akbar's son, was a 'gift of God',[29] not necessarily given to enforce God's law but rather to 'ensure the contentment of the world.'[30] Such ideas, scattered throughout the *Tuzuk* document of Jahangir's reign and other sources, indicate continued acceptance of the legitimacy of tem-poral power, stripped of theocratic trappings, in Indo-Mughal political thought. It began with a modern intellectual orientation with consider-able silences and moved towards a cosmological order. Though that journey was never completed, it did animate a large bureaucracy, the *Mansabdari*, which was supposed to realize the divine will.[31] But unlike Christianity, Islam in India was opened to the *dharma*-complex, which put the *Mansabdari* in an uneasy location, for those who composed it were nego-tiating a path between Islam's originary causality and context.

Animated by this retreating modernist abstraction, those who com-posed the bureaucracy, the *mansabdars*, were certainly not the public ser-vants of modernity, as defined by Max Weber.[32] However, they met some of Weber's criteria and it was this bureaucracy that conducted the Empire's foreign relations. That it did so delegitimizes modernity's claim that it invented the means for conducting foreign relations today. The similar-ities with current bureaucracies include hierarchy, for *mansabdars* were organizationally embedded in a regular mode of ranking, though it was organized by status rather than wealth, and etiquette reflected and rein-forced hierarchies.[33] There were in addition to the King's household sev-eral departments, which officers of the government managed at the centre and in the provinces, according to established manuals, the *dastur-ul-amal*. This incipient departmentalized system tended to impart to Mughal officials certain qualities of public service. Officers were graded and paid according to the number of troops and horses expected to be maintained and supplied. As the terms and conditions of service were governed by no fixed principle of contract or covenant, they could be appointed or dismissed at will as personal servants. Non-nobles could also be incorporated, and this contributed to the regionalism that challenged the central authority of the Emperor.[34] To clarify: All nobles were *mansabdars*, but all *mansabdars* were not nobles.[35] The interpenetration of the institutions of the army, nobility and officials meant that the *mansabdari* grew complex and interconnected with no clear borders demarcating function. Akbar organized this bureaucracy on a military basis and there were hardly any officers of state who did not have a *mansab*.

At the pinnacle of the bureaucracy was the *Grand Vizier*. Next came four ministers: the *Diwan*, responsible for revenue and finance; the *mir bakshi* responsible for administration and army organisation; the *sadr*, head of ecclesiastical and judicial departments; and the *mir saman*, Chief Executive Officer in charge of the state factories and stores.[36] Notably, there was no foreign minister—for foreign affairs were also family affairs. There were however foreign relations, which despite being enwrapped by family, necessitated the despatching of ambassadors, their reception and the negotiation of binding treaties. Although it was modern and founded on religion, as much as what the practitioners had been exposed to, it was a bureaucratic apparatus and a precursor to the present. This bureaucracy is what conducted the foreign relations of the Indo-Mughal Empire. It meant that diplomacy became the product not of God's will, but of a God-man, even while the notion of a divine being was being nationalized intellectually by Abu al-Fazl. This is why notions of the 'other', implicit in modernity, never made the Empire intent on obviating, much less obliterating, non-Muslims.

The silence in Islam, along with what it encountered in the subcontinent, made the state that grew out of this prolonged period of intercivilizational contact capable of tolerating contact and even negotiations with British commoners.[37] This was aided by commonalities in the mundane practices of diplomacy. These are near identical to the *Mb*—which discounts, at the level of practice, the civilizational uniqueness of diplomacy claimed by modernity. What is however unique along civilizational lines is how diplomacy was structured, the rationale for conducting it. The Indo-Mughals' aim was to not assimilate, as might be expected from the binarism implicit in Islam. Of course the binarism that emerged from Christianity as modernity could have easily emerged in Islam. Its very silence about context could be interpreted in the manner in which Christianity came to be by modernity. This is what happened with Mirza who was opposed as much for practical as for intellectual reasons to Akbar, because he was adjusting the Islam of the Qur'ān. Mirza's concern was to assimilate the Indo-Mughal Empire precisely because he was entrapped by modernity and hence viewed the world in binary terms. In his eyes, Akbar's contextuality would have quite naturally rendered him an 'other'.

What Akbar's deconstruction permitted was a diplomacy unlike Mirza's, because it came very close to the *Mb's* lesson to act contextually. In the context of the Empire, this was to maintain it rather than throw it into religiously motivated expansionism as decreed by the divine plan. To demonstrate the devaluing of time by the advocacy of space, one diplomatic example is presented. That it is from the 1500s also means that this practice predates the entry of modernity proper, thereby discounting the notion that diplomatic action requires a dedicated foreign office. Also illustrated is that the Empire was completely at ease in practicing diplomacy with an entity similar in power and status to itself. These practices were recognized by the peer-Empires the Mughals dealt with, making for an international system like Europe in that it was both familial and religious. In the 16th century one such peer-Empire was the Ottoman, and what shaped relations was that sensibilities stemming from where the Mughals had come from were drastically changed by where they settled.

The Emperor Humayun, though indifferent to the Ottomans, seized the opportunity for establishing relations. This was possible because of the chance arrival of Admiral Sidi Ali Reis, who had been shipwrecked, in Delhi. That Indo-Mughal approval meant a great deal is attested to by the Ottoman's boasting of his master's superiority and his claim that Humayun said the Ottoman ruler was the only one worthy of the title Padshah.[38] Humayun was rather more practical in his approach to the admiral, who was made into an envoy. Sidi Ali Reis was made to transport a letter to the Ottoman Sultan, Suleiman the Magnificent.[39] However, Humayun died and his successor was Akbar, who in 1573 conquered Gujarat, thereby opening the sea-route to Mecca. What should have made for Islamic solidarity had exactly the opposite effect. Renewed contact with Central Asia resulted in the Indo-Mughals falling out with the Ottomans. The process began when several women of the imperial household and their companions departed for the Hajj in 1575 and set sail in October 1576. After a delay of a year due to the failure to obtain a Portuguese pass to travel, they finally set sail in October 1576[40] and returned to the Empire in 1581.[41] The trip demonstrates how the 'Indo' had already inserted itself into the Mughals. Having been exposed to new climes, the Mughals were already behaving in ways that were considered by West Asian Muslims as contrary to the Sharia.[42] Such blasphemous manners, combined with the visitors' largesse, caused great consternation amongst the West Asians. Upon receiving reports, the Ottomans swiftly ordered the Indo-Mughals to be returned home.[43] As Naimur Farooqi writes, 'Akbar's religious attitude seems to have scandalised the whole world of Islam,'[44] and, it would seem, so too did his women. Though Indo-Mughal records are silent about Akbar's reaction to the humiliation meted out to his women, his subsequent actions define a new hostility towards the Ottomans. Akbar stopped sending charity and Hajj caravans to the Hijaz and relations with the Sharifs of Mecca (who had acted upon Sultan's orders to expel the Indo-Mughals) were also suspended.

Akbar went so far as to contemplate an anti-Ottoman alliance with the Portuguese,[45] and despatched an abortive diplomatic mission in 1582 to realize that goal. So serious was the threat posed by Akbar that news of an alliance with the Portuguese in 1587 prompted the Sultan to immediately send 20 galleys to Yemen.[46] In addition Akbar not only rejected a proposal of the Ottoman governor of Yemen but had him put in chains and banished to Lahore. 'The reason for this,' observes Father Monserrate, 'is said to have been his [Akbar's] resentment at the arrogance of the ambassadors themselves and the king who sent them ....'[47] So powerful was the impact of the mistreatment of the women that the incident directly led to Akbar contravening Islamic precepts. Akbar turned down an Uzbek proposal for a triple alliance with the Ottomans against Persia.[48] Akbar's actions went against Islamic solidarity and also against *Realpolitik*. In not acting as a modernist automaton, Akbar reaffirmed that familial sentiment, that is context, overrode the notion of time governing all diplomatic practice.

In short, Mughal-Ottoman relations as commonplace diplomatic practice are remarkably similar to what modernity claims as its own. As today, relations were marked by personal communications at the highest level.

Ambassadors were tasked with obtaining specific goals, stationed at the foreign capital and abused to demonstrate antipathy without seeking war. Important decisions were made by the emperor. The difference between modernity and the Indo-Mughals was in terms of rationality, the underlying metaphysics. Though the Indo-Mughals began as moderns, they were transitioning out of being so. This meant that the purpose for diplomacy was not to assimilate. Diplomacy was not the means of conducting war to realize a utopia, but was rather conducted to negotiate a crowded world on the basis of context, and resorting to violence was only to safeguard oneself. This is why, though modern in origins, Indo-Mughal diplomacy contradicted modernity's very dynamic: to rely on violence to further what is understood as originary causality.

The coming of authentic, modern, European diplomacy

It was this Indo-Mughal Empire that the British approached. What occurred directly reverses the conclusions of modern analysis, because the British sought to tessellate into the world they encountered. This was possible because that world had been changed by the *dharma*-complex. However, the process was not without several false starts, which in themselves are worthy of evaluation, especially since they reveal that not only was Indo-Mughal diplomatic practice comprehensible to the British, but so were concepts including Indo-Mughal notions of sovereignty, conditionality and due process. This easy two-way understanding once again contests the view that diplomacy was invented in Europe and must be geared to its aim.[49]

The first envoy of modernity was Sir Thomas Roe. Sent by King James I to Akbar's son, the Emperor Jahangir, in 1614,[50] Roe landed in Surat in September 1615 and immediately collided with the Empire's bureaucracy. Having received only traders, Zulfikar Khan, the Governor of Surat, expected Roe to subject himself to customs inspection, but the Englishman insisted that his status as an ambassador excused him.[51] Status anxiety, patently, is not a quality limited to today's Indians. So important was status to Roe that he threatened to bypass Zulfikar Khan, and inform the Emperor directly of the 'barbarous usage of me, being ambassador to a mighty King in league with him, and come a far journey upon his royal word.' Shaken, the Governor asked Roe to discuss matters with him personally before proceeding to the Emperor's court. But 'it was too late',

said Roe, 'to offer me Curtesyes, especially under pretence of dishonour-
ing my Master: That it was the Custome of Europe to visit those of my
quality first, and that I durst not breake yt in penaltye of my head, have-
inge expresse Command from my Master to Mayntayne the Honor of a
free king, and to visit none but such as first did that respect due to his
Majestie and that therefore I would never doe vt.'[52] Browbeaten, the
Governor acceded and Roe proceeded to the Emperor who received him
with the status he desired.[53]

Roe's purpose was to negotiate a commercial treaty 'which should place
the position of the English in India on a firm and lasting basis and secure
them against all oppression by the provincial officials.'[54] The English
wanted a treaty or a comprehensive grant of privileges. However, in
August 1617, two years after his arrival, Roe wrote: 'Neyther will this
overgrowne elephant descend to article or bynde him selfe reciprocally
to any prince upon termes of equality, but only by way of favour admit
our stay so long as it either likes him or those that governe him.'[55] In
1618 Roe wrote, 'I am infinitely weary of this unprofitable imployment
… I am weary; yt it is impossible, and I will not stay yow an hower'.[56]
Roe finally received limited permission for Englishmen to reside in the
Empire and conduct trade. 'In other words, Roe completely failed in his
negotiation', but not because the Empire did not understand the British
or possess the concepts to conduct diplomacy. Rather, the Empire did
not want to negotiate a treaty that homogenized Indo-Mughal imperial
space, subject in large part to local rulers, simply to please the British.[57]

Despite the heterogeneity of the Indo-Mughal Empire, the categories claimed by modern diplomacy as its own were understood deep within
the Empire's hinterland. The diary of the Italian traveller Manucci who
accompanied the English Ambassador Lord Bellomont provides a
detailed glimpse of the bureaucratization of diplomacy and the ability of
the Indo-Mughal bureaucracy to adapt over huge geographic spaces and
to new norms. The first substantive difference between Roe's visit and
Bellomont's was at the moment of arrival. Bellomont too arrived in Surat,
but he received a very different welcome. The Empire—at least at the
port of Surat—had acclimatized to the arrival of English ambassadors.
Manucci noted that: 'When the governor of Surat heard of the ambassador's arrival, he ordered his secretary to pay him a visit. The message
thus brought was that rumour said he had come as ambassador, therefore he was requested to state whether this was true or not. It was nec-

essary for him (the governor) to send a report to the emperor Xaaiahan (Shahjahan), then ruling over the empire of the Great Mogul.'[58] The Empire had adapted.

Bellomont was given leave to travel to the court, but was taken ill and died in June 1656 within days of his arrival[59] in a relatively unpopulated area between two towns. Officials responded with a speed and in a manner suggesting that even in the hinterland, and in death, Indo-Mughals were fully cognizant with the procedures to be followed in such an unlikely event. The death also demonstrates that there was, in addition to sovereignty, also an official hierarchy that in extending all the way to the Emperor bound geography politically long before modernity. Manucci wrote:

We carried the body at once to a sarae called Orel [Hodal], between Agrah and Dihli, and, it being already late, we did not bury him that night. The official at the sarae sent notice to the local judicial officer, who hastened to the spot, and, putting his seal on all the baggage, laid an embargo upon it. I asked him why he seized and sealed up those goods. He answered me that it was the custom of that realm, and that he could not release the things until an order came from court, they being the property of an ambassador.[60]

Only a deep familiarity with process explains the speed and assuredness with which the Empire's servants were able to respond. However these very qualities also permitted them to exploit the diplomatic apparatus. In doing so they demonstrate that the processes of Empire were so well known that they could take advantage of it. One must, after all, know the processes to be able to exploit it, and so it was. Within days of the death:

two Englishmen appeared … dressed after the fashion and in the costume of the country, men in the service of the king Shahjahan. They informed me that they had come under the king's orders to carry away the property of the ambassador, which lapsed to the crown. To that I retorted by asking if they bore any order, whereupon they laughed …. Many a time did I entreat them for God's sake to make over to me what was mine; but … they scoffed at me, and said 'Shut your mouth; if you say a word we will take your horse and your arms away.' The belongings were removed to Delhi 'where the Englishmen deposited the property in a sarae, put seals on the room doors, and told me to go about my business. … I expressed my astonishment that they should lock up in a sarae room property that they said belonged to the king. I asked them angrily whether the king had no other place in which to store the goods he owned; but they knew quite well that the property did not belong to them, and that they were taking the king's name in vain, solely in order that they might get hold of other people's goods.[61]

Not only were key ideas prevalent in the hinterland, in addition Lord Bellomont's mission exposed the capacity of the Empire to adapt and change protocols. The impunity with which officials were able to act with Manucci, lie to him and try to rob him of his possessions also underlines that what Akhil Gupta calls 'unspectacular corruption', is not new to India, nor was the exalted person of an ambassador exempt from it.

The next envoy was Sir William Norris, and his encounter reveals that the Empire was familiar with the idea of conditionality. Norris inexplicably chose to break with established custom and landed at Masulipatam on 25 September 1699. This was out of line with established procedures and Norris had to make his way to Surat, the landing point of his predecessors. He reached Surat the next year and nearly a year passed before he was able to set out for the Mughal court in January 1701. When he arrived at the court, Emperor Aurangzeb reminded Norris of an offer made by letter by the English to protect the seas from pirates. Aurangzeb made this an indispensible condition for the granting of any treaties to the British.[62] Unable to meet the condition, Norris departed in November 1701 without achieving any treaty or bettering Britain's situation in India in any way.

After these abortive attempts the British adopted a different tack with unprecedented results. In 1714 the Surman Embassy, named after its leader John Surman, made its way from Calcutta with the intention of acquiring a Mughal document—a *firman*—establishing their right to tax thirty-eight villages in Bengal. That they wanted a *firman*, a binding document granted by the Emperor himself to a supplicatory power, indicated the British envoys' willingness to acquiesce to local norms and practice. Rather than forcing their own codes, the harbingers of modernity intended to insert themselves into the Empire's legality. The British were also well aware of various grades of imperial documents and would not be satisfied with anything but a *firman*. In contrast to earlier missions, the Embassy was composed of commoners already stationed in India as opposed to nobles sent out from England.[63] There was talk of including Manucci, thereby rebutting the notion that the British, in contrast to the Indo-Mughals, understood sovereignty as a strict and impermeable concept. However, Manucci was left out because he was thought too old.[64]

Although the Embassy was practically flexible and adaptable, it was burdened by prejudice. This early instance of 'othering' revealed itself in the belief that the Indo-Mughals were disorganized and debased, the practical expression of this being corruption. Despite being proved wrong practically, the Embassy was unable to discard its beliefs. They proved so debilitating that they risked Britain's position in India. This was of great concern because between Roe's and Norris's missions the 'English (had) extended their settlements along both coasts of India' through a series of local agreements with Governors acting on behalf of the Emperor. Besides, in 1683 the East India Company (EIC) had been converted from a 'private adventurer' to 'an incorporated society invested with certain sovereign powers by the Sovereign of Great Britain',[65] and hence needed to safeguard its sovereignty. To this purpose, the English had been fortifying their bases in India. 'But fortified settlements cost money to keep up and must be supported by revenues. Consequently, they must needs approach the Mughal, for the land in India was his alone, and it was his to make grants of territory great or small.'[66] In short, the British simultaneously resorted to diplomacy in order to trade, and to pay for military facilities to protect that trade. It was the beginning of a type of diplomacy that, though practically tessellating, was expressive of a completely alien rationality.

That the Embassy took over three years to achieve its goal is surprising only if read in terms of its willingness to accede to the established order based on shared practical concepts. What prevented the tessellation from progressing, however, was the British rationale, geared as it was to 'othering' Indo-Mughals. Modernity's rationale propelled the British into practices that were detrimental to achieving their aims. However, that they so easily changed is testimony to their practical adaptability, undermined as it was by their rationality. It made them regard Indo-Mughals as the 'other' and it expressed itself as prejudice. Some Armenians seized upon this. They claimed to know the processes of the Court and how to negotiate. It was a ruse. The Armenians and their Indo-Mughal compatriots at the Court were most likely motivated by the desire to obtain the gifts the British had brought, under the mistaken prejudice that the Emperor's imprimatur could be bought. The Embassy's tendency to manufacture and then deride the 'other'—because of its metaphysics—led to their falling under the Armenians' spell and the disbursal of cash and gifts to bribe officials. In thinking this would help, they were comprehensively deceived. Bribes undoubtedly were accepted, but they played no role in Surman getting his *firman*. It was only after he removed himself from the influence of the Armenian Cojah Seerhaud and his contacts, stopped trying to bribe his way into Court and began following established codes and procedures (which he already knew) that Surman found success. It came to the British because they were able to not only adapt but also, for a moment, set aside their prejudices. Underlying all of this is the obvious will to assimilate into the prevailing order rather than usurp it. The final agreement met nearly all requirements and it was granted under the Indo-Mughal legal code.

The willingness to be assimilated becomes momentous because the Embassy travelled under the Union Jack—fully accredited negotiators on behalf of another sovereign. Seerhaud demanded parity with his companions and was also given a flag, thereby once again denying differences in the notion of sovereignty between the Indo-Mughals and the British.[67] As agents of the Crown the diplomats were keen to maintain their status and took great care in the appearance of their party. In this they matched the Court's concern with dress and formality.[68] 'Considering Everybody Ought to make a handsome appearance' the party procured the finest clothes available and even provided themselves with palanquins plated with silver.[69] The convoy for the four envoys was a hundred and sixty bullock wagons strong, each creaking under a load of more than half a ton.[70] Much of the luggage was gifts, but a large part was private merchandise. An even larger retinue of servants followed the embassy including a trumpeter, a clockmaker, ten carpenters, thirty spadesmen and twelve hundred porters, along with wagoners and drivers.[71] The size of the party was a sign of how major an undertaking this was, of the importance accorded to the mission and the Emperor.

The willingness to accede to the Indo-Mughals was not limited to the abstract level of treaty. It was practical too, in how the negotiations were to be conducted and who in practice was to set the tenor for negotiations. Early in the Embassy, Seerhaud made it clear that 'unless he had the Entire management of the *Durbar* he would not proceed' and so began to manoeuvre the British towards his Indo-Mughal allies. As interpreter, Seerhaud's role was critical to the party and his demands had to be considered. He wanted to control the Embassy's access to court and to further this aim produced a letter from an Armenian padre called Daniel, who claimed familiarity with Delhi and offered to help. Daniel recommended two Mughals at court, Caundora (Khan Dauran) and Salabat Khan. They became the principle guides to the British. That they were willing to be guided, and not just by Armenians but also by Indo-Mughals, is yet more evidence of the intense desire of the British to insert themselves into the prevailing system. Upon entering Delhi in July 1715 they were advised by another padre and, concerned with 'Aggrandizing our first appearance', scattered money as they entered the city, thinking this would enhance their status. Surman notes that Salabat Khan received them. He took them to Khan Dauran 'who received us very Civilly assuring us of his protection and good Services.' Surman was optimistic: 'The great favour Khan Dauran is in with the King gives us hopes of Success in this undertaking, He assures us of his protection and says the King has promised us great favours.'

Things appeared to be proceeding well, but prejudice was to undermine their efforts from almost the start of the mission. The next day Surman records he met 'his Majesty', refers to Khan Dauran as their 'Patron', and most intriguingly reported: 'We are Assured by our friends that the Vizier is only titular, the Executive power lying Chiefly in the other; So that,' he explained to his superiors at Fort William in Calcutta, 'what we are now about to doe, is Entirely our Interest. For which reason Agreed that we first visit Khan Dauran; next, the Vizier; and Last of all Tuccurrub Caun.'[72] What had transpired is that Seerhaud, Khan Dauran and Salabat Khan had won Surman's confidence by ensuring that the Embassy was received in Delhi and promising access to the Court. In doing so, the British both placed themselves in the hands of Armenians and Indo-Mughals but also, and deliberately, ignored the established rituals and protocols of the *mansabdari* system. This is why Surman explained with such care to Calcutta that he was not going to make contact with the Vizier. They were to pay dearly in wealth and time for letting their prejudiced view, that only by deviant ways could one petition the Court, get the better of them. Yet this did not contradict their avowed aim to slip into Indo-Mughals ways; it only showed that they fundamentally misunderstood those ways.

The British quickly got down to preparing their petition, and as they were so close to the court, Indo-Mughals supplanted the Armenians as guides. As Surman records, Khan Dauran was 'the main instrument of our affairs.' In addition, Surman wrote that 'the methods we are at present taking, is consistant and the advice & Councill of Zeyau-d-din Khan' who was introduced to the party by Khan Dauran. Nearly a year later their influence was still strong and Surman recorded: 'As for our business we were resolved nott to goe to the Vizier … as Khan Dauran him-self directed.' Under the advice of these two, the embassy compounded its earlier error, but in doing so continued to demonstrate its ability to practically adapt to what was thought to be Indo-Mughal customs. Hence, instead of proceeding to meet the Vizier—who was the most powerful authority after the Emperor—the British paid visits to several minor officials. In doing so, they deliberately insulted the Vizier by, for instance, visiting his younger brother's deputy. The consequence of these flagrant violations was that British requests were not brought to the Emperor's notice. The Embassy's correspondence suggests that the Emperor was distracted with other matters at the time, and in a desper-ate attempt to ensure that the Embassy was not forgotten they resolved that 'our best policy is to be always near the King … that we might Even then negotiating our business.'[73]

Intent on assimilation, Surman was quite capable of this when it came to practical matters. In August 1715—within a month of entering Delhi—the party prepared their petition for the Emperor in Persian, not English. Nowhere in the diary is it indicated that local usage was per-ceived as degrading. Surman was unencumbered by such petty concerns. The petition was shown to an official who condensed the document and made other modifications without changing its gist. On Khan Dauran's instructions the petition, along with a sizeable 'gift', was prepared for the Emperor in November. A letter confirms that the main conduit for con-sultations between the British and Khan Dauran was Seerhaud—who had initially introduced the two parties. Mughal protocol demanded that the petition be handed to the Vizier and that he would forward it to the Emperor. The British therefore broke with established—and known—protocol and instead chose to give the petition to Khan Dauran, who was a deputy *bakshi* or treasury officer. Khan Dauran did get around to sub-mitting the document, but it was returned with a note that treasury offi-cials examine it. The British attempt to short-circuit Indo-Mughal custom had failed, but this did not stop them from trying again. Yet, for the first time Surman's diary indicates a hint of displeasure with how things were proceeding. He complained, 'for altho' our affairs are fallen into the Patronage of one of the most able men in this Court to dispatch them if He pleases, yet his dilatory method of proceeding is such as must make us pursue our designs with patience ….' Tellingly, Surman was also informed that Khan Dauran required further gifts.[74]

Despite their practical flexibility the treasury had responded to the British petition in a most peculiar way. The key British demands were ignored—that is, the *firman* regarding Bengal. The first article of the British petition requested that a *firman* that would allow the 'English Company pay no Custom, in Indostan, Suratt Excepted.' There was no reply to this. On other points the treasury stated that either it had no knowledge of the various matters or it could not comment on particular demands because it fell outside the treasury's jurisdiction. So in response to the second article, which stated:

In Culcutta ye Company have a Settlement D: Culcutta, Govindpore, and Sootaluty (dihi Kalikata, Govindpur and Sutanuti); which 3 towns being near ye Factory, His deceased Highness Azzimuth Sha gave to be rented by ye Company. The rent of these 3 towns abovementioned, according to ye Kings books, amounts to 1194.14, and Something more; which is yearly paid into ye Treasury. We humbly petition, that ye renting off Severall other towns, that are near ye above towns; and whose rent amounts to near or about 800 rupees may be granted to ye Company, That the Rent shall be yearly, and duely paid into the Kings treasury by us; and that particular care shall be taken, to make them flourish.[75]

The reply from the treasury was:

… The particulars off these towns are nott in ye books, neither were they given from the King. They have a Perwanna under Izzut Cauns Seal for them pursuant to Azzimuth Sha's Nishaun: By which it appears 3 Towns Culcutta etc. In ye purgunna of Ammerdabad, and Subaship of Bengall have been bought from Munoredutt & other Jemidars and a Bill off Sale obtained, when ye Daun off Bengall gave them possession. As for ye Other Towns we have nott their names by which to render An Account. The Duan may be wrote to, That An Account be sent to Court.[76]

Faced with what can only be termed as bureaucratic resistance, and was certainly understood as such by the British—Surman, in keeping with his prejudice, comments that officials expected further gifts—they had no choice but to proceed with submitting their petition to the Emperor. This was returned swiftly. After all, in matters diplomatic, the Emperor took the bureaucracy's advice, though not bound by it, and it had already, to all intents and purposes, rejected the EIC document.[77]

This strange episode is in need of critical exegesis, because it is the identifying characteristic of the Embassy and occurred despite the British ability to change and adapt in matters conceptual (treaty), practical (Seerhaud and his Indo-Mughal allies) and linguistic (Persian). The only explanation therefore is that they remained entrapped by their prejudices, which were in fact shaping their adaptations. In other words, although the British were adaptable, it was nearly always misdirected owing to their metaphysics of 'othering'. In terms of the structure-of-structures, the British were incapable of exceeding their time by operating in time and space, that is, of learning from the space they were in that there were other times in operation. So when, within days of the rejection, a second petition was drawn up and sent to Khan Dauran for presentation, it was accompanied by a series of bribes. Unsurprisingly, they had no effect. The primary demand for a *firman*, Surman informed his superiors, 'By a mistake of the mutsuddys was omitted.' It could have been bureaucratic incompetence, the diary does not dwell upon it, but this was the most important British demand and hence specifically required the Emperor's sanction. But Surman was dealing with low ranking officials who had not the authority to grant what was desired. It is therefore likely that the omission was deliberate, a means for court minions to deal with requests above their pay-grade while ensuring they kept on receiving presents.[78]

Faced with a blockade, engineered by its own rationality, the Embassy began to fester. The negotiators could not understand why they had not made any progress since they thought powerful and influential courtiers, even in a corrupt court, were advising them. Yet the British continued following practices—not keeping to the Court's hierarchy, and paying bribes—that they knew to be incorrect, despite the lack of result from this course of action. Ultimately, Surman wrote with alacrity that when their chief adviser, Khan Dauran, was 'put in mind of our Petition, He was very surprizingly asked what Petition? have not I done all your business ....' Surman continued, 'This strange forgetfulness made us in very pathetick terms inquire … what we might expect after so many promises of having our business effected to our satisfaction when we had so long and patiently waited and been at so great an expense to be thus answered was very surprizing, and What we did not nor could not expect in the least.'[79] Surman undoubtedly was in a poor state, he had put himself in the hands of Indo-Mughals, and sought to become a part of the pre-existing structure, but nothing had been achieved.

The debilitating limits Surman's rationality imposed upon his actions served to undermine the man's natural tendency for flexibility and to learn and adapt. In this, Surman cannot be faulted because it was not a matter of changing his opinions about Indo-Mughals. That he was capable of. But for him to accept them as similar to himself in terms of ethics required ejecting his proto-modernistic view of the world altogether, and that was something he was incapable of. He wrote:

daily experience might convince us of the strange carriage and forgetfulness of that great man' and he received this 'further light, Viz.t that Khan Dauran had been advised by his own Mustsuddies, that it was not his business to perswade the King to sign our Petition contrary to what He had formerly desired, but that it was better to get signed upon it Cootbulmooluck whose business it was, as Vizier to advise the King what things were proper to be granted us, We find this was chiefly levelled against our Petition for Divy island and the ground round Calcutta now desired. We were in hopes that in case We could have got those Petitions granted us by the means of Khan dauran tht afterwards the Vizier would not gain say or at least by a little bribery it might have passed, there has been severall endeavours made to get an opportunity to speak with Khan Dauran so as to convince him but none has been procureable, We fear the Petition in this interim may be gone in and will come out signed as beforementioned.[80]

His prediction was correct. In March the Emperor returned the British petition for the second time. This time there were precise instructions that it must be submitted to the Vizier. The advice was sound but the English would not take it and clung to their original preconception: the court was debauched and bribery was the ticket to a *firman*. Their refusal to change cannot be attributed to some inherent inflexibility—the Embassy has already demonstrated its ability to adapt and learn repeatedly. But that very flexibility was misdirected; the inability of the British to cast off their prejudice accounts for their lack of progress.

In short, the British thought they were inserting themselves into the Indo-Mughal world, but they misunderstood that world. Unsurprisingly, given their preconceptions, the Embassy's next move was to fall back on their prejudice once again. And so, the British mounted a major campaign to buy a variety of court officials. In this, the British were quite holistic. They even tried to bribe minor officials including clerks because Surman thought he had to spread his largesse further afield and even to the 'Duanny Writers, who att that time wrote what they pleased on Each Phird: According to which naturally flowed the Kings Assent or deny-all.'[81] What he had taken upon himself was a comprehensive campaign of bribery, which was very different from the Empire's practice of sending a few choice gifts with its ambassadors for another king.

Operating flexibly, but incapable of transgressing their metaphysics, the British did exactly the opposite of what the Emperor himself had instructed them to do—deal only with the Vizier, whose prerogative it was to deal with foreign embassies. In choosing to ignore the advice, the British continued in their rut and became distracted, squabbled amongst themselves and attracted even more hangers-on keen to take advantage of the Embassy's largesse. When the British next submitted their petition they again offered massive bribes. To the *diwan-i-khailisah* they offered seven thousand rupees; to the head clerk, Bhog Chand, ten thousand rupees; and to their subordinates twelve hundred.[82] Knowing the British were keen to buy people, those who were accepting bribes responded by feeding the Embassy with favourable reports about the progress of their petition in the hope of extracting further payoffs. Not till 22 July 1716 did the British discover that they had been deceived throughout their negotiations and that the treasury was no more favourably disposed towards them than before. The Embassy's requests for a *firman* had failed. Instead, what the minor officials did was agree to the British petition but under the authority of a *Husbul Hoocum*, and that was very different from a *firman*. Surman knew that the latter was issued by the Emperor and legitimate throughout the Empire. It was essential for the British to have such a document, because they needed to show it to the various governors they dealt with in the far corners of the Empire. A *Husbul Hoocum* would not convince independent minded governors.[83]

As far as the servants of the Court were concerned, they of course were unable—by their own highly ordered practice—to grant a *firman* unless the petitioner personally approached the Vizier, who upon consenting to receive the petitioner considered his proposal and then ordered the bureaucracy to process the demand with whatever modifications the Empire saw fit. Simultaneously, the junior Indo-Mughals the British were dealing with had no intention of giving up the handsome presents being distributed. In effect, the British were granted not a treaty as they wanted but simply an order, and both parties knew that it was an entirely different type of document from what was sought, because it lacked the status of a treaty. At wit's end, Surman threatened to leave Delhi, and at another point he thought of going to the Vizier.[84]

The diary exudes a palpable sense of disgust at the lack of progress, but the situation was about to change. Another context had unforeseen implications for the negotiations. Events in Western India came to the Embassy's assistance. The Governor of Surat, Haidar Quli Khan, wrote to the Emperor that the English were seriously discontented and that if they were not speedily satisfied they would withdraw; Surat would there-fore suffer a loss in trade. The Emperor and Khan Dauran both read the letters, for the Empire was perpetually concerned with the seas and the Western port in particular, because it was religiously significant; Surat was where Muslims departed for the Haj. For four days nothing hap-pened. Then, suddenly, the Embassy was granted access to Khan Dauran who had taken to ignoring their requests for an audience. Presumably, the matter having come to the Emperor's notice, the Vizier took a per-sonal interest and advised the Khan to stop toying with the British. The Embassy also records on 9 September—just days after the letters from Surat had arrived—'Visited the Grand Vizier'.[85] Perhaps Surman was embarrassed at making much more of the visit in his diary, given that he had taken great pains in earlier letters to explain why he had not approached the Vizier. Yet more delays led to further ructions within the British party, and on 9 November Seerhaud—who originally suggested the course of action followed diligently by the Embassy for some 17 months—'confessed, that the Seaw [required for the *firmans*] cannot be given, without our petitions First going to the Vizier, and receiving his perusal and Approbation.' Having been told that the most rewarding course for action was to keep to standard operating practices of the Court, the British rapidly changed tack. Yet the magnitude of the change would never be evident in the nonchalant way in which it is recorded: 'The Phirds (*firmans*) were all carried to the Grand Vizier from the Duanny, who according to his kind disposition, After perusing them, Ordered the Duan Colsa to carry them immediately to the King and get them Signed, which was done accordingly.'[86]

Having already logged, as if only in passing, that he had so dramatically changed tack, Surman keeps to that casual style in recording the success of their mission. It too is written as if it were an afterthought. All Surman wrote was: 'For the Vizier as is usuall making a mark to petition, so his Majesty Signed his Assent to all that those papers contained.'[87] Presumably more could be expected of their success in the diary given Surman's emo-tionalism at other critical moments. The silence is deafening and what it indicates is that Surman quite evidently was in an inexplicable quandary, for the court had in practice disproved his prejudice. In the meanwhile, the Vizier's role was not yet complete. Surman reported that:

before they could proceed any farther there was a necessity to receive the Vizier's approval, accordingly it was carried there yesterday, and was received very candidly but pursuant to custom must again go to the King, but that there might be no loss of time the Vizier kindly ordered the Duan Colsa to carry them himself thither and get them signed, which was accordingly done, so I hope now they are pretty well passed, next Follows the Vizier's Signing and then we shall get the orders for drawing up the Phirmaund which as soon as received we shall Dispatch ....[88]

The momentary modification of the prejudice that had long held them back, harnessed with their natural willingness to become participants in an Indo-Mughal world, led to the British finally doing the right thing, and it obtained the desired result. That their case was processed rapidly suggests that there was nothing in the British petition that was in itself inimical to the Emperor. He, however, had paid no attention to them because they were going about the matter in completely the wrong way. The Court was not being lobbied in the correct manner for the British were not keeping to the right protocols. Upon succeeding by keeping to them, Surman's response hints at the analytical chaos he had been thrown into. It would soon pass.

As for what enabled Surman to succeed, it was not his personal abilities. They were incapable of surmounting his rationality, for it was only capable of being reflexive within itself, never able to look into other contexts. This is why he became so disgusted with his lack of progress. The only way he could conceive of the 'other' was in negative terms, and so the failure was due to his having to deal with debased people. What finally ensured success was the case of Surat. It directly affected the Emperor and he had to take matters into his own hands and advise the British to follow established forms. Having followed it, the Emperor was in a position to respond, and he responded positively. So quick was the resolution that Surman was caught off-guard:

We might have Expected the Vizier in whose power itt was, would have stop'd our business on this occasion or caused many delays the Sure way to squeeze a Sum of money, which must have been very larger. Butt he has behaved himself with far more generosity, Our papers no sooner reaching his hands, than they received dispatch; which encourages us to believe he will not be hereafter troublesome.[89]

The overwhelming power the proto-modernist rationality had over British thought and action is revealed by this entry: the expectation of uncivilized behaviour. It indicated that Surman's moment of analytical chaos had passed and his rationality had reasserted itself. The entry reinforces the limitations of modern reflexivity which, being limited to their own timeline, was incapable of assessing contextually. This was true right to the end of the mission. The Emperor, having benefited from the British doctor's attendance, was loath to see him go. The Embassy, despite its accumulated experiences over years, once again turned to Khan Dauran and he once again proved ineffectual. Finally, it was the Vizier who enabled the doctor and his party to leave.[90] That the British turned to Khan Dauran rather than the Vizier is inexplicable, for it contradicted experience—the British had achieved nothing through Khan Dauran and his advice to bribe their way through. The Vizier secured them their goals—in the context of the letter from Surat—but even so they shied away from him. In short, the British, though displaying remarkable adaptability in the realm of the practical, were unable to cast aside the fundamental prejudice that shaped their practice. The Indo-Mughals remained corrupt in Anglo-Saxon minds. This was 'othering' at work, because the belief was held despite the evidence contradicting it. The British had not begun practicing a diplomacy that sought to assimilate. However, a key feature of such a diplomatic practice was already evident: alienating binarily.

Conclusions

The Indo-Mughals followed an altogether different trajectory to the British, and the potential to become modern was never realized. This is because though Islam is like Christianity, the former was ameliorated by its own silences which permitted the absorption of the rationality whose kernel is *dharma*. The influence of the *dharma*-complex converted the Mughals into Indo-Mughals. The impulse to use diplomacy to assimilate was removed. Rather, diplomacy became a tool to avoid war and improve the present. This setting is what the British found and they were able to tessellate into this pre-existing structure. That was also their aim, but it was undermined by the tessellation being motivated by a rationality that totally misunderstood the Indo-Mughals regardless of what they did.

What is curious is not how wrong modern analysis is, but that moderns distort what they claim to be unchangeable: 'history'. These distortions become apparent because contrary to claims, the rationality of Indo-Mughal society was neither erased nor replaced by modernity. Indeed, it sought to efface itself! The facts therefore render the modernist story about its spread a fabrication intended, given modernity's dynamic, to sequester the Indian past. In reality all Surman's Embassy was able to do was practically adopt the practices of the Indo-Mughals, in part because they were so similar, but not its rationale. The Embassy was unable to transcend itself and move beyond the anarchical-binarism at the core of Christian inspired modernity and practice a reflexivity of both time and space. Their prejudices therefore remained despite Surman's actual lived experience during the mission. Nevertheless, Surman's success meant that a proto-modern rationality with a far greater potential to realize itself was now established in the sub-continent, and it is to the way it shaped the evolution of Indo-Mughal diplomacy that we turn next.

5

DEATH OF DIPLOMACY

The soldier completed and more than completed what the ambassador began.

— C.R. Wilson[1]

Having established a foothold in the sub-continent by tessellating into the practices of the Indo-Mughal Empire, the British East India Company (EIC) overthrew the Empire and replaced it with the British Raj. Its formation, for modernizers, is a paradigmatic reorganization of the subcontinent, for it resulted in modernity. Undisclosed in these renditions is that this was a phenomenal task practically. A landmass greater than today's India, highly fertile and supporting a population three times as dense as Europe's at the time, is supposed to have been converted in terms of rationality—something defined as stable in the *longue durée*.[2] Central to this process was diplomacy, and it itself was changed.

Tracking change is facilitated by Surman's vectors: an unchanging prejudice alongside practical adaptability. The first overrides experience and its power to do so stems from anarchical-binarism's valorization of time. It means that the 'other' must be converted to realize utopia. Hence the European interregnum saw what is inevitable to all modern diplomacy: the extermination of the 'other'. The Indo-Mughals' diplomacy of reciprocity and communication was erased by the new rationality of anarchical-binarism, which reached its zenith with the invention of 'race' understood as coterminous with nation.[3] 'Othering' was no longer civi-

165

lizational, it became biological. Diplomacy became an exclusively British affair, conducted solely by the Raj and for itself and in opposition to a segment of humanity. As for modernist reflexivity, limited to its own time, it was completely unable to transcend itself despite prolonged exposure to the subcontinent's *dharma*-complex. Yet, the rationality of anarchical-binarism was operationalized through the existing circuits of the Empire. This required Indo-Mughals' cooperation; this, in an early example of the 'fourth possibility', was made possible by the EIC amply displaying Surman's other quality: practical adaptability.

In brief, pre-existing diplomatic practices were harnessed by modernity but they were put to an altogether new purpose, generating violence on an unprecedented scale. As Athar Ali writes: 'the survivals of the Mughal Empire were subverted to a new use, and not employed to resurrect anything resembling the old Empire. That empire had its own inequities, but these, to be fair to it, were of a different form and content altogether.'[4]

Diplomacy-as-battle

Analysis on British aims in the subcontinent has so far identified two guiding principles: wealth extraction, and a domineering insecurity about the ability to do so. These were organized by the vectors Surman exposed. The search for wealth is what brought the colonizers to India, which in turn produced insecurity about the ability to realize their goal. Feeding into each other, these two aims propelled the EIC into redefining diplomacy as it existed in the Empire intellectually. The purpose of diplomacy was changed from communication and negotiation to secure the present, to assimilation to realize the future.[5] Under the EIC, diplomacy became a militarized tool as it came with the constant threat of war, only to be expected from a rationality defined by violence. All of this aggregated to diplomacy-as-battle. Underpinning the change was a shift in rationality from a unified cosmos to anarchical-binarism, which made for 'othering' or the positing of vast swathes of humanity beyond humanity. This permitted the unrestricted extraction of wealth from the Empire by the EIC, and opened the 'other' to more dramatic violence which the EIC could not imagine being inflicted on oneself. Combined, this was the full ventilation of diplomacy motivated by anarchical-binarism and it could only be realised outside Europe.

This is because Europe's notions of alienation, though highly developed, were regularized by treaty within Europe. In the encounter with non-moderns, however, modernity was free to practice its logic to its logical conclusion: denigration in order to assimilate. The first step was to finance the various missions to disperse and establish modernity. 'Othering' permitted this by sanctioning wealth extraction on an unprecedented scale. This is quite clear from the texts the Raj has left behind. Phrases such as the 'drain of wealth' and 'Annual Plunder' were mentioned as early as 1783 in *The Ninth Report of the Select Committee*.[6] In his study of the *Report*, Romesh Dutt explains the nature and size of this drain of wealth.[7] Britain formalized its demands early on. From Bengal the 'articles of tribute' were 'investment', which was the 'clear acknowledged Tribute from Bengal to England', 'direct Tribute' from the other British bases in India, private transfers, and finally, the transfer of income from trade to England.[8] Harry Verelst, Clive's successor as Governor, in assessing the impact of these extractions wrote: 'Whatever sums had formerly been remitted to Delhi were amply reimbursed by the returns made to the immense commerce of Bengal ... How widely different from these are the present circumstances of the Nabob's dominions! ... Each of the European Companies, by means of money taken up in the country, have greatly enlarged their annual Investments, without adding a rupee to the riches of the Province.'[9]

Irfan Habib, using conservative calculations, suggests that 'the tribute amounted to nine per cent of GNP [Gross National Product]—a crippling drain for any economy.'[10] Javier Esteban, in a study of net transfers between India and Britain between 1772 and 1820, concludes that 'seemingly negligible magnitudes in terms of national income can reveal their significance when placed in a meaningful context.'[11]

In extracting tribute the British were quite different from the Empire, but not in the way the British perceived it. Undoubtedly the British insisted they were different; they had to, for the teleology of modernity self-defines itself as uniquely capable of taking everyone to somewhere better;[12] anarchical-binarism could have it no other way, for implicated in the project is the very identity—the nobility—of modernity. The modern had to be ontologically different from those in the 'other' category. In practical terms Dina Khoury and Dane Kennedy argue: 'This conviction has its origins in European efforts in the nineteenth century and before to contrast themselves with "Oriental despotisms," presenting their

own states and societies as progressive, liberal, and modern while por-
traying their counterparts to the east as static, oppressive, and archaic.'[13]

Being better meant the colonized was worse, and this justified modernity, in particular the drain of wealth. This was a more substantial difference, because what the British missed is that progress paradoxically
entailed new and far more rapacious means of wealth extraction. In practice this was the enhancing of trauma, because unlike earlier empires,
modernity drained away wealth, to itself, to finance its universalization.
As Khoury and Kennedy write:[14]

> The Raj coerced its subjects and squeezed wealth from them. India garrisoned
> one of the largest armies in the world in the nineteenth century, a massive force
> that differed markedly from the increasingly nationalized armies of Europe. Like
> other agrarian empires the Raj relied mainly on land revenues. On various occa-
> sions its demands pushed peasants to the brink of disaster, and beyond.[15] The
> government also assessed "home charges" on India, an annual transfer of mil-
> lions of pounds to the British treasury.[16]

Even if modernity was not any more rapacious than the Empire, but
only changed the manner in which revenue was raised,[17] what is overlooked is that the purposes revenue was put to remained static. In the
colonized world, the white homelands benefited from some degree of
wealth extraction from the colonies, and the white colonies benefited
from a degree of reinvestment of colonial taxation, but very little of this
occurred in colonial India. There, a series of wars absorbed revenue leaving little for reinvestment. As Douglas Peers summarizes: 'Unlike white
settler colonies, where economic development was not hindered by having to bear much by way of military costs, colonies of conquest—especially India—found much of their wealth siphoned off to supporting
military forces, and hence the reality in British India, at least in light
of expenditure patterns, was not much different from previous regimes.'[18]
As the techniques employed by the Raj to raise taxes improved, a greater
proportion of revenue was channelled to diplomacy-as-battle. By the
1800s, military charges had shot up as an overall percentage of charges.
In 1834–35 military charges were 59% of net charges, and by 1851 military charges were some 60% of net charges. During this period, military charges grew by 44%, but revenue by just 35%.[19] Henry Lawrence
calculated that by the mid-1800s the 'expense of the army, including
the deadweight, is eleven millions a year, or nearly one-half the revenue of India.'[20]

The income from the Raj had to be protected not only because it furthered modernity but also because that rationality instinctively feared the 'other', a fear that continues today as anxiety about being overrun by the East.[21] At the time, fear of a return to a non-modern state or regressing from the utopia modernity promised coagulated to become an 'empire of opinion'.[22] Peers traces it to the 19th century British historian John Malcolm. He wrote: 'The only safe view that Britain can take of her empire in India is to consider it, as it really is, always in a state of danger.'[23] Viewing itself as the unique fruit of civilization and encountering many depraved 'others' in need of civilizing, the civilization of modernity naturally sees itself as threatened until its eventual victory. That Malcolm was indicative of British opinion is shown by the high regard he was held in. 'No man,' wrote the *United Services Journal* in 1845, 'better understood the habits and feelings of our subjects in that part of the world than Sir John Malcolm.'[24]

The insecurity Malcolm put his finger on engulfed officials. Governed by anarchical-binarism, they resorted to a permanent reliance on the army to manage their fears. They had to, for the only possibility within their metaphysics was to be assimilated or assimilate. That was why Thomas Munro, in the year he became Governor of Madras, remarked that 'in this country we always are, and always ought to be prepared for war'.[25] He was echoed by Charles Metcalf, later to become Governor-general, who wrote: 'the main object of all the Acts of our Government [is] to have the most efficient army that we can possibly maintain.'[26] A contemporary of Malcolm wrestled with defining this 'empire of opinion' and concluded that 'it is difficult to attach definite meaning, unless it be the opinion of our ability to crush all attempts at insurrection.'[27] A very similar definition was reached by the soldier-diplomat David Ochterlony, who argued that he understood 'empire of opinion' to mean 'above all the Military strength of the Rulers, remains unexhausted and invincible.'[28] As the British embarked upon a 'general offensive against Oriental governments', to bring about modernity they naturally and simultaneously spread the very violence that modernity is supposed to contain by militarizing society.[29]

The result of anarchical-binarism, then, was the extraction of wealth from the 'other' combined with a fear of the 'other'. Managing these twin concerns led to the rise of the 'garrison state' which Peers defines as militarization of the decision making process, prioritizing the military in resource allocation and emphasizing 'the threat or application (usually in a very public way) of military force as a means of securing political and strategic objectives.'[30] All of this is inherent in anarchical-binarism—since modernity is about displacing all rival rationalities—but the Raj's susceptibility to it was exacerbated by the cohesiveness and insularity of the British community in India and its domination by the military. An estimate of the European population of India in 1830 lists 36,409 officers and soldiers, 3,550 civilian employees of the EIC, and 2,149 Europeans not formally attached to either the EIC or the military.[31] Furthermore, the only public opinion that counted in the Raj was that of the tiny expatriate community, and it was resolutely opposed to retrenchments.[32] 'The persistence of a militarized state in India was assured for as long as there was a consensus that British rule could never depend for its survival upon the willing cooperation or passive acquiescence of the Indian people,' writes Peers.[33] Indeed, there was no scope for cooperation with the Empire because modernity, trapped by its own timeline, cannot empathize with its 'other'. Hence, while there might not have been an officially sanctioned ideology of expansion, for much of the period up to 1858, institutionally, culturally, and—most significantly—ideologically there was a predilection for violence. It produced conquest, which was of course inevitable as the aim was assimilation. Modernity required it. As one contemporary commentator reflected: 'During these sixty years India has had Governors-generals of all qualifications and temperaments, yet very few of them have avoided war.'[34]

This emphasis on violence arising from anarchical-binarism led to the deletion of the Empire's rationale for diplomacy by making it synonymous with war. This is because the 'British were never in a position to subdue completely all potential threats, alliances were crucial and the army played a major role.'[35] Sanctioned by the Empire's *firman* obtained by the Surman Embassy, British rule in Bengal rapidly fell in line with its rationality and became 'an absolute government, founded not on consent but on conquest,' noted the 19th century jurist James Fitzjames Stephen.[36] In short, diplomacy was militarized, for the aim was to conquer the 'other'. The means was to seize provincial rulers' 'sovereignty'. This was the target because, as Michael Fisher notes, by the mid-18th century virtually all of the regional courts of India governed their states independently *de facto* from the Emperor. Nevertheless, they remained nominally subordinate to his sovereignty. The rituals of these regional

courts acknowledged the Emperor's sovereignty even as the rulers themselves governed autonomously. This was why a regional ruler dispatched
a *wakil* rather than an *ilchi* or *safir*: a representative rather than a full
ambassador who could only be dispatched by the Emperor.[37] It was
through militarized diplomacy that first the provincial rulers', and then
the Emperor's sovereignty was captured. At play was a finite game: the
assimilation of geography to modernity.

The first project of assimilation was to subsume local rulers' 'sovereignty'. This category, known to both East and West, exposes modernity's hypocrisies and how they generate violence. As Fisher writes, the
EIC developed a 'peculiar role … with respect to both the British and
the Mughal sovereigns and to other Indian Rulers.'[38] To begin with, the
Surman Embassy sought to implant the British within the Empire's sovereignty, and in 1772 the practice of operating within the Empire's sovereignty was regularized with the EIC formally acknowledging the
Emperor's sovereignty. Yet, simultaneously, the EIC never renounced the
British crown's sovereignty. This was impossible for the EIC, being modern, viewed itself in terms of the 'other', which required the maintenance
of the self. Instead of investing themselves in India, adding themselves
to the warp and weft of Indo-Mughal society, they chose dual-sover-
eignty and hence deceived Indo-Mughals.[39]

None of this would have come to pass if the Raj had operated on the
basis of a cosmic rationality. Indeed, it would not even have raised the
question of adding oneself to the Empire, for the basic premise is that
everything is variation. The British would have viewed themselves as no
more than a variation of the Empire (and vice versa). This was of course
impossible, and so Robert Clive, the man who is viewed, along with
Warren Hastings, as instrumental in 'securing' India, charted a violent
course. Under Clive began the practice of what he called 'the masked
system', that is, administering in the interest of the EIC while maintaining the sham sovereignty of the Empire. This was patently something
that only anarchical-binarism made necessary, because provincial rulers
retained their own authority while maintaining the Emperor's sovereignty. Such a course of action was however impossible for moderns,
because it amounted to being assimilated, and by a reprehensible 'other'
too. If it came to pass, it would signal an intolerable turning away from
progress-through-history.

Modernity however does present the option of a cosmopolitan Raj. A
modern concept, it would enable the British to remain within the con-

fines of anarchical-binarism because all that the cosmopolitan does is tolerate, not dissolve what remains an intractable divide between self and other. Cosmopolitanism could have delimited violence against the 'other', but the entire basis of a cosmopolitan Raj would have been a total lack of empathy. In other words, intellectually a modern understanding would prevail, and given the heterogeneity of the Empire the Raj inherited, society would live on the brink of totalizing violence. The only solution would have been for the British to presume a unified cosmos; only it could have outlawed theoretically the violence of both deception and then assimilation. But this was of course beyond the conceptual horizons of the builders of the Raj. It was too serious about itself to even risk entertaining the notion of playing with itself.

And so cosmopolitanism, the least damaging expression of modernist thought, was never attempted. Operating in an international society devoid of European commonalities, the British became all the more willing to deceive Indo-Mughals, and wage diplomacy-as-battle. The violence towards the Empire began soon after Surman's contract. While individual breaches are not of concern, they become significant by their abundance. It was enough for a British sea captain to remark:

The injustice to the Moors consists in that, being by their courtesy permitted to live here as merchants we under pretence protected all the Nabob's servants that claimed our protection, though they were neither our servants nor our merchants, and gave our dustucks or passes to numbers of natives to trade custom free, to the great prejudice of the Nabob's revenue; nay, more, we levied large duties upon goods brought into our districts from the very people that permitted us to trade custom free, and by numbers of impositions … caused eternal clamour and complaints against us at Court.[40]

As the captain noted, the injustices went beyond the particular and assumed a more generalist tone. Injustice was institutionalized. Alongside came a completely new way of conducting diplomacy. The Empire used force but it was for diplomatic purposes, for instance through a show of force to enable negotiations. British diplomacy on the other hand was synonymous with violence. A British diplomat did not negotiate but laid down an inflexible demand that could not be met and would inevitably result in war. The first instance of diplomacy-as-battle came about with the EIC breaching the contract Surman had negotiated.

The EIC encroached on the territory of Siraj-ud-Daula who ruled an area approximating today's Bengal, Bangladesh and parts of Orissa or a territory approximately the size of France.[41] In doing so they challenged his sovereignty. What it also signalled was the beginning of the end of diplomacy as a means of negotiation and its conversion into a means of assimilation. The Nawab responded to British 'injustice' by capturing Fort William in 1756. It was, G.J. Bryant writes, 'a bargaining counter to bring the presumptuous East India Company to heel, not to eject them, whereas, the prompt British response … under Clive was to retake it by storm without prior negotiation.'[42]

In doing so the EIC 'adopted a basic psychological maxim about the conduct of war. This was always to force the pace and to seek battle with the "country" armies and never to reject it when offered by the other side.'[43]

So ended diplomacy as a means to negotiate a crowded world, of ensuring requirements between all parties could be met via empathy. Within a few months, Clive went on to force the famous showdown at Plassey. That victory resulted in the EIC replacing Siraj-ud-Daula with its own *nawab*, Mir Jafar. Though Plassey was no great battle militarily, its political consequences were momentous. Although it was unintended at the time, the victory made clear to all that the British were not wary of using diplomacy as war, and this practice eventually resulted in the seizure of the *diwani*—or the right to tax directly—in 1765.[44] With it, the richest and militarily most secure province in the Empire passed into the EIC's hands. The seizure of Bengal permitted the British to meet their aim of making the modernist project self-sustaining, for now Bengal's tax revenue could be used to bankroll the superimposition of modernity on the subcontinent.[45]

The geography under modernity was expanded by diplomacy-as-battle because it was by definition aggressive rather than conciliatory, for there is no room for negotiation with equals in modern diplomacy. For instance, Robert Orme, the first military historian of the Raj, wrote in the 1760s: 'Inactivity or retreat in war is never in Indostan imputed to prudence or stratagem, and the side which ceases to gain success is generally supposed to be on the brink of ruin.'[46] Modernity could not retreat, to do so would be to turn away from 'history'. Clive wrote in 1765: 'The Influence of the British Empire in India is founded in some degree on our effective Power but more perhaps on the Credit of former Successes and the Reputation of our Arms.'[47] The entwining of military power with diplomacy sealed the Empire's diplomacy of negotiation.

Furthermore, the nobility that modernity ascribes to itself means that not only does it have to expand, but it cannot remain satisfied with operating in a 'masked' manner. Modernity after all is the future, it is destiny. To cloak itself is therefore an abomination. Making itself known in its full glory demanded wresting sovereignty for itself to enable it to declare itself.[48] Practically, modernity had to pay for this need, and so, upon seizing the *diwani*, Clive wrote to inform the Directors that the EIC 'now became the Sovereigns of a rich and potent kingdom,' and not only the 'collectors but the proprietors of the nawab's revenues.'[49] Nicholas Dirks writes that in 'elevating the Company to the status of a state, Hastings was concerned to declare British sovereignty over all of the Company's possessions, and to assert "British sovereignty, though whatever channels it may pass into these provinces, should be all in all."'[50] In 1773 Hastings encouraged that the 'sovereignty of this country [be] wholly and absolutely vested in the Company,' and that he be the sole "instrument" of this sovereignty.'[51] Driven by an insatiable rationality, the British could not rest. The laws of 'history' demanded that the entire Empire be denied sovereignty because modernity had to announce itself not for what it was, an escalating cascade of violence, but for what it thought it was.

The actual practice of usurpation of sovereignty required diplomacy-as-battle throughout the subcontinent because 'the Company in the later eighteenth century presumed that not only the Emperor but also many of the Indian regional Rulers with whom it dealt held sovereignty.'[52] Each became the target for a diplomacy-as-battle where the British ambassador was at the sharp edge of a military machine.[53] British diplomacy was therefore not about a show of force followed by discussion of terms, but about the combined deployment of armed forces and diplomats. It only facilitated the inevitable battle of subjugating. The novelty of such practice elicited much comment. One Indo-Mughal chronicler, Seer Mutakhareen, is indicative. Despairing at the senseless violence of the Europeans, he bore witness to the fact that they only stopped warring to 'take breath … in order to come to blows again and to fight with as much fury as ever.'[54] The result was inevitable. Fisher puts it like this: As the EIC 'gained military ascendancy over successive regions in India, its views on the sovereignty of the Indian rulers changed. Treaties with the Indian rulers transferred from them to the Company various rights normally held by a sovereign. British practice often reduced some of these very 'sovereigns' to the de facto status of puppets or virtually confined them within their own palaces.'[55]

The British innovation, then, was to reorder diplomacy with their rationality, which demanded its internationalization at the expense of all. This meant that the Empire's subordination of force to diplomacy was met by the British who had done the exact opposite. Though such a transposal is expected within modernity, the virulence with which diplomacy-as-battle was deployed was new. This was because the alienation at the centre of European society had been checked by treaty amongst royals who were interlinked by kinship. These ameliorating factors did not bind the modern with Indo-Mughals, who could therefore be cast as the depraved 'other' in need of either elimination or reform.

Replacing the Empire with the Raj was only however a primer (for it was physical) to the metaphysical purging and replacing by modernity that is pursued so violently. The only way of achieving this was to metamorphose the very rationale for practice by reordering the rationale for governance. This meant making its foundation anarchical-binarism. To do so, the British harnessed the Empire's diplomatic circuits to serve the metaphysic of the Raj. What happened then was the introduction of a British diplomatic apparatus, the Residency system, which was quite similar to what existed practically in the Empire. This commensurability permitted the British to absorb, wholesale, local diplomatic practices and talent, but with an altogether different purpose: wars of assimilation. Despite its exposure, just as Surman could not exceed the boundaries of his rationality, nor could the state he laid the foundations for. The reason was that modernity's timebound reflexivity was unable to transcend its rationality. But victory, which was what was sought, as understood within modernity's finitudes was possible because of that other quality Surman displayed: adaptability. It too was replicated by those who inherited his mantle.

Battle practices

While the Raj was rationally unable to engage the rationality of the Empire, it was quite able and willing to appropriate the existing practice of diplomacy. Practical adaptability was the cornerstone of the Raj; it was how modernity took root in the subcontinent and was promoted by the easy tessellation of British diplomats into the Empire's established practices. That tessellation was possible because of commonalities, which undermines the idea that diplomacy was a European invention. The Raj's preparations to expand into the Empire's hinterland exposed other commonalities. Most significant was the Residency system, which was the means whereby the British injected their rationality into Indo-Mughal diplomacy. It was the Residency system that subverted the Empire's diplomatic practice and purpose by putting them to an altogether different purpose: diplomacy-as-battle. The process began with the very design of the Residency system which was intended to be slotted into, and was, the existing Indo-Mughal system of ceremony and precedence.[56] That the British were able to do so successfully was because they, like the Empire, had been managing a similar international society similar, which made for commonality. In Europe, writes Fisher:

the institution of permanent diplomatic missions only developed during the sixteenth century. Prior to that time, embassies had been exchanged between major European states but the cost and the regular 'disputes about precedence and ceremonial … led to the appointment of agents or residents, who were not entitled to the same ceremonial honours as ambassadors.'[57] The title 'Resident' continued in Europe till the end of the 18th century. Thus, when agents of the Company were sent to reside at the courts of India's major princes in the 1760s, the title of Resident fit their understanding of their own role.[58]

This system was not incomprehensible to the Indo-Mughals. In fact, it fit into their practices which

likewise had diplomatic conventions and regulations to which the Company had to conform. Ambassadors were regularly sent from one sovereign to another.[59] At a lower lever, agents, wakīls were exchanged among high Mughal officials and were sent to represent a high official at the Imperial court in his absence. Since the Company accepted Mughal sovereignty in 1772, the designation of its representatives as Residents, translated as wakīls in the Persian, instead of Ambassadors, fit into Mughal practice as well.[60]

The Residents were therefore, to begin with, diplomats as classically understood by both the British and the Empire. Studies of Mughal diplomatic practices note the similaritiess between the Residency system as it developed in Europe and what developed in medieval India. Neither, for instance, had a system of permanent diplomatic missions as modern states do,[61] and all these features, the product of operating in similar international societies, made for Europe's easy comprehension of the practices they found in the subcontinent. Both societies were also managing violence, but in very different ways. The Empire's rationality tempered violence by making its diplomats negotiate to maintain both parties, whereas European diplomacy's assimilative tendencies forged by anarchical-binarism were checked by the Treaty of Westphalia.

The Residency system began as the diplomatic arm of 'a regional state, powerful but treated on the basis of equality by other regional powers.' Early on, many Residents were deployed at the request of local powers, and on their part, many princes maintained *wakils* in the Raj's outposts at Calcutta, Bombay and Madras to represent themselves.[62] The 'political line' served more as a diplomatic body as understood by the Indo-Mughals and was expected to operate in the manner of the Surman Embassy, rather than as the agents for diplomacy-as-battle to conquer and control the Empire's provinces.[63] Modernity however had to terminate the equality and reciprocity afforded to all regional players by the diplomatic system operating under the umbrella of Mughal sovereignty. This had to done because modernity held that nothing could be its equal. This is why, in the years after Plassey, the EIC transmuted from a body of merchants to a regional power, then to *primus inter pares* amongst the provincial rulers, and finally emerged to replace the Empire by converting it into the Raj. Diplomacy-as-battle enabled this process by eliminating diplomacy as negotiation. The process culminated in 1877 when the British took over sovereignty from the Empire. Victoria, the British Queen, took the title of 'Empress of India' and the new rulers organized the Imperial Assembly.

The replacing of the Empire with the Raj, conducted as it were in the realm of concepts, was the changing of rationalities. Replacement, however, was only possible through many appropriations arising from a set of commonalities. Ironically, even after the Empire had been commandeered, there was continuity in terms of bodies. Mughal diplomacy was an extension of a body (the royal person), whereas the Raj's diplomacy was founded on the irreconcilable separation of bodies. In addition, the human resourcing of both regimes was almost identical.[64] Like the *mansabdari* system the Raj too relied on soldiers. The bulk of the EIC's 'political' officers came from the military, and between 1823 and 1857 military officers made up the bulk of Residents.[65] The military reached its apogee in the late 1830s, early 1840s, when some 80 annual offices were in military hands and just 30 in civilian.[66] Many more soldiers were sent to India than administrators. On average, 37 writers (the entry level appointment in the civil service) were sent from London annually between 1802 and 1833, as compared with 258 cadets.[67]

There were differences within a broadly similar rubric. The Empire viewed men-of-arms as a status symbol. However, the British sent officers because they were cheaper than civil servants, and there would have been many more were 'it not for the explicit and repeated orders of the Court of Directors in London.'[68] In 1808, for example, 'The Court [of Directors] observed that altho' they had not absolutely prohibited the nomination of Military Officers to be public Residents they nevertheless should have great satisfaction in seeing those Situations occupied by Civilians.'[69] Such directives died out completely between 1812 and 1840, but expressions of the Directors' prejudice against military officers were later renewed. One of the main complaints the Directors had against Governor-General Ellenborough in 1842, and apparently a factor in his recall, was his large-scale use of military officers in civil employment.[70] However, the militarization trend continued. Overall, Fisher finds that between 1764 and 1858 the military made up 52.7% of the total annual offices of Resident, and in the less prestigious office of Political Agent, 57.9%.[71] But the crucial difference between the two sets of soldiers was that those who administered the Raj operated under the dynamic of anarchical-binarism. Not only did they therefore have a predilection for war—being military men—but their rationality made diplomacy synonymous with war.

As for modernity's appropriations, they took two principal forms. The more significant was the assimilation of the Empire's personnel. In part this was because they knew how things worked and the modernizers lacked texture. The Raj therefore became dependent on a crucial layer of diplomats who were non-Muslim but had served the Empire. That they appear to have crossed over without any anomie is indicative of the 'fourth possibility'. But first, the group of people who transferred their allegiance were the *munshi*s (from Arabic, 'one who creates, produces, or composes'). A *munshi* was not proficient only in Persian (the language of the Empire) but also in English, making him mediator and spokesman and also a key personage in the formulation of tactics to further British policy.[72] The British, however, were only interested in the *munshi*s for their practical knowledge. This is why *munshi*s rarely appear in official histories, though much of what the Raj did could not have happened without their aid. Fisher, having compiled an index of the identities and service records of 523 *munshi*s between 1764 and 1857, concludes that 'it is clear how much the Company relied on this traditional Islamicized service elite in its efforts to gain mastery of the Persianate court ritual. By analysing the backgrounds of these Indian subordinates, it is clear that the prime qualification for appointment as Munshi was knowledge of the Persianate conventions of the diplomatic world of India.'

Essential to the Raj's operations, *munshi*s signify a cosmological rationality at a late stage of the Empire. Their conduct once again demonstrates that while modernity cannot contain the cosmological, the latter can, and it may even make use of modernist rationality. This is the 'fourth possibility', and very different from Surman's and the Raj's practical adaptability, for neither comprehended the Empire's rationality and the possibilities it contained. Instead the Raj, like Surman, was limited to taking the Empire's practices on board to further modernity. *Munshi*s on the other hand were conscious of the difference between their rationality and the modern base of the Empire. Yet *munshi*s were able to switch to first the Empire, then the Raj, and without any trace of anomie or any cognitive dissonance. This is taken as evidence that they were cosmologically minded rather than modern. This is all the more noteworthy because the *munshi*s first Persianized themselves and then served the Raj, despite the feelings of distance and contempt by each of the two ruling groups (especially the British) towards the other. That they were able to do so is testimony to the extent to which the *dharma*-complex and its assumptions continued to motivate these officials. This is unsurprising because the subcontinent's rationality had already modified the Empire's Islamic *raison d'être*. In other words, despite the originary claims to uniqueness made by both Empire and Raj, they remained for *munshi*s no more than variations of a theme: rulers. Being rulers, they were uniquely imbued with the power to dispense patronage, and it was for these very practical reasons that the *munshi*s migrated from a declining power to the Raj.

A cosmological explanation for *munshi*s is called for because earlier explanations of their ability to seamlessly transition into the Empire and then the Raj play havoc with causality. Sanjay Subrahmanyam and Muzaffar Alam, for instance, first identify practices and then retrospectively use a modern category to explain them. The category is 'composite culture' which was produced by the Empire. However, all that it can reveal is why the Empire accepted *munshi*s, not what made *munshi*s excel at transferring themselves into the Empire without any violence to themselves. This process is indicated by what made the Empire itself ready to accept them. For Subrahmanyam and Alam this is due to the Empire being secular, and they show this by referring to the educational texts for *munshi*s.[73] That material 'fell into a branch of knowledge that was regarded as secular, in the sense of being distinctly this-worldly and largely devoid of religious or theological connotations.' But once again, the authors do not seek to explain why this was so. A means to ascertain this is, as has been demonstrated, the silences within Islam that permitted an intellectual shift, and it was aided by the lesson of the *Mb*. In practice Akbar continued the move initiated by Humayun, and thus the Mughals became Indo-Mughals by intellectually reordering themselves,[74] ejecting aspects of their modernist framework upon exposure to the cosmological intellectual context they found themselves in. However, this did not make the state secular, because that term implies a logic arising from modernity. It was implanted into India long after the rise of the Empire and its *munshi*s by the Raj. In other words, practices that appeared to be secular were motivated by an altogether different logic that made them something else, and arose from a cosmological rationality. In short, the state became accepting because of exposure to the same rationality that made *munshi*s seek out the state.

Subrahmanyam and Alam also argue that the state's 'composite culture' made for the 'moral universe' of the *munshi*s. This, however, is to presume that state created society, whereas the process is always two-way, especially when the state's modernist rationality had already been ameliorated by exposure to non-modern society. To return to Subrahmanyam's and Alam's argument, having located the *munshi* in the state they turn to the autobiography of a *munshi*, Nik Rai,[75] and conclude that he 'comfortably straddles a diversity of cultural and literary heritages'. Nik Rai's 'moral universe' is understood as emanating from the state because the 'philosophical universe within which he [Nik Rai] conceives of all matters, is impregnated with Persian, and with all the richness of the 'secular' tradition that Indo-Persian represented by the seventeenth century.' In short, the presumption is that the state makes society. But this state-centric reading is undermined in the example of Nik Rai because he 'is of course aware that he is not a Muslim'. Yet he admired and imitated the great *mir munshi* Abu al-Fazl, and he was surely not alone in this. Though steeped in the Empire's culture, Nik Rai remained enough of a non-Muslim to find it distasteful that Aurangzeb, 'in consideration of matters external to spirituality … made a mosque from a temple'. With irony Nik Rai wrote: 'Look at the miracle of my idol-house, o Sheikh. That when it was ruined, it became the House of God.'[76] The point is that though Subrahmanyam and Alam make the *munshi*'s 'moral universe' a function of the state, they also undermine their interpretation by showing the *munshi*'s distaste for the state, and that is directly tied into the society that preceded the Empire. Hence, at least for Nik Rai, society precedes the state, as does his rationality. This is also in keeping with the cosmic argument for why *munshi*s functioned as they did, using the state to further themselves. This was possible because the state, though originating in a modern rationality, was never understood as such by the cosmological *munshi*s. In short, the *munshi*s used the modernizing state by making themselves modern in terms of practice but to further goals manufactured in context, and in doing so maintained their cosmological rationality. In other words, this was an early example of the 'fourth possibility'.

Meanwhile, another form of appropriation was the Raj harnessing local practices to implement policies founded on the 'other'. An indication is what happened to the intelligence network. It was one of the most important local apparatuses appropriated because intelligence, while crucial to any diplomatic service, was essential to diplomacy-as-battle. Oddly, the wholesale co-opting of the Empire's intelligence system meant that the Raj also fell foul of the same problems that plagued the Empire. In appropriating, the Raj not only put the apparatus to service modernity, but modernized the intelligence network itself by inserting Europe's rationality. The result was the deletion of aspirations and freedoms for the people who made it function, thereby ending the possibility that is the 'fourth possibility'.

To understand this regression in possibilities is to chart what the British appropriated, how and to what purpose. The target for appropriation was the Mughal information-gathering network, the *akhbar nawis*, which 'from the Mughal period down to the twentieth century, continued as the medium by which changing kinds of information have been gathered, conveyed, and presented. Each period has had its own definitions of information and its own role for the *akhbar nawis*. The continuities and the changes in this office thus reflect the shifting political world of India for nearly five centuries.'[77]

The term *akhbar nawis* comes from the Arabic root *kh-b-r*, 'to know'. It came to denote 'news, information, advices, intelligence; notification, announcement; report, rumour, fame; story, account.'[78] And *nawis* means 'writer'.[79] Just as the Mughals drew upon extant forms but reformulated them to arrive at a definition of 'information' and the means to control it compatible with their own cultural and political values,[80] so too did the EIC. The origins of the system can be traced to the *A'in-I Akbari*, which lays out detailed prescription for their use.[81] One type of *akhbar nawis* was the flow of information from the provinces to the imperial court. Here as well, Akbar established the original model.[82] However, the court had to constantly modify the network because writers got co-opted by the regions they reported on. To start with, Emperors appointed writers called *sawanih nigar* ('untoward events writer') to the provinces—apparently incognito.[83] Later this official took charge of the provincial postal system (*dak*), thus revealing his official status.[84]

An overlaying complicated the original network, and permitted its appropriation. The cause of the overlaying was the Empire's dissolution. During this period, provincial governors made themselves hereditary rulers in their regions and regional courts modelled themselves on the Empire's court. Each ruler extended his *akhbar nawis*, *wakil*s, and other agents into the other major courts of the time. Further, each ruler posted *akhbar nawis* in the territories under his control. Conversely, each court became the object of manipulation and scrutiny by the numerous *akhbar nawis* and *wakil*s stationed there by rival and allied rulers. The modifications to the institution of the *akhbar nawis* reflected an altered political context.[85] The growing role of the EIC led to it also becoming the target of *akhbarat*. For instance the message sent to the Maratha *Peshwa* (ruler) in 1775, which warned: 'The English chiefs have sent couriers to inspect the palaces and forts and all the country leading to the Deccan. After getting the information they intend at the end of the rainy season to march towards Jhansi and Kalpi. Please order your mokasadars ['official holding revenue shares from villages'] not to allow the dak of the English couriers to be posted anywhere; slay them wherever found.'[86]

In 1779 an *akhbar nawis* reported to the *Peshwa* that 'Hasting ... posted relays of palki-bearers [sedan chair carriers] to the number of 350 men, from Calcutta to Kotah.'[87] These intelligence systems possessed long memories. Eight years later the *Peshwa*'s newswriter reported the EIC had upgraded the system: 'The English have set up a camel-post in the place of runners, from Lucknow to Delhi, in order to get the quickest news of the Emperor's Court and Sindhia's camp.'[88]

From being a target for *akhbar nawis*, the British succeeded in subordinating it and using it against its inventors. It was the repetition of Surman's practical adaptability on a sub-continental scale. The changes the British instituted were not in the realm of practice, which is why Indo-

Mughals sought to transition into the Raj, for they expected the same rewards, and responsibilities, as during Empire. In other words it was the 'fourth possibility', of using modernity to enhance themselves, and was brought about by a reflexivity that noted changes in context: the dissolution of Empire and the appearance of a new ruler that could provide employment. So easy was it for Indo-Mughals to transition that in 1770 the *Naib Nazim* (Deputy Governor) of Bengal took it upon himself to instruct the EIC as to the 'proper' forms for an intelligence agency:

It is an ancient custom in Hindostan and has always been adopted by Emperors that whenever it was expedient to appoint officers of the crown upon any urgent business three persons selected under the officers, namely, the Darogha [manager], the writer of occurrences [*waqi 'a nawis*], and writer of reports [*sawanih nigar*] and besides this another channel of intelligence was secured by a proper distribution of hircarrahs [messengers] as a check upon the others that no connections might be privately formed or Partialities shown to particular people. The three public officers wrote a separate detail; and the hircarrahs kept a secret diary of the transactions of the officers. I would recommend that in the present case the same method be pursued, and three persons be appointed of good capacity who might not be influenced by prejudice or diverted from their duty by connections and friendships....[89]

The EIC followed his advice and appointed the agents he nominated.[90] The Deputy Governor was not the only example of fluid movement, which also took place between the centre of the Empire and the Raj. In 1782, one of the Emperor's highest officials offered to shift his allegiance to the EIC. Ghulam Muhammad Khan, who identified himself as the Manager of the *Mughal Imperial Intelligence Service* Office, wrote: 'I am an old Servant of his Majesty and am employed by His Majesty Shah Allum in giving him Intelligence received from every quarter of Hindustan. ... I am desirous to engage in your Service.'[91] That Muslim courtiers were just as capable of transitioning as Nik Rai had been is yet further evidence of how far the Islamic state had been reordered by its context.

The Raj's reflexivity made it incapable of such change. Instead, it appropriated local practices to further itself. The appropriation shaped every step the Raj took in its diplomacy-as-battle, for each Resident maintained under him an intelligence service and 'Intelligence Office'. Their activities were clearly understood by the locals, which is why the Poona court in 1795 objected to the Resident's appointment of a newswriter to that court. In the Resident's words, the proposed newswriter, 'being an Intelligent person likely to give me valuable good Information ... the vague objections of the Durbar seem dangerous in Precedent as liable to an unlimited Extension.'[92] If one ruler could exclude a EIC newswriter, so could all rulers. The EIC therefore insisted on the appointment.

That a great deal of importance was placed on this network is also illustrated by the EIC's complaints if reports from a region diminished.[93] That the newswriter was also put under severe pressure reinforces the significance of the network to the EIC's diplomacy. For example, the *akhbar nawis* at Jaipur wrote in the third person that should he be dismissed from the EIC's service and protection, 'the Court of yepoor will wreak its vengeance by imprisonment and seizure of his household, for opposing the orders and the acts in general of ... that Government ....'[94] The EIC's intelligence services were so significant that there were attempts to co-opt it. The *wazir* of Kabul proposed that the EIC's newswriter in Peshawar share information with him. The EIC immediately rejected this.[95] Additionally, an *akhbar nawis* or other agent at Calcutta could obtain for a ruler valuable advance notice of the Resident's orders. In 1844, Awadh's ruler and his court, and even members of the Residency staff, learned the Governor-General's secret instructions to the Resident before the Resident himself. The Resident complained:

[A] copy of this identical letter arrived at Lucknow three days before the original reached me and its contents were actually known to the King, Minister and one or two others before I was myself aware of them.... [M]y Head Intelligence Writer, previously to the perusal of the original, read out to me a letter which tallied with it nearly word for word...[96]

From the 1700s to the imposition of crown sovereignty in 1858 the human resources and the apparatuses of the Empire were all put to another use. This practical adaptability is however no substitute for the reflexivity that modernity is supposed to be capable of. Indeed, nothing of the sort came to pass and the Raj's adaptability was used to further its dynamic: anarchical-binarism. In terms of reflexivity, the Raj never exceeded its own rationality to produce even an iota of change, never even recognized what the 'other's' terms were. In other words, anarchical-binarism came to dominate diplomacy and the effects were startling. A practice for communicating and negotiating to prevent war was made into a tool of war. The changes were only possible because the British easily comprehended the Empire's diplomatic practice, which undermines the claim that diplomacy as it exists today is a modern invention.

Fisher notes that the Empire's practices, which modernity used, persisted to the mid-19th century. Adding, for instance, Christian dates to the *Hijri* dates in *akhbarats* however no more modernized Indo-Mughals than Indian numerals Indianized Europe.[97] What did change was however far more significant, for it was at the level of rationality which transformed the very purpose of pre-existing practices.

The victory of battle-diplomacy

A genealogy does not seek to detail every event. Yet it cannot but not note that the broad processes being outlined faced considerable resistance, though it ultimately failed to stem the onset of modernity. The struggle the Raj faced shaped the nature of the confrontation if not the inevitable outcome: the termination of diplomacy as a means to make the present liveable, turning it into a function of anarchical-binarism. The story of diplomatic resistance is tangible in the practice of gift-giving. The Raj had great difficulty with this, even though the Raj succeeded finally in eliminating the Empire's rationality for gifting and made it a function of modernity.

Natasha Eaton shows how the EIC attempted to transform the notion of 'gift' and its place in diplomacy in India. Within a broad tessellation of the idea of 'gift' there were two views. In the prevailing cosmos the 'gift' was used to form and maintain the Empire's polity. Subordinates 'offered valuable tributes—*nazr*, and received in return *khil'at*—robes minutely graded in the vocabulary of rank and occasion from the wardrobe of the ruler, signifying a certain incorporation into the king's body as well as the body politic.'[98] Kingly charisma consisted in giving 'excessively'—kings styled themselves as the 'embodiment of hospitality.'[99] In contrast the Raj viewed the inlaying of its employees into the Empire's gift rituals with anxiety and suspicion. They saw 'these practices as bribery and extortion innate to "Oriental despotism."'[100] At the heart of the matter lay the EIC official's abuse of Indo-Mughal gifting. In response to 'escalating charges of corruption,' the Regulating Act of 1773 barred British officials from receiving land, money, and jewels from Indians.[101] Under the 'reformed' regime, 'gifts [were] allowed … to have legal validity … only if they were given for reasons deemed satisfactory in British courts of law, which proposed new taxonomies of gifts and new ideas of political expediency.'[102]

Hastings wanted to replace the Empire's gifting with a gift that in design and in symbolic value was English—the painted portrait:

In eighteenth-century Britain, portraits played a key role in strengthening kinship networks: two dimensional images were believed to convey a certain presence of the absent donor through the mediation of likeness.[103] The dissemination of portraits extended to the diplomatic realm, and no ambassador quitted Britain without likenesses of the reigning monarch. While these canvases evoked his presence, they did not stand in for the absent sovereign (as in France), a practice that the British abhorred as 'despotic.'[104]

In keeping with British tradition, Hastings promoted his own portraits-as-gift because he 'believed that the British rulers of Bengal must conduct a foreign policy within a diplomatic system comparable to that of Europe.' Hastings attempted to ground this in extant Indian notions of diplomacy as being 'face-to-face relations'.[105] To do so, he supplemented English ideas of diplomacy with his interpretation of Akbar's munificent artistic practices. As Abu al-Fazl recorded: 'His Majesty himself sat for his likeness and also ordered to have the likenesses taken of all of the grandees in the realm. An immense album was thus formed; those who have passed away have received new life and those who are still alive have immortality promised them.'[106] However, this practice had little to do with portrait-exchange, the new conception that Hastings was trying to insert into extant practice.

Instead of following EIC orders to reform themselves, Indo-Mughals made new requirements as part of resistance in a world where their ability to practice diplomacy was rapidly contracting. An example is Awadh, which was targeted for British expansion in the 1770s. In response to the Nawab of Awadh Asaf ud-daula's threat to write to George III if the EIC did not reduce his payments, Hastings came to the capital, Lucknow, and spent five months there.[107] Shortly after Hastings' arrival the heir to the Empire fled from Delhi to take refuge at Lucknow, where he sat to the English painter Zoffany brought by Hastings, prompting Asaf to do the same.[108] However, Asaf quickly disposed of his portrait by giving it to a disgraced EIC official. It was a gesture of contempt for EIC policy. To add insult, Asaf organized a series of lavish entertainments for Hastings—directly contradicting EIC policy, and increasing Awadh's debts to the EIC, but in keeping with Indo-Mughal norms.[109] One of the court poets wrote: 'At the time of his [Hastings'] departure, the exalted Nawāb gave gifts to Hastings' men in such large numbers that no one could ever imagine. Every person of any note was given a horse, an elephant and a fine robe.'[110] The poet was commending a return to what had been common parlance in earlier diplomatic practice. But Hastings left Lucknow having failed to secure any agreements, and horrified at the expense Asaf had indulged in. Asaf acted as he did because having been denied the practice of diplomacy, he 'wanted to project the image of an exalted emperor who gives to his subordinates and allies in dazzling, potlatch-like public displays of munificence, but this contradicted Hastings' parsimonious governance.'[111]

Asaf's artistic—and ultimately futile—response to the demise of diplomacy as he knew it built on the Empire's incipient pan-Indianism in the political consciousness of its subjects. The strengthening of this consciousness was as much spurred on by the perpetual insecurities of the Raj, expressed in equal measure against one and all. It meant an increase in surveillance to an unprecedented scale, and brought new pressures to bear on the informants. From about 1775, for example, the *Nawab* of Arcot sent *akhbar nawis* to Calcutta because the Raj was unable to effectively tap into the intelligence network.[112] Arcot was relied upon because it had effective newswriters and informants in the courts of the Marathas, Hyderabad, and the Mysore rulers. Under pressure for more information, the *Nawab* asserted that by disclosing the intelligence he was putting 'the life of his newswriter … at stake.'[113] In pushing existing practices to the limit, the British cast their nets more widely and plumbed deeper than the Indo-Mughals had. An EIC official urged Residents to report virtually everything about the world the EIC was entering: 'The utility of collecting every possible information respecting the disposition, genius, talents, character, connections, views, interests, revenues, military strength, and even domestic history of those Princes or people, with whose affairs our own happens to be interwoven or related, either immediately or remotely, must also be equally clear.'[114]

The response to this violence—one of its least invasive forms of violence under the Raj, for it did not in itself threaten life—spurred in Indo-Mughals a new notion of the political geography of India in a colonized globe.[115] For the first time a series of princes mounted direct diplomatic initiatives to the British Queen in London. More than thirty embassies to the British court in London were made to seek recourse from the practices of the Raj. These 'counterflows' were minor in comparison to the diplomatic onslaught of the Raj which undermined the Empire's sovereignty and denied the princes' diplomacy, but in mounting their missions, locals learnt how to take advantage of European inventions such as printing by publishing cheap pamphlets to circulate their stories[116] and learned how to lobby the British parliamentary system.[117] Some secured advantages in London for their rulers, but these were subsumed by the EIC's overriding emphasis on a diplomacy of conquest.

It was within this new consciousness of a colonized globe, and just as Indo-Mughals were reaching out farther than they had ever before, that modernity struck its final blow. Though diplomacy-as-battle had been regularized and the denizens of the Raj had to inhabit the world it created, there was enough of older forms in them for them to transcend their present to practice what they knew had existed in another context. In short, provincial rulers continued to choose older concepts of diplomacy. The moment when it could have flowered by communicating with peoples across the globe was also the instant of its mortality. The death of diplomacy was a result of the rationality of the 'other' achieving its zenith in two distinct ways: maintaining the racial purity of the Residency system, and subsuming all diplomacy to that system. Riding on anarchical-binarism, the EIC could not simply convert the 'other' to modernity—that is, make Indo-Mughals into moderns. They would require Indo-Mughals to assume the modern notion of opposites coming together. The result—hybrids—is certainly how the British perceived Indo-Mughals in their service. There was however a problem: as Homi Bhabha writes, hybrids are by definition 'half acquiescent, half oppositional, always untrustworthy.'[118] This is precisely why, and as early as 1782 the Commander-in-Chief of the EIC's armies, wrote: 'At present, excepting at the Court of the Nizam, we are obliged to depend on Intelligence coveyed to us thro' black agents as the views of every other Power of Hindostan and whose reports it is but too natural to suppose are calculated to suit their own Interests.'[119]

Others agreed, citing Indians' lack of judgement and fidelity.[120] The old notion of debasement of local people from Roe's time continued. One Resident wrote, 'it is vain to expect honesty from any Native Servant, who is not placed beyond the Reach of ordinary Temptation.'[121] That no lessons about negotiating with locals had been learnt from Surman's negotiations in 1717 is testimony to modernity's incapacity to reflect in context.

Despite modernity resolving that Indo-Mughals in their service were hybrids, which is the only way modernity could account for them, there is no reason to assume Indo-Mughals were hybrids. Rather, like *munshi*s, Indo-Mughals joined the Raj because it was only a variation on a theme: rulers. However, the true magnitude of the difference from older rulers was to emerge piecemeal. An incident in 1791 was the threshold for one Indo-Mughal, when he realized that the Raj was motivated by a rationality that sought to eliminate him. The realization was precipitated by the death of the Resident at Nagpur. His chief assistant, an Indo-Mughal, thought he would get the job, as did a young British lieutenant—a purely military, non-political man. Each wrote independently to the Governor-General asserting his right to replace the late Resident. The Governor-General supported the British lieutenant and ordered the Indo-Mughal to serve him. It was the unravelling of a unified cosmos for the Indo-Mughal, the dawn of the realization that the Raj was not the Empire. Rather than produce opportunities, the Raj made Indo-Mughals no more than functionaries in practices that aimed to eliminate the very people it employed. Rather than allow himself to be demoted to the 'Character of Common News Writer,' he resigned.[122]

While this official extricated himself from diplomacy, entire states were being systematically barred from practicing any diplomacy at all. In combination this was the beginning of the end of Indo-Mughal diplomacy, not just in terms of the local rationality but as an absolute: diplomacy henceforth was to be an exclusively British affair, conducted to the tune of anarchical-binarism. The way in which this was achieved was by transferring all diplomatic communication to the Residents. In doing so modernity was furthered because there was no possibility for diplomacy to be used as a technique for negotiation. Delinking diplomacy from its communicative purpose completed its harnessing to battle.

Beginning in 1793, the EIC managed to induce some fifty-five states to agree by treaty to channel all foreign political contacts through the Resident.[123] A typical treaty laid down that the ruler in question abjured any 'negotiation or political correspondence with any European or Native power without the consent of the said Company.'[124] On their part, rulers sought to avoid such restrictions on their foreign relations. Rulers maintained *akhbar nawis* in all the courts and states of interest to them, well beyond the power of the EIC to prohibit.[125] In practice, however, the British expected all states to observe this restriction from as early as the Resident could enforce it. In the case of Nagpur, for example, the Raja would not conclude a treaty prohibiting all communication until

1826, nevertheless the EIC forbade the practice as early as 1813. While the EIC did not literally forbid rulers from having a foreign policy, it simply insisted that all communication pass through its hands![126] In practice it meant that the Residents could communicate with each other and coordinate their efforts while the princes were forbidden to correspond with anyone except through the EIC.

The assumption of paramountcy in 1858 made the British the pre-eminent power in the land, but the removal of military insecurities did not mean the end of 'othering'. It continued, for what was being constructed was a citadel of modernity. To allow in the 'other' would have undermined the self, and so the purity of the Political Line in terms of 'race'—that is, the only language obvious enough for a binary logic—was stringently maintained. That this was in the teeth of opposition indicates that Indo-Mughals who had not realized the situation like the Resident's assistant in Nagpur persisted in believing that the British too saw themselves as inextricably intermeshed with Indo-Mughal society. For that society, the British were not alien, but simply rulers. In short, the dynamic of 'othering' was yet to be internalized, though some were no doubt mimicking. In either case, the state was viewed as a means of progress, regardless of what the state thought of them. In understanding the state so, Indo-Mughals continued to act in accordance with the 'fourth-possibility', as the *munshi*s had, and sought to use modernity to further themselves in the present.

And they succeeded. In response to agitation, Indians began to be very slowly admitted into the Indian Civil Service (ICS) from the 1860s. One of the earliest was Bihari Lall Gupta, who though able to negotiate worlds without anomie was only able to do so with *jugar*. Entering the ICS necessitated crossing the 'black waters' to London. Gupta knew his family would oppose his plans and so kept them secret. That he had to both run away from home and borrow the money to travel from his far wealthier friends was confirmed by his granddaughter, my grandmother. The *jugar* of his act may be approached by Gayatri Spivak repeatedly talking about herself having done the same as Gupta, despite the security of doing so about a century later and coming from a much richer, not to mention supportive family.[127] In service Gupta went on to initiate the challenge to the law by which Indian officers, even though in executive and judicial charge of districts, were disqualified from trying European offenders, which came to be known as the Ilbert bill controversy.[128] With the likes of Gupta managing to overcome the impossibilities of what modernity deigned 'tradition' and more tangibly economics, the Raj no doubt felt threatened, and so it barred natives from the Residency system in 1877.[129] It was not until May 1918 that the first Indian, Abdul Qaiyum, after lifelong service as a supporting officer, was carefully selected for the Political Line because his appointment would not cause 'an embarrassing precedent' as he was to retire within a year.[130] It was as recently as 1925 that the first Indian, K.P.S. Menon, entered the Political Line from the ICS in keeping with standard practice for Indians (that is, whites in the colonial terminology, in which those called Indians today were called 'natives'). His appointment did not open the gates to the Indianization of the Political Line and natives were well aware of the reason. It was binarism, which had encrusted into racism, and that is why in 1935 three natives raised the issue of whether 'White colour' was a requirement for the Line in the Assembly. The reply was, 'Not as far as I am aware'.[131] As W. Murray Hogben writes, the reluctance of the British to Indianize the political line even on the eve of independence may be traced to 'a certain sense of racial or moral superiority' founded on the assumption that the locals 'lacked character'.[132] It was, in short, the belief that modernity would be imperilled if left to the non-modern.

Conclusions

Having established a foothold in the Empire, the Raj sought to repudiate it and replace it. This was necessary because of the rationality that governed the Raj, and the means to establish modernity was via practical adaptability. This is why B.N. Pure writes:

It can hardly be suggested that the British evolved their own administrative organisation independent and exclusive of the one they inherited. ... [A] policy of festina lente was followed to enable them to understand properly problems connected with administration of people whose language, culture and tradition were entirely unknown to them. Many of the administrative institutions of the preceding ruling families were retained permanently, laws and usages left undisturbed, and reforms in administration postponed.[133]

The journey from tessellation to hegemony was only possible because at the level of practice what the British encountered was no different from their own experience. Diplomatic practice in the Empire had been modified by the context the Mughals found themselves in. The result was what is mistakenly called a 'secular' understanding of diplomacy. It is this mistaken assumption that leads Subrahmanyam to argue that '"modernity" represents a more-or-less global shift, with many different sources and roots, and-inevitably-many different forms and meanings depending on which society we look at it from.'[134] To do so is to deny modernity the very value it attaches to itself, does a disservice to the term by making it a meaningless sponge, and ignores not just the past of the remarkable agents of the Empire, but also their abilities to transition without anomie into the Empire and then the Raj.

If, as modernists are wont to view it, Europe's long gestation produced a 'maximum rationalization of intelligence' predicated upon substantial numbers of persons being 'legally empowered and psychologically disposed to carry on mental production at the highest level of operation without being [disabled by] private or public inhibitions or barriers',[135] then surely the entry of modernity was a 'regression' in India. Instead of transcending 'particularistic restraints of family, kin, caste and class and allow their minds to wander within 'neutral zones' provided by institutions free from political and religious dictate'[136] the Raj reinforced Indo-Mughal barriers (a militarized bureaucracy with funds being put in service of not development but diplomacy-as-battle); deconstructed a cosmological diplomatic service (the *munshi* was firmly placed in a secondary position); and introduced the all-encompassing notion of 'race' to create an impermeable biological barrier, ultimately denying Indo-Mughals the right to practice their own diplomacy or a role in what was being constructed. But modernists continue to think of this as progress because it is articulated within a finite rationality in awe of time, whereas in trying to correct this misconception by acting in context Indo-Mughals changed those boundaries by incorporating space. Whether the finitude of the alien rationality succeeded in overwhelming the *dharma*-complex in post-independence India to make it a modern nation-state in the realm of the international is what we explore next.

6

DIPLOMACY REBORN

My life is my message.

— Mohandas Gandhi.[1]

The most important thing about our foreign policy is that it is part of our great historical tradition.

— Jawaharlal Nehru[2]

The moment of independence is theorized as the victory of modernity.[3] It is called many things, most ominously the 'cunning of reason', for once again it is believed that modernity is reason and it is presumed to order the Indian intellect.[4] If it does, then Indian diplomats have assumed an originary state of Hobbesian 'warre'.[5] Such readings arise not from the absence of what Sunil Khilnani calls 'cool-headed interpretation',[6] but from the active avoidance or negation of Indian 'authoritative sources'. The result is analytical chaos, engendered by the use of modern, rather than practitioner's, categories to interpret diplomacy in independent India.

To resolve this disarray, the present chapter outlines a set of categories and their percolation into the practice of the geobody's diplomacy. The most significant category is the *dharma*-complex, because the architects of Indian diplomacy drew upon it to conceptualize and engage what moderns call the 'international'. The most pernicious manifestation of anarchical-binarism, it is a zone where violence on a scale only possible of nation-states is legitimate. India however embarked on an impossible possibility: to reorder this zone diplomatically. Central to this diplomacy was not anarchical-binarism but Mahatma Gandhi's cosmological rationality. Gandhi engaged the *Mb's dharma*-complex, synthesized it to make for truth and made it the basis for a politics so different from power politics-between-nations that it is termed the art-of-politics.[7] In doing so Gandhi made two key contributions. He found the means to practice politics in consonance with the cosmos, that is to defend it without harming those seeking to destroy it,[8] and in doing so he resolved the *Mb's* paradox of how a rationality that sanctions all copes with that which chooses to destroy.[9] Gandhi handled this inconsistency by reconceptualizing violence into aggressive-violence and resistance or *satyagraha*. The bifurcation does not deny violence but makes it mutable. Resistance is violence but qualitatively different from aggressive-violence, because it does not seek to criticize, much less to impose and destroy. Resistance is therefore in purpose, practice and result different enough from aggressive-violence to be non-violent. Putting this into effect entailed 'reckless courage', not to realize a future but to live in consonance with the cosmos now.[10] In doing so he demonstrated the most audacious example of the 'fourth possibility': the delivery of freedom instantaneously by resorting to an irenic metre and so making possible politics by the impossibility of power politics.

At least three centuries of modernist thought from Hobbes onwards—and a much longer intellectual tradition—were short-circuited by Gandhi's innovations within a tradition of *dharma*. This intellectual revolution came to life internationally with Gandhi's death, when his mantle passed to Jawaharlal Nehru. Though starting as a modern, Nehru was distinguished from mimic-men by moving towards Gandhi's art-of-politics and then deploying its practice, *satyagraha*, to the acme of anarchical-binarism, the 'international'. Undoubtedly Nehru wrestled with the art-of-politics, and being able only to grasp the practical in it, made *satyagraha* into an ideal. This reductionism of rationale to idealized practice is why it does not sit easy with the institution expected to perform it: the Ministry of External Affairs (MEA). Lacking formal training in the rationality that makes requisite the art-of-politics, the MEA keeps to Gandhi's example in the manner of rote learning as opposed to the instinct of logic. Indian diplomacy therefore became practically Gandhian, but by being purely principled, opened itself to an unanswerable challenge: why choose this principle over that? And yet, Gandhi's rationale as principled Nehruvian diplomacy persisted. Finally, just how strictly principles have been adhered to is exposed by the incoherence of modernist explanations being resolved when diplomacy is studied by the cosmological heuristic.

Gandhi's engagement with dharma

Gandhi's contribution to the escape from European hegemony is well known, but the attempts to reel him—and by implication India—into the West's conceptual categories continue unabated. A case in point is the statement, 'There is no such thing as absolute morality for all times. But there is relative morality which is absolute enough for imperfect mortals that we are.'[11] It leads to ascribing a lack of belief, and perspectivalism, to Gandhi. Manfred Steger does this by following Joan Bondurant to once again entrap Gandhi within nationalism. Steger imposes modernist order on Gandhi[12] to argue that he unthinkingly reproduces the divisions inherent to modernism, that his project is 'marked by violence at its origin … a mirror image of the European nationalist discourse with its conceptually violent assumptions of moral superiority, culturally specific claims to a universal truth, and invidious comparisons.'[13] Organizing such readings is a tension internal to modernity: the oscillating status of truth being either oppressively totalizing or hopelessly individuated. In this replay of the clash between Prakash and O'Hanlon/Washbrook what is lost once again are Indians and the terms in which they comprehend the world.

From an unchanging perspectivalism, Lloyd and Susanne Rudolph swing to the other extreme to render Gandhi postmodern.[14] It is an incredible assertion because superimposed on Gandhi is an anarchical state of nature, that is, the conceptual assumption interlinking modernity with postmodernity and overlooked by followers of the latter.[15] To return to Roland Barthes, postmodernity simply multiplies the already existent notion of author—descended directly from the idea of God—by making everyone an author. All this does is proliferate the sources of conflict, and indeed makes it state of man. This is so because postmodernity follows modernity and therefore reproduces the idea of the author which itself is the conflict generating idea.[16] However, Gandhi was operating in an altogether different intellectual stream with no author to start with. The aspiration to be an author was not rendered commonplace by

Gandhi, it never existed in his *metis* which put Gandhi's subsequent modifications on a path that the Rudolphs miss because they begin with the premises of their intellectual setting—fad[17]—rather than the subject's. This is why, for instance, they claim that Gandhi's postmodernity is 'situational truth' and arose from his reading of the *Mb's Gita*.[18] This is an impossible conclusion—if the reader possesses texture—because, as Simon Brodbeck shows, the *Gita* is about causality, and how it ought to be viewed as not limiting but expressive of the infinite possibilities presented by the cosmos, a conclusion Gandhi himself arrives at. In taking Gandhi's reading of the *Gita* as 'situational truth' the Rudolphs capture the *dharma* element in him. What they miss is highest-*dharma* or the truth of situated truth in the *dharma*-complex or what Gandhi calls truth. This makes for a completely different ontological trajectory, refuting the Rudolphs' attempt to enclose Gandhi just as he negated the tyranny of their intellectual setting decades earlier.

In modernity's crude terms Gandhi is sublime,[19] discerning the road he crafted and how it led to India's foreign policy—and in contradistinction to modernity—requires fashioning a space for his thought. A first glimpse at how this may be done is provided by Akeel Bilgrami, who identifies the oscillating status of Gandhi's understanding of truth as a 'spectacular misreading'.[20] Bilgrami contrasts Gandhi with John Stuart Mill's *On Liberty*. It argues that objectivity is never something we are sure to attain; we must therefore be made modest about our truth, not impose it, and must tolerate difference. But Bilgrami is wrong to write, 'truth for Gandhi ... is an experiential notion,'[21] for what he has identified is only one aspect of Gandhi's truth, it is contextual truth or *dharma*. Indeed Gandhi does hold to this, which is why he said, pointing to his breast, the 'seat of authority lies here,' and continued, 'I exercise my judgement about every scripture, including the Gita.'[22] Gandhi did indeed give pride of place to *antahkarana* or the individual's truth rather than *sruti* (revealed texts), *smrti* (traditions) and *acara* (expected conduct),[23] but this is only one part of the complex that is truth. Left out is the allied notion of highest-*dharma*. Despite missing this, Bilgrami correctly surmises that the 'pervasive diffidence and lack of conviction in opinions which is the character of the epistemology that Mill's argument presupposes, is entirely alien to Gandhi.'[24] This is not because of context, but rather because of the underlying truth of contextual truth. It means that unlike Mill—who is wracked by uncertainty—toleration is a non-issue for Gandhi, but neither does this lead him to condemn. How and why this is so lies beyond the explicative powers of modernity and postmodernity. It is only by exceeding their limitations that Gandhi may be laid bare in the manner he sought to with his writing, and with him, Indian diplomacy.

To do so it is necessary to engage Gandhi on his own terms. Bilgrami, though incisive, cannot do this because he places Gandhi within the context of 'the Radical Enlightenment'[25] and thereby does not keep to Gandhi's experiential notion of truth. In short, like anthropologists, historians and international relations scholars, philosophers too fail to make Indians 'authoritative sources'. Even when their ways are identified, they are not used as the basis of the hermeneutic. The point is not that Gandhi's thought might have been presaged—and then erased—in Europe, but that maintaining the integrity of Gandhi's experiential philosophy requires focusing on his experiences and his reflection on them. Rather than recreate Gandhi's world to contextualize him within it, this genealogy maintains his rationality by keeping with producer-centred-research (PCR) and starting with the event, Gandhi himself, to recreate his intellectual context in his terms. The raw material is his vast corpus of writings, and it is navigated not via modernist philosophers, but by developing a method from the writings itself.[26]

One word suffuses the writings. Appearing more than 3,500 times the word is *dharma*. What does it mean and where does it come from? Identification is complicated by the accusation—reminiscent of modernity's reaction to the *Mb*—that Gandhi's writings are a 'jumble' devoid of coherence.[27] Never alienated from the texture of his civilization, Gandhi was intimate with the *Mb*. Between 1905 and 1947 he directly referred to or quoted from it nearly 300 times, patiently studied it, translated entire sections of it, encouraged its study—and in doing so learned and repeated in lectures the *Mb's* lesson, which is why he emphasized the user's pre-eminence.[28] Gandhi's reliance on the text is an obvious texture for understanding him. It provides a context to identify his understanding of *dharma*. Important is that Gandhi understood the text as 'a profoundly religious book, largely allegorical, in no way meant to be a historical record. It is a description of the eternal duel going on within ourselves, given so vividly as to make us think for the time being that the deeds described therein were actually done by human beings.'[29] Such a view motivated another accusation, made of him in his time: 'the ideal of truth is a Western conception … in the East, craftiness and diplomatic wile have always been held in much repute.'[30] As an example of modernity's extension from containing Indo-Mughals physically to containing India's intellect, Gandhi's response is instructive for it contains the texture to decode the purpose of his politics:

At the time of writing, I never think of what I have said before. My aim is not to be consistent with my previous statements on a given question, but to be consistent with truth as it may present itself to me at a given moment. … But friends who observe inconsistency will do well to take the meaning that my latest writing may yield unless, of course, they prefer the old. But before making the choice they should try to see if there is not an underlying and abiding consistency between the two seeming inconsistencies.[31]

The first part of his texture for his actions is the 'experiential' that Bilgrami highlights, and it is identical to the *Mb's dharma* which is contextual and presupposes a unified whole. One must act in accordance to what the situation calls for, for truth is certain within the practitioner's context (for instance, the optic for representation this work is operating in). So contextual truth, as Gandhi understands it, 'fractures' the Western moral tradition both intellectually and practically.[32]

But this is only the beginning, for there is also a synthesis remarkable in modernity's language. The second part of Gandhi's statement, the 'underlying and abiding consistency' of his pronouncements, is indicative of something that eludes modernity and its descendants. And that is the truth of contextual truth. This second type of truth is the general lesson of the *Mb* made explicit, or an abiding truth: what Alfred Hiltebeitel calls highest-*dharma*. It is the highest because it is to know the truth that each situation produces its own truth. This lesson is what Gandhi replicated from the *Mb*, and in combination with *dharma* made for what is called the *dharma*-complex and what Gandhi called truth. However, this is not a *Diktat* because since truth is based on the truth of contextual truth, anyone may refute it. But to be truthful is to know also that the rejection is a product of context, and in doing so the actor reinforces the truth that is contextual truth.

Descended from the *Mb*, this civilizational notion is complicated by Gandhi's use of 'morality'. It requires unpacking because it slips into ideology in modernity. After all, modernity is a morality tale—Christianity—repackaged as ideology. For Gandhi, morality was something alternative and he wrote, 'I do not know of any *dharma* which is opposed to or goes beyond morality. *Dharma* is morality practiced to its ultimate limits.'[33] Elsewhere he expanded on *dharma* itself:

Dharma does not mean any particular creed or dogma. Nor does it mean learning by rote books or even believing all that they say. Dharma is a quality of the soul and is present, visibly or invisibly, in every human being. Through it we know our duty in life our relation with other souls. It is evident that we cannot do so till we have known the self in us. Hence dharma is the means by which we can know ourselves. We may accept this means from wherever we get it, whether from India or Arabia.[34]

Dharma is personalized, hence it is not dogma but is abiding, which makes it appear contradictory—but it is not, because by *dharma* and morality what Gandhi meant is highest-*dharma*, which is experiential because it may only be grasped through experience. The experiential makes for the very opposite of modernity's engagement with the non-modern. Indicative of it is Piers Vitebsky's noting that 'local knowledge is often total, by virtue of the very fact that it is local.'[35] This is correct, but for Gandhi this knowledge is only total in the local. What is missed by modernity is Gandhi's added layer, that there is a total knowledge, and that local knowledge is total in the locality that generated it. It is this dual and simultaneous operation that makes for Gandhi's truth.

Gandhi's edging towards this rediscovery is in keeping with truth because he recognizes the multiplex and inherently unstable—in the sense that it is in a process of constant reorganization—quality of the society he emerges from and its distinctiveness from what produced modernity: 'Hinduism … is ever evolving. It has no one scripture like the Quran or the Bible. The Gita itself is an instance in point. It has breathed new life into Hinduism. It has given an original rule of conduct.'[36]

From flux arises continuity contra *intertextualité* to make for intertextuality.[37] There are substantial implications for 'tradition'. It is for Gandhi something to be honoured, pondered and reproduced, rather than being made the object of systematic destruction as it is by modernity. However, that does not make progress into a cumulative process. Truth is not progress-through-history and Gandhi, following the *Mb*, was explicit about this: 'Dharma does not lie in giving up a custom simply because no reason can be given for it. On the contrary dharma consists in respecting the customs of the society of which one is part, provided these do not go against morality. … A person who gives up a practice because he cannot see any reason for its continuance is unwise and wilful.'[38]

Giving up tradition is therefore not something Gandhi rejects whole-sale, but Gandhi disapproves of capricious calculations against tradition. The right to revoke time exists only because a neutral cosmos permits calculations in time and space. One may be capricious about time only by disengaging from time and space: society. Otherwise it was imperative to participate:

Today, the dharma of our times is to spin and so long as the sadhu [holy man] is dependent on society for his daily needs, he must spread the dharma of the age by practising it. ... It is a different matter, however, if he eats left-overs lying around, does not care to cover himself, and lives in some unapproachable and unseen cave away from society. He is then free not to observe the dharma of the age.[39]

'Gandhi is not an absolutist, idealist or a theoretician but a man rooted in the ground reality of human condition and predicament. Unlike Kant he never loses right of the real complex "lived" situations that human beings face in their day-to-day life.' However, the error in this reading is the belief that Gandhi is following Kant and 'pleads for imperatives which are categorical enough for mortals like us whose life is not black and white but bears many hues of gray.'[40] This is the error which Steger, Bondurant, Bilgrami and the Rudolphs make. The error arises from Gandhi not being used as an 'authoritative source', that too to explain himself! His *metis* is ignored and instead, a rationality stemming from Christian morality is imposed upon him. But Gandhi's rationale is under-pinned by the *Mb*'s notion of a cosmos unified by relations and neutral at inception.[41] It is why Gandhi could assume everyone was moral,[42] and begin to conceptualize a means of acting truthful not because of a past or in the future. Implicit is the avoidance of violence, which distinguishes Gandhi's politics from modernity, for beginning with anarchy it assumes that everyone must be made moral through violence or, as postmodern-ists call it, 'discipline'.[43]

Gandhi's art-of-politics

It is Gandhi's insight into the *Mb*'s lesson that enabled him to manage his context in an astounding manner by developing an entirely new type of politics, or rather inventing politics itself, since all that existed in its absence was power politics. Faisal Devji, following Shruti Kapila, calls Gandhi's move the 'spiritualisation of politics'.[44] But the term 'spiritual' will only do if what Gandhi did is recognized for what it was: building upon the *dharma*-complex to make for a manner of conducting politics unseen before him. Quite how he did this is disclosed by Gandhi's aim. Unlike modernity, for Gandhi the very instant of acting had to be expressive of truth as every moment is expressive of the cosmos—past, present and future—and it ought to be maintained. Gandhi, in short, negated modernity's distinction between the real and the ideal, since everything is both by virtue of existing. What this meant is that actions are not about realizing the ideal or changing the very nature of the cosmos, but simply are in line with the cosmos. In other words, to act is to act knowing there are no fruits to be gathered, for actions are simply in line with the cosmos. Replaying the *Gita's* lesson, Gandhi arrives at it because he engaged it.[45]

What is also explicit in the *Gita* is that to be in line with the cosmos does not open the doors to anarchy. It is this lesson that produced Gandhi's original contribution: devising a means of acting which preserved and defended the cosmos while avoiding the *Mb's* contradictory sanctioning of violence to defend. Gandhi had to proscribe violence because the cosmos necessitated maintenance in all its contexts, for they in combination made the cosmos. The practical manifestation of this was *satyagraha*. That this practice is only the most mundane outcome of a coherent intellectual rationale quite alternative, since at its core is the unified cosmos, is why what Gandhi developed is termed an art-of-politics. The word politics is retained for the same reason the word rationality is used. That politics is understood in a modern manner does not discount it from being an altogether different set of practices originating in a rationality alternative.[46] The success of the art-of-politics—for it is realized at the moment of its enactment—is also the most stunning example of the 'fourth possibility', for Gandhi's action can only function by embracing modernity, thereby repealing it to establish a violence-free zone now.

How Gandhi was able to arrive at this solution to the violence endemic in earlier politics is clarified if Gandhi's understanding of violence is adopted. To do so is to begin with the commonplace notion that violence is pervasive. Johann Galtung, for instance, defines violence 'as the cause of the difference between the potential and the actual.'[47] He is preceded by Gandhi who wrote that 'no action is altogether innocent' of violence. In short, violence is inherent not just in realizing a desire but in the very act of living. Nor is violence limited to the material,[48] because that is only a facet of the cosmos. Gandhi, therefore, is after a comprehensive reordering of the practices of life based on a rationality that must delete violence now.

But violence is entrenched in the very act of living, which means that Gandhi was quite aware that the certitude of non-violence was unrealizable; but this, as Gandhi wrote did not 'vitiate the principle itself'.[49] Gandhi, then, was striving for what in modernity's terms is an unrealizable principle, and in that striving delivered what for modernity remains undeliverable. Gandhi started by identifying violence's constituent parts. As he wrote, the 'difference between one action and another lies only in the degree of violence involved.' The degree, which in keeping with *dharma* can only be judged relationally, permits two broad classes of violence: aggressive-violence and resistance. The latter is violence since it opposes, but it is ontologically different from aggressive-violence since resistance directs violence into the resister. This is damaging, but at least not to another element of the cosmos, and is done with full self-knowledge of the effect of the violence—something impossible when violence is directed outward. To be able to do so requires courage; hence as Devji shows, Gandhi sought to learn from an SS officer of the Third Reich, no less, the 'art of throwing away my life for a noble cause.'[50] The manner in which the courageous act of directing violence within becomes resistance is via purpose. The purpose of the resister is to always appeal to the person being resisted.[51] And so, Gandhi's aim was an end free of criticism achieved without criticism,[52] for the end is the beginning because all is the cosmos.

This makes for a practical means of acting quite differently from modernity. For instance, while the modernist inflicts violence to incorporate the 'other', the resister acts on the basis of being interconnected with all, or what the MEA calls empathy.[53] This approach licenses what Robert Klitgaard calls sympathy in the modernist. Sympathy is what the resister is attempting to elicit, thereby refuting the modernist notion of alienation. Klitgaard adds that for the resistance to succeed it requires the target to be a 'maximizer' not an 'absolutist', because if the target can absolutely commit to defeating the resister then the latter commits suicide,[54] which of course is unbearable because with the resister also perishes truth. That the British succumbed to Gandhi's resistance proved his rationality capable, because the British made Gandhi's resistance successful by reacting to it with enough sympathy to stop furthering modernity. What the British did was revoke the very notion of the 'other' in practice. However, Gandhi knew this was not the end of modernity, for it is impossible to elicit sympathy from all; he wrote, 'Fasting can only be resorted to against a lover, not to extort rights but to reform him, as when a son fasts for a parent who drinks. I fasted to reform those who loved me. But I will not fast to reform, say General Dyer who not only does not love me, but who regards himself as my enemy.'[55]

With someone as intractable as Reginald Dyer (the officer responsible for the Amritsar massacre in 1919) there was only disappointment. Yet this did not refute truth, and to keep with it is also why Gandhi could not dictate the terms of the resistance. Gandhi, though constantly encouraging the *satyagrahi* to internalize great violence, never set out what the extent of sacrifice ought to be. Only the actor could decide this and the purpose was not simply to differentiate the actor from others, but to also distinguish amongst the recipients of one's sacrifice. Devji argues that this 'ostensibly unequal treatment, both of oneself and of others, produces real equality in an almost communist sense, as in the famous shibboleth "from each according to his ability, to each according to his needs". And it does so by turning the subject who distinguishes and differentiates into someone who by that very token is able to see everything equally.'[56] In short, resistance was the only logical way to act if one was to keep to the cosmos, but the nature of that resistance was dependent on context.

This overriding concern with keeping to truth also meant that violence had to be stemmed. As Gandhi explained: 'While the end is truth, non-violence is the means of attaining it. In such matters, the means cannot be separated from the end. Hence I have written that truth and non-violence are the two sides of the same coin.'[57]

The end is truth because it is the realization that highest-*dharma* is impossible without *dharma*. Practically, it is the moment Dennis Dalton calls a 'personal liberation, an attitudinal revolution within'.[58] It arises at the instant it is operationalized, but how it arises remains unclear because of the refusal to treat Gandhi as an 'authoritative source'. Instead there are oscillations between imposed notions, which cloud more than they reveal. 'Goodness is a sort of mysterious contagion,' writes Bilgrami,[59] and for Klitgaard Gandhi's acting virtuously leads to the greatest utility.[60] Neither can account for the instant when morality manifested itself in Sir Charles Napier as a moment of doubt about his annexation of Sindh. It was at this moment that he was properly entwined with those he had conquered by empathy.[61] It is this that the art-of-politics intends to produce through resistance, thereby maintaining truth by both defending it and acting in consonance with it. And it is because of the need to maintain the integrity of the art-of-politics that there was no possibility for Gandhi to dictate the terms of any resistance. To do so would have fatally undermined truth itself. Gandhi therefore had to find a means of putting into play the art-of-politics without any coercion. As Gandhi elaborated: 'If I want to deprive you of your watch, I shall certainly have to fight for it; if I want to buy your watch, I shall have to pay you for it; and if I want a gift I shall have to plead for it; and, according to the means I employ, the watch is stolen property, my own property, or a donation. Thus we see three different results from three different means.'[62]

Only truthful means could suffice, which is why Gandhi had to also safeguard truth in a truthful way: without violence, for that is inimical to the cosmos. Hence he spoke of harmonization: 'I consider it to be man's achievement to harmonise dharma and the ultimate aim of life, truth and swaraj: swaraj and government by all, the welfare of the country and the welfare of all. That alone is the path that leads to moksha, that alone is what interests me. None of my activities are carried on with any other end in view.'[63]

The difficulty—and strength—in harmonization lies in it being a result of time and space. All Gandhi sought to do was to keep to truth, but so spectacularly did he do so that he inadvertently became an exemplary exemplar. In this he was aided by the consistency with which the imperial space that he inhabited along with millions, manufactured violence. It is through this that the Raj made truth obvious, along with the right way to deal with untruth. 'Reason,' as Gandhi said, 'has to be strengthened by suffering and suffering opens the eyes of understanding.'[64] It made for an entirely different style of politics with alternate consequences. For instance, Gandhi's attractiveness lay not in his charisma or flamboyance—which set other leaders apart from the masses—but rather in his partaking along with millions of others in the Raj's consistent production of suffering. It unified. Gandhi behaved so because truth is the 'solidarity' of common experience, unlike modernity for which, Richard Rorty notes, truth is 'objectivity'.[65] But of course experiential truth makes for objective truth, something Rorty once again misses.

The result of harmonization produced another dramatic innovation: a state, but unlike what is found in the *Mb* and any modern nation-state. This alternative state, a 'sovereignty of the people based on pure moral authority',[66] was Gandhi's final aim. It is apparent to the textured reader that the very name for the zone he was crafting, *Ramarajya*, was 'the kingdom of God on earth'.[67] God naturally is truth, which is also why Gandhi's project is nothing like modernist progress towards 'Heaven on Earth'.[68] Founded at the instant of *satyagraha* being performed, it is evident that a coalition of such actors makes for a *Ramarajya*.[69] To put it differently, *Ramarajya* is achieved in a context at the moment of *satyagraha*, rather than at some future date. Gandhi's innovation also did away with what modernity idealizes, a long violent past to realize utopia. In making the state contingent on the practice of *satyagraha*, Gandhi nationalized the education of kings in the *Mb* to include everyone. The result of nationalizing the *Mb's* lesson was not however a nationalist state. To have craved that was to get 'English rule without the Englishman. You want the tiger's nature, but not the tiger; that is to say, you would make India English. And when it becomes English, it will be called not Hindustan but Englistan. This is not the Swaraj that I want.'[70]

Swaraj did not mean a non-political situation nor a non-state but a state that exceeded modernity's 'history' and animated by the meeting of aggressive-violence with non-violence. Gandhi aimed at an area founded on an altogether different ontology expressed in the practice of *satyagraha*. Such a state had not only to be maintained, but also to seek out all forms of violence—including modernist violence—and engage it, for to do otherwise was to tolerate untruth, which amounted to revoking truth. This is why Gandhi wrote: 'Truthfulness is even more important than peacefulness. Indeed, lying is the mother of violence,'[71] but Gandhi could not be the one to tell anyone how to keep to truth, for that was dependent on context.

Nevertheless, the very practice of *satyagraha* remains an act of violence that undermines the *Ramarajya*. Making it completely consonant with truth is to do away with violence altogether, even *satyagraha*. Such a situation is only possible if *satyagraha* is used to secure a context which does not require resorting to *satyagraha*. In practice this is to do away with modernity, for it warps the very fabric of the cosmos. But how? Instructive is Gandhi's analogical answer to a question about the Polish resistance to Nazi Germany: 'Supposing a mouse in fighting a cat tried to resist the cat with his sharp teeth, would you call that mouse violent? ... In the same way, for the Poles to stand valiantly against the German hordes vastly superior in numbers, military equipment and strength, was almost non-violence. ... You must give its full value to the word "almost".'

The resistance qualified as a *satyagraha* because violence was pitiful in the context of the threat; the violence was defensive and also intended to produce sympathy in the Allied powers—who had sacrificed Czechoslovakia[72]—so that they honoured a treaty to defend Poland. But the reason Gandhi inserts the qualifier 'almost' is not because he is anyone to dictate to Poles what form their resistance ought to take, nor because this was not a *satyagraha*. Gandhi's 'almost' was an acknowledgement of the fact that all existence was violent, but *satyagraha* was different enough from aggressive-violence to make it non-violence. What Gandhi's reply also conveyed was the necessity and applicability of his art-of-politics in the realm of what is hailed as the 'international', for the word itself is now an alluring caste mark denoting not just speed, excitement and adventure but also new analytic possibilities—note the rise of global or interconnected histories. What is missed in this mania for internationalism is the violence contained in the very category itself.

Gandhi's personal struggle, no matter how inadvertently, succeeded in establishing *Ramarajya*, but his protégé Nehru was left to fight Gandhi's battles all over again in the most pernicious expression of the modernist project: the international. Born into a modern context, India was defined by boundaries that quite literally contained the *Ramarajya*. How then could India act in consonance with truth in a world of aggressive-violence? As Ajay Skaria notes, 'Ramarajya is inseparable from the practice of *satyagraha*,'[73] but how could a *Ramarajya* practice *satyagraha* in the radically altered context that is the international? Recognizing the complexity of practicing the art-of-politics in the international, Gandhi cautioned that India's size meant it could not organize itself into an army, because preparedness was synonymous with violence. He wrote, 'if we take that path [to meet violence with 'our superior violence'], we will also have to choose the path of exploitation like the European nations.'[74] The quandary for Nehru, then, was to maintain truth by acting truthfully, that is, defend truth in a truthful manner in the fullest expression of anarchical-binarism.

Nehru: the principled Gandhian

Demonstrating whether Nehru did this requires sketching what he was trying to do, but to do so in the derived language of Indian international 'history' as it has been written and rewritten would fatally undermine the attempt. This is because extant work refuses to treat him as an 'authoritative source' and instead deploys a binary heuristics that results in nothing less than a caricature of a man. Attempts to ameliorate this 'analytic-violence', however mistakenly, turn to heuristics when the problem lies in the hermeneutics that make for binary heuristics. The purpose, then, is to resolve analytic-violence both by modernity and within it, by exegesis that keeps to the text itself.

These concerns explain why this PCR once again returns to the practitioner himself and keeps to his terms. This is to note that undoubtedly Nehru was not part of 'the first Asian social group whose mental world was transformed through its interaction with the West'.[75] Nevertheless, he was sufficiently Westernized to be alienated from the texture of his own civilization. To argue so is simply to restate his own understanding of himself; after all, Nehru did write at length about his discovery of India.[76] Nehru's alienation was emblematic of his modern rationality, but he was moving from it towards a rationality articulated most effectively by Gandhi. Nehru expressed this when he wrote: 'Gandhiji was a very difficult person to understand; sometimes his language was almost incomprehensible to an average modern.'[77] Nehru therefore began as a modern, but progressively moved from modern finitudes to Gandhian truth. Gandhi attributed Nehru's movement to their shared geography.[78] In this Gandhi was too modest, for he was also the foremost explicator of the geography's rationality and Nehru knew it. That is why he followed Gandhi, and why Gandhi chose Nehru as successor. The manner in which Gandhi put it is illuminating: 'Somebody suggested that Pandit Jawaharlal [Nehru] and I were estranged. This is baseless. Jawaharlal has been resisting me ever since he fell into my net. You cannot divide water by repeatedly striking it with a stick. It is just as difficult to divide us. I have always said that … Jawaharlal will be my successor. He says whatever is uppermost in his mind, but he always does what I want. When I am gone he will do what I am doing now. Then he will speak my language too.'[79]

Gandhi's prophecy proved correct, for Nehru did adopt Gandhian language. The modern argument that the use was instrumental, to gain the legitimacy to act internationally by crafting a unifying identity internally, is an example of analytical dissonance. Such an explanation cannot account for the awkward detail that if instrumentality was Nehru's value and generated policies capable of securing interests, then there was no reason to cloak it. Unless, of course, Nehru could not be openly instrumental because of some antipathy towards it in the psyche of his electorate. This makes for an extraordinary contention. Not because it remains to be substantiated, but because it means that Indians do not countenance instrumentality in international relations, even if it secures interests, and instead prefer either self-delusion or doing without the fruits of instrumentality. In any case, such counterfactuals arising from the presumed practice of entire populations are beyond a work resolutely focused on intellectual categories expressed in individuals' actual practices.

To keep to such a method discounts the instrumental hypothesis practically, for the costs of cloaking such a rationality mount quickly. Indicative is the US Ambassador Loy Henderson's acerbic cable to the Secretary of State, Dean Acheson, in 1951 that Nehru is 'constitutionally unhappy when he [is] not leading some cause of downtrodden peoples … particularly Asian or colored peoples … against real or imagined oppression.'[80] Simultaneously, Nehru's recourse to Gandhian language—words such as 'honour' and 'high responsibilities'—actually delayed aid and perpetuated famine in the same year.[81] And in any case Nehru refused to act instrumentally and sell material that might be used in a nuclear war, to secure grain supplies.[82] Gandhian language and actual practice neither then granted the legitimacy to act internationally nor secured interests. Meanwhile, within India, recourse to Gandhi was actually a dangerous gamble. Gandhian language actually eroded Nehru's political capital because his electorate was dying, but on the other hand he might have been gaining moral points for being principled. As for identity, the failure of foreign policy due to Gandhian language could only produce a negative identity, one founded on failure. Nothing in what Nehru said and wrote shows this to have been his intention. Therefore, given the costs and uncertainty it is impossible to maintain that Nehru's recourse to Gandhi was instrumental, as claimed by modernist analysis.

Yet the hypothesis of the instrumental use of Gandhi persists, which is why modernist readings fluctuate between two heuristics and end up insisting that Nehruvian diplomacy is either realist or idealist.[83] A more sophisticated view, because of its return to causality, is Srinath Raghavan's heuristic that 'an admixture of liberal values and realist outlook … predisposed Nehru to favour coercive rather than controlling strategies.'[84] Any strict totting up of the facts, as is done for Nehru's time by Raghavan, will inevitably note that Nehru is coercive, in that when met with aggressive-violence he did not shy away from it but sought to challenge it—but, crucially, from another register. However, Raghavan has identified a practice of politics that cannot arise from the admixture of liberalism and realism—that is, from John Locke and Hobbes—because though the two seek to manage violence, their means are incompatible.[85] Indeed this is why Raghavan uses these two opposing categories to classify Nehru, for he perplexes the heuristics available to modernity. There is however a far deeper contradiction within liberalism, which harmonizes it with realism: they are both crafted from the same fabric, which is violence.[86] This compatibility is what makes both entirely incompatible with Nehru, for he neither was in awe of violence nor relied upon it. Instead Nehru managed violence from Gandhi's register. This becomes evident if analysis reliant on a combination of limited categories, resulting in an unstable heuristic, is cast aside for exegesis or the interpretation of Nehru in terms of his own intellectual contexts.

One such context that cannot be ignored is his movement towards Gandhi. Nehru grasped his way towards Gandhi, but not to use him as a cloak, for the intentionality thesis is hollow. The reason for Nehru's moves only begin to become evident if what he and Gandhi say about each other are taken sincerely, that is, if both are taken as 'authoritative sources'. To return to the principal players, in combination, is to realize the full weight of Nehru's struggle to reorder his intellectual setting and simultaneously imbues Gandhi's statement about Nehru's origins with a new significance: both, by virtue of sharing a cultural geography, draw upon the same civilizational resources. Nehru too engages the *Mb*, and his interpretation is familiar: 'Without this foundation of dharma there is no true happiness and society cannot hold together … for "the entire world of mortals is a self-dependent organism." Yet dharma itself is relative and depends on the times and the conditions prevailing, apart from some basic principles, such as adherence to truth, non-violence. These principles endure and do not change, but otherwise dharma, changes with the changing age.'[87]

This shared understanding with Gandhi permits moving towards what Raghavan's editors call for: deep and hard thinking about whether the Indian state's strategic thinking is a derivative discourse.[88] Raghavan's facts show that it is not—hence his invented heuristic. Avoiding the dissonance at the core of this heuristic is imperative, for it is founded on two heuristics that are themselves—as generally presented—irreconcilable with each other and Nehru's explanations. In other words, two wrongs do not make a right. Indeed they only cloak the full extent of Indian aims, that is, the possibilities impossible within modernity, which is why another set of categories arising from Nehru's engagement with Gandhi is vital.

While the move towards the art-of-politics manages Nehru's engagement with Gandhi without dismissing either, what is also clear is that Nehru was never able to fully grasp it. At the core of Nehru's struggles is that he understood *dharma* as contextual truth, but what he missed is that this is a facet of truth, the other component being highest-*dharma*. This connection does gain on Nehru but he never quite grasps that underpinning all of this is a causally neutral cosmos. That this is what necessitates non-violence is lost on Nehru. Instead he makes non-violence a principle, and in the process what is left out is what Gandhi developed from a logical rationalization of his rationalising base.

The result was the replacement of the integrated actor by one principled in the school of Gandhian practice. The difference lies in logically keeping to the art-of-politics and steeling oneself to act in a principled manner. That the latter became Nehru's way was possibly due to Gandhi making experience the means of the art-of-politics to manifest itself. 'In spite of the close association with Gandhi,' wrote Nehru, 'for many years, I am not clear in my own mind about his objective. I doubt if he is clear himself.'[89] Furthermore, Nehru's coming from modernity made it difficult for him to comprehend Gandhi's language.[90] Yet Nehru was moving towards replacing modernist assumptions with non-violence. The problem was that he simply replaced one set of originary ideas (anarchy, binarism) with another: non-violence.[91] A stage in this journey was his struggle with *satyagraha* as the means to conduct international relations. Nehru's modernist sensibilities clashed with Gandhi's in the summer of 1940. The outcome was a compromise resolution. Quoted at length in *Discovery of India*, it is significant because the author accepts non-violence as the framing principle for international politics.[92] This was the practical result of Nehru's incomprehension of the logic of Gandhi's rationality.

In a sense Nehru stuck with modernity, for he maintained modernity's notion of a coloured origin rather than a neutral cosmos. None of this detracts from the significance of his breakthrough, for he made the origin not anarchical-binarism but non-violence. This was Nehru's move-ment, but not much changed in the next decade. Within a year and a half of independence, Nehru reminded parliament: 'We were bred in a high tradition under Mahatma Gandhi. That tradition is an ethical tradition, a moral tradition and at the same time it is an application of those eth-ical and moral doctrines to practical politics. That great man placed before us a technique of action which was unique in the world, which combined political activity and political conflict and a struggle for freedom with certain moral and ethical principles.'

In using the word 'moral', Nehru replicates Gandhi's language and concept of truth or highest-*dharma*. In noting Gandhi's integration of both politics and violence with morality to maintain morality, Nehru is once again inching towards the art-of-politics. Yet the modernist in him remains. In the same speech Nehru said, 'We have to keep in mind those very ideals to which we have pledged ourselves so often.' These ideals are non-violence and truth, which Nehru said were for Gandhi an 'article of faith', and it is precisely this error that prevented Nehru from grasping the fundamental insight that motivates the art-of-politics: a unified and neutral cosmos. However, Nehru is travelling. He also said that 'we should do our utmost to live up as far as we can to that standard, but always judging a problem by the light of our own intelligence; otherwise we will fail.'[93] In short, Gandhi's comprehensive package, the art-of-politics, is at this time for Nehru a doctrine where non-violence has been reduced from the result of a coherent philosophy to an 'article of faith' central to the maintenance of a moral self.

Nehru never became fully consonant with Gandhi's thought. This was evident in an interview with Rustom Karanjia in 1960.[94] That text, closer to a debate than an interview, provides a clear indication of Nehru's ratio-nality towards the end of life and during the time of the China crisis. A standard issue mimic man because he was moving in the opposite direc-tion to Nehru, Karanjia reproduced the old binaries—science versus tra-dition—and asked if Nehru used Gandhi instrumentally: 'the Gandhian era ended with the assumption of political power by the Congress. The year 1947 ushered in what is universally hailed as the Nehru epoch of our country. Should I be right in the inference that from Freedom onwards, you used the Gandhian means to serve the Nehru ends ....' Nehru demolished Karanjia's instrumental reading founded on divisive-ness by answering:

You are wrong in using words like the Nehru epoch or the Nehru policy. I would call ours the authentic Gandhian era and the policies and philosophy and philosophy which we seek to implement are the policies and philosophy taught to us by Gandhiji. There has been no break in the continuity of our thoughts before and after 1947, though, of course, new technological and scientific advances since have made us re-think in some ways and adapt our policies to the new times. But here also Gandhiji was in many ways prophetic. His thoughts and approaches and solutions helped us to cover the chasm between the Industrial Revolution and the Nuclear Era. After all, the only possible answer to the Atom Bomb is non-violence. Isn't it?

Nehru is, quite plainly, a principled Gandhian. This was both his strength and his weakness because by missing Gandhi's integrity, Nehru had to be brave to keep to Gandhi's 'principles'. Of course, if his logic were understood then Nehru would be motivated by much more than a man or principles, he would realize that his actions had to be non-violent to be in consonance with the cosmos itself.

The certitude of Nehru's answers about the role of Gandhi in India's foreign policy led Karanjia to mount a sort of defence for the modern. He did so by suggesting that Nehru had 'gone beyond non-violence to the discovery of a more positive solution to this threat of the atom bomb in Panch Sheel or the Doctrine of Peaceful Co-existence.' Evident is the modern's inability to tolerate what is evidently the operation of another rationality. However, Karanjia's hopes were dashed because Nehru's reply was:

All that was inherent in Gandhism. In fact, this approach of Panch Sheel, co-existence, peace, tolerance, the attitude of live and let live, has been fundamental to Indian thought throughout the ages and you find it in all religions. Great emperors like Ashoka practised it and Gandhiji organised it into a practical philosophy of action which we have inherited. There was no place for the 'cold war' in Ashoka's mind, and Gandhiji gave the world the most practical substitute for war and violence by bringing about a mighty revolution with the bloodless weapon of passive resistance.

Nehru's diplomacy is quite evidently Gandhian. Nehru has also learned that Gandhi developed a philosophy and that it is lodged in practice and provides a means of acting. The interview now reached a crescendo, for the real question about which the debate revolved was what is the rationale for Nehru's actions. Karanjia defended what Nehru had cast aside by attacking him. Karanjia finally asked if the 'conviction amongst pro-

gressives that Gandhiji broke and emasculated your earlier faith in scientific Socialism with his sentimental and spiritual solutions' was true.
Nehru replied:

Some of Gandhiji's approaches were old-fashioned, and I combated them ....
But on the whole it is wrong to say that he broke or emasculated me or anybody
else. Any such thing would be against his way of doing things. The most important thing he insisted upon was the importance of means: ends were shaped by
the means that led to them, and therefore the means had to be good, pure and
truthful. That is what we learnt from him and it is well we did so.

Nehru accepted the metaphysics of context. He noted that this did
not permit breaking or emasculating because that is aggressive-violence.
Nehru therefore made the connection between means and ends. Nehru
also inverted the modernist notion of sacrificing the present to realize
the future. But nowhere did Nehru say he understood the link between
contextual truth and highest-*dharma*, which is at the nub of Gandhi's
art-of-politics. This is why Nehru repeatedly emphasized that he follows
a man, rather than the *dharma*-complex.

Arguably Nehru did not have to grasp what was Gandhi's truth, since
he was not a philosopher-king, only a king. As king he put into practice
the practical elements from a rationality alternative not because he
grasped it but because he was, said Manmohan Singh repeatedly, 'a stal-
wart, committed to Gandhi'.[95] Though his integrity was reduced to principles, they were enough to inaugurate an unprecedented invention
enabling a diplomatic practice 'of a different kind, carried on in a different register, at odds with and in defiance of power politics.'[96] This was
Non-Alignment,[97] and though its inventor was unaware of the consistency that produced it, the policy kept with Gandhi's art-of-politics by
doing away with modernity's telos to deliver freedom immediately in a
courageous act. This is because to be non-aligned is not to succumb to
the sticks and carrots meted out by the soliciting superpowers, but to
actively engage that violence with resistance. In doing so the Non-Aligned
Movement (NAM) crafts, in the face of the miasma that is the international, a unity that is denied intellectually by modernity and practically
by borders.

Nehru had moved a great distance from modernity by replacing its
anarchical binary foundations with the principle of non-violence.
Notwithstanding this, Nehru never completed his journey because he
remained principled. What this means for the practice of Indian diplo-

macy is that while it is startlingly different from modern diplomacy, intellectually the difference is muted by the reliance on the notion of the principle. Also explained is why Nehru's inheritors in the main operate—at best—mechanically, by rote learning of principles because they are 'good' rather than on the basis of insight into why they are virtuous. Insight is desired because it provides flexibility by making for a reflecting, intertextual actor as opposed to the modernist automaton. Despite having its intellectual basis undermined, practice remained resolutely Gandhian. 'Everything we do is in Gandhi,' said a top diplomat, reiterating how Indian diplomats replicate—as principle—Gandhian thought over 60 years of Indian diplomacy, from first Foreign Secretary (FS), K.P.S. Menon, to the first National Security Advisor (NSA), J.N. Dixit.[98]

The diplomatic apparatus

The MEA's diplomacy, though capable of realizing the possibilities offered by the art-of-politics by keeping to its techniques, cannot operate with the élan engendered by logical understanding. The reasons for this lie only partly with Nehru being hobbled by his principled approach. Nehru's approach was compounded by his material: the MEA's mimic men who were travelling in the opposite direction to him. He stopped their trajectory and rendered them no more than functionaries to put into practice an art-of-politics reduced to principles. Nor could Nehru ever trust them, for to be principled is an act of great will engendered by a mentor. Nehru had Gandhi, but what of the MEA? Nehru knew that an even greater amount of will was required of its staff because they were drawn from the Residency system which was backward, authoritarian and exploitative in style in the words of one product, K.M. Panikkar—the man who invented the term Southeast Asia.[99]

These functionaries were drawn from the 600 or so non-whites who had been reluctantly let into the Indian Civil Service (ICS). Of them about 100 opted for Pakistan.[100] The remainder, of whom only a handful had served in the Political Line, along with some new recruits made up the foreign policy establishment of independent India. Their input was limited to enacting Nehru's principles, for he feared his bureaucrats would be unable to replicate his own intellectual movement. 'Of one thing,' Nehru said he was 'quite sure': (in very Gandhian language) '... no new order can be built up in India so long as the spirit of the ICS pervades our administration and our public services ... the ICS and similar service must disappear completely, as such, before we can start real work on a new order.'[101] Hobbled from inception, it meant that the MEA was never able to perform with the dynamism that Gandhi was able to produce in his engagements (which had nothing of course to do with how others thought what his encounters should be).

Nehru to a degree was able to reproduce this by the sheer will of his commitment to Gandhi, but in this he was well aware of the limitations of his officers, writing that the 'services were fossilised in their mental outlook. They were wedded to bygone and obsolete methods and refused to move with the times ... It remains to be seen how long we can function in these circumstances. The experience of the past three or four months has shown us that the conduct and attitude of the officers has not changed.'[102]

Yet Nehru had to rely on these people to operationalize the *Ramarajya*. He therefore persisted in attempting to reboot his staff with a completely new software which he saw himself as uniquely familiar with. In practical terms the result was Nehru leading on all significant matters and the MEA declining into a highly hierarchical organization, under constant scrutiny because it was presumed incapable of living up to Gandhi's principles. As Nehru wrote, 'checking and constant supervision are necessary.' But Nehru did not do this for mundane reasons, for he added, 'To hold up work for petty sanctions from distant authority is not only to delay but to waste money and energy. It is not sufficiently realised that time in this context is money.'[103] And so, Nehru was trapped between principles and micro-management. As he also wrote: 'Constant supervision is, of course, always necessary,' but he must carry it out in a way that does not 'impede work'.[104] The vice-like grip Nehru and the MEA found themselves caught in was due to the conversion of Gandhi's art-of-politics into principle.

Yet the MEA did function, admirably at times. Indicative is the manner in which Nehru put to work G.S. Bajpai. A former ICS officer, he has been characterized as a British 'stooge,'[105] and had clashed with Gandhi on personal[106] and political matters.[107] Yet Nehru relied on him almost completely on matters international, to the surprise of many including the Cabinet Secretary Vishnu Sahay. When he questioned the wisdom of employing Bajpai, Nehru replied: 'That may be, but almost before I have completed a sentence, the man produces a draft perfectly stating my views and conclusions. He does it so well that I then have merely to sign without even altering a comma.'[108] Bajpai, a mimic man par excellence, was the perfect technocrat. But that is all Nehru permitted of him, to put in place—not formulate—policy and to do it not just well, but tastefully.[109]

That the mimic men were not called upon to devise policy is evident during the most significant crisis during Nehru's tenure—the China confrontation—when Bajpai opposed the Prime Minister's (PM's) policy and was ignored.[110] Such a course is impossible for modernists, but contextualizing Nehru in Gandhi can explain the reason: Bajpai was ignored because Nehru was certain that his course had to follow Gandhi, understood not as modernity understands him, but in terms of the rationality he modified and kept to. That Nehru brushed aside contrary advice also gives the lie to the Australian diplomat, Walter Crocker's, assessment that Nehru's Office was plagued by 'sycophancy, personal ad-hoc approaches, and mixture of amateurishness and subjectivity,' because only a few senior officers had access to the PM.[111] Bajpai had access and opposed and was ignored, but Crocker could not grasp the reason for this, and instead resorted to his modernist hermeneutic to explain away the working of the MEA with 'amateurishness and subjectivity'. This early example of analytical-violence was inevitable because Crocker was unfamiliar with the texture of Indian diplomacy; otherwise Crocker would have known that Nehru's office was not a failure because the purpose was not to be 'modern' at all. And yet, to this day, the charge of Indian diplomacy being childishly incapable persists. What is inexplicable, however, is that popularizers, for instance Ramachandra Guha, refuse to take Nehru as authoritative, even about himself. Instead Guha continues to analyze Nehru with reference to Crocker—a man limited by his own intellectual tradition to conceptualizing diplomacy as nothing else than the will to assimilate.[112]

On an altogether different road, Nehru put the Non-Aligned Movement (NAM) into operation. While its very alterity may only be accounted for in terms of the *metis* of the *Mb* interpreted by Gandhi, NAM was nevertheless the product of the principled operationalizing of the art-of-politics. A Cabinet Secretary at the time highlighted how Nehru, as the sole spokesman for that tradition, inculcated it singlehandedly into the foreign policy of the state:

In the field of defining policies, the Prime Minister's role has been overwhelming. Take foreign policy. It was his [Nehru's] special genius to establish that, in the circumstances of his time, non-alignment was the right policy of India. In this he was far in advance of his advisors. If he had followed the advice of people around him, India would have started as an aligned State …. Of our foreign policy, it may truly be said he was both the architect and the main implementer.

Nehru's 'special genius' was of course his ability to stick to a principled stance. However, Nehru was clear that not many in the MEA were capable of reproducing his principled stance. The ICS officer S. Kesava Iyengar who was Principle Secretary to Nehru confirmed the low opinion Nehru had of his like:

I think it would be correct to say that while he was most kindly and considerate to many of us in the service as individuals, he did not think of us, as a class, as being particularly distinguished. We were there to do a job. Some of us were good and some mediocre, but we were not people with whom it was appropriate for him to discuss the pros and cons of the kind of problem that was thrown up to the Prime Minister of India. In other words … one did not get the impression that one had any share in the making of decisions.[113]

Even a member of the first cabinet wrote: 'My five years experience in the Cabinet [was] that no one would say a word against Nehru. … and even Cabinet members dared not oppose him, let alone the civil servants.'[114] It meant that power coalesced in the Prime Minister's Office (PMO) and the PM made decisions, because at the dawn of the *Ramarajya* Nehru was loath to trust any of the bureaucrats he inherited, for they were deemed incapable of being as principled in the Mahatma's ways as Nehru himself was. This was exacerbated by the fact that Nehru was incapable of training his officers. All he could do as a principled follower was to excoriate them for being unable to live up to Gandhi's example. Indeed Nehru found it easier to rely upon himself than to train a new cadre. 'One result was that External Affairs Ministry did not get into the habit of producing situation reports stating the considerations, analysing them and presenting options. There was a marked tendency to wait for the word from the PM himself.'[115] The PM became the prime repository for principled Gandhian policy and the MEA simply a cypher, owing to a lack of training in the ways of principled Gandhian action.

This lack of training explains why diplomacy remains centralized—far in excess of any other policy area—in the PMO to this day. In the 123 Agreement negotiations the decision to negotiate was the PM's and only a handful of people—less than a dozen—played a role in formulating the negotiating position and participated in the actual negotiations. That the

THE MAKING OF INDIAN DIPLOMACY

officers who participated were not the top people, such as the Secretaries who assisted the FS (though both Shyam Saran and Shivshankar Menon were instrumental), is because the PMO relied on the total-evaluations process.[116] This was necessary because the conduct of foreign policy is a principled matter, which therefore necessitates a total-evaluations process. All this keeps to the past.

The PMO's grip on all matters pertaining to foreign policy continued unabated from Nehru's time to today. For instance, the establishment of the foreign intelligence service, the Research and Analysis Wing (RAW). The PM's singular role is described by a former FS, Rajeshwar Dayal:

> One day the Director, RN Kao, came to me with a brief typewritten note and asked for my signature … the request was made casually, as though it was a matter of minor routine. But one glance at the paper took me aback. [it said a new service for external intelligence was to be created and that the MEA should include the names of the operatives to ensure cover …] When I asked when the decision was taken I was told blandly that it had been taken by the PM! It seemed extraordinary that a far reaching decision which so obviously and intimately concerned External Affairs should have been taken without a word of consultation with that Ministry.[117]

Though decisions remain prime ministerial, officers do—on occasion—have some ability to influence policy on practical matters. Brajesh Mishra was therefore able to force his point on the PM when Mao Zedong smiled at him. Most officers however are not principled enough to push their case—some do not have the principles.[118] This becomes apparent in the type of policy papers put up to the FS and ultimately the PM. It was only as recently as 2004 that the chiefs of the various territorial divisions began to actually 'stick their neck out' and put forward actual policy decisions. Until then, territorial division heads put up a series of options to the FS. It was under FS Shyam Saran that they were encouraged to not stop at putting forward options but to also state what ought to be done, 'because they are supposed to be the experts.'[119]

A few weeks before his death Nehru is reported to have said his greatest failure was not to have succeeded in decolonizing the modernist mentality of the administration: 'I failed to change this administration. It is still a colonial administration.'[120] The solution to Nehru's quest escaped him because of his fundamental inability to grasp Gandhi's thought. Despite this failure, the moves toward a representative bureaucracy have been the back door through which Gandhi's rationality has been reintroduced into the state, for the people who compose it today are not modern at inception. Positive discrimination, under way for decades, began in 1951, with reservations for groups designated Scheduled Caste/ Scheduled Tribe (SC/ST). The policy received a great impetus in 1979 when candidates were allowed to take the entrance exams in any Indian language. With this, the services were opened to a mass of people who had always been excluded from positions of authority.[121] Major changes followed, the most momentous being the broadening of positive discrimination to 50% in 1992 by the Mandal Commission. It spurred on the proliferation of non-modern peoples and ways into an Imperial and Anglicized bureaucracy.

Yet the MEA remains a principled rather than a rational actor, because it attempts to live up to Gandhi's integrity via Nehru's principles. The only means to restore the consistency at the heart of Gandhi's thought and the tradition he drew upon is to surface in the diplomats who compose the MEA the logic implicit in their actions and expressed by Gandhi and implemented by Nehru: in short, to make manifest the art-of-politics. Doing so will permit diplomats to escape from the confines of rote learning principles—frequently muddled, as my attachment taught me, with passion incorrectly expressed in the language of nationalism—to be able to actually perform to the maximum what is rendered permissible by Gandhi's, that is their rationality. The remarkable practices that compose their lives are evidence enough. In other words, the example is the instinctive manner in which diplomats access the state—that is, realize impossible possibilities with unprecedented efficiency and effectiveness. To be fair, the outcome of the MEA's deliberations is really no different from the purpose of its staff, because actions continue to be generated by an instinctual rationality of being and acting (no matter how misunderstood): the art-of-politics. What is lost, however, is efficiency, and the reason is the burden of being principled.

Satyagraha *in practice: Pakistan and China*

It was in the context of this intellectual shift, started but never completed, that Nehru was overtaken by events: war with Pakistan and China. In other words he engaged the international without ever having grasped the art-of-politics or having made the MEA principled enough (something only necessitated, of course, by the positing of an ideal). The Pakistan and

China conflicts are archetypical exegetical sites as they rumble on both materially and also intellectually in the absence of explanations in the language of the protagonists. The purpose in recounting the two conflicts, then, is not to describe details again, but to demonstrate how those details are only sensible if read in categories that have never been used to understand them. To view the conflicts in terms of the art-of-politics is therefore to make for exegesis free from the vacuities of instrumental readings and not undone by contradictions within the category for analysis.

Nehru has already provided the appropriate categories to understand his actions. There is his general acceptance of non-violence as the frame for diplomacy and Gandhi's rationality, albeit followed in a principled manner. This approach is apparent in a speech about the two crises made in August 1963:

First of all, right at the beginning, after our independence there was a general background of our not spending too much money on the army … We decided to save money on defence and apply it to industrialisation … We hoped that the cease-fire in Kashmir (1st January 1948) would result in some kind of settlement and we saw no other country likely to attack us and so we decided to reduce the strength of our army.[122]

Nehru sought to prepare for conflict, but in Gandhi's sense—that is, never to recoil from aggressive-violence but to seek it out and match it with resistance. It made for his 'no war' pact with Pakistan, because for him it was an article of faith to engender change non-violently. When this was accepted in 1956, Nehru was jubilant for he had new confidence in the ability to act truthfully. As he told Parliament in 1956: 'It is not by military methods or threats of war or by talking to each other from so-called positions of strength that we shall come nearer … We can develop strength in other ways, strength in friendship, in cooperation and through raising the standard of our people.'[123] But within a year his tone changed. He acknowledged that 'Pakistan's mind was tied up with violence and hatred against India' but his belief in Gandhi's ideas, understood as a principled stance, stood: 'At any rate we are not going to reply in kind. We will continue to be friendly with them.'[124] That he felt he alone was principled enough to follow Gandhi in the international realm was clear in 1962 when Nehru said: 'We are getting out of touch with reality in the modern world, and we were living in an artificial atmosphere of our own creation.'[125] He could not know how correct he was, but also how misunderstood he would be.[126] Realizing that he had been misconstrued, as speaking of administrative failure arising from detachment from everyday India, Nehru strenuously clarified soon after the initial comment: What I meant was that this world is cruel. We had thought in terms of carrying the banner of peace everywhere and we were betrayed. China betrayed us; the world has betrayed us. Our efforts to follow the path of peace have been knocked on the head. We are forced to prepare for a defensive war, much against our will.'[127]

Nehru was learning that not only was he the only principled Gandhian actor on the international stage, but also he could not elicit the required response with the fluid ease his mentor did with the Raj. Though Nehru learned this, he was incapable of realizing that the reason might have been his having misunderstood his mentor's rationality.

Yet Nehru persevered, and the ground for doing so were laid for him by Pakistan's invasion of Kashmir, which provided an opportunity for a perfect example of *satyagraha*. It is well known that the King of Kashmir's response to the invasion was to transfer responsibility to the populist politician, Sheikh Abdullah, and that Gandhi thought he was the true representative of Kashmiris. Abdullah asked for Indian help, which was conditional on accession to India. Abdullah agreed. The King signed the instrument of accession and Indian troops, after having fought for imperialism in one guise or another for nearly three centuries, for the first time fought an action that can only be termed a *satyagraha*. Regardless of how the action is conceived elsewhere, for Gandhi and India the soldiers were resisting immorality, for Pakistan's violence was aggressive-violence and therefore a total negation of truth.[128] The resistance, though by an army, was different enough from the violence that Pakistan attempted to be classed as non-violent.

The difference between the use of force by Pakistan and by India lay in no one aspect of the clash, but in the entire set of calculations that produced it. Pakistan's immorality began with aggressive-violence, but it could have been an act of resistance incomprehensible to the Indians. Gandhi however had no doubts, because Pakistan lied about the invasion. The denial meant Pakistan could not be moral, for truth does not need to be cloaked. In brief, *dharma* makes for individuated truth and Pakistan (for ease) is entitled to its *dharma* and to act upon it. For Gandhi this was highest-*dharma* and in combination with *dharma*, the answer was truth. However, Pakistan's lies were only necessitated because the practices were not in consonance with truth but something else, which could not be uttered for that would reveal it for what it was. This was compounded by the unwillingness to cease hostilities. Gandhi said: 'If there are raids from outside the frontier of Kashmir, the obvious conclusion is that it must be with the connivance of Pakistan. Pakistan can deny it. But the denial does not settle the matter. … They keep saying that they want an amicable settlement but they do nothing to create the conditions for such a settlement.'[129] Some time later he added: 'I can understand it if every outsider leaves Kashmir and no one interferes from outside or sends help or complains. But I cannot understand it if they (Pakistan) say that they themselves will remain in Kashmir but that others should get out.'

Gandhi's inability to understand arose from his experience of *satyagraha*. His traditional target, the British, by and large maintained his faith by responding in a truthful way, which gave him the courage to expect the same from India's Muslims—the very people Pakistan sought to radicalize because they were expected to operate on the basis of fragmentation. However, Pakistan was unable to undo the centuries-old permeation of Islam by the rationality of *dharma*. Indeed Kashmir is where one of the earliest translations of the *Mb* had been made. Gandhi knew however that Pakistan would be unable to radicalise Indian Muslims for a different set of reasons. As a *satyagrahi* he was courageous and willing to bear violence to minimize its effects as part of the wider project of maintaining the truth, and in doing so he always gave the benefit of the doubt because the base assumption was not an 'other' but another. It made him say of Indian Muslims: 'Why should we not so conduct ourselves that any conflict between India and Pakistan becomes impossible? We must be brave and trust the Muslims. If later they violate the trust you can cut off their heads.'[130] The invasion received no moral or any support from Indian Muslims. Gandhi's trust arising from his notion of a unified cosmos ensured that Pakistan's attempts at radicalization were destined to fail.

But was this *satyagraha*? Gandhi said, 'I do not agree that the armed force our Government has dispatched to Kashmir has committed aggression there.'[131] The troops for Gandhi were resisters, but resistance itself is a form of violence, which is why Gandhi found it 'barbarous' that he had to resist.[132] But evidently this was a *satyagraha* because of how it was made sense of. The action was in keeping with the art-of-politics, and was therefore contextual. This is why Gandhi turned to the Kashmiri people, to explain the *satyagraha*: 'The simple fact is that Pakistan has invaded Kashmir. Units of the Indian army have gone to Kashmir but not to invade Kashmir. They have been sent on the express invitation of the Maharaja and Sheikh Abdullah. Sheikh Abdullah is the real Maharaja of Kashmir. Muslims in their thousands are devoted to him.'[133]

What ensured the action was *satyagraha* was that it kept to the cosmological approach. First, India's defence of Kashmir enjoyed the sanction of both the King (the old regime perpetuated by the British) and Sheikh Abdullah. In short, there was popular support and across the board, thereby matching the numerous contexts which made for Kashmir in light of an armed aggression that threatened to engulf all in the state. The action was also a *satyagraha* because it had no intention of exceeding the goal of maintaining *Ramarajya* by extending territorial control—rather, territory was sacrificed. But this did not make for the very modern notion of sacrificing the present for the future, for those who sacrificed themselves had no future. Instead all there was on offer was the present where action was conducted to live truthfully by defending it. For India not to have done so would have meant yielding to aggressive-violence, and hence made for a betrayal of the truth. Gandhi's secretary Pyarelal knew this. He wrote: 'It was therefore right for the Union Government to save the fair city by rushing troops to Srinagar. He [Gandhi] would not shed a tear if the little Union force was wiped out bravely defending Kashmir like the Spartan at Thermopylae.'[134] The analogy is not perfect but within the art-of-politics, Indian resistance is perfectly sensible. As Ganeri writes, 'what is in question is not how the practice is made, but how it is made sense of, and that is what preserves each of the virtues involved as itself an intrinsic good.'[135]

Kashmir demonstrated that it was possible for a state to perform Gandhian policy. However, the China war remains contested for a plethora of reasons coalescing around not a dearth of facts but analysis of those facts in a manner ignorant of the decision maker's *metis*. The result is analysis riddled with ruptures that form, for instance, in Alastair Lamb's and Neville Maxwell's work because of their inability to follow the wealth of accumulated evidence to the conclusion it presents.[136] In short, they follow the White Rabbit but refuse to enter the rabbit hole. Instead, they manage the lacuna in their explanations by retreating and reproducing a modern mentality and foisting it upon Nehru, which is inexplicable as these categories appear nowhere in the texts Nehru has left behind or in his practice of diplomacy.[137] The only other explanation, of course, is that Nehru was an arch-liar. To see how Lamb and Maxwell impose their rationality is to return to the genesis of the crisis. It originates with a difference in where the border was, and India's handling of the matter is understood as aggressive-violence, 'cartographical aggression'. For Lamb, 'the official Indian interpretation of documents did not accord with what the documents in question actually said,' and a 'senior official in the Indian High Commission in London,' to whom Lamb presented his findings, 'could not have been less interested.' Lamb essentially forwards Maxwell's analysis arguing that India's aggression over maps is what led to war. The milestones of this story are that from 1959 India refused to negotiate with the Chinese, whose border agreements during the 1950s and 60s with numerous other countries are taken as a symbol of good faith by Lamb and Maxwell. Neither finds India's legal case credible. Both forward a wealth of detail to argue for India's inability to understand the 'historical' position. Both then hypothesize that the explanation for Indian aggression is that the Chinese claim on Aksai Chin, if taken seriously, would weaken India's case against Pakistan, and this made Nehru resort to occupying disputed territory: the Forward Policy.

Explicit in this reading is the imposition of a modernist mentality, and implicit is another assumption, the assertion that Indians are incapable of managing international relations peacefully. Such postulations are necessary because it is only with them that what is incalculable in terms of modernist interpretation can be calculated. Intending to resolve this analytic-violence, Raghavan accumulates even more facts that serve to ameliorate it (as the totting up of everything in a causal universe undoubtedly does). However, an unwieldy and contradictory intellectual setting—liberal realism—is used to integrate the light shed by the new facts. This logical incoherence is easily avoided by adopting the most salient fact of them all: the category Nehru himself said he relied upon, Gandhi.

Once again, to take Indians as 'authoritative sources' is to present practice in context. Raghavan's detailed work highlights the immediate context. It was a note by the Indian Ambassador in Nanking, K.M. Panikkar, stating that with Britain's withdrawal, India became 'in law the successor to British rights in Tibet.'[138] This was couched in a deeper contextual and practice-based reading of the past, expressed in Nehru telling parliament that the border from Nepal to Ladakh was defined 'chiefly by long usage and custom'.[139] The invasion of Tibet altered the context by bringing China proper up to India in 1950. This worried Nehru but he remained committed to seeking 'some kind of understanding of China'.[140] Meetings between Panikkar and the Chinese Premier Zhou Enlai followed, but the latter remained silent on the border issue. This broad context was narrowed by FS K.P.S. Menon in 1952 seeing 'on the walls of the Military Academy in Chengtu, a map, showing China as it was and ought to be and including large portions of Kashmir. This is perhaps the real reason for the Chinese reluctance to discuss the problem of Tibet with us.'[141]

Always sensitive to context, Nehru feared 'some kind of gradual spreading out or infiltration.'[142] Faced with China's refusal to discuss the issue, Nehru, under Panikkar's guidance, enacted a policy of strengthening India's position.[143] In practice this meant safeguarding truth in its physical expression—*Ramarajya*. It required emphasizing the common experiences that underlay the freedom struggle.[144] If the experience that made for a *Ramarajya* was remote in the borderlands, arguably Peking was even more distant. India's strategy, then, was a principled extension of Gandhi's attempts at harmonization, and it began because the Chinese chose to ignore the issue, which is why once again in 1953 the border was not discussed.[145] That Nehru chose Pannikar's option is indicative, for he could have gone with Bajpai's advice that rather than acquiesce in Chinese silence, India ought to push for a final settlement.[146] Bajpai, an arch modernist, had always been a critic of Nehruvian foreign policy which he read as confined to 'protestations of non-alignment in Cold War and to senseless chatter about colonialism, racial discrimination, etc.'[147] What Bajpai missed is that Nehru could not enforce a final agreement over and above the people in those regions, for to do so would amount to ignoring them and that would contradict truth. But this did not mean fleeing from aggressive-violence, for that too would betray truth. As Raghavan concludes, 'the nub of Pannikar's argument' was that 'so long as China was unwilling to rake up the matter, India should use the time to make its position effective in the frontier areas, where its administrative hold was weak and its political position fledgling.'[148]

And so Bajpai was ignored and India followed Pannikar's policy. That Nehru opted for this indicates that what was put in place was Gandhi's art-of-politics in its fullest expression: *satyagraha*. Nehru was willing to wait, to surface the morality which propelled him in the border regions and create a *Ramarajya* rather than force an agreement with China over the heads of the border peoples, which would undermine everything he, as a principled follower of Gandhi, believed. As a probationer upon his return from one of the still disputed regions said, 'I saw orders from the 1960s saying that [the region] should be integrated socially and politically into India.' He added, 'but today [people living there] look across the border to China and want to join them because they are so much more developed.'[149]

During negotiations with China Nehru's conviction that the Chinese would respond in the correct manner, in the context of pressures from within his polity, was shaken. Committed to negotiating the border issue at some point, Nehru began to prepare and issued a directive for definitive new maps and the establishment of check posts.[150] The new border placed Aksai Chin—an area in the Western sector of the border—within India. This has been taken by Maxwell as conclusive proof of Indian aggression, manifested in the bid to unilaterally settle matters.[151] However, such a reading takes no account of China's unwillingness to discuss the border. Nehru therefore decided to prepare a case so as to avoid being presented by a *fait accompli* akin to Tibet's annexation. Lamb, speculating about the origins of the map of 1954, writes: 'Where did this border come from? Perhaps it was simply that someone in the Survey of India merely copied from some old and dusty file left over from British times and the product of British Russophobia.'[152] The point is not where it came from, but that Zhou Enlai did not object to it.[153] Later China upped the ante and surreptitiously encroached on territory—which was at best contested—by building a road.[154]

It produced a 'sense of disquiet' in Nehru.[155] In 1957 Zhou visited India and yet again did not question India's portrayal of the border.[156] As late as 1960 Nehru and the MEA were unconvinced about protesting against Chinese incursions into Aksai Chin because it was, from India's perspective, contested territory, not sovereign territory.[157] India, in short, staked a claim but kept open the option of negotiating the sector, without pushing the issue. It was a case of meeting aggressive-violence but without replicating it. The situation changed with China changing the terms of the engagement. From not wanting to discuss the border, Zhou swung to claiming that the entire boundary was not demarcated,[158] and manufactured a critical moment in India-China relations.[159] The dissolution of the entire border by China—given its behaviour in both Tibet and Aksai Chin—could not be ignored by a modernist, but is vital to the art-of-politics given its focus on contextual action. An explanation for the change in China's position might have been India's granting refuge to the Dalai Lama in 1959.[160] It was at this juncture, in 1960, that Sarvepalli Gopal returned from London and convinced Nehru that India could draw the line at Aksai Chin.[161]

Gopal had an assistant—Jagat Mehta of the MEA—whose commentary on the map mission sheds crucial light on the mentality governing India's diplomacy. Mehta writes that 'the vast literature on the India-China boundary question overlooks the fact that our report was not a doctoral thesis on the merits of the case. It was advocacy to support the given stand of our government.'[162] The given stand was of course founded on a contextual understanding of where the *Ramarajya* was hemmed in, and though it was not debated in parliament or in cabinet until 1959, neither did China question the stand. Meanwhile there had been a series of clashes which Nehru took as the 'culmination of progressive Chinese unfriendliness towards India'.[163] Bolstered by Gopal's report and increasingly wary of Chinese intentions, Nehru wrote: 'Such a basis for negotiations would ignore past history, custom, tradition and international agreements.'[164] Once again, it was practice that guided his position, but he was becoming increasingly doubtful about the expectation of the correct moral response from the Chinese.[165]

Having defined the terms of the debate explicitly—using Gopal's maps—a *satyagrahi* is however willing to wait it out, accept violence inflicted on the self in the attempt to inculcate a moral response. India, that is Nehru, at first glance proved incapable of bearing the costs of *satyagraha*. There was the notion of an exchange of territory, but as Nehru wrote: 'If I give them that I shall no longer be Prime Minister of India—I will not do it.'[166] It was not the threat of dissolution that prevented Nehru from a territorial swap but the lack of virtue demanded by the strictest of *satyagrahi*s: Nehru was unwilling to sacrifice his prime ministership. However, this reading is misplaced because it contradicts the rationality that produced it. The art-of-politics cannot take over territory to the point of re-colonization, because that is to betray truth. Senior cabinet members thought that Nehru would be 'out of office as Prime Minister' if he ceded territory to the Chinese,[167] and it is precisely in thinking that it was to save himself that the proponents of this view expose the threat that Nehru was meeting. Surrounded by modernists in the MEA, and parliament, the only means of conducting the art-of-politics in the international was Nehru. In short, if he went it would mark the end of the *Ramarajya*. Its preservation is also what ruled out a land swap because it may not have resulted in a 'final settlement'. The fear was that Aksai Chin would be the 'thin edge of a wedge,' and would be used by China to prise more territory from India because of how China had changed its nego-tiating position.[168] As Mountbatten observed, Nehru 'was greatly shaken by their duplicity'.[169] If India did accede to Chinese demands there was no knowing, given past behaviour, where that road would lead. At the close of the 1960 summit between China and India the position had become intractable. The MEA Secretary General N.R. Pillai explained, 'if they (India) gave way now on this matter, it will only encourage the Chinese to feel that they were weak and to press even more ambitious claims later'.[170] Furthermore, in the crucial area of Aksai Chin, Zhou was unwilling to concede anything. He insisted that China had all along been in effective control of the area shown by their claim lines, something that clearly illustrated Chinese dishonesty because all China had done was maintain a stony silence, never contesting India's position.[171] In other words, to give in to the Chinese would have eradicated truth. Thus the only option was to continue to match the Chinese, but not in their idiom, rather in the language of the art-of-politics, and that is precisely what was done. Ultimately, the Forward Policy arose from Nehru aspiring to establish the truth of his stated position (open to contestation but unchal-lenged) by harmonizing the border regions to create a *Ramarajya* as sug-gested by Pannikar, rather than arriving at a resolution over the heads of the people who would have been directly affected. To do so was to act in terms of the art-of-politics by facing aggressive-violence, but without resorting to aggressive-violence both within and without the state. It is in this sense that, as with Pakistan, Nehru was entitled to act to defend truth, but it was, to use Gandhi's word, 'barbarous' that he had been made to do so.

Conclusions

To present the Pakistan and China crises in terms of what is probably the most significant relationship in Indian history should not be a nov-elty. Unexpectedly it is, which may have something to with the fact that restoring that relationship to its rightful place in—to use modernity's categories—the 'history' of the 'modern nation-state' also does away with those classifications. But it was not to stem modern analysis's complicity in the reordering of entire populations that such a move was made. Rather the purpose was to eliminate analytical-violence and untenable heuristic devices. Doing so was possible by tracing the percolation of ideas between Nehru and Gandhi (though only one side of what undoubtedly was a two-way flow has been presented) to reveal the art-of-politics and Nehru's use of it. When Indian diplomacy is viewed in the terms of that intellectual exchange, the credibility of both is restored. Deleted too is the contention that Nehru was insincere, and negated is the notion that his mentor, a man who could reach out across the abyss modernity created and touch its intellectual wastelands, would have no impact on the workings of the state he helped create. That the art-of-politics can satisfy the exegetic impulse by keeping to the practitioners without recourse to violence is testimony to how successfully Nehru stuck to his principles, and disproves the belief that India practiced a 'derivative' diplomatic practice, that is power politics. We now turn to the question of whether principled Nehruvianism continued beyond his term.

7

VIOLENCE OF IGNORANCE

India will … not prepare for or think in terms of any aggression or dominion over any other country. Defence thus becomes purely defence against external aggression or internal disorder.

— Jawaharlal Nehru[1]

Verifying whether the *Ramarajya* capitulated to modernity after Nehru requires a consistent terrain for exegesis. Nuclear diplomacy provides the ideal landscape for it is coterminous with the modern nation-state and also exceeds its 'history'. Nuclear policy is also the only facet of Indian diplomacy to have been subjected to both the analytical tools in modernity's quiver: realist and postcolonial (poco). These two schools however simply replay the clash between O'Hanlon/Washbrook and Prakash. At the empirical core of both readings is the same linear story: the 123 Agreement (123) as the culmination of a process beginning with idealism, and followed by a period of 'ad hocism'.[2] In keeping with their belief in uniformity of meaning across time and space, realists understand this story as India finally becoming modern by learning to speak the modernist language: deterrence. For realists, replication of their analytics is progress. Yet practice defies categorization, and therefore Indian permutations of realist theory that naturally cannot break out of progress through aggressive-violence are sought.[3] Meanwhile, pocos politicize the material to once again argue that meaning cannot be fixed: the atom is either for development or for security. The process that for realists led to

231

maturity becomes regress for pocos, for it reveals India as incapable of containing the atom and succumbing to its violence.

In other words, most of what India has done is irrational for one, and incompetent for the other. Implicit in both renditions is violence almost programmatic in its virulence, for Indian practice is understood to be, in some form or another, ignorant. This is 'not a simple antithesis of knowledge. It is a state people attribute to others and is laden with moral judgement,'[4] writes Mark Hobart. The attribution of ignorance is required because extant research is conducted on the basis of a morality alien to the subject. It is to eliminate this difference that violence is deployed, and it extends from denigrating Indians as irrational to denying them their rationality via a host of dismissals and avoidances. Indeed, so alternative is the subject's morality that modernists recoil from it by actively disengaging from the state.[5] But if the metric for explicative success is the degree of analytic-violence required in making a coherent case, then the assumption ought to be that Indians are rational. To do so is to tackle modernist violence by not retreating, but engaging the state and keeping open the possibility of alterity rather than attempting to straitjacket practice. To do so exposes the Ministry of External Affairs (MEA) as subaltern because its international peers cannot understand it, yet politicians, knowing this full well, use incomprehension to their advantage. The subaltern therefore speaks but cannot be understood, but that is no barrier to progressing.

Analytical violence

The overarching violence of poco analysis lies at its inception, because the possibility of an alternate rationality is theorized out. Indicative is Srirupa Roy who intends to 'understand nuclearisation through the lens of socio-cultural and historical analysis,'[6] but precisely this is denied to the state. Instead there is that stale old story about the state: its denizens deleted themselves in an attempt to mimic modernity, forever trapping themselves within modernity's confines. The extent of this intellectual closure may be charted in Itty Abraham's monograph where he theorizes that the 'postcolonial is a specific condition in the global condition of modernity' and that this is a 'rationality in ordering human affairs'. For Abraham, then, the intellectual gates are closed by the assumption that modernity equals rationality, or at a minimum the rationality that became dominant as Indians began to mimic. The gates are locked shut by another conflation: that the aspiration to better the human condition is the desire to become modern. In doing so Abraham surfaces a phenomenal hubris: that only modern rationality produces the desire to better the human condition. Impossible is the 'fourth-possibility', that a non-modern rationality could seek progress, by appropriating modernity itself to achieve goals in line with the appropriating rationality. It is the inability to entertain this alterity that leads to poco violence.

Since Indians are mimicking modernity, pocos interpret Indian aspirations to transform the human condition as a 'problem' arising out of the time-lag between non-modern and modern. The aspirants are destined to an 'endless search for "modernization" and "development"' because the modern is presumed always to be just beyond reach. Furthermore, postcolonial Indians are presumed to be obsessed about boundaries.[7] They have to be, because to mimic one has to identify and delineate what is to be copied, and this is inescapable: it is presumed that the only possible future is the West's and that Indians want it. This series of assumptions and conflations produces analytical, at best, conundrums. For instance, M.V. Ramana and C. Rammanohar Reddy in a volume by eminent intellectuals—who may not all be postcolonial, but Ramana appears in Abraham's collection—argue that the 'major casualty of the nuclear dream shared by India and Pakistan is peace.'[8] It is an astounding claim. A sentence eliminates an entire sequence of peaceful overtures by making Indian actions a function of modernity. Avoiding such errors requires engaging the state on its own terms, something postcolonials resolutely refuse to do. Indicative is Raminder Kaur who abjures studying the state because states are the 'protagonists of rationality'. As with Abraham and all pocos, the underlying assumption is that rationality can be nothing but modern. Somehow the state elite are impervious to—or have instantaneously, at the moment of becoming part of the state, cast off—the logics, thoughts and practices of the society from which they emerged![9]

In short the political culture of the state is *a priori* presumed disconnected from the society that produced it, something maintained by the absence of any real knowledge about the people who compose the state, purely because no analyst has ever sought to enter it and study it in its lived reality.

In the absence of producer-centred-research (PCR) there is only analytic-violence, enhanced by moderns being mortified by the possibility of alterity. For instance, in documenting a practice common to all nuclear programmes, secrecy, what is explicit is analytic-violence: Ramana finds in secrecy the undermining of the very ideal that nuclear weapons are supposed to safeguard: democracy.[10] But why is the Indian elite obsessed with security? Sunanda Datta-Ray inadvertently shed light on this through his experience arising from conversations with a top general, the FS and the PM. Datta-Ray makes the implicit point that secrecy can only be made sense of in terms of broader sensibilities and makes for not an all-encompassing field, but issue-based practices.[11] The entire state is certainly not secrecy-obsessed. PM Manmohan Singh has repeatedly spoken of the need for 'declassification' to aid long-term strategic thinking, and thereby, tangentially, critiqued the bureaucracy's obsessive secrecy.[12] In a conversation he dwelt upon the bureaucracy's resistance to making itself less opaque. Singh recounted with admiration the relative openness of the US where George W. Bush introduced him to White House staff including interns, some of whom were of Indian origin. PM Singh asked rhetorically: 'if they can be so open, why cannot we.'[13]

The obsession with secrecy can only be comprehended if the practitioners of secrecy are permitted their rationality. To do so divulges how the practice of secrecy is not inimical to democracy but enables it. Secrecy is what precluded me from participating in a trip to Bombay because, the FS explained, 'some of these programmes [were] only open to government servants.'[14] On the probationers' return, general questions about the visit were met by a wall of silence. The questions were innocuous to the point of banality: Where the probationers stayed; What they did; Did they go to the nuclear facility? [They did] What was it like? One probationer muttered 'national secrecy' to explain his silence. Another explained that at the LBSNAA they had taken an oath, which they embraced as the denial of some rights—such as free speech—guaranteed by the Constitution.[15] However another, in private giggled, 'they don't want to talk about it because it gives them status!' She added that:

I was talking to one of the scientists and he was saying … "Why for all this secrecy? It's just to hide incompetencies here. And as for this national security business … we use all these private contractors and all their records are public. If any Chinese want to find out what we do, all they have to do is go look at the private companies records!" These peoples [the probationers] heads are spinning now with all this secrecy![16]

The quote not only provides researchers interested in the nuclear apparatus with an avenue to interrogate it but also illuminates another, hidden, metre for bureaucratic secrecy. It might be a Weberian attempt to insulate oneself from criticism,[17] but what is intriguing is that secrecy is a means of maintaining the status that has been accorded to bureaucrats. As this probationer made apparent, secrecy is a means of differentiating themselves from the bulk of the citizenry, and is especially required by those who themselves have risen from low status. In short, secrecy in terms of bureaucrats—who, let it not be forgotten, are also citizens—is enabling and empowering which presumably is the aim of democracy. In other words, the practice of secrecy is only seemingly similar to modernity because the purpose of engaging in it is not to undermine democracy, but realize its benefits for a specific group of citizens. In rendering familiar practices unfamiliar these citizens discount the rationality supposed to have been internalized by mimesis, for these practices of secrecy have a rationality altogether their own.

The poco analysis of secrecy, though crude, is only a primer to the analytic-violence which engulfs nuclear diplomacy. The most crude, yet ubiquitous, methodological means of maintaining the fiction of a modernist rationality administering the planet is to misunderstand, condemn or completely avoid uncontainable practices and contexts. These analytic practices are crucial because they drive the poco argument by eliminating the possibility of alterity. For instance, Karsten Frey argues that India's nuclear diplomacy oscillated between security concerns (or materialism) and something termed 'moral exceptionalism' which arose from Mohandas Gandhi and Jawaharlal Nehru, and now Indians are motivated by status-seeking in violence.[18] He can make the claim only by discounting as 'unrealistic' Indian practices of disarmament, which has an entire department devoted to it at the MEA (DISA or Disarmament and International Security Affairs). Frey wilfully negates Indian practices because they reveal a rationality[19] unique in its pursuit of an alternative to what modernity has brought us to, and that is a nuclear free world.

Every time such methods are employed they cause violence by dismissing practitioners. Fissures in modernist analysis are exposed, for these are moments of interpretive failure managed by aggressive-violence. Rather than annihilate practices that do not fit into imposed paradigms, this exegesis ejects the paradigm and offers a new one arising from the logic expressed by practice. It is vital that this is done, because discriminatory methods lead to an intellectual cul-de-sac. For instance, while the bureaucratic-secrecy argument correctly identifies a malaise but misunderstands it, the status-seeking argument misunderstands nuclear status—based on deleting the practices of nuclear diplomacy and entire departments—and concludes that Indians are in awe of a 'nuclear myth'. It is on this basis that Indian practices are condemned as 'morally prohibitive'. Myths, of course, for a modernist are irrational, and when connected to the nuclear, abhorrent.[20] The argument does not deny the role of status, but the poco error is, like Prakash earlier, to leave unexplored local notions of status and its purpose.

In this pocos, though committed to ambivalence, are ironically quite unequivocal in their condemnation of the state. The cost is that poco strictures conceal possibilities inexplicable to modernity. For instance, poco explanations cannot posit behaviour that eschews aggressive-violence, and resists nuclear coercion through *satyagraha*, while simultaneously harnessing the atom to eradicate poverty: using the atom to delete, both within and without aggressive-violence while not succumbing to it and thereby protecting the local rationality that necessitates those deletions. Incapable of comprehending this possibility, pocos reproduce mimicry: India aspires to modernity, a defining symbol of which is the atom, and ultimately, like any modernizing state, proves incapable of preventing the violence contained in the atom from infecting society.[21] The position is untenable, not least because it ignores key practices and dismisses the method by which Indian diplomats calculate the purpose of science and technology. In missing all of this, Frey is indicative in his mistaken interpretation that there is a 'strong tendency of India's elite to perceive themselves as victims.'[22] Even if correct, this does not explain why these perceptions persist, because they cannot do so within modernity's bounds—just another reason why they must be overcome.

Enclosing the atom: satyagraha

It is for these reasons that poco beliefs are ejected for the art-of-politics as the metric for analysis. But there is one further poco hurdle: its atomic metaphysics, that is, the atom's 'ambivalence'. This posits that the atom may be used for development or for security. In this reading, national development and national power are coterminous and development's unstated outcome is to increase state power. Nuclear energy is a fluid sign and there is the presumption that it inevitably becomes a tool of power, reflecting the paranoia of the Hobbesian state.[23] The failing of this reading is that there is no differentiation between types of power. It is quite evidently understood as no more than aggressive-violence, so that the curative effect of power in improving individual and societal conditions is denied.[24]

To trace India's understanding of atomic power is to follow Jawaharlal Nehru. Though having begun a modern and untrained in nuclear analysis, Nehru was, relative to pocos, positively subtle in his understanding of power. This is why Nehru could embrace modernist technology—much as the MEA uses modernist hierarchy—and enclose it in practice, within his principled Gandhianism. This meant that there could be no slippage to violence, which is inherent in modernity's encounter with the atom. This state of affairs continued until at least the 1990s and would be quite evident if it were not subsumed by the modernist attributing ignorance to Indians, founded as it is on the active denial of the possibility of Indians being 'authoritative sources'.

To explain just how Nehru was able to contain the atom within non-violence requires turning to the foremost explicator of its logic, Gandhi, and his engagement with science. Gandhi feared not science but the modernist rationality of science slipping into society, infecting it to create a 'scientific rationality'.[25] This was centred on the notion that experimentation revealed the cosmos as brute, the implication being that the self was external to the cosmos and could manipulate it. Gandhi rejected this understanding of science. For Gandhi, operating within the *dharma*-complex, the self was inextricably implicated in the cosmos. Thus Gandhi's solution to the creep of 'scientific rationality' was to use science in an altogether different manner: science as an expression of contextualism, that is, *dharma*. What Gandhi did was to avoid misconstruing science as modernity had, and he did so by highlighting the very particularity that defines science: the experiment. After all, it is conducted in carefully delineated circumstances. In underscoring this, Gandhi negated the generalizability of any experiment beyond its contexts. Science, in short, was the *dharma-complex*.

India's relationship with the atom therefore had to be anything but modernity's experience, which began with violence. This could never become India's metric because, as Gandhi's work makes evident, that is intolerable to a cosmological rationality. The atom therefore became a tool to improve one's situation in line with the cosmos and incapable of being used for aggressive-violence. Abraham would misunderstand that this is no more than a 'discursive shift in the meaning of nuclear energy',[26] because moderns are limited by debilitating presumptions that make for putting everything to violent purposes. This is why Indian moves must for pocos be dismissed as semantics, and such acts are yet another moment of interpretive failure managed violently.

What is dismissed as semantics however made for the actual practice of peaceful nuclear diplomacy. Its context was the enclosure of nuclear research by the state in 1948 with the Atomic Energy Act (AEA). It made for the securing of the atom to an alternative register. This coincided, in the 1950s, with international opinion that nuclear energy could solve many economic ills.[27] However, India noted the ambivalence of nuclear power and, wary of its military uses, chose a path alternative to modernity by being the first state, in April 1954, to suggest a 'Standstill Agreement' calling for the suspension of nuclear testing. By that time there had already been 65 tests. Despite these, in 1957 Nehru baldly stated the policy that continues to guide the Indian state: 'No man can prophesy the future. But I should like to say on behalf of any future Government of India that whatever might happen, whatever the circumstances, we shall never use this atomic energy for evil purposes. There is no condition attached to this assurance, because once a condition is attached, the value of such an assurance does not go very far.'[28]

Within months of Nehru's statement, China made it known that it would start developing a nuclear weapon.[29] A few years later Nehru said that if nothing were done to reign in the weaponization of the atom, then 'it may become almost impossible to control the situation.'[30] Yet, in the aftermath of the border war with China, India's nuclear programme was not diverted towards military purposes.[31] This was despite calls to weaponize in the face of possible nuclear annihilation at the hands of the Chinese (and Russians).[32]

Meanwhile, the China war sensitized Nehru about the costs of applying principled Gandhianism in the international. In a nuclear conflagration, the cost would instantaneously amount to what Klitgaard calls 'suicide'. Such an unbearable act of violence was of course totally antithetical to truth—which had to be defended in a truthful manner, that is, through resistance. This explains why in 1964 Nehru wrote in the margins of a note that nuclear energy contained 'a built-in advantage of defence use if the need should arise.'[33] Those words are widely misunderstood by moderns as the start of the slippery slide to the violence inherent in the atom. Yet practice confounds this position, for despite the disappointment of Pakistan, the shock of China and the nuclearization of the world, Nehru did not cross what a diplomat calls the '*Laxman rekha*' or the threshold to weaponization.[34] Nehru stuck to his convictions to the end of his days. Just before death in May 1964 he said: 'We are determined not to use weapons for war purposes. We do not make atom bombs. I do not think we will.'[35]

Nehru's fixing of the atom in a peaceful register was only possible by recourse to a rationality unconnected with anarchical-binarism. Secured to the art-of-politics, the atom was used to forward it. Practically this meant using the atom to safeguard the cosmological from aggressive-violence without replicating it. Such a reading avoids modernist analytic-violence that converts Nehru's action into inaction arising from a fundamental inability to make up his mind: ambivalence. This violence is easily managed by reconnecting him to his principled understanding of Gandhi.[36] The heuristic then least violent to the actors is the art-of-politics.

The fixing of policy in that heuristic meant that post-Nehru governments were also unencumbered by ambivalence. Instead New Delhi consistently sought out aggressive-violence just as Gandhi did, to convert it via resistance. In practice, therefore, the Chinese nuclear test in September 1964 could not derail Nehru's policy. Unsurprisingly, postcolonials find this inexplicable. Frey is indicative in his incomprehension and is perplexed by India not responding with weaponization, attempting alliances or negotiating a nuclear umbrella.[37] Weaponization would, of course, mean playing the game of Mutually Assured Destruction (MAD), and that is power politics *in extremis*. Similarly, nuclear alliances or a nuclear umbrella would mean acquiescing to the MAD power's logic. All three would mean acceptance of the modernist paradigm, divide the cosmos and thereby undermine the art-of-politics.

India instead sought to protect its rationality by seeking out the aggressively-violent in an attempt not to escape from the bordered and violent world modernists had created, but to unify it. The means was to seek reassurances from both nuclear powers that they would not target India.[38] However, PM Lal Bahadur Shastri failed to obtain guarantees and initiated in November 1965 the Subterranean Nuclear Explosion Project (SNEP), which when completed would put the country three months away from a test.[39] Shastri initiated SNEP under immense pressure from parliamentarians unable to absorb the pain inherent in nuclear *satya-*

graha—annihilation, which itself is a negation of truth.[40] It would be an imposition of modernity to view SNEP as a derailment of *satyagraha*, but what is debatable is how brave India was to resort to SNEP. The answer had already been delivered by Gandhi who said that what is of significance is not the extent of the sacrifice, but the reasons for performing it. In this, India kept to its avowed position of sacrificing for resistance rather than aggressive-violence,[41] and SNEP was resistance because Shastri only initiated it after failing to convert the world to non-violence by delegitimizing the most violent weapons in existence.

The 'semantics' of the pacific rationale that had enclosed the atom was apparent in practice again in November 1965. A proposal, a full five years before the Non Proliferation Treaty (NPT), for a 'treaty to prevent the proliferation of nuclear weapons'[42] was made by India at the United Nations (UN). Despite it being doomed to produce no results, in early 1966, and before the NPT came into effect, Indira Gandhi scrapped SNEP.[43] That she was able to do so is another demonstration of her ability to keep to her father's principles by maintaining a *satyagraha* befitting Gandhi. To his rationality the NPT was impossible because it further divided the cosmos. A former Indian FS, M.K. Rasgotra, captured what the NPT meant in practice: 'The white man has it, it's safe in his hands… the yellow man has also come along because he's been cooperating with the white man, it's safe in his hands. But the brown man is not good enough to guard and hold these weapons. This is the mentality of nuclear apartheid, which they've been promoting for some time.'[44]

That view was widely held. The founder of India's nuclear doctrine, K. Subrahmanyam, recorded that the US, the chief proponent of the NPT, clandestinely supported Israel and South Africa in developing the bomb and tolerated the crypto-nuclear weapons status of Japan and the Federal Republic of Germany.[45] Hugh Gusterson expanded on Subrahmanyam's point years later. The NPT divided the world on a temporal metric—simply stating that all who had tested a weapon by 1967 were nuclear powers. This arbitrary date became the legal anchor for a global nuclear regime 'increasingly legitimated in racialized terms'.[46] In such a situation, India's calls for the nuclear powers to move towards total disarmament were ignored. At work was a profoundly Orientalist discourse which, argued Gusterson, sees 'we' (the West) as rational and disciplined, while 'they' are the mirror opposite. This view entraps moderns, for unable to entertain the possibility of an alternative rationality, they dismiss Indian practices as irrational or mimesis.[47]

The 1974 test was undoubtedly a watershed, but nor for the reasons paraded by standard issue 'histories'. What became evident with Pokharan I is the subaltern nature of the state, which is only to be expected given that it operated to a tune at odds with modernity. Gayatri Spivak defines subaltern as being denied the 'lines of social mobility',[48] that is, the impossibility of what is said being understood by the hegemonic discourse.[49] Abraham inadvertently exposes the state's subaltern position by expertly delineating the incomprehension of modern (Western) politicians towards India's nuclear diplomacy.[50] But once again, there is no explanation as to why India's language was incomprehensible, because Abraham does not let the subaltern speak. Instead India is muted by a retreat into poco's analytic frame, 'ambivalence', to argue that the test triggered a period of ambivalence about what direction the nuclear future should take. In doing so, pocos once again do not focus on Indian policy makers, but approach them through the West (in Abraham's case the NPT framework). Crucially, its inabilities to read are transferred onto India as an incapacity to speak. For example, the test for India was a 'peaceful' explosion but was misread as India's seeking to claim for itself nuclear weapons status.[51] For Abraham to note the misreading is significant, but to then argue that this arose from Indian decision makers' inability to make up their minds and convey precisely what they meant is another act of violence, for it does more than silence. This is, as Spivak puts it, the 'ventriloquism of the speaking subaltern [and it] is the left intellectual's stock-in-trade.'[52]

Recognizing speech requires ejecting modern rationality—which in any case is unusable given that it rides on aggressive-violence—for the unadvertised role of the art-of-politics. In its terms, the 1974 explosion was a response to a deteriorating context (that is the rise of aggressive-violence), which demanded measures to safeguard truth. The context included China's testing not just nuclear bombs, but bombs launched seven times by airborne bombers.[53] That India's response stopped at a capacity-demonstration, rather than moving on to any effort to militarize the atom, is evidence of the continuance of *satyagraha* and this categorically denies ambivalence. To reiterate, as Gandhi stated, truth had to be defended but in a manner that did not reproduce aggressive-violence. To do this, one had to exist. In fact, suicide was an unbearable form of violence. Such a means of acting, by being misunderstood by at least the West, is why the state was subaltern.

To elaborate, India's subalternity becomes apparent if it is recognised that India did send a definitive message with the test but that it was directed at China, not the West for it is not the be-all and end-all of Indian diplomacy as Abraham supposes. This delegitimizes contentions that PM Indira Gandhi could not make up her mind and spoke in such muddled tones that she was bound to be misunderstood. To prove the modern charge that she was incapable requires verification of whether China misunderstood her, for the audience New Delhi was speaking to was in Beijing. In the absence of those records, a conversation the Canadian High Commissioner had with Mrs Gandhi in 1967 will have to suffice. The record comes to us via a secret cable sent by the US ambassador, Chester Bowles, to Washington. Bowles reported: 'With China at her [Mrs. Gandhi's] back, and Pakistan lurking on the sidelines, she foresaw no alternative but to keep open her option on the production of nuclear weapons.'[54] That the West understood the message suggests that China too got it. The explosion was therefore a definitive sign of capacity to Beijing.

However, the rest of the message was not understood by the world. What it failed to grasp was that the test was 'peaceful' because of its context: responding to overt weaponization with no more than a demonstration of capacity. Unlike China or the Great Powers, India had no will to power, notes a former Indian diplomat.[55] In other words, India could not but not respond to the material, but it chose to do so in terms not of aggressive-violence but of resistance to meet the requirements of a changing context. In the absence of a lexicon to comprehend it, the test has been called a 'political' response.[56] It was, but this was not power politics, but the art-of-politics. In other words, India's subaltern status was reinforced by no state realizing that aggressive-violence was being matched not in kind, but by resistance. This misunderstanding persists until today. Poco's 'ambivalence' and 'indecision' are what realists call 'ad hocism', and this perfect coincidence also silences the state perfectly. This is why anthropologists assume that India's nuclear test site—barren desert—was selected to display aggressive-violence against Muslims and colonizers.[57] The assumption is that India spoke back in the language of modernity, replied in kind (aggressive-violence) to both Muslim invaders and the West. The hypothesis elicited a bemused response from the former Bharatiya Janata Party (BJP) Cabinet Minister Jaswant Singh: 'Where should we have tested? The Sundarbans?'[58] In short, modernity's ascribing of incapacity is actually aggressive-violence disguised as analysis and the result is an orgy of violence that silences the Indian state. That the ventriloquism of the leftists coincides with the realists suggests an insidious collusion: analysts' complicity in the maintenance the realm of modernity which is directly threatened by the likes of Mrs Gandhi and Jaswant Singh, for they played to a tune that was pacific.

What finally exposes the utter incomprehension of modernist analysis in the face of the art-of-politics is the decision-making process surrounding the test. Worried about Western-style MAD diplomacy and wanting to terminate its hold on the world, Mrs Gandhi, like Shastri, dispatched a diplomat, L.N. Jha, to Moscow and Washington in 1967 to secure a guarantee to free India from nuclear blackmail. Like Shastri, Mrs Gandhi failed.[59] It was in this immediate context that Rajeshwar Dayal, stationed at South Block at the time, described the decision to test: 'There were no policy papers nor had there been any discussion on this crucial matter in the External Affairs Ministry.' Dayal had suggested drawing up background papers, Mrs Gandhi agreed, but on the appointed day for discussion Mrs Gandhi glowered, asking who had authorized their preparation. Dayal writes: 'I tried to refresh her memory, but she would have none of it. She said something about a "national decision", but we were not aware of any national decision or even debate in Parliament on the sensitive issue. At least three of us [the Secretaries in charge of the Defence, Finance and Foreign ministries] were greatly puzzled at our summary and inexplicable rebuff for carrying out what we conceived to be our assigned duty.'[60]

Dayal's report of the process leading up the explosion matches the contention that nuclear decisions have a lot to do with—as Jacques Hymans' writes—'the hearts of state leaders themselves.'[61] That even the US Embassy in New Delhi realized this was the case for Mrs Gandhi is disclosed by a particularly sensitive telegram signed 'Moynihan', dated January 1974.[62] Rather than assume nuclear decision-making was beyond her intellectual range, one may conclude that the fact that the decision was personal meant Mrs Gandhi felt no need to debate the matter. As Nehru's daughter, she was uniquely imbued with her father's principles, in turn extrapolated from Gandhi. In short, nuclear policy was crystal clear in her mind, even if it was principled rather than ensconced in the logic of the art-of-politics. Unable to explain her mind, modernists accuse her of not insanity but 'ad hocism', and in doing so make the remarkable contention that a woman who had managed to steer an entire country was unable of clarity of thought and purpose when it came to nuclear matters.[63] In doing so they repeat the charge similar to the ones made against the *Mb* and Gandhi, and for the same category of reason: the lack of will to investigate on practitioners' terms. In brief, then, the silencing of a woman was in turn the muting of an entire people.

Yet India persisted in speaking its indecipherable language, for it was the only one it was capable of enunciating. Undoubtedly policy during those years was violent because it opposed aggressive-violence, but the opposition was conducted in a manner totally removed from aggressive-violence. To embrace it would have meant deterrence. However, Mrs Gandhi denounced deterrence as 'untenable'.[64] Her diplomacy in the lead-up to the test illustrated the point. The test itself was a message in resistance and the audience was not the West, though it like its current explicators silence the subaltern. However, Mrs Gandhi had more important concerns on her mind: China. It was to counter it that she continued to speak her father's language and rather than weaponize, continued her *satyagraha* which by being misunderstood maintained India's subaltern status.

The status of status

The final stage of India's nuclear diplomacy was the programme's weaponization and formalization in 1998. Understood as the inevitable victory of modernity, the contention is best approached in terms of status because it entwines both practitioners and analysts. The latter, as usual, are polarized. Sumit Ganguly attributes all to security, insisting that 'prestige and status' were irrelevant to the decision to formalize weapons-status.[65] Pocos swing to another extreme. Frey argues security conditions were permissive of weapons acquisition, but not sufficient to weaponize and formalize the condition. The constant in this rendition is status. Indians sought status in Gandhian ideas and then military power because of India's 'acceptance of nuclear weapons as the currency in which the international status of states is measured.'[66] In doing so Frey too posits that Indians, if not modern to start with, are so now.

Evidently realists cannot comprehend polysemy, while pocos acknowledge it but only in their terms. Yet both conclude that Indians are modern. This contradiction internal to modernist analysis—India became modern because it accepted the irrelevance of status or because India acceded to modern notions of status—is produced by the confusion about status and compounded by the state's subalternity. The overlap between the two is consistent over several administrations from 1974 to today. Amongst them, Rajiv Gandhi's is the most significant, for he made the decision to weaponize.

The broad context for the decision was that Rajiv, like Shastri and Mrs Gandhi, operated in consonance with the art-of-politics. That is why he attempted to rein in nuclear proliferation.[67] He 'was genuinely against the bomb', said his scientific adviser, thereby negating the contention that India under him sought status as understood by moderns.[68] The Indian nuclear weapons elite replicated Rajiv's unconcern with modern status. Rajesh Basrur, after analyzing the key writings of the Indian nuclear weapons elite, concludes: 'nuclear weapons are viewed with less doubt and suspicion than in the past, though their limitations are acknowledged. They are certainly not privileged as the principal providers of the nation's security, which is widely seen in economic and social terms.'[69]

Nearly half of the members of the strategic elite interviewed did not consider nuclear retaliation necessary even in response to a minor nuclear attack. Basrur finds this a 'remarkable picture of restraint in the face of grave provocation.'[70] What is 'remarkable' is not the Indian elite's opinion, even though it displays a considerable ability to absorb the pain necessitated by *satyagraha*, but that Basrur finds it noteworthy. He does so because the very nature of subalternity precludes even the sympathetic modernist from understanding the subaltern's language. The only solution to the surprise alternating with incomprehension that dominates studies of Indian nuclear diplomacy is to adopt the language of subalternity, that is, the language of the Indian elite.

That language was matched in practice by Rajiv, whose 'first international act was to launch the Six Nation Five Continent Appeal for nuclear disarmament at a summit meeting in New Delhi in 1985.' Inescapably, however, Rajiv weaponized the programme, but this is not contradictory, a sign of modernist progress or postcolonial regression. Instead, the apparent contradictions of Rajiv's policies make sense if viewed in terms of the art-of-politics. One contradiction was that even after weaponization, India offered an 'Action Plan for Ushering in a Nuclear Weapon-Free and Non-violent World', of which Rasgotra wrote: 'It envisions a world without hate, fear and confrontation, a world which is a true democracy of nations. This, in Rajiv Gandhi's own phrase, is "India's millennial concept of the world as a family. This vision of a new world order is a spiritual vision, not unlike Jawaharlal Nehru's but closer, it seems, to Mahatma Gandhi's vision of the world.'"[71]

It was closer to Gandhi's as he had changed the nature of violence through the art-of-politics. Having seen the failure of his predecessors to ensure security through disarmament and then through a guarantee in a world predicated on nuclear annihilation, Rajiv saw no choice but to do what within the art-of-politics amounted to no more than tweaking India's position to ensure that truth prevailed by using resistance to respond to mounting aggressive-violence.[72] Weaponization was thus under way by 1989 but was in keeping with principled Gandhianism, which had earlier led to the noting of the military application of the atom by Nehru and the 1974 test.[73] The decision to weaponize, to recall Gandhi on Kashmir, was a 'barbarous' act,[74] but one nevertheless consistent with the art-of-politics. In short, resistance, not aggressive-violence, motivated weaponization and hence the continuation in calls for de-weaponization.

As for the decision, it encloses a vision of the self that is able to absorb considerable pain, and tracking its extent demonstrates that it was not a realist state that India aspired to. One of the first signs of pain was during the 1965 war with Pakistan, when 100 parliamentarians wrote to the PM calling for India to weaponize. That letter was provoked by the Chinese threat to open a second front to protect Pakistan. As the CIA Director James Woolsey testified in 1993: 'Beijing has consistently regarded a nuclear-armed Pakistan as a crucial regional ally and vital counterweight to India's growing military capabilities.'[75] That the decision to weaponize came some 20 years after the letter marks India's subalternity during those years in the face of the international. This status did not change with weaponization because it was prompted by an external threat, but that was only instrumental to maintaining the subaltern rationality. In other words, it was imperative to face aggressive-violence because anything else would betray the art-of-politics, which would also be betrayed by risking the deletion of oneself.

These twin concerns were evident in PM Atal Behari Vajpayee's letter to the US President explaining the tests.[76] Vajpayee believed China was using Pakistan to encircle India, thereby threatening the art-of-politics. There was of course no reason to assume this *a priori*, since China and Pakistan were free to trade, even in nuclear materials and technology. However, the fact remained that both countries had been aggressors. As the Indian diplomat Sisir Gupta put it in 1966: 'China may subject a non-nuclear India to periodic blackmail, weaken its spirit of resistance and self-confidence and thus without a war achieve its major political and military objectives in Asia. India's experience with China suggest that such a course of action is not only possible but probable.'[77] Secondly, neither Pakistan nor China could be trusted, given their history of duplicity, most sharply expressed in nuclear policy. As Zachary Davis observed, 'China's nuclear relationship with Pakistan, which has not signed the NPT and possessed an undeclared nuclear stockpile, has been at odds with its declared policy of not aiding proliferation.' The point was not that Beijing was not breaking any treaties, but that its 'behaviour remained inconsistent with non-proliferation norms in the post-Cold War period' and that this was being done in a surreptitious manner.[78] Such behaviour countered truth and simultaneously threatened India's truthful politics. To ignore this could have undone the art-of-politics, which would have been an abdication of truth.

India therefore sought out aggressive-violence but met it on an alternative register, and in doing so acted as a subaltern, for not only did modern states miss what was happening, but so too did pocos and realists. Quite how alternative the register was might be gathered from setting out the external context for weaponization. Though China had pledged no-first-use (NFU) in 1964, Beijing's total lack of clarity is what caused Indians to conclude that the threat to truth was increasing: 'I was completely unaware of what their policy was ... past experience does not reassure us. ... It's still the case ... a few months ago the PM [Manmohan Singh] said so ... he cannot understand Chinese aggressiveness,' says an FS from the 1980s.[79] In addition to Chinese nuclear policy being totally cloaked, the NFU pledge began to be contradicted from the late 1980s by People's Liberation Army (PLA) strategists. 'Very often one finds strategists arguing abstractly in favour of first strikes in conventional and nuclear war, even while claiming that China is committed to a second strike posture,' wrote Alastair Johnston three years before Pokharan II. He added, 'a number of Chinese strategists chafe at the possible operational restrictions imposed by NFU.'[80] Noting the tendency for 'a more obviously pre-emptive operational doctrine,' Johnston found it detailed in a Chinese document. It said: 'In a nuclear war, the first task of a strategic surprise attack is to "eradicate the enemy's nuclear surprise attack weapons and thus obtain nuclear superiority and strategic initiative. To this end the most important strategic objective becomes surprise-attacking the opponent's strategic missile bases, nuclear weapons aircraft and their bases, and nuclear submarines and related naval bases.'"[81]

Johnston also found a consistent Chinese definition 'of active defence in conventional conflicts' that conflated aggression and defence to China's advantage. As a Chinese document stated, a 'strategic counterattack carries the implications of a strategic offensive. From a political perspective, it makes more sense and is more advantageous not to call it 'attack' but to call it a 'counterattack'.'[82] Similarly, an exposition on limited war argued that the best time for a 'counterattack' was when the enemy was preparing to launch an attack but before its planes and missiles had left the ground.[83] Hence the very present threat of aggressive-violence waged through nuclear means had changed the context Mrs Gandhi had inhabited, and to keep with the art-of-politics it was necessary facing this new context. That India took no action until the mid-1980s does not suggest an abdication of duty; rather it is testimony to the ability to absorb pain and thereby keep to the article of faith enunciated by Nehru. In doing so, India continued to shy away from the idiom of aggressive-violence learnt by all the nuclear powers. Nor was India's ability to absorb pain irrational, but the rationality of the art-of-politics. Its distinction, as has already been noted, lay not in the extent of sacrifice (which was to be judged relationally) but that it was practiced for the correct reasons: that is, to keep to the art-of-politics.[84]

As for the tests themselves, it is an error to assume that Pokharan II was necessary to continue *satyagraha*. Since the crucial decision to weaponize had already been taken, the tests signified little materially. The main recipient of the message certainly thought so, hence China's subdued response.[85] A more compelling requirement was internal to the art-of-politics: preserve truth by not living a lie. India therefore weaponized in terms of the art-of-politics to meet a new context, and tested to preserve truth because it formalized the fact that it possessed weapons capability. To not formalize this would contradict truth—by living a lie that modernists gloss over with the term 'ambivalence'. As Gandhi had noted, the seeker of truth can have nothing to hide. To hide was in itself a negation of truth.[86] It was challenged by the ambivalence produced the moment India had a weapon. That India waited for about six years between acquiring a weapon and exposing it does not connote a temporary abandonment of the art-of-politics. A number of Indian administrations had come very close to testing but had been stopped for a variety of reasons.[87] In short, weaponization and the 1998 tests arose from the internal logic of the art-of-politics. In this status was all-important, for it was only by maintaining the atom's status in a peaceful register that India could keep its status as operating coherently within the art-of-politics. And so India continuously met aggressive-violence, but with resistance, thereby putting diplomacy beyond modernity's threshold. This is also why India remained subaltern, and is also why, at a loss to explain, all modernity continues to do is resort to analytic-violence.

Ultimately, maintaining India's status of eschewing aggressive-violence externally was meaningless if it were used to defend a polity wracked by that type of violence. This meant that India's engagement with the atom could not stop at the non-use of the atom for aggressive-violence externally, since the atom leant itself to eradicating such violence within. This brings us to the second aspect of Gandhi's notion of the *Ramarajya*. This required keeping to the art-of-politics to erase not only aggressive-violence without, but also aggressive-violence within. This symbiotic relationship also strengthened the art-of-politics by making for something worth the immense costs of defending via *satyagraha*. To India's harnessing of the atom for resistance externally was therefore added the elimination of aggressive-violence internally via development. Postcolonials correctly note this possibility, but their error is to miss the earlier fixing of the atom on a peaceful register, which meant that there could not be any slippage in the status of the atom. Undoubtedly pocos are right that the status of the atom is all-important, but it was manufactured in India according to a schedule unavailable to moderns, which is why they cannot explain—unless it is by inflicting analytic-violence—India's very peculiar dual use of the atom. That this could indeed work is why Stephen Cohen writes: 'The 1998 tests increased India's prestige and status, thus indirectly improving its net security.'[88] George Perkovich agrees.[89] It is the 'net' aspect, which intertwines the drive to eliminate aggressive-violence both externally and internally.

The friability of art

Realizing the internal facet of 'net security' provided the final impetus for the 1998 tests. They also demonstrate how in speaking, India remained a subaltern but was still able to progress. But this was also a process that imperilled the subaltern. That remained India's status even after the tests, because they were not designed to realize some modern status. The subaltern stubbornly kept to its status even after achieving nuclear weapons status, by adopting the operational doctrine of NFU. The art-of-politics was therefore maintained not only in theory but also in practice. India's NFU is theoretically in line with *satyagraha* because once again India matched aggressive-violence on an alternative register. The NFU does this through its 'promise' to never use the weapon first, and in making that promise chooses the only means of engagement capable of removing the threat of aggressive-violence from diplomacy while also providing the means of preserving the *Ramarajya*.[90] Furthermore, India's past practice imbued its NFU with a credibility lacking in China's pledge.

The imperilment of India's rationality may be first glimpsed in the manner in which the NFU was arrived at. The NFU's key proponent, K. Subrahmanyam, appears to have stumbled on it, thereby exposing the friability of the art-of-politics. Its brittleness was exposed with Nehru never quite grasping the tradition he owed allegiance to, and this was exacerbated by his not institutionalizing his principled Gandhian thought within the MEA. Yet decades later, Subhramanyam put into practice a policy that was in line with the art-of-politics. Subrahmanyam therefore provides a site to explore the production of *satyagraha* on the eve of the 21st century. His is therefore a cautionary tale of how not to craft a *satyagraha* because he mimicked, but he did not mimic modernity: Subrahmanyam mimicked Gandhi.

The site that is Subrahmanyam becomes one of intercivilizational contact, because though reared in small town India under the influence of Gandhi and Nehru, both of whom he admired,[91] he came to strategic language at the London School of Economics and Political Science (LSE).[92] Its language of power politics, by definition, could not express the rationality of non-violence that wafted through the society he was born into. In effect, there was a dissonance between modernity's categories and Subrahmanyam's intellectual apparatus, and the result was exclusion of the possibility of realizing the 'integrity' of Gandhian thought. Expressing a cosmic rationality in modernity's lexicon is of course impossible, which is why the latter cannot resolve the former. It is this incongruity that produced Subrahmanyam's inconsistencies.[93] In short, Subrahmanyam's failure was to not even entertain the notion of a subaltern rationality, but then again he was no philosopher. Rather than dismiss this as a symbol of failure, as postcolonials do, or as a sign of realism, it is far more productive to view him through his own texture and as the site for the production of a politics alternative reproduced by the state.

The dissonance in Subrahmanyam is revealed by the fact that despite his exposure to modernity at the LSE, he proclaimed a policy at best uncomfortable within modernism:

A future [security] strategy has to be based on a vision of non-violence ... turning away from conflictual to co-operative approaches .... There are no alternatives to such a strategy. Either humanity unites to survive, or it is bound to face a bleak future. ... We of this generation have a stark choice before us. Either we become saviours of our posterity or its executioners. Either we opt for life or shatter the future of mankind. Let us opt for life.[94]

The jarring effect of intercivilizational contact is in the error, manifest in the quotation, of following Nehru and making non-violence an 'article of faith', rather than keeping with Gandhi who, establishing himself on the *dharma*-complex, produced an art-of-politics which logically effaced aggressive-violence. Subrahmanyam's resorting to non-violence as talisman arose from partial understanding of the *dharma*-complex. Like Gandhi, Subrahmanyam understood that *dharma* was 'the rule of law and the ethics of the age' because in 'the Hindu way of life there are no god or prophet-given laws. *Dharma* is not immutable but is liable to change to be in consonance with changing times.' He also warned that 'the true Hindu way of life is in danger today but not from those who follow other religions. It is threatened by those who want to imitate others and abandon its essence, because they have misinterpreted it through the prism of dogmatic faiths.'[95] Clearly, Subrahmanyam understood *dharma* as context-dependent, and there is his warning against mimicking modernity. However, what was lost was the 'integrity' of Gandhi's truth, that is highest-*dharma* which in conjunction with *dharma* made for the *dharma*-complex. What this meant was that Subrahmanyam was incapable of understanding that *dharma* made for highest-*dharma* and they in combination made violence logically untenable.

By missing this, Subrahmanyam based himself not on the rationality that made violence untenable, but on the result: non-violence. Yet he understood *dharma* perfectly. The combination was incendiary, for it meant that he was free to apply non-violence contextually. What Subrahmanyam did by missing the *dharma*-complex was to make non-violence an article of faith to be applied in line with *dharma*. The effect was an appalling perversion of Gandhi's art-of-politics because Subrahmanyam was able to propose the discriminatory use of resistance or, in his words, 'non-violence as a resistance strategy had to be on a case-by-case basis: it cannot be treated as universally applicable against all aggressions in the world.' In other words, Subrahmanyam was incapable of comprehending two crucial components to the art-of-politics: that means matter, and that to act non-violently delivers freedom instantaneously because it means one is in consonance with the cosmos. This is because Subrahmanyam missed highest-*dharma* and with it the reason why everything was unified at inception. Thus the eschewing of aggressive-violence was reduced from the logic of the cosmos to mere expediency. In short, Subrahmanyam chose to avoid aggressive-violence only when it came to nuclear weapons, because their destructive power had shrunk the globe to a 'small space station'.[96]

What had happened was that a comprehensive rationality delegitimizing violence was under Nehru converted into something quite anaemic because the rationale's most mundane result—non-violence—was made into the fount of an ideology: principled Nehruvianism. This was then reduced to caricature by Subrahmanyam because he made the article-of-faith into a matter of expediency. But this was not the most corrosive effect of Subrahmanyam's devaluation.

The most acidic result of Subrahmanyam's reformulations arises from the curious paradox that in producing the NFU, Subrahmanyam made for a practice perfectly in harmony with the art-of-politics. Much like Nehru and others, Subrahmanyam in practice continued to behave like a *satyagrahi*. But in doing all this, Subrahmanyam was indulging in the very practice he decried: mimesis. Though he sought to mimic not modernity but Gandhi, mimicry within the context of non-violence as article-of-faith contained the charge that could explode the subaltern's rationality. To explain means first charting how the impossibility—untheorized by the theorists of mimicry, limited as they are to the binarism of East copying West—of Subrahmanyam mimicking Gandhi came to pass. This conundrum may be unravelled by another lesson Subrahmanyam learned from Gandhi, that 'violence was better than cowardice' and that 'non-violence [i]s the best method of conducting the struggle against domination.' But why struggle against domination? Gandhi's answer was that it was to defend a particular type of polity. Gandhi called it *Ramarajya* (which meant the deletion of aggressive-violence within) and Nehru tried to establish it in the borderlands during the China crisis. In contrast, for Subrahmanyam defence was to be made on a comparatively pedestrian basis—survival for survival's sake. In other words, non-violence was the 'best' way to match 'domination' but not the only way. All that made non-violence appropriate in matters nuclear was that everyone could die if aggression was matched with aggression. The cost of this devaluation was that not only was it possible for the polity to practice non-violence on a case-by-case basis without, but gone was the need to eliminate aggressive-violence within the polity to make for a society worth defending via the immense sacrifice entailed in resistance.

If Subrahmanyam's mimesis had fully taken over the state's rationality, then the *Ramarajya* would have been fatally compromised. This is because Subrahmanyam made non-violence into an article of expediency and deleted the necessity of using the atom for development. By no longer being compelled to keep to resistance because it was logical in terms of the cosmos or because it was, as for Nehru, an article-of-faith, India could have sought to mimic anything and anyone, including modernist violence. That would have meant a purely aggressive use for the atom, rather than using it to resist aggressive-violence within and without. If this had come to pass, then Perkovich's charge that India sought to manage itself by 'mimicking the once-derided big powers'[97] would have been correct. The threat then was the conversion of a rationale into rank expediency, for that act might have led to Nehruvian non-violence being replaced by something else by a practitioner incapable of the courage—which Nehru and subsequent PMs have displayed—required of the *satyagrahi*.

As it happens, India's subaltern, *Ramarajya*, status cut across the political divide and enclosed the BJP. The tests were after all a properly BJP decision and that party's highest functionaries played a delicately balanced game to maintain the *Ramarajya*—not modern status—by deleting aggressive-violence within and without. As has already been noted the tests were intended to regularize (in terms of the art-of-politics) India's weapons status, but more was demanded by the art-of-politics: survival for survival's sake was not sufficient, the internal aspect of 'net security' had to be realized. However, delivery was complicated by India's subaltern status, which meant that its language was indecipherable to the world. The BJP's quandary then was to make its subaltern self explicable. The way to do this was by creating a liminal zone where India could speak on its own peaceful register but be understood by modernity in the only language it understood: aggressive-violence. That the tests were pacific is because of the intent: to delete aggressive-violence within. In other words key Indian politicians, L.K. Advani and Jaswant Singh, knew, given their familiarity with the language of 'international relations', that the tests would be interpreted in terms of aggressive-violence rather than as the product of the art-of-politics.[98] Not only was this known, but the misunderstanding was required to manage the internal in terms of the art-of-politics.

The question remains: how could the liminal zone lead the abatement of aggressive-violence within? The answer lies first in the perception that the means to this goal is the US, which has long been regarded as crucial to ending the everyday violence Indians suffer within. The material reality is one of poverty and this status is unavoidable for formulations based on the art-of-politics.[99] As a very senior former FS said, 'We want to get our house in order.'[100] The way to do this was laid out in quiet tones by PM Singh: the international manufacturing market is controlled by China, but international trade is price sensitive and open to political manipulation; for India, manufacturing is a necessity, but for internal development; for the export market, what is required is to develop high technology, which is more resistant to price, demand and political fluctuations.[101] A high-ranking diplomat explained the point further: 'There is no interest in re-inventing the wheel. If the technology exists, we can improve it at a fraction of the cost, do their research and development for them at half the price then why not? That's what spurred on India … from at least Rajiv Gandhi's time.'[102]

The second part of the answer is that Washington had been consistently unwilling to help India realize the internal dimension of the art-of-politics. The paucity of technology transfers was indicated by the 1985 Indo-US Memorandum of Understanding (MOU) which increased 'dual-use' technology sales to India by 90% because the baseline was practically zero.[103] But the latest and most critical technology was not forthcoming, and the sale of the Cray supercomputer illustrates this best. The US feared India would illegally transfer the technology, and so negotiations dragged on for two years.[104] That US fears were unfounded explains why the suggestion outraged India's negotiator and FS, A.P. Venkateshwaren. His response was: 'Our record in this respect is impeccable. … at no point has any country felt that we have reneged on our commitments.'[105] India finally did obtain an inferior version, but it was to prevent such eventualities from repeating themselves that a means had to be found to communicate and realize the internal dimension. This was complicated by the fact that India sought to speak to the most modern power of them all and therefore attuned only to the language of coercion. India had to find a way of catching Washington's eye by being misunderstood as speaking modernity's language. In other words, the subaltern sought to speak and maintain its status, therefore it could only speak its own language. The only other option was to sacrifice the language of *satyagraha* for aggressive-violence. The danger of this possibility was expressed in an article. It was motivated by 1980s negotiations and appeared in the *Economic and Political Weekly*, entitled, 'Trading Non-alignment for high tech?'[106] The publication was a precursor for the debate that surrounded the 123 negotiations, testimony to the remarkable consistency of India's abiding fear of falling victim to a dangerous rationality.

The BJP audaciously managed this concern by forging the liminal zone, and it maintained India's subalternity by satisfying the internal dimension on its terms. This was even given voice. National Security Advisor (NSA) Brajesh Mishra—one of the handful of people involved in making the decision to test—in his two-page explanation for the tests made the usual reassurances that India would continue to act in a truthful manner, but closed by saying, 'The prime need is for peaceful co-operation and economic development.'[107] The government reiterated Mishra's message, word for word.[108] PM Vajpayee, noting that he was breaking with precedent by speaking about the tests at all, elaborated on what had been expressed by Mishra. Vajpayee pointed out that the tests were misunderstood as posing a threat, and then added: 'Happily, not all commentators missed the mark, especially those whose knowledge of India is not superficial. Richard Haass … pointed out that "what is at stake here are ties with a country with a billion people, a large and growing market and a robust democracy. Isolating India will not serve US economic or strategic interests ...."'[109] In other words, India sought 'net security' through the test,[110] but though this was expressed, India's subalternity meant that it was naturally misunderstood by the US, which imposed sanctions.

L.K. Advani in conversation said that this was expected by Vajpayee, but that it was immaterial in terms of an incalculable: that the tests would be misunderstood by the US as a will-to-power and result in India being able to access technology.[111] The gambit paid off. The tests were misheard as the language of aggression spoken by a state with an unimpeachable nuclear record. Eager to woo this supposedly modern, yet responsible state, the US dropped its sanctions and in 2001 the Next Steps in Strategic Partnership (NSSP) talks started. In short, and in direct contrast to China's ancient *Realpolitik* heritage,[112] India drew upon its *metis* to speak its own language for the purposes of maintaining the art-of-politics. This was interpreted in another lexicon, which counter-intuitively permitted India to challenge both external and internal aggressive-violence through resistance. The subaltern had spoken back, but without falling prey to the listener's language. And the means was to use strategically its very subalternity.

Conclusions

Realists expect everyone to respond to the material in the same way, thereby erasing the possibility of anything more than politics as aggressive-violence. Meanwhile, pocos imbued the atom with the capacity to overwhelm all politics. In doing so, both miss the ability to handle the atom via localized conceptions of status. The error is to be expected as modernity was dealing with a subaltern. This becomes obvious in that the rationale for matching aggressive-violence without had little to do with realist or poco rationales and everything to do with maintaining the art-of-politics. It in turn also necessitated the elimination of violence within the polity. The means to do so was to capitalize on the state's subaltern status by using it strategically to communicate with a modernity that only understands coercion. The trick was to do so without coercing aggressively. That this was impossible for India was because the atom had been fixed on a peaceful register decades before. In other words, India's newly acquired nuclear weapons status was mistakenly understood as signifying the same rationality that it did in the West's case. India's new status was sought not because the aim was to emulate the practitioners of aggressive-violence, but to keep to the art-of-politics. By keeping to a rationale that seeks to delete aggression, India's nuclear status remained embedded in a consistently Nehruvian register. India therefore could not use its nuclear weapons status as modernity does. All of this of course made no sense to modernity because, convinced of its own rationality, its analysts can never indulge in PCR. That this lack of knowledge was only one way did not however help India. It had to communicate in terms of its subalternity to keep to its rationality. Hence miscommunication was converted into the means to engage the US to maintain the cosmos by deleting aggressive-violence both within and without. None of this, obviously, was about emulating modernity's obsessions with power, it was about dealing with power from a pacific register and to forward that itinerary. In other words, while modernity sought strength, India played with strength to forward peace.

CONCLUSIONS

IN THE SHADOW OF POWER POLITICS

Mahatma Gandhi used to say, we have our doors and windows open to the free flow of ideas, yet we have confidence in ourselves that we will not be overwhelmed by any of them. I want more of our citizens to appreciate this reality.

— Manmohan Singh[1]

What has been traced is the improbable evolution of a homespun solution to the problem of violence intrinsic not just to modern diplomacy, but to the very politics within which it is located. Its pervasive aggression is neatly evaded by the everyday politics of those who constitute the state and the state itself. Thus accepted ideas of not only the possible, but also the quantifiable are defied. The 'governed have succeeded, in the teeth of severe opposition from the dominant sections,' notes Partha Chatterjee. The ruled now rule, but their aim was never to 'bend and stretch the rules of bourgeois politics and rational bureaucracy to create forms of democratic practice' that have 'become unrecognisably different'. What they produced was so at inception because they began not with Europe. Plotting the paths generated by alternate beginnings requires not living in hope that 'some day a great storywriter will appear to give [their productions] new names and a new language,' but listening to the people and the state they constructed, and doing so now, for it is the only means to dismount from the paramount delusion of our times that the be-all, if not the end-all for the Indian state is Europe.[2]

This archaic belief upon which all analysts continue to ride is most startlingly discredited by the eschewal of aggressive-violence, for at the core of Indian practice is a central assumption: the unified cosmos, that is, the structure-of-structures. Irenic by definition, it makes for a very particular kind of politics palpable in the very practices of the state. Termed the art-of-politics, this is not at a remove from everyday politics, but is everyday politics, and works in consonance with another result of the central assumption: a reflexivity alternative, that is, the 'the fourth possibility'. What sets both apart from prevailing—that is modern—conceptualizations is that they operate in time and space, while modernity is limited to time alone. Indian independence, then, was a moment of manœuvre, but not as it continues to be read, because the Indians who matter never became trapped by a repressive past or a delusive future. Rather, what continues from then to now is an intense reconstruction of the present. This is conducted in a manner abnormal for modernity, because its norm is instrumentality for violence is its means to deliver peace. Such inconsistency is impossible for today's diplomats because from the time of Yudhisthira, the lesson has been that means must match ends. What this means is that modernity need not be delegitimized; it is fundamentally illogical in terms of India, that is the geobody's, rationality.

The logic of this alternative rationale discloses scintillating possibilities. Modernity would do well to at least try to understand these opportunities. To start, the fundamental premise of the geobody's political style has diagnostic implications. This is not to deny that the structure-of-structures is a category, but what sets it apart is that it arose from subjects. After all, it was only by deciding to conduct producer-centred-research (PCR), and therefore reading practice in terms of the practitioner's categories, that this exegesis strategically exposed modernity's finitudes. More interesting is the perplexing proposition that the denial of representation resulting in miscommunication need not be a hindrance. Indeed such a situation might be the only vector permitting a pacific politics that remains uncontaminated by modernity while seizing its mechanical animals. To do so discounts the delusion that progress is the sole handmaiden of power politics. Meanwhile, as the international is the artery for the (mis)communication that enables progress on non-modern terms, it is no longer a zone for anarchical-binarism but the moral plain interlinking everything. There is therefore no essential difference between the spaces within national boundaries and those separating them. This is why the geobody's diplomatic purpose is disconnected from modernity because by being devised in an interlinking zone, purpose is calculated and realized relationally rather than in terms of binaries. This is exactly why the need to rely on modernity to reform oneself never arises. What however is necessary is empathy. In contrast to the modern understanding of the 'international' as an unbridgeable gulf separating various 'others' (in theory and practice, note the West's anxieties about immigrants), for the subaltern the 'international' is the interlink making possible an empathy that modernity is incapable of reciprocating. It is empathy that erases the superficial veneer that claims intellectual certitude under the title of modernity, to make for not politics, but the art-of-politics.

Modern politics ironically is what enables the cosmological to thrive, for the entire rationality is founded on maintaining truth in a truthful way. This is possible because the geobody perfectly understands modernity (for it is explicable to the former, while the reverse is impossible) and occurs constantly. For instance, national borders, by operating on the principle of the 'other', are something individual subalterns must negotiate. Yet the struggle that modernity's borders impose on the least powerful is just another example of how the truth that is the cosmos is maintained, for the effort of slipping across borders undermines the 'other' and replaces it with another. Similarly, the geobody's nuclear policies seek to collapse artificial and discriminatory boundaries founded on that old chestnut: race. In other words, the 'international' is an incitement to practices made possible only by the very existence of the modern. In exposing the practices of resistance, then, what has been demonstrated is that the circumscribed not only exists but also is the geobody's means to engage modernity.

Practically, geobodic resistance is near perfect, owing to mechanisms arising from the rationality that in turn maintains it. Foremost are 'total evaluations', but these have resulted in a monopoly of knowledge held by a tiny minority within the Ministry of External Affairs (MEA) itself. Differentiation within the bureaucracy and between officers in the MEA may be understood via Weber's sociology of knowledge. For him bureaucracy is the 'exercise of control on the basis of knowledge.'[3] The knowledge, in the MEA's case, is the cosmos, but what Weber misses is that this knowledge may not be uniformly available to all within the bureaucracy. It is familiarity with this knowledge that 'total evaluations' verifies. To be found fit ensures significant postings but in the (frequent) absence of anyone knowledgeable enough, those at the very least competent at fire fighting get whatever job is going, including the top job.

Weber also misses the point that control need not be paper travelling through proper channels. The MEA is much more. In short, the MEA is a repository of a particular type of knowledge, but this is not the prerogative of all within the organization, and therefore there is control within the organization, based not on paper but on holistic management. This protects the rationale, but limits it to a tiny handful. What this means is that the geobody's rationale remains to this day quite unintelligible not only to the vast majority of those who compose the MEA, but also to the moderns it seeks out. To elaborate, for the geobody, accepted lines of representation, founded as they are on the use of domineering power, are unavailable and unusable, for they betray the cosmological. This is what makes the geobody subaltern. However, it is precisely this—in modernity's terms—deficiency that enabled communication with modernity during the 1998 tests! The very incomprehensibility or inaudibility of the subaltern, then, is what illustrates the operability of the art-of-politics in the shadow of power politics.

There is nothing new to any of this, for it has been going on since at least 1947. Enabled by an underlying consistency that has existed over the *longue durée*, this is what permits communication with modernity. Constancy also undermines the hegemonic equation that makes India synonymous with 'modern nation-state'. This conflation is more than unfortunate, for it makes for an unbearable tension with 'India as civilisation'. Vinay Lal even argues that the modern nation-state erased 'India as civilisation'.[4] Implicit in such a reading is binary-anarchism which is illogical in terms of what is being described, and the cause is methodological incompetence. In the light of PCR, what is evident is that modernity never engaged India's rationality but only sequestered Indian practices during colonialism. Evident too in the exegesis of post-independence diplomacy is that if the metric for successful explanation is the degree of analytic-violence required to make sense of events, then patently the art-of-politics is a far more useful heuristic than modernity. The consequence is an inescapable implication: there is a fundamental misfit between modernity and what happens today in the corridors of power. In other words, to even contemplate the MEA and the structure it is a part of in terms of modernity is profoundly wrong. Far better to face truth and classify the geobody as a *Ramarajya*. Truth has nothing to hide, for the *Ramarajya* is not the constricted category of the blinkered rationality that produced 'religion', but the goal of Gandhi's philosophical precision.

And yet, the enabling heuristic is blatantly contradicted by individuals' recourse to violence. It would be an error, however, to assume that the culprits lie beyond the cosmological. Their failures are the product of erroneous calculations based on the real that is context and arising out of context, rather than on the basis of some instrumental construct such as nationalism. It is their resolute materiality that makes such diplomats no more than distortions of the structure-of-structures. When they do not keep to the heuristic's logic, it is because they miss the full potential of their own rationality rather than because they contradict it or have abandoned it. This is so for the entire spectrum of violence, be it the outcome of individual weaknesses, a lack of consideration or the seductions of modernity, all enhanced by rampant misunderstanding of the rationale that motivates and compounded by a lack of knowledge. For instance, a diplomat announced during the hectic run-up to the election of the twelfth president, 'the leaders are busy politicking about a largely ceremonial Constitutional position [the Presidency] ... who has time to care about poor India.'[5] Whether he was being sanctimonious is debatable, but what is not is that the officer did not know that the presidency is what the president makes of it—but then again, nor do New Delhi pundits. Prized for being the products of 'history', they yet do not have access to facts, nor have they learned what they do have access to.[6] That is why diplomats and commentators miss the point that the seventh President, Giani Zail Singh, was no rubber stamp. This all-pervasive ignorance is magnified by the overwhelming bulk of post-2000 entrants finding the most thrilling aspect of their work not the incitement to challenge the political, for that is too demanding for them, but encounters with what they call 'VIPs'. The exhilaration of shaking hands with politicians and having 'snaps' taken with Bollywood film stars early on in a diplomat's career never dissipates. Six years into their careers some continue to upload pictures on *facebook* to comments such as '*kya baat hai*' or in the vernacular, 'What fantastic news!' Nor is this a new phenomenon, and it continues to burn brightly post-career. For instance, all that a memoire tantalizingly entitled *A Diplomat Reveals* actually lays bare are the string of VIPs whom the author, like other officers, has linked himself with, playing the roles of glorified chauffeur, host and guide.[7]

And finally, they entirely miss the logic of practice, which is evident in diplomats' crass self-publicizing. When Mani Shankar Aiyar claimed authorship of Rajiv Gandhi's call to disarmament at the UN, Sunanda

Datta-Ray mentioned that Muchkund Dubey (a former FS) said he had drafted the speech. It is testimony to Aiyar's wit and presence of mind that without a moment's hesitation he both backtracked and maintained his credibility by countering: 'Dubey wrote it, but I translated it into English.' In their enthusiasm for self-publicity officers regularly contradicted each other during the fieldwork. More recently, Salman Haider (another former FS) did so by refuting a diplomat in the very same anthology. Haider's self-glorification defies common knowledge as he goes on to cheekily imply that the 'Look East' policy—the first foreign policy innovation since Non-alignment—was an invention of the bureaucracy, when as is all too well known, it was Narasimha Rao's.[8] The mismatch, then, between the politicians who give the MEA its bearing and diplomats scrambling for credit may be gauged by the fact that the politics of these policies lie beyond the will to be named, because motivating them is the logic of the people, finessed by Gandhi, expressed through politicians and implemented after a fashion by bureaucrats.

What is of concern is not the pedestrian quality of individual peccadillos, but that the perpetrators imperil the art-of-politics. The danger was manifest in the advice on the Iran vote and the pointless furore that was Sharm al-Sheikh. Most lethal is the possibility of mimicking modernity, because non-violence had been raised from the most minor consequence of a cosmic rationality to an ideal. Elevation is what devalues the cosmological. A little knowledge is indeed a dangerous thing, and this deadly devaluation makes plain the urgent need to nationalize the lesson Nehru failed to fully grasp: Gandhi's truth or the *Mb*'s *dharma*-complex. It is this lacuna that led to a prescient former Western High Commissioner in New Delhi, who has written several scholarly pieces about the *Ramarajya*, dolefully noting that though 'practice is perfectly logical in a very different kind of register, [practice can be] logically articulated by very few, no more than one or two diplomats at Headquarters at any one time.' The problem is not that the overwhelming bulk of the diplomatic service threatens to undermine what began with the *Mb*, for most have absolutely no say in policy during their entire careers, but that officers convey the wrong impression—as happened with the Secretary introducing Menon as an arch-liar. As the High Commissioner said instructively: 'Politicians on the other hand are far more conversant with the logic of your diplomacy … tracing it back to Gandhi. But your diplomats seem to be completely at sea.'[9]

Intellectualizing the Ramarajya

What is required, then, is to manage the inevitable failures of individuals to make for the effective operationalizing of the motivating rationality. Doing so requires surfacing the sanctity of the everyday logic apparent in the humdrum lives of the *Ramarajya's* denizens and making manifest how it shapes the *Ramarajya*. In other words, making the cosmological obvious to the people who unthinkingly work within its parameters and stray from it, and in doing so reiterate that it is the baseline for both individuals and society. An everyday example illustrates how this could be done. Many of Calcutta's inhabitants, in the face of the violence that is not having anywhere to defecate, regularly do so against the outer walls of houses. Householders have struck back not with violence—hiring guards—but by plastering onto walls images of gods.[10] Their remarkable efficacy lies not in teaching that the mundane is divine but in reminding people that it is so. Similarly, diplomats need prompting and the means to do so is to totally reinvent the means of entry and training.

Since this is not a school inspector's report[11] the description of training will be indicative, but what is evident is that job security guarantees underperformance and at great expense to the taxpayer. Training starts with a 'Foundation Course', diplomats call 'Fun Course'[12] and continues with over a year of desultory classes and a tour of the *Ramarajya*, tellingly called '*Bharat Darshan*'—that is, the viewing of something sacred and enhanced by a month-long district attachment. The experience is hugely varied because probationers—and officers—may do as they please with their time, and so their experience in the district ranged from huddling in snow-covered *dak* bungalows and smoking endless quantities of high quality marijuana to lolling on warm beaches with a car and driver at hand. Then there is a six-month desk attachment at the MEA, and finally one or two years learning a language abroad. All of this is a matter of great leisure—by the standards of any major multinational—because job security is only threatened by the most flagrant of violations becoming public knowledge. When there is apprehension amongst probationers and their families, it arises not from the ability to perform and fear of losing one's job. Rather, as a probationer put it: 'They're all getting married before they go abroad because heaven forbid they marry a westerner … and if they come back with a black … my god!' The statement was confirmed by another probationer's deep secrecy surrounding the

acquisition of a girlfriend because she was 'white'. The girlfriend's won-
derment at the apparent 'delayed onset of puberty' of her boyfriend, who
was in his late 20s, confirms the need to reform a training schedule.
Rather than education, what is provided is unaccountable pleasure in the
comparative social freedom afforded by Western society and reinforced
by a guaranteed income and little responsibility. It is a trend that continues, at considerable public expense, throughout many bureaucratic lives.

The *Ramarajya's* diplomacy cannot be left to the proclivities of individual temperaments. The current scheme needs to be rationalized to
delete miscalculations and frivolity and instead make for an education
of the sort Yudhisthira received, but taught in today's language and with
Gandhi's lesson incorporated. At the core of such an education can only
be what organizes the *Ramarajya's* diplomacy: the cosmos and all that it
entails. A manual of the type available at the Lal Bahadur Shastri National
Academy of Administration (LBSNAA) is all that is required, along with
a qualified teacher,[13] but the very simplicity of this requirement belies
the difficulty of achieving it. Matters are aided by the fact that the overall theme of the training is in any case already lodged in Gandhi—but a
micro rather than macro understanding of him.[14] It is only once this blinkered understanding has been broadened and inculcated in diplomats
that other lessons on note taking, writing—anything at all—in English
(a skill woefully lacking, as I discovered during the classes I taught) and
more specialized knowledge can be imparted. The reason is that the job
of the MEA officer is fundamentally a political one, but with a twist. The
officer is expected to manage politics but with the art-of-politics, as is
patently obvious in the diplomacy of the very elite: politicians. Diplomats
therefore have first and foremost to be fluent in the rationale of the
Ramarajya. Once conceptual clarity is achieved, then outside specialists
may be brought in to manage specifics.

Such an education outflanks a modernist conundrum. This is the tension between, to use modernity's language, the intellectual who espouses
truth and the public-intellectual who descends into the practical.
Swinging, in true bipolar fashion, between these two categories, the modern world cannot reconcile theory with the practical. Julien Benda's *La
Trahison des clercs* makes the distinction,[15] by noting that what puts 'public' into 'public-intellectual' is pragmatic criteria for human action and
denial of the supranational force of truth. This is because the public-intellectual scorns the universal for the particular, regards man as distinct from

his fellows instead of as a part of the whole, and exalts the practical over the spiritual. 'Worst of all, he has become the high-priest of the irratio- nal, glorifying the instinct, the subconscious, all the non-rational char- acteristics of man, as against the speculative and logical powers of the mind.'[16] This binary tension shapes the practice of modern intellectuals. Václav Havel reproduces Benda, warning that 'utopian intellectuals should be resisted in favour of the other type of intellectual: those mindful of the ties that link everything together, who approach the world with humility, but also with an increased sense of responsibility, who wage a struggle for every good thing.'[17] On the other hand is David Milne's con- clusion upon analysis of US defence intellectuals, that is, the top diplo- mats: 'Being driven by an overarching value system is often a virtue. America's victory in the Cold War was undergirded by a strong central principle: that liberty was inextinguishable and the West's pluralist vir- tues were preferable and superior to communist monism.'[18]

This unresolvable modern quandary dissolves in cosmic terms. Within that conception, what Havel and Milne do is disconnect highest-*dharma* from *dharma*. Havel emphasizes the former but denies the latter, and Milne is no better for reversing Havel. Their ways cannot do for the *Ramarajya*, for it is truth and that is the combined operation of *dharma* and highest-*dharma*. What this makes for is a completely new type of diplomat for whom the model cannot be the US, if only because its arch diplomats, the defence intellectuals, 'did not know very much'.[19] The new- ness of the proposed diplomat is that he knows but not in modernity's bipolar terms. Rather, the *Ramarajya's* diplomat ought to be one who has already harmonized to advise, that is, know the civilizational rationality that is truth and that is the *dharma*-complex whose political reality is the *Ramarajya*.

To harmonize requires selecting diplomats willing and able to do so, but that does not imply the recreation of an ideology. No idea is being imposed, only a 'common frame of reference' being surfaced, and its very implicitness makes success all the more likely.[20] What this requires is a dedicated MEA entry system capable of selecting people who want to learn and perform. This is patently not the case now. For instance, LBSNAA in the face of depredation introduced mixed housing. An Indian Administrative Service (IAS) probationer and relative explains: 'The men, especially those from the IITs live like animals and its expected that the women will have a soothing effect on the men.'[21] What is required is to obliterate the wildly differing standards within the organization by levelling the quality of the intake. The result will be a uniform exercise of power in a manner totally new—at any rate to modernity. Indubitably, it will take many years for the MEA to perfect such a system. However, since most diplomats are not required to do much more than conduct mundane organizational tasks day in day out, there is no need to totally re-educate the MEA. Instead the PM must place far greater reliance on advisers by appointing them heads of mission, to leave the routine to career diplomats, for if they may be entrusted with anything, it is 'booking flights, hotels ... organising pick-ups'. Nor can advisers only come from within the administrative system, as recommended by Naresh Chandra, because what his task force does not account for is the problem of individual failure reproduced by the inappropriate incentive that is job security.

Not only do systemizers miss all of this, they also remain incapable of learning the *Ramarajya's* rationality. Moderns appear fated to be trapped in an iterating groove. Uneven and Combined Development (UCD) is just one recently fashionable example of how stale ideas circulate. UCD's repetitive shibboleth is modernity's bland claim that the international is composed of differentiated societies, making it the 'dimension of social reality which arises specifically from the coexistence within it of more than one society'. Justin Rosenberg restates the obvious in writing all societies have coexisted, which means inter-societal interaction has been a permanent feature of, and determinant influence on, each individual society, via 'diplomacy'.[22] But UCD is mimicry, a replaying of Taylor and van der Veer. The only difference is that the zone for intermix is named, the 'international'. While diplomacy is given its due, what remains unchanged is that the zone is understood as producing hybridity. A fundamentally modern theory thereby reproduces modernist notions of bipolarity and anarchy[23] to deny diplomacy the possibility of being any more than the means to manage binary violence in an anarchical world. Even UCD's idea of hybridity ensuring that old patterns do not repeat themselves replicates Kaviraj's limited conception of reflexivity.[24]

It is to be hoped that this is the last tactic (for UCD is not strategy) to contain non-moderns by maintaining Europe's intellectual relevance now that its economic centrality has been decisively displaced. But what does this re-treading of well-trodden ground, this exercise of analytic power, tell us about power? Nothing at all. UCD, like the rationality that spawned it, remains incapable of going beyond explaining its theory of a network of uneven nodes of power interacting (perhaps like a complex hydraulic pumping system, an analogy that also explains Freud's mechanistic understandings). There can be no reconceptualizing of power in a radical way, because UCD is a tool of modern hermeneutics and it seeks, at the very least, to straightjacket subjects by analysis. In short, UCD is aggressive-violence. This is inadvertently exposed when UCD attempts to decentre Europe by foregrounding the 'international', but winds up parroting the old idea: Europe may not define today's world, but it would not exist without Europe.[25]

The failures of individuals, the monopoly of knowledge that causes it, and the aggression of modern analytics provide an ultimately practical reason why it is vital to know the logic Gandhi unveiled. In the absence of Gandhi's insight, to keep to his example meant that the arch diplomats—politicians—had to be highly principled, for what was called for, and continues to be delivered, is tremendous courage and self-discipline: the internalizing of great aggressive-violence and responding not in kind but with *satyagraha*. It is to lighten the burden of being principled in the face of annihilation by an ideology that sanctifies violence that the logic behind the *Ramarajya's* practice must be 'nationalized'. The distinction is between operating on the basis of rules learnt by rote (or violence) and in an instinctual manner that defines the very pinnacle of the state, making it a *Ramarajya*. This exegesis sought to expose its logic. To know it makes for impossible possibilities, for the contrast with modernity is stark. In John Carse's terms the difference between modern diplomacy and the *Ramarajya's* diplomacy is this: modernity plays to win, the *Ramarajya* plays to continue play.[26] For modernity, the rules may not change; the rules of the *Ramarajya* must change. Modernity plays within boundaries; the *Ramarajya* plays with boundaries. Modernity is serious; the *Ramarajya* is playful. Modernity wins titles; the *Ramarajya* has nothing but its name. Modernity plays to be powerful; the *Ramarajya* plays with strength. Modernity consumes time; the *Ramarajya* generates time. Modernity aims to win eternal life; the *Ramarajya* aims for eternal birth.[27]

There is no scope for ambivalence, for the choice is ineluctable: practice a diplomacy of infinite possibilities now or remain confined by endless impossibilities.

NOTES

INTRODUCTION

1. Paul R. Brass, 'India, Myron Weiner and the Political Science of Development', *Economic and Political Weekly*, vol. 37, no. 29, 20–26 July 2002, p. 3031.
2. Henry Kissinger, *Does America Need a Foreign Policy? Towards a Diplomacy for the 21ˢᵗ Century* (New York: Free Press, 2001), p. 154.
3. Manmohan Singh, 'Reply by the Prime Minister in the Lok Sabha to the debate on Civil Nuclear Energy Cooperation with the United States' in Avtar Singh Bhasin (ed.), *India's Foreign Relations—2006* (New Delhi: Geetika Publishers, 2007), 11 March 2006, p. 439. Pranab Mukherjee, 'Speech of External Affairs Minister Pranab Mukherjee in the Lok Sabha on Civil Nuclear Energy Cooperation with the US after adoption of the Henry J. Hyde Act by the US Congress' in Avtar Singh Bhasin (ed.) (2007), 18 December 2006. Anand Sharma, 'Interview of Minister of State Anand Sharma with the daily Tribune' in Avtar Singh Bhasin (ed.) (2007), 20 February 2006. US negotiators were surprised to learn India saw things so. See comments by Nicholas Burns in: 'Joint Press briefing by Foreign Secretary Shivshankar Menon and U.S. Under Secretary of State for Political Affairs Nicholas Burns' in Avtar Singh Bhasin (ed.) (2007), 7 December 2006, p. 1601.
4. Deep K. Datta-Ray, 'Singh gets nuclear deal despite the horse trading,' *South China Morning Post*, 8 July 2008; Deep K. Datta-Ray, 'Dawn of India's brave new nuclear world,' *South China Morning Post*, 9 September 2008.
5. Deep K. Datta-Ray, 'Prime exemplar of courage,' *The Straits Times*, 10 July 2008.
6. Arun Shourie, conversation, his residence, New Delhi, 1 June 2007.
7. Manmohan Singh, 'Interview of Prime Minister Dr. Manmohan Singh on Charlie Rose show' in Avtar Singh Bhasin (ed.) (2007), 27 February 2006, p. 1464.
8. Deep K. Datta-Ray, 'Raising India's pulse without selling its soul,' *South China Morning Post*, 13 August 2008. See also 'Pranab assails Rice remarks,' *The Hindu*, 30 January 2007, http://www.hindu.com/2007/06/30/stories/2007063057770100.htm
9. On the India-specific separation plan, see *Implementation of the India–United States Joint Statement of July 18, 2005: India's Separation Plan—presented to Parliament on 11 May 2006,*' in Avtar Singh Bhasin (ed.) (2007). 'Government of India's note to the IAEA', IAEA Document INFCIRC/731. See 'Agreement between the Government of India and the International Atomic Energy Agency for the Application of Safeguards to Civilian Nuclear Facilities,' in Avtar Singh Bhasin (ed.), *India's Foreign Relations—2008* (New Delhi: Geetika Publishers, 2009).

10. IFS Officer no. 1. Senior Congress cabinet member no. 2, conversation, his office, New Delhi, 8 December 2008.

11. For a useful overview of 'Gaia' theories see Connie Barlow, *From Gaia to Selfish Genes: Selected Writings on the Life Sciences* (Cambridge, MA: MIT Press, 1991). Recently fashionable again, 'Global Historians' when attempting to be more than comparative, do exactly what Liberals, Marxists and Realists do: presume the categories invented in Europe apply to all regardless of time and space. See Gyan Prakash, 'Writing Post-Orientalist Histories of the Third World: Perspectives from Indian Historiography' and 'Can the 'Subaltern' Ride? A Reply to O'Hanlon and Washbrook' in Vinayak Chaturvedi (Ed.), *Mapping Subaltern Studies and the Postcolonial* (London: Verso, 2000). See also Rosalind O'Hanlon and David Washbrook, 'After Orientalism: Culture, Criticism and Politics in the Third World' in Vinayak Chaturvedi (Ed.) (2000).

12. Gayatri Chakravorty Spivak, 'Can the Subaltern Speak?' in Cary Nelson and Lawrence Grossberg (eds), *Marxism and the Interpretation of Culture* (Chicago: University of Illinois Press, 1988), p. 281. And let it be remembered that the subaltern is revealed in her meaning by Spivak!

13. M.K. Narayanan, 'Observations of Shri M.K. Narayan Governor of West Bengal at the release of the book Looking East to Look West: Lee Kuan Yew's Mission India authored by Shri Sunanda K. Datta-Ray,' Calcutta, 18 February 2010. See http://rajbhavankolkata. gov.in/WriteReadData/Speeches/BOOK%20RELEASE%20LOOKING%20EAST%20 TO%20LOOK%20WEST.pdf

14. Gayatri Chakravorty Spivak, *Can the Subaltern Speak?* (Abbreviated by the author), in *The Post-colonial Studies Reader*, 2nd ed. (Oxford: Routledge, 2006), p. 28.

1. DELUSIVE UTOPIA

1. Alasdair MacIntyre, 'Review of Beyond Marxism by Vrajendra Ray Mehta,' *Political Theory*, vol. 11, no. 4, November 1983, p. 623.

2. Raymond Cohen, 'Putting Diplomatic Studies on the Map,' *Diplomatic Studies Programme Newsletter*, 4 May 1998; Paul Sharp, 'For Diplomacy: Representation and the Study of International Relations,' *International Studies Review*, vol. 1, no. 1, 1999. IR denotes the academic discipline of 'International Relations'.

3. C.M. Constantinou, *On the Way to Diplomacy* (Minneapolis: Minnesota University Press, 1996).

4. Martin Wight, 'Why is There no International Theory?' in Martin Wight and Herbert Butterfield (ed.), *Diplomatic Investigations, Essays in the Theory of International Politics* (London: Allen & Unwin, 1966), p. 18. Despite Wight's bemoaning the lack of investigations into diplomatic society in 1966, to this day there are only a handful of article length investigations of diplomats in foreign ministries, and no book length investigation of a Western foreign ministry, let alone a non-Western diplomatic service.

5. For instance, Inayatullah and Blaney, though castigating the discipline of IR for taking scant note of non-Western practitioners, remains a critique from within IR, rather than an engagement with the objects of study. See Naeem Inayatullah and David L. Blaney, *International Relations and the Problem of Difference* (London: Routledge, 2004).

6. Stephen Hopgood, 'Socialising IR,' *GSC Quarterly* no. 10, Fall 2003; Smith Simpson, 'Of Diplomats and Their Chroniclers: Review of Craig and Loewenheim,' *Virginia Quarterly Review*, vol. 71, no. 4, 1995.

7. Hidemi Suganami, 'Japan's Entry into International Society' in Hedley Bull and Adam Watson (eds), *The Expansion of International Society* (Oxford University Press, 1984).

8. Raymond Aron, *Peace and War: A Theory of International Relations*, trans. Richard Howard and Annette Baker Fox (New York: Doubleday & Company, 1966), p. 287.

9. Iver B. Neumann, 'To be a Diplomat,' *International Studies Perspective*, vol. 6, no. 1, 2005, p. 72.

10. Sudipta Kaviraj, 'In Search of Civil Society' in Sudipta Kaviraj and Sunil Khilnani (eds), *Civil Society: History and Possibilities* (Cambridge University Press, 2001), p. 316; Ashis Nandy, 'The *Politics of Secularism* and the Recovery of *Religious Tolerance*,' *Alternatives*, vol. 13, no. 2, 1998.

11. Jonardon Ganeri, 'Contextualism in the Study of Indian Intellectual Cultures,' *Journal of Indian Philosophy*, vol. 36, 2008, pp. 560–61.

12. Even challenges to Realist anarchy theory take anarchy as the start-point for theorizing. See Hedley Bull, *The Anarchical Society* (New York: Columbia University Press, 1977), pp. 24–5; Hedley Bull, 'Hobbes and International Anarchy,' *Social Research*, vol. 48, no. 4, Winter 1981; Kenneth N. Waltz, *Theory of International Politics* (Reading, MA: Addison-Wesley, 1979); Hans J. Morgenthau, *Politics Among Nations: The Struggle for Power and Peace* (New York: Alfred A. Knopf, 1967); Alexander Wendt, *Social Theory of International Politics* (New York: Cambridge University Press, 1999), pp. 249 & 309.

13. Hedley Bull, 'Society and Anarchy in International Relations' in Herbert Butterfield and Martin Wight (eds) (1966), p. 35.

14. Thomas Hobbes, *Leviathan, Cambridge Texts in the History of Political Thought*, ed. Richard Tuck, (Cambridge University Press, 1996), pp. 88, 140.

15. Bertrand Russell, *A History of Western Philosophy* (London: George Allen & Unwin, 1946), p. 556. See also Robert P. Kraynak, 'Hobbes, Thomas (1588–1679)' in Adam Kuper and Jessica Kuper (eds), *The Social Science Encyclopaedia* (London: Routledge, 2005), p. 637.

16. Hedley Bull (1977), p. 39.

17. Hedley Bull, *Intervention in World Politics* (Oxford University Press, 1984), p. 122; Martin Wight, *Systems of States*, ed. Hedley Bull (Leicester University Press, 1977), p. 128.

18. Reinhart Koselleck, *The Practice of Conceptual History: Timing History, Spacing Concepts*, trans. Todd Samuel Presner *et al.* (Stanford University Press, 2002), p. 235. IR assumes progress to mean Westernization. See Jacinta O'Hagan, *Conceptions of the West in International Relations Thought: From Oswald Spengler to Edward Said* (Basingstoke: Macmillan, 2002), p. 126–9.

19. James Der Derian, 'Mediating Estrangement: A Theory for Diplomacy,' *Review of International Studies*, vol. 13, no. 2, April 1987.

20. Gregory Feldman, 'Estranged States: Diplomacy and the Containment of National Minorities in Europe,' *Anthropological Theory*, vol. 5, no. 3, pp. 223–4.

21. James Der Derian, *On Diplomacy: A Genealogy of Western Estrangement* (Oxford University Press, 1987), p. 51.

22. Der Derian (1987), p. 59.

23. Luke 2: 9–13, quoted in Der Derian (1987), p. 66.

24. Ibid., pp. 105–16.

25. Ibid., p. 7. The Pope, sensing decline of the Catholic Church's power, ineffectively declared the Treaty of Westphalia null and void by the bull *Zelo Domus Dei*. See p. 111.

26. Ibid., p. 127–8.

27. Anarchy's supposed rival is 'hierarchy' where a Leviathan orders the cosmos. As the cover of Hobbes' book states, once again demonstrating the Christianity underpinning cool modernist theory: 'There is no power on earth to be compared to him.' (Book of Job 41.24). For 'hierarchy' see David A. Lake, '*Escape From the State of Nature: Authority and Hierarchy in World Politics*,' *International Security*, vol. 32, no. 1, 2007.

28. Adam Watson, *Diplomacy: The Dialogue between States* (London: Methuen, 1982), p. 31; Barry Buzan, 'From International System to International Society: Structural Realism and Regime Theory Meet the English School,' *International Organization*, vol. 47, no. 3, Summer 1993. The connection between this rationality and diplomacy is made by Wight: see Martin Wight in Martin Wight and Herbert Butterfield (eds) (1966), pp. 96–7.

29. Georg W.F. Hegel, *The Static & the Dynamic Philosophy of History & the Metaphysics of Reason: George Wilhelm Friedrich Hegel* (Albuquerque, NM: American Classical College Press, 1977), p. 112.

30. 'The theme of "the Other"—and specially what constitutes the otherness of "the Other"—has been at the very heart of the work of every major twentieth-century Continental philosopher.' See Richard J. Bernstein, *The New Constellation: the Ethical-Political Horizons of Modernity/Postmodernity* (Cambridge, MA: MIT Press, 1992), p. 68. Furthermore, 'Western philosophy is in essence the attempt to domesticate Otherness, since what we understand by thought is nothing but such a project.' See Rodolphe Gasché, *Tain of the Mirror: Derrida and the Philosophy of Reflection* (Cambridge, MA: Harvard University Press, 1986), p. 101.

31. George W.F. Hegel, *The Philosophy of History*, trans. J. Sibree (New York: Dover Publications, 1956), p. 173. Hegel was not the first to make an essential difference between India and Europe; his intellectual world derived from Johann Gottfried Herder and Friedrich Schlegel. See Helmuth von Glasenapp, *Das Indienbild deutscher Denker* (Stuttgart, 1960), pp. 14–32; Wilhelm Halbfass (1988), pp. 86–103.

32. Ronald Inden, 'Orientalist Constructions of India,' *Modern Asian Studies*, vol. 20, no. 3, 1986.

33. James Der Derian (1987), p. 23.

34. Ibid., pp. 170, 316–17.

35. Orvar Löfgren, 'The Nationalization of Culture,' *Ethnologia Europaea*, vol. 19, 1989, pp. 21–2.

36. James Der Derian (1987), pp. 28, 209.

37. James Der Derian, *Virtuous War: Mapping the Military-Industrial-Media-Entertainment Network* (Boulder, Colorado: Westview Press, 2001).

38. James Der Derian (1987), p. 51.

39. G.R. Berridge, Maurice Keens-Soper and T.G. Otte, *Diplomatic Theory from Machiavelli to Kissinger* (New York: Palgrave, 2001), pp. 1–2.

40. Paul Sharp, 'Revolutionary States, Outlaw Regimes and the Techniques of Public Diplomacy' in Jan Melissen (ed.), *The New Public Diplomacy: Soft Power in International Relations* (Basingstoke: Palgrave, 2005).

41. Postmodernity, which is supposed to signal the end of the modern, unfortunately denies the possibility of progress and originality, and fundamentally is embedded in the rhetoric of the modern. See Jean-François Lyotard, *The Postmodern Condition: A Report on Knowledge*, trans. Geoff Bennington and Brian Massumi (Minneapolis: University of Minnesota Press, 1984); Jean-François Lyotard, *The Differend: Phrases in Dispute*, trans. Georges Van Den Abbeele (Minneapolis: University of Minnesota Press, 1988), p. 202.

42. J.D.B. Vincent and R.J. Vincent (eds), *Order and Violence: Hedley Bull and International Relations* (Oxford University Press, 1990), p. 472; Judith N. Shklar, *Ordinary Vices* (Cambridge, MA: Belknap Press of Harvard University Press, 1984), p. 8; Michel Foucault, *The Archaeology of Knowledge*, trans. A.M. Sheridan-Smith (London: Routledge, 1972), p. 229; Michel Foucault, *Discipline and Punish: The Birth of the Prison*, trans. A.M. Sheridan-Smith (Harmondsworth: Penguin, 1977), p. 151.

43. G.R. Berridge in Alan James (ed.), *A Dictionary of Diplomacy* (New York: Palgrave, 2001).

44. Hedley Bull's 1977 essay is entitled 'The Anarchical Society'. It has been noted that anarchy is socially constructed. See Ronie D. Lipschutz and Judith Mayer, *Global Civil Society and Global Environmental Governance* (Albany: State University of New York Press, 1996), p. 102.

45. Dilip P. Gaonkar, 'On Alternative Modernities' in Dilip P. Gaonkar (ed.), *Alternative Modernities* (Durham, NC: Duke University Press, 2001), p. 14.

46. Dipesh Chakrabarty, *Provincializing Europe: Postcolonial Thought and Historical Difference* (Princeton University Press, 2000), p. 4.

47. Dipesh Chakrabarty, *Habitations of Modernity: Essays in the Wake of Subaltern Studies* (University of Chicago Press, 2002), pp. xxi, xx.

48. Charles Taylor, 'Two Theories of Modernity,' *Public Culture*, vol. 11, no. 1, 1999, pp. 169, 173.

49. Peter Van der Veer, *Imperial Encounters: Religion and Modernity in India and Britain* (Princeton University Press, 2001), pp. 3–8.

50. Rukin Advani quoted in Deep K. Datta-Ray, 'You have to protect your imprint,' *Times of India*, 18 March 2011.

51. Sumit Ganguly, *Conflict Unending: India–Pakistan Tensions since 1947* (New York: Columbia University Press, 2001).

52. Thorstein Veblen, *The Higher Learning in America: A Memorandum on the Conduct of Universities by Business Men* (New York: B.W. Heubsch, 1918), p. 4.

53. This is left as a question as much as a statement, because there is no research on the rationality of migrant academics. What is certain is that in IR, academics such as Sumit Ganguly are hobbled by their uncritical parroting of Anglo-Saxon theory and seeking to enclose India within its rationale.

54. Talcott Parsons, *Societies: Evolutionary and Comparative Perspectives* (Englewood Cliffs, NJ: Prentice-Hall, 1966); Talcott Parsons, *The System of Modern Societies* (Englewood Cliffs, NJ: Prentice-Hall, 1971), p. 29.

55. Theodore H. Von Laue, *The World Revolution: The Twentieth Century in Global Perspective* (New York: Oxford University Press, 1987), pp. 4–6.

56. Niklas Luhmann, *Die Gesellschaft der Gesellschaft, Erster und zweiter Teilband* (Frankfurt am Main, 1997), p. 151.

57. James D. Faubion, *Modern Greek Lessons: A Primer in Historical Constructivism* (Princeton University Press, 1993), p. 113.

58. Shmuel Eisenstadt, 'Multiple Modernities,' *Daedalus*, vol. 129, no. 1, Winter 2000, p. 3.

59. Ibid., pp. 4, 22–6. For a very useful critique of how reflexivity is activated within moderns see Philip Carl Salzman, 'On Reflexivity,' *American Anthropologist*, vol. 104, no. 3, September 2002.

60. For instance, the French Revolution brought modernity to Europe and inaugurated a new world era by erasing the past with the Year One. See Benedict Anderson, *Imagined Communities: Reflections on the Origin and Spread of Nationalism* (London: Verso, 1983), p. 193; Bernard Yack, *The Fetishism of Modernities: Epochal Self-consciousness in Contemporary Social and Political Thought* (Notre Dame, Ind.: University of Notre Dame Press, 1998), pp. 108–11; Immanuel Kant, *The Metaphysics of Morals*, trans. Mary J. Gregor (Cambridge University Press, 1991), p. 182. Even opponents of the Revolution saw it as the harbinger of modernity. See Alexis de Tocqueville, *The Old Régime and the French Revolution*, trans. Stuart Gilbert (Gloucester: Peter Smith), 1978, p. vii.

61. Shmuel Eisenstadt, 'Cultural Traditions and Political Dynamics, The Origin and Mode of Ideological Politics,' *British Journal of Sociology*, vol. 32, no. 2, June 1981; Shmuel Eisenstadt, 'Comparative Liminality: Liminality and Dynamics of Civilizations,' *Religion*, vol. 15, no. 3, 1985; Adam Seligman, *Order and Transcendence: The Role of Utopias and the Dynamics of Civilizations* (Leiden: E.J. Brill, 1989), pp. 1–44; Eric Vogelin, *From Enlightenment to Revolution*, ed. John H. Hallowell (Durham, NC: Duke University Press, 1975).

62. Renato Ortiz, 'From Incomplete Modernity to World Modernity,' in Daedalus, vol. 129, no. 1, Winter 2000.
63. Sudipta Kaviraj, 'Modernity and Politics in India,' *Daedalus*, vol. 129, no. 1, Winter 2000, pp. 138–40.
64. Philip Carl Salzman, *American Anthropologist*, 104, 3, 2002.
65. Shmuel Eisenstadt, *Revolutions and the Transformation of Societies* (New York: Free Press, 1978), p. 172.
66. Johann P. Arnason, *Civilizations in Dispute: Historical Questions and Theoretical Traditions* (Leiden: E.J. Brill, 2003), p. 29.
67. Benjamin Nelson, 'Civilizational Complexes and Intercivilizational encounters' in Toby E. Huff (ed.), *On the Roads to Modernity: Conscience, Science and Civilizations, Selected Writings by Benjamin Nelson* (Totowa, NJ: Rowman and Littlefield, 1981), pp. 80, 92.
68. Sudipta Kaviraj, *Daedalus*, Winter 2000, p. 137.
69. Navnita Chadha Behera, 'Re-imagining IR in India,' *International Relations of the Asia Pacific*, vol. 7, no. 3, 2007, p. 358.
70. There is also the question of whether modern categories can comprehend non-Western rationalities. In any case categories create subjects, thereby distorting them.
71. Jonardon Ganeri, *Philosophy In Classical India: The Proper Work of Reason* (London: Routledge, 2001), p. 4.
72. Maurice Bloch, *How we Think they Think: Anthropological Approaches to Cognition, Memory and Literacy* (Boulder, CO: Westview Press, 1998), p. 6.
73. Kenneth E. Wilkening, 'Culture and Japanese Citizen Influence on the Transboundary Air Pollution Issue in Northeast Asia,' *Political Psychology*, vol. 20, no. 4, 1999, pp. 705–6.
74. Jonathan Friedman, *Cultural Identity and Global Process* (London: Sage, 1994), p. 27.
75. Braudel used '*la longue durée*' to refer to the 'almost timeless history' of the relationship of humans to the natural environment; see Fernand Braudel, 'Histoire et sciences sociales. *La longue durée,*' Annales E.S.C., vol. 13, *1958*.
76. Nietzsche never described anything approximating a 'genealogical approach'. His writings however provide a means to map a genealogical approach. See Friedrich W. Nietzsche, *The Will to Power*, trans. W. Kaufmann and R.J. Holhngdale (New York: Vintage Books, 1968); Paul Saurette, 'I Mistrust All Systematizers and Avoid Them: Nietzsche, Arendt and the Will to Order in International Relations Theory,' *Millennium Journal of International Relations*, Vol. 25, No. 1, March 1996.
77. Max Weber, *From Max Weber: Essays in Sociology*, trans. & ed. H. H. Gerth and C. Wright Mills (New York: Galaxy, 1958), pp. 13–31.
78. Donald A. Nielsen, 'Rationalization, Transformations of Consciousness and Intercivilizational Encounters: Reflections on Benjamin Nelson's Sociology of Civilizations,' *International Sociology*, vol. 16, no. 3, September 2001, pp. 411–12.
79. Murphy Halliburton, 'Social Thought & Commentary: Gandhi Or Gramsci? The Use of authoritative sources in anthropology,' *Anthropological Quarterly*, vol. 77, no. 4, 2004.
80. James Der Derian, 'The Conceptual Cosmology of Paul Virilio,' *Theory Culture Society*, vol. 16, no. 5–6, 1999.
81. Eric Blondel, 'The Question of Genealogy' in Richard Schacht (ed.), *Nietzsche, Genealogy, Morality: Essays on Nietzsche's Genealogy of Morals* (Berkeley: University of California Press, 1994), p. 310.
82. Ulf Hannerz, 'Cosmopolitans and Locals in World Culture,' *Theory, Culture and Society*, vol. 7, no. 2–3, 1990, pp. 239–40.
83. Immanuel Kant, 'Toward Perpetual Peace', in H.S. Reiss (ed.), *Kant: Political Writing* (Cambridge University Press, 1991); Jürgen Habermas, 'Kant's Idea of Perpetual Peace,

with the Benefit of Two Hundred Years Hindsight' in James Bohman and Matthias Lutz-Bachman (eds), *Perpetual Peace: Essays on Kant's Cosmopolitan Ideal* (Cambridge, MA: MIT Press, 1997), p. 117.

84. Jürgen Habermas, *The Inclusion of the Other: Studies in Political Theory* (Cambridge MA: MIT Press, 2001).

85. J. Duvernay-Bolens, 'Un trickster chez les naturalistes: la notion d'hybride,' *Ethnologie Française*, vol. 23, no. 1, 1993. For an overview of recent uses of the notion of hybridity see Deborah A. Kapchan and Pauline Turner Strong, 'Theorizing the Hybrid,' *The Journal of American Folklore*, vol. 112, no. 445, 1999.

86. Gerard Delanty, *Inventing Europe: Idea, Identity, Reality* (Basingstoke: Macmillan, 1995), pp. 45–6.

87. Theodore H. von Laue (1987), pp. 43–5.

88. Donald A. Nielsen, *Three Faces of God: Society, Religion and the Categories of Totality in the Philosophy of Émile Durkheim* (Albany: SUNY Press, 1999), pp. 13–16; Benjamin Nelson, 1981, pp. 203–5.

89. Benjamin Nelson (1981), p. 84. Nelson drew on Émile Durkheim and Marcel Mauss. See Émile Durkheim and Marcel Mauss, 'Note on the Notion of Civilization', trans. Benjamin Nelson, *Social Research*, vol. 38, no. 4, 1971, p. 812.

90. Civilizations of course are forever changing, owing to internal pluralism as much as international encounters, but that does not make for a total revision of the civilization, for that would negate the concept itself. See Robert Cox, 'Thinking about Civilizations,' *Review of International Studies*, vol. 26, no. 2, Dec. 2000, pp. 217, 220; Benjamin Nelson, 'Civilizational Complexes and Intercivilizational Encounters,' *Sociological Analysis*, vol. 34, no. 2, 1973.

91. James Der Derian (1987), p. 1. Poststructuralists obsess about origins, thereby betraying their modernist roots despite the literary turn. For instance Derrida privileges the collision of text and reader as 'origin'. See Jacques Derrida, *Of Grammatology*, trans. Gayatri Chakravorty Spivak (Baltimore: Johns Hopkins University Press, 1976), p. 162. The point of course is to verify the nature of those collisions in carefully delineated circumstances.

92. Michel Foucault (1972), pp. 139–40.

93. Frederick Errington and Deborah Gewertz, 'The Individuation of Tradition in a Papua New Guinea Modernity,' *American Anthropologist*, vol. 98, no. 1, 1996. David Miller, *Modernity: An Ethnographic Approach* (Oxford University Press, 1994).

94. Martin Wight and Herbert Butterfield (eds) (1966); Hedley Bull (1977), pp. 24–5; Kenneth N. Waltz (1979); Hans J. Morgenthau (1967); Robert O. Keohane and Lisa L. Martin, 'The Promise of Institutionalist Theory,' *International Security*, vol. 20, no. 1, Summer 1995; Helen Milner, 'The Assumption of Anarchy in International Relations Theory: A Critique,' *Review of International Studies*, vol. 17, no. 1, January 1991; Keneth A. Oye (ed.), *Cooperation Under Anarchy* (Princeton University Press, 1986).

95. The problem with constructivists is that they first assume the international is anarchical, and then they can conceptualize politics in this realm as only Hobbesian, Lockean or Kantian. See Alexander Wendt, *Social Theory of International Politics* (New York: Cambridge University Press, 1999), p. 309.

96. Constructivists assume locals are Europeanized because they operate in anarchy. See Tarak Barkawi and Mark Laffey, 'The Post-Colonial Moment in Security Studies,' *Review of International Studies*, vol. 32, no. 2, 2006, pp. 331–2.

97. Friedrich W. Nietzsche, *The Will to Power*, trans. Walter Kaufmann and R.J. Hollingdale (New York: Vintage Books, 1967).

98. Navnita Chadha Behera, 2007, p. 360.

2. IRREPRESSIBLE PRESENT

1. Bruno Latour quoted in Deep K. Datta-Ray, 'The only shibboleth the West has is science,' *Times of India*, 4 April 2011.
2. Christian Godin, 'The Notion of Totality in Indian Thought,' trans. Richard Stamp, *Diogenes*, no. 189, nol. 48, no. 1, 2000, p. 58.
3. Edwin Lutyens had no time for Indian architecture and the buildings were actually designed by Baker. See Robert G. Irving, *Indian Summer: Lutyens, Baker, and Imperial Delhi* (New Haven: Yale University Press, 1981).
4. Even theorists use modernity as a sponge term; see Carola Dietze, 'Toward a History on Equal Terms: A Discussion of Provincializing Europe,' *History and Theory*, vol. 47, no. 1, February 2008; Dipesh Chakrabarty, 'In Defense of Provincializing Europe: A Response to Carla Dietze,' *History and Theory*, vol. 47, no. 1, February 2008.
5. At best there is silence about the theoretical resources and self-understandings of locals. See Jonardon Ganeri, 'Intellectual India: Reason, Identity, Dissent: Amartya Sen and the Reach of Reason,' *New Literary History*, vol. 40, no. 2, pp. 248–9. Europeans, of course, assert that everything current was born in Europe, in terms of theory and in practice. On theory see Iver B. Neumann, *Russia and the Idea of Europe: a Study in Identity and International Relations* (London: Routledge, 1996). For a practical example see Deep K. Datta-Ray, 'New club rules,' *South China Morning Post*, 12 July 2012.
6. See Anthony Smith, *The Ethnic Origins of Nations* (Oxford: Basil Blackwell, 1986); Crawford Young, *The Politics of Cultural Pluralism* (Madison: University of Wisconsin Press, 1976); John L. Comaroff, 'Humanity, Ethnicity, Nationality: Conceptual and Comparative Perspectives on the USSR,' *Theory and Society*, vol. 20, no, 5, October 1991. Recent works include Albert Breton, Gianluigi Galeotti, Pierre Salmon, and Ronald Winterobe (eds), *Nationalism and Rationalists* (New York: Cambridge University Press, 1995); Ernst B. Haas, *Nationalism, Liberalism, and Progress: The Rise and Decline of Nationalism* (Ithaca, NY: Cornell University Press, 1997).
7. For the instrumental view of Indian nationalism see G. Aloysius, *Nationalism without a Nation in India* (Oxford University Press, 1997), pp. 217–18. See also Partha Chatterjee, 'Nationalism as a Problem in the History of Political Ideas' in Partha Chatterjee, *Nationalist Thought and the Colonial World: A Derivative Discourse* (Tokyo: United Nations University and London: Zed Books, 1986); Partha Chatterjee, *The Politics of the Governed: Reflections on Popular Politics in Most of the World* (New York: Columbia University Press, 2004), p. 85.
8. Even if there is an unrealized surplus to modernity, it is still derived from Christianity and hence an imposition. See Javed Alam, 'The Composite Culture and its Historiography,' *South Asia*, vol. 22, Special Issue, 1999.
9. Slide on Evolution supplied by MEA. The slide is from a database which is used every year to induct probationers.
10. 'Indian Foreign Service, A Backgrounder.' Available at MEA Website. http://meaindia.nic.in/mystart.php?id=5002
11. IFS Officer no. 2.
12. IFS Probationer no. 9.
13. IFS Probationer no. 2. Similar comments were later made by IFS Probationers no. 4, 7, 12, 15. Every probationer I put the hypothesis to agreed. Most enthusiastic were IFS Probationers 4, 5, 16, 20.
14. That secularism is in itself an outgrowth of Christianity provokes another set of quandaries that are not followed here. For the religious origins of secularism see William E. Connolly,

Why I Am Not a Secularist (Minneapolis: University of Minnesota Press, 1999), pp. 19–25. See also Charles Taylor, *A Secular Age* (Cambridge, MA: The Belknap Press of Harvard University Press, 2007).

15. For high-modernist approaches to this, see Harold A. Gould, 'Lucknow Rickshawallas: The Social Organization of an Occupational Category' in Harold A. Gould (ed.), *Caste Adaptation in Modernizing Indian Society* (New Delhi: Chanakya Publications, 1988); Milton Singer, 'Industrial Leadership, the Hindu Ethic and the Spirit of Socialism' in Milton Singer (ed.), *When a Great Tradition Modernizes: An Anthropological Approach to Indian Civilization* (New York: Praeger, 1972). For late-modernist critiques which, rather than denying the reality of local existence, subsume these phenomena into 'cosmopolitanism', see James Ferguson, *Expectations of Modernity: Myth and Meanings of Urban Life on the Zambian Copperbelt* (Berkeley: University of California Press, 1999).

16. The homogeneity of the post-independence state was broken by its leader's policies of positive discrimination explained below. See also Partha Chatterjee, 'The Nation in Heterogeneous Time,' *The Indian Economic and Social History Review*, vol. 38, no. 4, 2001.

17. George Orwell, *Nineteen Eighty-Four* (London: Secker and Warburg, 1949), Part I, Chapter 3, p. 32.

18. Hence this is not a circular understanding of time, often used to divide the cosmos into East and West. See Akhil Gupta, 'The Reincarnation of Souls and the Rebirth of Commodities: Representations of Time in East and West,' *Cultural Critique*, No. 22, Autumn 1992.

19. Wilhelm Halbfass, *India and Europe: An Essay in Understanding* (Albany, NY: SUNY, 1988), p. 375.

20. See Gyan Prakash, 'Writing Post-Orientalist Histories of the Third World: Perspectives from Indian Historiography' and 'Can the 'Subaltern' Ride? A Reply to O'Hanlon and Washbrook' in Vinayak Chaturvedi (ed.), *Mapping Subaltern Studies and the Postcolonial* (London: Verso, 2000). See also Rosalind O'Hanlon and David Washbrook, 'After Orientalism: Culture, Criticism and Politics in the Third World' in Vinayak Chaturvedi (ed.) (2000).

21. Underpinning this is anarchical-binarism. Halbfass is a good example of this. He decontextualizes Christian missionaries in India, thereby removing from them the Christian tenet of fulfilment, and then states that they got this from Indians! See S.N. Balagangadhara, 'Understanding and Imagination, A Critical Notice of Halbfass and Inden,' *Cultural Dynamics*, vol. 3, 1990, pp. 390–91.

22. Filippo Osella and Caroline Osella, *Social Mobility in Kerala: Modernity and Identity in Conflict* (London: Pluto Press, 2000), p. 9. Filippo Osella and Katy Gardner, 'Migration, Modernity and Social Transformation in South Asia: an Overview,' *Contributions to Indian Sociology*, vol. 37, no. 1 & 2, 2003, pp. xii-xiii. Modernity is recognized as being conceptually empty, so why use it to contain non-Westerns?

23. Of course, subalterns were never totally silenced. See Susie Tharu and K. Lalita (eds), *Women Writing in India: 600 BC to the Present*, vol. I (New York: Feminist Press, 1991).

24. Gyan Prakash follows Ashis Nandy, *The Intimate Enemy: Loss and Recovery Of Self under Colonialism* (New Delhi: Oxford University Press, 1983).

25. Prakash's moves are nihilistic because they are encumbered by Western disillusionment. For a critique of postcolonial approaches in IR see Albert Paolini, *Navigating Modernity: Post-Colonialism, Identity and International Relations* (Boulder, CO: Lynne Rienner Press, 1999), pp. 98–101.

26. For a similar move exposing equivalence between two opposing authors see Kunal M. Parker, 'The Historiography of Difference,' *Law and History Review*, vol. 23, no. 3, Fall 2005.

27. Even the over-analyzed category of *bhadralok* is unfixable. See Tithi Bhattacharya, 'A World of Learning: the Material Culture of Education and Class in Nineteenth-century Bengal' in Crispin Bates (ed.), *Beyond Representation: Colonial and Postcolonial Constructions of Indian Identity* (New Delhi: Oxford University Press, 2006); Swapna M. Banerjee, 'Subverting the Moral Universe: 'Narratives of Transgression' in the Construction of Middle-class Identity in Colonial Bengal' in Crispin Bates (ed.) (2006).

28. Gyan Prakash, 'Can the 'Subaltern' Ride? A Reply to O'Hanlon and Washbrook' in Vinayak Chaturvedi (ed.) (2000).

29. There is nothing intrinsically non-modern about the myth, it may be a tool of modernity. See Eric Strand, 'Gandhian communalism and the Midnight Children's conference,' *ELH*, vol. 72, no. 4, Winter 2005.

30. The hallmark of studying the past. See Samuel Huntington, *The Third Wave: Democratization in the late Twentieth Century* (Norman: University of Oaklahoma Press, 1991).

31. Jean-François Lyotard (1984), pp. xxiv. This is not Bhabha's antireferential approach (for such knowledge is impossible) but is contextual, the contexts of diplomats. See Homi K. Bhabha, *The Location of Culture* (London: Routledge, 1994), p. 256. Nor does the task have to be awkward: see Albert Paolini (1999), p. 58.

32. Given the uniqueness of this exercise, this section has benefited from Jules Naudet, '"Paying-Back to Society": Upward Social Mobility among Dalits,' *Contributions to Indian Sociology*, vol. 42, no. 3, 2008.

33. Preneet Kaur, Lok Sabha Unstarred Question No. 4201, 19 February 2014. See http://www.mea.gov.in/lok-sabha.htm?dtl/22943/Q+NO+4201+SC+ST+AND+OBCs+IN+FOREIGN+SERVICES.

34. Many of these were in a mix of Indian languages (including Hindi, Bengali, Tamil, Malayalam, Bhojpuri, and various other languages), especially during parties and in group situations. I however am only fluent in English.

35. David Arnold and Stuart Blackburn, *Telling Lives in India: Biography, Autobiography, and Life History* (Bloomington: Indiana University Press, 2004), p. 10.

36. Some politicians were happy to have conversations attributed to them, but most were not.

37. Matthew Sparke, *In the Space of Theory: Postfoundational Geographies of the Nation-state* (Minneapolis: University of Minnesota Press, 2005).

38. Manu Goswami, *Producing India: From Colonial Economy to National Space* (Chicago University Press, 2004), p. 4.

39. David Arnold and Stuart Blackburn (2004), pp. 4–5.

40. Arlene B. Tickner, 'Seeing IR Differently: Notes from the Third World,' *Millennium: Journal of International Studies*, vol. 32, no. 2, 2003, p. 304.

41. The cosmos is indeed the cosmos. It is not a modernist universal, a coagulation of nations and citizens or a product of governmentality: the finite totals produced by national censuses. Nor is the cosmos totalizing or homogenizing, but the total of everything that exists, because it exists. There is no futile search for origins. As for the future, what comes into existence is a product of the cosmos by virtue of either being discovered by or being descended from an element within the cosmos. It exists before 'the world' (modernity) and therefore contains it, rather than having been displaced by it as argued by Benedict Anderson, *The Spectre of Comparison: Nationalism, Southeast Asia and the World* (London: Verso, 1998), p. 44.

42. M.K. Gandhi, 'Discourses on the Gita,' 4 April 1926, in *The Collected Works of Mahatma Gandhi* (Electronic Book) (New Delhi, Publications Division Government of India, 1999, 98 volumes) (Henceforth CWMG-EB), vol. 37, p. 118. The EB has been used because the 97 documents left out of it are of little relevance to this work. See Tridip Suhrud, '"Re-

editing" Gandhi's Collected Works,' *Economic and Political Weekly*, vol. 39, no. 46, 47, 20 November 2004.

43. James Der Derian (1987), pp. 51–9, 105–16.

44. J.P. Singh Uberoi, *The European Modernity: Science, Truth and Method* (New Delhi: Oxford University Press, 2002), p. 27. Uberoi's work encompasses Der Derian type theories within the broader framework of modernity.

45. See Homi K. Bhabha, 'Difference, Discrimination and the Discourse of Colonialism' in F. Barker, P. Hulme, M. Iversen and D. Loxley (eds), *The Politics of Theory* (Colchester: University of Essex, 1983), pp. 194–211; Homi K. Bhabha, 'Of Mimicry and Man: The Ambivalence of Colonial Discourse' in Homi K. Bhabha (1994), pp. 121–31. Hybridity can only exist within the assumption of modernity. See K. Mitchell, 'Different Diasporas and the Hype of Hybridity,' *Environment and Planning D: Society and Space*, vol. 15, 1997, p. 534.

46. When Spivak writes: 'We are always after the empire of reason, our claims to it always short of adequate,' she is talking about people like herself, modernized and struggling within it. There is no need to presume that 'we' includes the hundreds of millions of people in India or that their reason of a unified cosmos is either not 'reason' or after modernity's 'reason'. See Gayatri Chakravorty Spivak, *Post Colonial Critic: Interviews, Strategies and Dialogues*, ed. Sarah Harasym (London: Routledge, 1990), p. 228.

47. This possibility was demonstrated in epic Europe, long before modernity seized the continent, see R.N. Lebow, *A Cultural Theory of International Relations* (Cambridge University Press, 2008), p. 485.

48. Gyan Prakash (2000).

49. Homi K. Bhabha (1994), p. 241.

50. Gayatri Chakravorty Spivak, *Post Colonial Critic: Interviews, Strategies and Dialogues*, ed. Sarah Harasyn (London: Routledge, 1990), p. 72.

51. Anomie is of course part and parcel of modernity. See Jürgen Habermas, *Knowledge and Human Interests*, trans. Jeremy Shapiro (London: Heinemann, 1972), p. 348.

52. Manmohan Singh, 'Speech by Prime Minister Dr. Manmohan Singh at the Foundation Stone laying ceremony of Jawaharlal Nehru Bhavan to house the Ministry of External Affairs' [14 February 2006] in Avtar Singh Bhasin (ed.) (2007), *India's Foreign Relations—2007* (New Delhi: Geetika Publications, 2008); Manmohan Singh, 'Address by Prime Minister at the Pravasi Bharatiya Divas' [7 January 2007] in Avtar Singh Bhasin (ed.); Manmohan Singh, 'Remarks of Prime Minister at the Fortune Global Forum' in Avtar Singh Bhasin (ed.), 29 October 2007.

53. In 2004 modernity began to theorize relational ways of being, or tropes, as opposed to standard formulaic structured understandings of human relations. See Janet Carsten, *After Kinship* (Cambridge University Press, 2004).

54. Brian A. Hatcher, "'The Cosmos is One Family" (Vasudhaiva Kutumbakam): Problematic Mantra of Hindu Humanism,' *Contributions to Indian Sociology*, vol. 28, no. 1, January 1994.

55. Different but not alienated. In fact the crow loves the deer and the jackal engages both. An interrelated cosmos.

56. Some come very close to this approach, but ultimately remain restrained by their starting hypothesis of otherness. See Kathinka Froystad, *Blended Boundaries: Caste, Class and Shifting Faces of 'Hinduness' in a North Indian City* (New Delhi: Oxford University Press, 2005).

57. James Coleman, 'Social Capital in the Creation of Human Capital,' *American Journal of Sociology*, vol. 94, no. 1, 1988, pp. 100–01.

58. Milton M. Gordon, *Social Class in American Sociology* (Durham, NC: Duke University Press, 1958), p. 189.

59. See Alain de Boton, *Status Anxiety* (New York: Pantheon, 2004).
60. James C. Kimberly, 'Status Inconsistency: A Reformulation of a Theoretical Problem,' *Human Relations*, vol. 20, no. 2, 1967.
61. Constitution of India, Articles 309–311. IAS Officer no. 3.
62. IFS Officer no. 7.
63. Michael Billig, *Banal Nationalism* (London: Sage, 1995), pp. 6–8.
64. IFS Officer no. 16.
65. IFS Officer no. 12. On familial relations see Indrani Chatterjee (ed.), *Unfamiliar Relations: Family and History in South Asia* (New Delhi: Permanent Black, 2004).
66. 'Civil Services witness 25 % rise in aspirants,' *The Economic Times*, 25 March 2009. http://articles.economictimes.indiatimes.com/2009–03–25/news/28435314_1_civil-services-private-sector-aspirants
67. See Barry Barnes, *Understanding Agency: Social Theory and Responsible Action* (London: Sage Publications, 2000).
68. IFS Probationer no. 2.
69. Christopher Fuller, Harpriya Narasimhan, 'Information Technology Professionals and the New-rich Middle Class in Chennai (Madras),' *Modern Asian Studies*, vol. 41, no. 1, 2007, p. 143.
70. IFS Probationer no. 7. Similar comments were made by IFS Officer no. 2 & 9 & IFS Probationers no. 12 & 15, IAS Probationer no. 1. *Gora* is a pejorative term for whites.
71. IFS Probationer no. 3.
72. IFS Officer no. 4
73. IFS Officer no. 38.
74. Mani Shankar Aiyar, interview, 3 February 2008, his residence, New Delhi.
75. IFS Officer no. 11.
76. IFS Officer no. 18.
77. IFS-R Officer no. 21. For a theorization of the compatibility of family loyalty with state loyalty see Muzafer Sherif and Carolyn W. Sherif, *Groups in Harmony and Tension: An Integration of Studies on Intergroup Relations* (New York: Harper, 1953), p. 44.
78. Mani Shankar Aiyar, interview, Aiyar's residence, 3 February 2008.
79. IFS Officer no. 17.
80. IFS Probationer no. 8. Nearly every probationer expressed similar sentiments. Most vocal were IFS Probationers no. 2, 12, 15.
81. See Barbara Simpson, 'Pragmatism, Mead and the Practice Turn,' *Organisation Studies*, vol. 30, no. 12, December 2009.
82. IFS Probationer no. 4.
83. Corruption is defined usually as the misuse of authority for private gain. See Arnold J. Heidenheimer (ed.), *Political Corruption: Readings in Comparative Analysis* (New Brunswick, NJ: Transaction Books, 1978), pp. 3–28. Corruption is also equated to legal violence. See Kate Gillespie and Gwenn Okruhlik, 'The Political Dimensions of Corruption Cleanups: A Framework for Analysis,' *Comparative Politics*, vol. 24, no. 1, October 1991, p. 66. Corruption is also viewed not in terms of legal definitions and their violations but of the standards against which 'corruption' is measured. See Akhil Gupta, 'Narrating the State of Corruption' in Dieter Haller and Cris Shore (eds), *Corruption: Anthropological Perspectives* (London: Pluto Press, 2005), p. 78.
84. IFS Officer no. 30.
85. IFS Probationer no. 16.
86. IFS Probationer no. 20.
87. As opposed to what is argued by Gyan Prakash (2001).

88. IFS Probationer no. 20.

89. Said while Aiyar was meeting new diplomats before his lecture, Mani Shakar Aiyar, 'India of my dreams', Lecture at Foreign Service Institute, 27 August 2007. There is no record of this lecture in Avtar Singh Bhasin (ed.) (2008).

90. IFS Probationer no. 5. For a standard modernist, in this case paternalistic, take on tribal education see Lauren Alcorn, *Indigenous Education at Crossroads: James Bay Cree and the Tribal People of Orissa* (Bhubhaneshwar: Sikshasandhan, 2006).

91. Paul Virilio, *Speed and Politics: An Essay on Dromology*, trans. Mark Polizzotti (New York: Semiotext(e), 1986), p. 142.

92. John C. Torpey, *The Invention of the Passport. Surveillance, Citizenship and the State* (Cambridge University Press, 2000), p. 7.

93. William E. Connolly, 'Speed, Concentric Cultures, and Cosmopolitanism,' *Political Theory*, vol. 28, no. 5, October 2000.

94. Ibid., p. 609.

95. Even wealthy merchants may be subalterns. See Douglas Haynes, 'From Avoidance to Confrontation? A Contestory History of Merchant-state Relations in Surat, 1600–1924' in Douglas Haynes and Gyan Prakash (eds), *Contesting Power: Resistance and Everyday Social Relations in South Asia* (New Delhi: Oxford University Press, 1991).

96. Ronald B. Inden, *Imagining India* (Oxford: Basil Blackwell, 1990), p. 197.

97. These are processes of the particular. See Noam Chomsky and Michel Foucault, 'Human Nature: Justice Versus Power', in Fons Elders (ed.), *Reflexive Water: The Basic Concerns of Mankind* (London: Souvenir Press, 1974), p. 180.

98. The central government body that conducts the entrance exams for the all-India services.

99. Arundhati Ghosh, 6 May 2008, conversation, India International Centre, New Delhi.

100. The word is often misued by Indians who have a vague conception, drawn from English literature (that is, the literature of England), about a group of people they have never met.

101. IFS Probationer no. 13.

102. IRS Probationer no. 1; comments replicated by IRS Probationer no. 4 & 5. IRS Probationers no. 2 & 3 gave much more mundane reasons: 'getting a job with a good living standard'.

103. The evidence for this contention was garnered from several interviews and conversations, particularly IFS Officers no. 1, 2, 3, 8, 24, 26, 27, 34, 42, 44 and IFS Probationers no. 2, 7, 11, 12, 21, 22, 23 and IAS Probationer no. 2.

104. IRS Probationer no. 4.

105. On this class see B.B. Misra, *The Indian Middle Class: Their Growth in Modern Times* (Bombay: Oxford University Press, 1961).

106. See Chapter 1, section on hybridity.

107. Jawid Laiq, 'Diplomatic Impunity,' *The Outlook*, New Delhi, 27 September 1999. See: http://www.outlookindia.com/article.aspx?208153 See also Aurobindo Ghosh, *The Ideal of Human Unity* (Madras, 1919), p. 298. For a detailed discussion see Bishwanath Prasad, *The Indian Administratitive Service* (New Delhi: S. Chand, 1968), pp. 19–21; Nagendranath Ghosh, *Comparative Administrative Law* (Calcutta: Butterworth, 1919), p. 298.

108. V.P. Menon, *The Story of the Integration of Indian States* (London: Longmans, Green, 1956), p. 204. Menon writes that Sardar Patel proposed that five or six Maharajahs or near relatives should be incorporated into the services. The Nawab of Rampur requested Lord Moutbatten to recommend his son's name to Sardar Patel for induction into the newly established Central Service. The Viceroy wrote that the son was a 'high class Muslim' who has a 'charming wife', and the Sardar let him into the service. See also Durga Dass (ed.), *Sardar Patel's Correspondence, vol. VIII* (Ahmedabad: Navjivan Publishing House, 1973), pp. 367–8.

109. Barbara N. Ramusack, *The Princes of India in the Twilight of Empire: Dissolution of a Patron-client System, 1914–1939* (Columbus: University of Cincinnati, 1978), p. 244.

110. See Homi K. Bhabha, 'Difference, Discrimination and the Discourse of Colonialism' in F. Barker *et al.* (eds), *The Politics of Theory*, (Colchester: University of Essex, 1983), pp. 194–211; Homi K. Bhabha, 'Of Mimicry and Man: The Ambivalence of Colonial Discourse,' *October*, 28, pp. 125–33, p. 126; Homi K. Bhabha, 'Surviving Theory: A Conversation with Homi K. Bhabha' in F. Afzal-Khan and K. Seshadri-Crooks (eds), *The Preoccupation of Postcolonial Studies* (Durham, NC: Duke University Press), 2000, p. 370.

111. Jawaharlal Nehru, 'A Historic Milestone in Cooperation' in Sarvepalli Gopal, Ravinder Kumar, H. Y. Sharada Prasad, A. K. Damodaran and Mushirul Hasan (eds), *Selected Works of Jawaharlal Nehru*, Second Series, Vol. 28, 1 Feb.–31 May, 1955, p. 549.

112. Singapore's first Chief of Staff, Brigadier-General Kirpa Ram Vij, quoted in Sunanda K. Datta-Ray, *Looking East to Look West: Lee Kuan Yew's Mission India* (Singapore: ISEAS Press, 2009), pp. 125–9.

113. P.K. Varma, 'The Bureaucratic Bazaar, Uncivil Service,' *The Pioneer (Foray)*, New Delhi, 6 August 2000.

114. Prasenjit Duara, 'Why is History Antitheoreatical?' *Modern China*, vol. 24, no. 2, April 1998, p. 105.

115. A.N.D. Haksar, 'Shine off the Foreign Service,' *Hindustan Times*, New Delhi, 16 August 1992; A.N.D. Haksar, 'Mandalisation and the Foreign Service,' *The Pioneer*, New Delhi, 4 Sept. 1994.

116. Rajeev Deshpande, Rema Nagarajan and Vishwa Mohan, 'Changing face of the Indian civil servant,' *The Times of India*, 16 January 2010. http://articles.timesofindia.indiatimes.com/2010–01–16/india/28118492_1_civil-services-entrance-exams-upsc

117. Jivat Thadani, IAS, conversation, IIC, New Delhi, 20 March 2011.

118. No. 36033/5/2004-Estt.(Res.), Government of India, Ministry of Personnel, Public Grievances & Pensions, Department of Personnel & Training, 14 October 2004. See http://circulars.nic.in/WriteReadData/CircularPortal/D2/D02adm/36033_5_2004_01April2005.htm

119. Article 340 of the Indian Constitution empowers the government to create such classes, and in 1955 2,339 groups were designated as belonging to the Other Backward Castes (OBC). The 1980 report of the Mandal Commission (established to 'identify the socially or educationally backward') recommended that, in addition to the 23% of government jobs reserved for the Scheduled Caste and Scheduled Tribes, a further 27% be reserved for the OBC. In 1990, V.P. Singh announced plans to implement this recommendation. In 1992 India's Supreme Court upheld jobs reservation for the OBC but ruled that: (i) reservation was not to extend to more than 50% of the population and (ii) that groups within the OBC category who were manifestly not disadvantaged (the 'creamy layer') were to be excluded from reservation.

120. Retired IFS-R Officer no. 1.

121. Two multiple choice papers in General Studies (150 questions in two hours) and an Optional paper (120 questions in two hours).

122. IAS Officer no. 2.

123. IFS Probationer no. 14. Similar comments were made most pointedly by IFS Probationers no. 2, 3, 8, 9, 10, 15, 17, 20.

124. D.S. Chauhan, 'India's Underprivileged Classes and the Higher Public Service: Towards Developing a Representative Bureaucracy,' *Review of Administrative Sciences*, vol. 42, 1976, pp. 39–55.

125. 'Lessons in English for today's diplomats,' *The Times of India*, 16 January 2010, http://articles.timesofindia.indiatimes.com/2010–01–16/india/28116854_1_foreign-service-foreign-language-regional-languages. IFS-R no. 3.

126. A.N.D. Haksar (1992 and 1994).

127. IFS Officer no. 1. Also IFS Officers no. 5, 34, and 38.

128. Pranab Mukherjee, 'Appointment of High Commissioners/Ambassadors,' Lok Sabha Unstarred Question No. 1209, 29 November 2006. See: http://meaindia.nic.in/mystart. php?id=220212069

129. Preneet Kaur, Lok Sabha Unstarred Question No. 4201, 19 February 2014. See http://www.mea.gov.in/lok-sabha.htm?dtl/22943/Q+NO+4201+SC+ST+AND+OBCs+IN+FOREIGN+SERVICES

130. Preneet Kaur, Lok Sabha Unstarred Question No. 1648, 10 August 2011. Seehttp://meaindia.nic.in/mystart.php?id=500418071

131. Sachin Parashar, 'MEA reviews choice of steno as North Korea envoy,' *The Times of India*, 13 June 2012. See: http://articles.timesofindia.indiatimes.com/2012–06–13/india/32214184_1_ifs-officers-stenographer-mea

132. IFS Officer no. 1.

133. Saran did one stint in the West as a First Secretary in Geneva. After him Shivshankar Menon became FS and similarly also did just one stint in the West as a First Secretary.

134. Natwar Singh, conversation, his residence, New Delhi, 4 June 2007. This was long after my first encounter with him.

135. Constitution of India, Articles 309–311; IAS Officer no. 3.

136. IFS Officer no. 5; also IFS Officers no. 27 and 38.

137. IFS Officer no. 21.

138. IFS Officer no. 14.

139. IFS Probationer no. 6.

140. Public Service Commission, Examination Notice No. 04/2012-CSP, 11 February 2012.

141. World Bank, *2011 World Development Indicators* (Washington, 2011), p. 25. See http://issuu.com/world.bank.publications/docs/9780821387092/52?mode=a_p

142. IFS Probationer no. 12.

143. IFS Probationer no. 5.

144. IFS Probationer no. 7. Other probationers tangentially agreed, particularly IFS Probationers no. 2, 4, 8, 9. Some justified the practice.

145. IFS Officer no. 15. Comments repeated by IFS Officers no. 24, 34.

146. Special Correspondent, 'Steno envoy sparks 'caste war',' *The Telegraph*, 9 June 2012. See http://www.telegraphindia.com/1120609/jsp/nation/story_15589174.jsp#.T9mObistiiY

147. See Max Weber, *The Protestant Ethic and the Spirit of Capitalism* trans. Talcott Parson (New York: Scribner, 1930). On the ways in which the PWE engenders prejudice see Christian S. Crandall, 'Ideology and Lay Theories of Stigma: The Justification of Stigmatization' in Todd F. Heatherton, Robert E. Kleck, Michelle R. Hebl and Jay G. Hull (eds), *The Social Psychology of Stigma* (New York: Guildford Press, 2000); Sheri R. Levy, Antonio L. Freitas and Peter Salovey, 'Constructing Action Abstractly and Blurring Social Distinctions: Implications for Perceiving Homogeneity among, but also Empathizing with and Helping, Others,' *Journal of Personality and Social Psychology*, vol. 83, 2002; Felicia Pratto, James Sidanius, Lisa M. Stallworth and Bertram F. Malle, 'Social Dominance Orientation: A Personality Variable Predicting Social and Political Attitudes,' *Journal of Personality and Social Psychology*, vol. 67, 1994; Diane M. Quinn and Jennifer Crocker, 'When Ideology Hurts: Effects of Feeling Fat and the Protestant Ethic on the Psychological Well-being of Women,' *Journal of Personality and Social Psychology*, vol. 77; Irwin Katz and R. Glenn

Haas, 'Racial Ambivalence and American Value Conflict: Correlational and Priming Studies of Dual Cognitive Structures,' *Journal of Personality and Social Psychology*, vol. 55, 1988; Christian S. Crandall, 'Prejudice against Fat People: Ideology and self-interest,' *Journal of Personality and Social Psychology*, vol. 66, 1994.

148. IFS Probationer no. 1. Emphasized by IFS Probationer no. 2, 3, 6, 13, 14, 16, 20; and by nearly every IFS Officer.

149. Diplomats anticipated problems—such as teacher absenteeism—in achieving an education because they know their locality. On anticipation and education success see Raegen T. Miller, Richard J. Murnane and John B. Willet, 'Do Teacher Absences Impact Student Achievement? Longitudinal Evidence from One Urban School District,' *Educational Evaluation & Policy Analysis*, vol. 30, no. 2, June 2008, p. 196.

150. IFS Probationer no. 21. As became quickly apparent, such difficulties were the norm for many officers and probationers.

151. On 'innovation' within modernist bureaucracy see M. Harris, 'Technology, Innovation and Post-bureaucracy: The Case of the British Library,' *Journal of Organization Change Management*, vol. 19, no. 1, 2006.

152. IFS Probationer no. 21.

153. These are experiential differences, not elitist interpretations of supposed 'ideas of India' fabricated by analysis based on the false binarism of elite/mass implicit in practically all works. For an example see Sunil Khilnani, *The Idea of India* (London: Hamish Hamilton, 1997, Chapter I).

154. This is in contrast to Benedict Anderson (1983), p. 44.

155. See Ranjita Mohanty and Rajesh Tandon (eds), *Participatory Citizenship: Identity, Exclusion, Inclusion* (New Delhi: Sage, 2006).

156. Research and Information System for Developing Countries. 'The RIS is actually the MEA's back office,' said the person I was speaking to. Economist at Research and Information System for Developing Countries, 10 August 2011, conversation, India Habitat Centre, New Delhi.

157. Low Choo Ming, 'Reflections of 33 Years in Diplomacy' in Tommy Koh & Chan Li Lin (eds), *The Little Red Dot: Reflections by Singapore's Diplomats* (Singapore: World Scientific Publishing, 2005), pp. 223–32.

158. S. Jaishankar, interview, High Commissioner's residence, Singapore, 5 January 2008.

159. M.K. Narayanan in conversation with Harish Khare and Siddharth Varadarajan, 'This is as good a text as one can possibly get,' *The Hindu*, 28 July 2007 http://www.hindu.com/2007/07/28/stories/2007072855121300.htm; M.K. Narayanan in conversation with Harish Khare and Siddharth Varadarajan, 'I don't think the country is yet willing to recognise the U.S. is a benign power,' *The Hindu*, 30 July 2007. http://www.hindu.com/2007/07/30/stories/2007073053941100.htm

160. IFS Officer no. 35.

161. Standing Committee on External Affairs (2006–07, 14th Lok Sabha), Fifteenth Report, Ministry of External Affairs, Demands for Grants (2007–08) (New Delhi: Lok Sabha Secretariat, April 2007), p. 13.

162. IFS Officer no. 1, repeated by IFS Officer no. 40.

163. IFS Officer no. 29.

164. Ibid.

165. IFS Probationer no. 23.

166. IFS Officer no. 39

167. IFS Officer no. 36. Several probationers also mentioned this.

168. IFS Officer no. 39.

169. *Ministry of External Affairs Annual Report 2011–2012* (New Delhi: Policy Planning and Research Division, MEA), p. 147.
170. IFS Probationer no. 14.
171. IFS Probationers no. 11 & 17.
172. IFS Officer no. 32.
173. IFS Officer no. 40. The point was repeated with varying degrees of outrage by older diplomats. Several younger diplomats seemed to be satisfied that nothing more taxing than providing a 'taxi service' was to be expected of them.
174. IAS Officer no. 4. Similar views were held by a large number of senior diplomats and two ministers.
175. IFS Officer no. 40.
176. IFS Probationer no. 9.
177. In Foucault's and then Deleuze's conceptualization, dispositif is the deployment of power to achieve a totalizing objective. Both the deployment, and use, of power are however cloaked. This is because power is not top-down and overwhelming but operates through a range of micro-operations which superficially appear to be dispersed and disconnected.
178. Philip Slater, *The Chrysalis Effect: The Metamorphosis of Global Culture* (Brighton: Sussex Academic Press, 2008), p. 248. Gilles Deleuze, 'What is a dispositif?' in *Michel Foucault: Philosopher*, ed. and trans. Timothy J. Armstrong (New York: Routledge, 1992).
179. Discussion between several probationers and myself. Emphasized in 66 of the 70 interviews.
180. See Michael Adas, 'South Asian Resistance in Comparative Perspective' in Douglas Haynes and Gyan Prakash (eds) (1991).
181. Neera Chandhoke, '"Seeing" the State in India,' *Economic and Political Weekly*, vol. 40, no. 11, 12–18 March 2005, p. 1039.
182. Sherry B. Ortner, *Making Gender: The Politics and Erotics of Culture* (Boston: Beacon Press, 1996), p. 148, speaks of a 'quiet effective agency'.
183. IFS Probationer no. 3.
184. In 2001, average literacy was still 65%. Female literacy is around 54%. See Nitya Nanda, 'The Indian Growth Story: Myths and Realities,' *Journal of Asian and African Studies*, vol. 44, no. 6, 2009, p. 747. Teacher-pupil ratios for primary and upper primary declined from 1:24 and 1:20 in the early 1950s to 1:43 and 1:38 in 1999–2000. Rural health care programmes remain underfunded and what exists is used inefficiently, forcing rural users to access the urban health care system, and almost half of all children below 5 years in India are underweight. See Ravi Duggal, S. Nandraj and A. Vadair, 'Health Expenditure Across States (Special Statistics),' *Economic and Political Weekly* (15—22 April 1995).
185. IFS Probationer no. 9.
186. Amartya Sen, *Development as Freedom* (New York: Alfred A. Knopf, 1999).
187. On the failures of the state and yet its continuing centrality see Sudipta Kaviraj, 'The Modern State in India' in Sudipta Kaviraj and Martin Doornbos (eds), *Dynamics of State Formation: India and Europe Compared* (New Delhi: Sage, 1997).
188. Martin Wight, *Power Politics*, ed. Hedley Bull and Carsten Holbraad (London: Leicester University Press, 1978), p. 58.
189. Boaventura de Sousa Santos, *Towards a New Common Sense: Law, Science and Politics in the Paradigmatic Transition* (New York: Routledge, 1995), pp. 274–81.
190. J.C. Kimberly, 'Status Inconsistency: a Reformulation of a Theoretical Problem,' *Human Relations*, vol. 20, May 1967, p. 171.
191. For a treatment of mobility see S.M. Miller, 'Comparative Social Mobility,' *Current Sociology*, vol. 9, no. 1, 1960.
192. De Neve notes that modernity always involves mobility. See Geert De Neve, 'Expectations

and Rewards of Modernity: Commitment and Mobility among Rural Migrants in Tirupur, Tamil Nadu,' *Contributions to Indian Sociology*, vol. 37, no. 1, 2, 2003, p. 252. Contained, local acts of mobility are interpreted as linear progress probably because of the conceptual and historical Eurocentrism of much sociology and social-science. See Bryan Turner, 'Enclave Society: Towards a Sociology of Immobility,' *European Journal of Social Theory*, vol. 10, no. 2, 2007, p. 288.

193. Helen Constas, *Bureaucratic Collectivism: an Analysis of the Historical Examples of Pharaonic Egypt and Soviet Russia* (New York: New School for Social Research), 1954, p. 31.

194. Calvin Morrill, 'Culture and Organization Theory,' *Annals of the American Academy of Political and Social Science*, vol. 619, no. 1, 2008, p. 35.

195. H.M. Höpfl, 'Post-bureaucracy and Weber's "Modern" Bureaucrat,', *Journal of Organization Change Management*, vol. 19, no. 1, 2006, p. 10.

196. Jack Goody, *The Logic of Writing and the Organization of Society* (Cambridge University Press, 1986), p. 92.

197. Composed of the FS, and the Secretaries handling East, West, Economic Relations and Commerce. See Ministry of External Affairs, Statement of Boards, Councils, Committees and Other Bodies, 21 March 2012, http://www.mea.gov.in/staticfile/rti/4_1_b__vii.pdf.

198. IFS Officer no. 6.

199. Dan Kärreman and Mats Alvesson, 'Cages in Tandem: Management Control, Social Identity, and Identification in a Knowledge-intensive firm,' *Organisation*, vol. 11, no. 1, 2004, p. 152.

200. John F. McCarthy, 'Short Stories at Work: Storytelling as an Indicator of Organizational Commitment,' *Group & Organization Management*, vol. 33, no. 2, April 2008; Graham Sewell, 'The Discipline of Teams: The Control of Team-Based Industrial Work Through Electronic and Peer Surveillance,' *Administrative Science Quarterly*, vol. 43, no. 2, 1998; Graham Sewell and James R. Barker, 'Coercion versus Care: Using Irony to Make Sense of Organizational Surveillance,' *Academy of Management Review*, vol. 31, no. 4, 2006, pp. 934–61.

201. Brajesh Mishra, '"Mao's Smile" Revisited: Sino-Indian Relations during an Important Period,' *Indian Foreign Affairs Journal*, vol. 1, no. 4, 2006.

202. Brajesh Mishra, conversation, his residence, New Delhi, 8 June 2007. It is also the system used by the Boston Consultancy Group (BCG), except that the BCG system permits the appraiser to refer to earlier appraisels when conducting the performance review. This is backstory is not immediately available in the MEA to the reviewer. BCG Consultant, interview, consultant's residence, London, 10 February 2010.

203. Rick Iedema, *The Discourses of Post-Bureaucratic Organization* (Amsterdam: John Benjamins Publishing Company, 2003), pp. 131 & 200; see also Charles Perrow, *Complex Organizations: A Critical Essay* (New York: Random House, 1986), pp. 157–77.

204. Letter from Foreign Secretary's Office: No. 6923/FS/08, 24 July 2008.

205. Sachin Parashar, 'MEA reviews choice of steno as North Korea envoy,' *Times of India*, 13 June 2012. See: http://articles.timesofindia.indiatimes.com/2012–06–13/india/322 14184_1_ifs-officers-stenographer-mea

206. IFS Officer no. 38.

207. Shyam Saran bypassed three batches.

208. Veena Sikri quoted in, Rashmee Sehgal, 'MEA woman invokes RTI on Menon,' *Asian Age*, 15 March 2007.

209. 'Gender bias? IFS officer seeks answers from CIC,' *Times of India*, New Delhi, 18 March 2007. See http://articles.timesofindia.indiatimes.com/2007–03–18/india/27881973_1_ foreign-secretary-veena-sikri-gender-bias

210. See See Rajiv Sikri, 'Appointments and disappointments, Foreign Secretary controversies: Questions that deserve answers,' *Asian Age*, 28 March 2007. Rajiv Sikri, 'When transparency is foreign,' *Asian Age*, 29 March 2007.

211. Cable 151154: 'Indian Iran retort might lay groundwork for nuclear movement,' *The Hindu*, 24 April 2008. See: http://www.thehindu.com/news/the-india-cables/the-cables/article1571890.ece

212. Rajiv Sikri, 'Will Iran spoil the Indo-US party?', *The Asian Age*, 4 August 2007. Reproduced online at South Asia Analysis Group: http://www.southasiaanalysis.org/%5Cpapers24%5Cpaper2322.html

213. Reed J. Fendrick, 'Diplomacy as an Instrument of National Power' in U.S. Army War College, *Guide to National Security Policy and Strategy*, ed. J. Boone Barholomees, Jr., p. 179.

214. Shiv Shankar Menon, [Untitled], Foreign Service Institute, New Delhi 17 August 2007. There is no record of this speech in Avtar Singh Bhasin (ed.) (2008), for it was intended for probationers.

215. Rajiv Sikri, 'India's Foreign Policy Priorities in the Coming Decade,' ISAS Working Paper, no. 25, 25 September 2007. This paper forms the kernel of his book: Rajiv Sikri, *Challenge and Strategy: Rethinking India's Foreign Policy* (New Delhi: Sage, 2009), pp. 45, 49.

216. See Rajiv Sikri, 25 September 2007. Sikri writes that 'hard-nosed self interest' should be the rationale for diplomacy (p. 5) which presumably means realizing the aspiration to be a 'great power' (p. 49) since no other rationale is provided. Becoming great for greatness' sake is possible if 'existing power centres, including the US, become relatively weaker' (p. 45). In other words, he advocates a binary understanding of power totally at odds with a cosmological rationality. It is also contradicted by his time-bound manner, with no reference to context, of arriving at the goal of being a 'great power'.

217. Even a reviewer who shares Sikri's naivety and writes a glowing review of Sikri's book notes this. See P.S. Jayaramu, 'Critiquing Indian Foreign Policy,' *International Studies*, vol. 47, no. 2–4, April–July 2010, p. 450.

218. Interview with External Affairs Minister K. Natwar Singh by Karan Thapar for BBC programme 'Hard Talk-India' [8 April 2005] in Avtar Singh Bhasin (ed.), *India's Foreign Relations—2005* (New Delhi: Geetika Publishers, 2006), p. 46.

219. Internal MEA documents written by Sikri have not been seen. The point was made by IFS Officer no. 24. Siddharth Varadarajan states he had seen a document by Sikri for the PM which objected to India's Iran position, see Siddharth Varadarajan, 'Taking stock of the Indo-US nuclear deal', in *The Hindu*, 17 August 2007, http://www.hindu.com/2007/08/17/stories/2007081755871300.htm. Sikri confirmed that the document was written and overturned by the PM. Sikri writes the 'vote at the IAEA in September 2005 referring Iran's case to the UNSC was a foreign policy disaster' in Rajiv Sikri, 25 September 2007, p. 27. See also Rajiv Sikri, 'Will Iran spoil the Indo-US party?', *The Asian Age*, 4 August 2007.

220. Kenneth N. Waltz, *Theory of International Politics* (1979), pp. 73. On the inapplicability of Waltz even within the paradigm of modernity see Barry Buzan and Lene Hansen, *The Evolution of International Security Studies* (Cambridge: Cambridge University Press, 2009).

221. Manmohan Singh, conversation, 7 Racecourse Road, New Delhi, 21 May 2008.

222. On surviving see Sherry B. Ortner, 'Resistance and the Problem of Ethnographic Refusal,' Comparative *Studies in Society and History*, vol. 37, no. 1, January 1995, pp. 173–93. On this type of ambivalence see Catherine Casey, *Work, Self and Society: After Industrialism* (London: Routledge, 1995).

223. Manmohan Singh, conversation, 7 Racecourse Road, New Delhi, 25 May 2008.

224. Manmohan Singh, 'Statement of Prime Minister in Rajya Sabha on the India-US Nuclear Agreement' [17 August 2006] in Avtar Singh Bhasin (ed.) (2007), pp. 461–2.

225. Manmohan Singh, 'Speech by Prime Minister Dr. Manmohan Singh at the Foundation Stone laying ceremony of Jawaharlal Nehru Bhavan to house the Ministry of External Affairs' [14 February 2006] in Avtar Singh Bhasin (ed.) (2007), p. 141.

226. See Introduction. That it is used to describe the situation in the MEA's compilation of documents is indicative. See Avtar Singh Bhasin (ed.) (2006), Preface, p. 10. The PM does not shy away from the term either. Manmohan Singh, 'Reply by the Prime Minister in the Lok Sabha to the debate on Civil Nuclear Energy Cooperation with the United States' [11 March 2006] in Avtar Singh Bhasin (ed.) (2007), p. 439. These vectors are explored in Chapters 5 and 6.

227. Sharon Traweek, *Beamtimes and Lifetimes: The World of High Energy Physicists* (Cambridge, MA.: Harvard University Press, 1988).

228. Deep K. Datta-Ray, 'Nuclear deal marks birth of the Knowledge Economy,' *South China Morning Post*, 7 October 2008.

229. Deep K. Datta-Ray, 'Positive energy,' *Daily News and Analysis*, 1 October 2008.

230. K. Subrahmanyam, conversation, his residence, Noida, 27 April 2008.

231. See Stanley Hoffmann, 'An American Social Science: International Relations,' *Daedalus*, vol. 106, no. 3, 1977, p. 58; Timothy Dunne and Nicholas J. Wheeler (eds), *Human Rights in Global Politics* (Cambridge University Press, 1999); Ken Booth, 'Security in Anarchy: Utopian Realism in Theory and Practice,' *International Affairs*, vol. 67, no. 3, 1991. On power organizing European IR thought see Uday Singh Mehta, *Liberalism and Empire: A Study in the 19th Century British Liberal Thought* (Chicago University Press, 1999); Naeem Inayatullah and David L. Blaney, *International Relations and the Problem of Difference* (New York: Routledge, 2004).

232. Shivshankar Menon, 'Speech by Foreign Secretary Shivshankar Menon at the Observer Research Foundation on "The Challenges Ahead for India's Foreign Policy"' [10 April 2007] in Avtar Singh Bhasin (ed.), 2008.

233. Siddharth Varadarajan, 'BRIC, IBSA not keen to support sanctions against Iran,' *The Hindu*, 18 April 2010. http://www.thehindu.com/opinion/columns/siddharth-varadarajan/article402185.ece?css=print

234. 'Cable 149884: Iran's Ahmadinejad to visit India,' *The Hindu*, 21 March 2011. http://www.thehindu.com/news/the-india-cables/the-cables/article1556942.ece

235. In 2012 India and Iran found a way of circumventing US sanctions. See 'India and Iran reach oil pay deal despite sanctions,' BBC, 8 February 2012. http://www.bbc.co.uk/news/business-16940415

236. Shivshankar Menon, 'Speech by Foreign Secretary Shivshankar Menon at the Observer Research Foundation on "The Challenges Ahead for India's Foreign Policy"' in Avtar Singh Bhasin (ed.), 2008, 10 April 2007, p. 207.

237. For a very self-satisfied take on anthropology by anthropologists see Benjamin Soares and Filippo Osella, 'Islam, Politics, Anthropology,' *Journal of the Royal Anthropological Institute*, vol. 15, no. 1, May 2009.

238. 'Cable 180629: Menon favours closer cooperation following Mumbai terror attacks,' 30 November 2008. http://www.thehindu.com/news/the-india-cables/the-cables/article1562923.ece

239. Katy Gardner and Fillipo Osella, 2003, pp. v–xxviii.

240. In IR this idea of progress entwines Marxists who propound the theory of 'Uneven and combined development' and realists.

241. IFS Officer no. 37.

242. IFS Officer no. 36.
243. IFS Officer no. 19.
244. IFS Probationer no. 10.
245. The processes are subtler than Jaffrelot's mono-dimensional, progressional contention that the low-caste are at the forefront of a 'silent' revolution. See Christophe Jaffrelot, *India's Silent Revolution: Rise of Lower Castes in North India* (London: C. Hurst & Co., 2003).
246. Geeti Sen, 'Preface: National Culture and Cultural Nationalism' in Geeti Sen (ed.), *India: A National Culture?* (Thousand Oaks, CA: Sage, 2003).
247. DPS: R.K. Puram, teacher, conversation, her residence, New Delhi, 1 February 2008.
248. Katy Gardner and Filippo Osella, 2003, pp. xii-xiii.
249. IFS Probationer no. 1.
250. IFS Probationer no. 3 & Customs Probationer no. 4.
251. IRS Probationer no. 4.
252. Akhil Gupta (2005), p. 29.
253. On job cynicism see P. Fleming and G. Sewell, 'Looking For "The Good Soldier, Švejk": Alternative Modalities of Resistance in the Contemporary Workplace,' *Sociology*, vol. 36, no. 4, 2002.
254. Emile Durkheim, *Suicide: A Study in Sociology*, ed. George Dimpson, trans. John A. Spaulding and George Simpson (New York: Free Press, 1968). For a discussion of the 'anomie hypothesis' see C. James Richardson, *Contemporary Social Mobility* (London: Francis Pinter Publishers, 1977), pp. 189–227. This organizes much work on social mobility and presumes that rapid social mobility causes identity and mental tensions. On social mobility and mental disorder see Earl Hopper, *Social Mobility: A Study of Social Control and Insatiability* (Oxford: Basil Blackwell Publishers, 1981); R. J. Kleiner and S. Parker, 'Goal-striving and Psychosomatic Symptoms in a Migrant and Nonmigrant Population' in M.B. Kantor (ed.), *Mobility and Mental Health* (Springfield, IL: Charles C. Thomas, 1963), pp. 189–203.
255. Ruohui Zhao and Liqun Cao, 'Social Change and Anomie: A Cross-national Study,' *Social Forces*, vol. 88, no. 3, March 2010.
256. See Emile Durkheim, *The Division of Labor in Society*, trans. George Simpson (New York: Free Press, 1949); Emile Durkheim (1968). See also Robert K. Merton, 'Social Structure as Anomie,' *American Sociological Review*, vol. 3, no. 5, 1938, pp. 672–82, and Robert K. Merton, 'Anomie, Anomia and Social Interaction: Contexts of Deviant Behaviour' in Marshall B. Clinard (ed.), *Anomie and Deviant Behavior: A Discussion and Critique* (New York: Free Press of Glencoe, 1964). For a useful correlation of the two see Ruohui Zhao and Liqun Cao, March 2010.
257. Jim Cullen, *The American Dream: A Short History of an Idea that Shaped a Nation* (New York: Oxford University Press, 2003), pp. 6–7, 10.
258. Michael I. Norton and Dan Ariely, 'Building a Better America—One Wealth Quintile at a Time,' *Perspectives on Psychological Science*, vol. 6, no. 1, 2011.
259. Kenneth Burke, *Language as Symbolic Action: Essays on Life, Literature and Method* (Berkeley, CA: University of California Press, 1966).
260. For a very recent discussion see Alisha Coleman-Jensen, Mark Nord, Margaret Andrews and Steven Carlson, *Household Food Security in the United States in 2010* (ERR-125, U.S. Dept. of Agriculture, Econ. Res. Serv. September 2011), http://www.ers.usda.gov/Publications/ERR125/ERR125.pdf
261. Quoted in Ashis Nandy, 'The Beautiful, Expanding Future of Poverty: Popular Economics as a Psychological Defence,' *Economic and Political Weekly*, vol. 39, no. 1, 3–9 January 2004. For a more up to date discussion (which shows that poverty remains endemic) see Rourke L. O'Brien and David S. Pedulla, 'Beyond the poverty line,' *Stanford Social Inno-*

vation Review, Fall 2010, http://www.ssireview.org/articles/entry/beyond_the_poverty_
line. See also Suzanne Macartney, *Child Poverty in the United States 2009 and 2010: Selected
Race Groups and Hispanic Origin*, November 2011. http://www.census.gov/prod/2011pubs/
acsbr10–05.pdf

262. 'Joint report of the Centre for Budget and Policy Priorities and the American Foundation
for Families,' quoted in Majid Rahnema, 'Global Poverty: A Pauperising Myth,' *Intercultural*, vol. 14, no. 2, Spring 1991, p. 21n. According to Michael Harrington, five million
American children live in poverty. On poverty amidst plenty, see Michael Harrington, *The
American Poverty* (New York: Holt, Rinehart and Winston, 1984).

263. William Connolly, *Identity/Difference: Democratic Negotiations of Political Paradox* (Minneapolis: University of Minnesota Press, 2002), p. 64.

264. IFS Officer no. 33. The more common answer was: 'Who knows what others will do,'
which implied not othering, but that there were too many unknown variables in another's
life to make predictions. IFS Probationers no. 2, 3, 4 & 8.

265. Modern analysis, premised on alienation, sees change as the product of forces pushing up
or down. On pushing up see Peter Michael Blau, 'Social Mobility and Interpersonal Rela-
tions,' *American Sociological Review*, vol. 21, no. 3, 1956; Alfred Schütz, 'The Stranger: An
Essay in Social Psychology,' *American Journal of Sociology*, vol. 49, no. 6, 1944, pp. 499–507;
Frederick C. Turner (ed.), *Social Mobility and Political Attitudes: Comparative Perspectives*,
(New Brunswick, NJ: Transaction Publishers, 1992). On pushing down see Pierre Bour-
dieu, *La noblesse d'Etat: grandes écoles et esprit de corps* (Paris: Les Editions de Minuit, 1989);
C.L. Dewes, C.L. Barney and Carolyn Leste Law (eds), *This Fine Place so far from Home:
Voices of Academics from the Working Class* (Philadelphia: Temple University Press, 1995);
Michael D. Grimes and Joan M. Morris, *Caught in the Middle: Contradictions in the Lives
of Sociologists from Working-Class Backgrounds* (Westport, CT: London Praeger, 1997).
Social change is seen to produce moral tensions, either guilt, betrayal or shame. See Vin-
cent de Gaulejac, *La névrose de classe: Trajectoire sociale et conflits d'identité* (Paris: Hommes
et Groupes Editeurs, 1999); Richard Hoggart, *The Uses of Literacy: Aspects of Working-Class
Life, with Special References to Publications and Entertainments* (London: Chatto and Windus, 1957); Jake Ryan and Charles Sackrey, *Strangers in Paradise: Academics from Working
Class* (Boston: South End Press, 1984); Janet Zandy, *Liberating Memory: Our Work and
Our Working-Class Consciousness* (New Brunswick, NJ: Rutgers University Press, 1995).

266. Gary Fine, 'Negotiated Orders and Organizational Cultures,' *Annual Review of Sociology*,
vol. 10, 1984, p. 241.

267. There are numerous works on negotiating style, and though lodged unselfconsciously
within the paradigm of alienation, they are nevertheless enlightening. On the limits of
modernist approaches to Indian negotiations see Rajesh Kumar and Verner Worm, 'Institutional Dynamics and the Negotiation Process: Comparing India and China,' *International
Journal of Conflict Management*, vol. 15 no. 3, 2004. On Indian negotiations, rather than
underlying rationales, see Douglas C. Makeig, 'War, No-War, and the India Pakistan
Negotiating Process,' *Pacific Affairs*, vol. 6, Summer 1987. On US negotiating style vis-à-
vis India see Kanti P. Bajpai, P.R. Chari, Pervaiz Iqbal Cheema, Stephen P. Cohen and
Sumit Ganguly, *Brasstacks and Beyond: Perception and Management of Crisis in South Asia*
(New Delhi: Manohar) (1995). On Chinese styles see Kenneth T. Young, *Negotiating with
the Chinese Communists: The United States Experience, 1953–1967* (New York: McGraw
Hill, 1968); Arthur Lall, *How Communist China Negotiates* (New York: Columbia University Press, 1968). On US styles within an administration see Gaddis Smith, *Morality,
Reason and Power: American Diplomacy in the Carter Years* (New York: Hill and Wang,
1986). On the possibility of changing styles: Hussein Kassim and Anand Menon, 'The

Principal–Agent Approach and the Study of the European Union: Promise Unfulfilled?' *Journal of European Public Policy*, vol. 10, no. 1, February 2003. Some works apply the modernist binary to argue for the learning of each other's styles (which of course does not imply manufacture of a 'third space,' only movement within a binary construct). See Y. Xia, 'Cultural Values, Communications Styles, and Use of Mobile Communications in China,' *China Media Research*, vol 2, no. 2, 2006. The duplicitous notion of a hybrid space is used by Raymond Clémençon, 'Global Climate Change and the Trade System: Bridging the Culture Gap,' *Journal for Environmental Development*, vol. 4, 1995. On brute power negotiation: Adrian Sherwin-White, *The Roman Citizenship* (Oxford University Press, 1973). M.A.R. Kleiman, *When Brute Force Fails: Strategic Thinking for Crime Control*, US Department of Justice (Washington: US Department of Justice, NCJRS, 2005). On devious negotiations see S. Brown, *Political Subjectivity: Applications of Q Methodology in Political Science* (New Haven, CT: Yale University Press, 1980). On internal politics shaping negotiation see Judith Mayer, 'Chapter 6: Environmental Organising in Indonesia: The Search for a Newer Order' in Ronnie D. Lipschutz and Judith Mayer (eds), *Global Civil Society & Global Environmental Governance: The Politics of Nature from Place to Planet* (Albany, NY: SUNY, 2002). On women's negotiation see Mary Caprioli, 'Democracy and Human Rights versus Women's Security: A Contradiction?' *Security Dialogue*, vol. 35, no. 4, 2004.

268. Leigh L. Thompson, *The Mind and Heart of the Negotiator* (Upper Saddle River, NJ: Prentice Hall, 2001), p. 10.

269. Hoffman's theory about people being predisposed to empathy is about moral socialization reliant on relationality. Secondly, empathy does not necessarily equate to reproducing another's sentiments. See Martin L. Hoffman, *Empathy and Moral Development: Implications for Caring and Justice* (Cambridge University Press, 2000), p. 30.

270. IFS Officer no. 1.

271. Sigmund Freud, *Civilization and its Discontents* trans. and ed. James Strachey (New York: W.W. Norton, 1961), p. 90.

272. Manmohan Singh, 'Statement of Prime Minister in Rajya Sabha on the India-US Nuclear Agreement' in Avtar Singh Bhasin (ed.) (2007), 17 August 2006, p. 472.

273. See Indo-US 123 Agreement, 1 August 2007. http://www.hindu.com/nic/123agreement.pdf

274. Deep K. Datta-Ray, 'Test match,' *South China Morning Post*, Hong Kong, 9 August 2007.

275. IFS Officer No. 1.

276. That the PM used Machiavelli to delineate the dangers for the initiator of such change does not make him Machiavellian, but rather demonstrates how the founders of modernity may be incorporated into a unified system. See Manmohan Singh, 'Statement of PM in Rajya Sabha on the India-US Nuclear Agreement' [17 August 2006] in Avtar Singh Bhasin (ed.) (2007). Machiavelli of course is a cornerstone for modern governmentality. See M. Foucault, *History of Madness*, trans. J. Murphy and J. Khalfa (London and New York: Routledge, 2006).

277. Note from Foreign Secretary's office: No. 9475/FS/2007.

278. Manmohan Singh, 'Statement of Prime Minister in Rajya Sabha on the India-US nuclear agreement' [17 August 2006] in Avtar Singh Bhasin (ed.) (2007), p. 471.

279. Ibid. See 'Implementation of the India-United States Joint Statement of July 18, 2005: India's Separation Plan Tabled in Parliament on May 11, 2006' in Avtar Singh Bhasin (ed.) (2007), p. 446.

280. Michael Blaker, 'Japan in 1977: an emerging consensus,' *Asian Survey*, vol. 18, no. 1, January 1978, pp. 48, 166 & 214.

281. Communication dated 25 July 2008 received from the Permanent Mission of India con-

cerning a document entitled 'Implementation of the India-United States Joint Statement of July 18, 2005: India's Separation Plan,' INFCIRC/731, 25 July 2008.

282. IFS Officer No. 1, 40. For how anarchy motivates this see Richard Bernstein and Ross H. Munro, *The Coming Conflict with China* (New York: Alfred Knopf, 1997). See also Harish Khare and Siddharth Vardarajan, 'NSA Interview: This is as good a text as one can possibly get,' *The Hindu*, 28 July 2007, http://www.hindu.com/2007/07/28/stories/2007072855121300.htm Harish Khare and Siddharth Vardarajan, 'I don't think the country is yet willing to recognise the U.S. is a benign power,' *The Hindu*, 30 July 2007, http://www.hindu.com/2007/07/30/stories/2007073053941100.htm For an overview of Clinton-Bush balance of power calculations vis-à-vis India see K.P. Vijayalakshmi, 'American Worldview and its Implications for India,' *South Asian Survey*, vol. 15, no. 2, 2008.

283. On Eurocentric history confounding IR's ability to comprehend Asian practice see David C. Kang, 'Getting Asia Wrong: The Need for New Analytical Frameworks,' *International Security*, vol. 27, no. 4, Spring 2003. Kang's methodology—but not his programme—is criticized by Amitav Acharya, 'Will Asia's Past be its Future?' *International Security*, vol. 28, no. 3, Winter 2003/04.

284. Deep K. Datta-Ray, 'Raising India's pulse without selling its soul,' *South China Morning Post*, 13 August 2008. See also Special Correspondent, 'Pranab assails Rice remarks,' *The Hindu*, 30 June 2007, http://www.hindu.com/2007/06/30/stories/2007063057770100. htm

285. NSA M.K. Narayanan in an interview first indicates that the US wants India as an ally against China, then discounts it and finally closes with surprise at US demands. See Harish Khare and Siddharth Vardarajan, 'NSA Interview: This is as good a text as one can possibly get,' *The Hindu*, 28 July 2007, http://www.hindu.com/2007/07/28/stories/200 7072855121300.htm

286. A complex and long running philosophical conundrum, the term is understood in its simplest sense. See Ian Deweese-Boyd, 'Self-deception' in Edward N. Zalta (ed.), *The Stanford Encyclopedia of Philosophy* (Spring 2012 Edition). http://plato.stanford.edu/entries/self-deception/

287. David S. Cloud and Mark Magnier, 'India not sold on closer military ties with U.S.,' *Los Angeles Times*, 6 June 2012. See http://articles.latimes.com/2012/jun/06/world/la-fg-panetta-india-20120607

288. Cable 232002: Scenesetter for USD(P) Flournoy's visit to India, 28 March 2011. http://www.thehindu.com/news/the-india-cables/the-cables/article1576896.ece

289. See Cable 232002: Scenesetter for USD(P) Flournoy's visit to India, 29 October 2009. http://www.thehindu.com/news/the-india-cables/the-cables/article1576896.ece and Cable 35111: Scenesetter for Mukherjee's visit to the States, 21 June 2005. http://www.thehindu.com/news/the-india-cables/the-cables/article1556768.ece

290. Cable 35111: Scenesetter for Mukherjee's visit to the States, 21 June 2005. http://www.thehindu.com/news/the-india-cables/the-cables/article1556768.ece

291. Cable 232002: Scenesetter for USD(P) Flournoy's visit to India, 29 October 2009. http://www.thehindu.com/news/the-india-cables/the-cables/article1576896.ece

292. Interview with IFS diplomat no. 38.

293. Cable 29834: Defence minister upbeat on Indo-US relations but…, 31 March 2005. http://www.thehindu.com/news/the-india-cables/the-cables/article1576942.ece

294. Cable 36415: PM and Pranab scoff at Leftist criticism of U.S. defence ties, *The Hindu*, 12 July 2005. http://www.thehindu.com/news/the-india-cables/the-cables/article1576915.ece

295. Pranab Mukherjee, 'Statement of Defence Minister Pranab Mukherjee in the Rajya Sabha

on the "New Framework for the U.S—India Defence Relationship"'[2 August 2005] in Avtar Singh Bhasin (ed.) (2006), New Delhi, p. 1399.

296. Cable 38759: MEA urges USG not to pursue status of forces agreement with India until ACSA agreement is concluded, *The Hindu*, 18 August 2005. http://www.thehindu.com/news/the-india-cables/the-cables/article1576910.ece

297. Cable 29834: Defense minister upbeat on Indo-US relations but…, *The Hindu*, 31 March 2005. http://www.thehindu.com/news/the-india-cables/the-cables/article1576942.ece

298. Andrew Bacevich, Email communication to author, 5 July 2011.

299. Cable 232002: Scenesetter for USD(P) Flournoy's visit to India, 29 October 2009. http://www.thehindu.com/news/the-india-cables/the-cables/article1576896.ece

300. Cable 30136: Scenesetter for Admiral Fallon's visit to India, *The Hindu*, 5 April 2005. http://www.thehindu.com/news/the-india-cables/the-cables/article1576936.ece

301. Deep K. Datta-Ray, 'Securing India's security,' *Hindustan Times*, 16 October 2007. http://www.hindustantimes.com/editorial-views-on/Platform/Securing-India-s-security/Article1-252663.aspx

302. Interview with a senior Singaporean official, Oberoi Hotel, New Delhi, 12 April 2011.

303. Chidanand Rajghatta, 'Wary of China but leery of alliance, US and India go into third strategic dialogue,' *Times of India*, 8 June 2012. See http://articles.timesofindia.indiatimes.com/2012–06–08/us/32123201_1_strategic-dialogue-alyssa-ayres-commerce-secretary See also David S. Cloud and Mark Magnier, 'India not sold on closer military ties with U.S.,' *Los Angeles Times*, 6 June 2012. See http://articles.latimes.com/2012/jun/06/world/la-fg-panetta-india-20120607

304. Sandeep Dikshit, 'Timothy Roemer resigns', *The Hindu*, 28 April 2011, http://www.thehindu.com/news/international/article1776184.ece

305. IAS officer 7.

306. Or for that matter Benjamin Franklin. See Paul W. Conner, *Poor Richard's Politicks: Benjamin Franklin and the New American Order* (New York: Oxford University Press, 1966), p. 156.

307. This required extensive negotiations by the PMO with Indian scientists who 'having had one bad experience … were….'. See also Manmohan Singh, 'Statement of Prime Minister in Rajya Sabha on the India-US Nuclear Agreement'[17 August 2006] in Avtar Singh Bhasin (ed.) (2007), p. 473. Manmohan Singh, conversation, 7 Racecourse Road, New Delhi, 13 June 2007.

308. Also see introduction for the pressures exerted both from within and without on India and India's negotiators.

309. IFS Probationer no. 18. Caste meanings and rankings are neither consensual nor compatible, and never approach the Dumontian (modernist) ideal of a universalized structure of hierarchy. See Dipankar Gupta, *Interrogating Caste: Understanding Hierarchy and Difference in Indian Society* (New Delhi: Penguin, 2000), Chap. 2, 3, 5.

310. Deep K. Datta-Ray, 'India finds a new elite in the grass roots,' *South China Morning Post*, 8 October 2007.

311. Frank Dikötter, '"Patient zero": China and the myth of the "opium plague"', Inaugural lecture (London: School of Oriental and African Studies, 2003).

312. Discussion with Probationer 19's father.

313. There was no comprehensible reply from the Probationer when we talked about this—which indicatesa flawed mental calculation, perhaps to bebe explained by the tensions caused by the move from unified cosmos to modernist thought. IFS Probationer no. 19.

314. Indo Asian News Service, 'Boundary issue not to affect growing India-China ties: NSA,' *Times of India*, 1 April 2010.

315. Deep K. Datta-Ray, 'Call it Chinese Arithmetic,' *Times of India*, 25 January 2011. http://articles.timesofindia.indiatimes.com/2011–01–25/edit-page/28368728_1_hu-chinese-state-china-s-president

316. IFS Officer no. 1.

317. IFS Officer no. 10.

318. For a critique of the traditional paradigms of 'amnesia' and 'repetition' see Pradip Datta, 'Historic Trauma and the Politics of the Present in India,' *Interventions*, vol. 7, no. 3.

319. 'Media Briefing by Official Spokesperson on the meeting of the SAARC Standing Committee' [17 April 2006] in Avtar Singh Bhasin (ed.) (2007), p. 657.

320. 'Fifteenth Report,' Standing Committee on External Affairs (2006–2007) (New Delhi: Lok Sabha Secretariat, April 2007), p. 17.

321. IFS Officer no. 3. See Pakistan Notification SRO no. 695(1)/2006, 1 July 2006, mentioned in 'Media briefing by Foreign Secretary on the conclusion of the first day of the SAARC Standing Committee Meeting in Dhaka, Bangladesh' [31 July 2006] in Avtar Singh Bhasin (ed.), 2007, p. 660.

322. MEA *Annual Report 2008–2009* (New Delhi), pp. 14–15. http://meaindia.nic.in/meaxpsite/annualreport/12ar012009.pdf

323. Ibid., p. 15.

324. Anita Joshua, 'Pakistan to switch to negative list for trade with India,' *The Hindu*, 29 February 2012. http://www.thehindu.com/news/national/article2947102.ece

325. The Indian High Commissioner in Islamabad said at the time, Pakistan's actions made no economic sense, 'nor has it contributed to the resolution of any political differences between India and Pakistan over the last 60 years.' See 'Media Briefing by Official Spokesperson on developments related to SAARC, specifically SAFTA' [7 July 2006] in Avtar Singh Bhasin (ed.) (2007), p. 659, footnote.

326. G.N. Curry, 'Moving beyond Post-development: Facilitating Indigenous Alternatives for 'Development',' *Economic Geography*, vol. 79, no. 4, 2003, p. 418.

327. Senior Congress cabinet minister no. 3, conversation, his office, New Delhi, 30 May 2008.

328. 'PM to clear air on terror delink today,' *The Times of India*, 29 July 2009. http://articles.timesofindia.indiatimes.com/2009–07–29/india/28185640_1_joint-statement-sharm-el-sheikh-balochistan

329. Siddharth Vardarajan, 'India, Pakistan positive on talks,' *The Hindu*, 16 July 2009. http://www.hindu.com/2009/07/16/stories/2009071661120100.htm

330. 'Text of India-Pakistan statement,' BBC News, 6 January 2004. http://news.bbc.co.uk/2/hi/south_asia/3372157.stm.

331. 'Holbrooke rubbishes Pak's Baloch allegations,' *The Economic Times*, 31 July 2009. http://articles.economictimes.indiatimes.com/2009–07–31/news/28447547_1_balochistan-joint-statement-afghanistan-richard-holbrooke

332. IFS Officer no. 3.

333. A senior Congress cabinet minister says, 'What does he [Pakistan's Prime Minister] know? He doesn't know half the things that are going on his country.' Senior Congress cabinet member no. 1, conversation, his residence, New Delhi, 12 July 2007. See also Farhan Bokhari, Daniel Dombey and James Lamont, 'Pakistan battles its Islamist offspring,' *Financial Times*, 13 December 2008. http://www.ft.com/intl/cms/s/0/9e49dd8a-c8b7-11dd-b86f-000077b07658.html#axzz1tXpGgGlu

334. Dinyar Patel, 'Our past is being moth-eaten,' *The Hindu*, 19 April 2012. See http://www.thehindu.com/opinion/lead/article3328939.ece

335. Lalu Prasad Yadav, Speech 'India of my Dreams', 28 June 2007. IFS Officer no. 25.

336. J. Van Maanen and S. Barley, 'Cultural Organizations: Fragments of a Theory' in P.J. Frost, L.F. Moore, M.R. Louis, C.C. Lundberg and J. Martin (eds), *Organizational Culture* (Beverley Hills, CA: Sage Publications, 1985).

337. Michel de Certeau, *The Writing of History*, trans. Tom Conley (New York: Columbia University Press, 1988), pp. xxv-xxvi.

338. Michel de Certeau, *The Practice of Everyday Life*, trans. Steven Rendall (Berkeley: University of California Press, 1998), pp. xix-xx.

339. James C. Scott, *Seeing Like a State: How Certain Schemes to Improve the Human Condition have Failed* (New Haven: Yale University Press, 1998), pp. 313, 424.

340. Michel de Certeau, Fredric Jameson and Carl Lovitt, 'On the Oppositional Practices of Everyday Life,' *Social Text*, vol. 3, Autumn 1980, p. 8.

3. THEORIZING THE UNCONTAINABLE

1. James L. Fitzgerald, trans. & ed., *The Mahābhārata, Book 12: The Book of Peace, Part One* (University of Chicago Press, 2004), p. 130, *Mb* 1.56.34.

2. R.N. Dandekar, 'The Mahabharata: Origins and Growth,' *University of Ceylon Review*, vol. 12, no. 2, 1954, p. 2.

3. Maurice Bloch, *Prey into Hunter: The Politics of Religious Experience* (Cambridge University Press, 1992); Maurice Bloch (1998), pp. 183–98.

4. Ibid. (1998), p. 6.

5. Yrjö Engeström, 'How We Think They Think: Anthropological Approaches to Cognition, Memory, and Literacy,' *American Ethnologist*, vol. 26, no. 3, 1999, pp. 750–51; Nigel Rapport, 'Context as an Act of Personal Externalisation, Gregory Bateson and the Harvey family in the English village of Wanet' in n Roy Dilley (ed.), *The Problem of Context* (New York: Berghahn Books, 1999), pp. 111–12.

6. Donald A. Nielsen, September 2001, p. 407.

7. See Chapter 6.

8. Shiv Shankar Menon [Untitled], 17 August 2007.

9. Harold Nicolson, *Diplomacy* (New York: Oxford University Press, 1964).

10. Lord Gore Booth (ed.), *Satow's Guide to Diplomatic Practice* (London: Longman, 1979), p. 451.

11. Also mentioned: intelligence, knowledge, discernment, prudence, hospitality, charm, industry, courage and tact. Menon mentioned 'precision', which Nicholson called 'accuracy'. See Harold Nicolson, *Diplomacy* (1964), p. 67.

12. Harold Nicolson, *Good Behaviour: Being a Study of Certain Types of Civility* (London: Constable, 1955), pp. 40–80, pp. 162–205; Horace Rumbold, *The War Crisis in Berlin July—August 1914* (London: Constable, 1944, p. xix).

13. Shiv Shankar Menon [Untitled], 17 August 2007.

14. Ibid.

15. As Chapter 2 noted, a significant reason why new diplomats do not put down the IFS as a choice is that they know nothing of diplomacy.

16. During a lecture by the author at the IIC.

17. IFS Officer no. 31.

18. Kwame A. Appiah, *In My Father's House: Africa in the Philosophy of Culture* (New York: Oxford University Press, 1992).

19. Tapan Raychaudhuri, *Europe Reconsidered: Perceptions of the West in Nineteenth Century Bengal* (New York: Oxford University Press, 1988), pp. ix, 345.

20. Sunanda K. Datta-Ray, 'The Last Ingabanga' in *First Proof: The Penguin Book of New Writing from India* (New Delhi: Penguin, 2005).

21. Martin Wainwright, *'The Better Class' of Indians: Social Rank, Imperial Identity, and South Asians in Britain, 1858–1914* (Manchester University Press, 2008).

22. Joël Candau, *Mémoire et identité* (Paris: Presses Universitaires de France, 1998), pp. 104–05.

23. IFS Probationer no. 22.

24. Amartya Sen, 'Indian Traditions and the Western Imagination,' *Daedalus*, vol. 126, no. 2, Spring 1997, p. 1; Bimal Krishna *Matilal, Mind, Language, and World: the Collected Essays of Bimal Krishna Matilal, vol. I* ed. Jonardon Ganeri (Oxford University Press, 2002), p. 21.

25. Archaeological evidence suggests that the events of the Mb took place around 900 BC. Romilla Thapar, *A History of India*, Vol. 1 (Baltimore: Penguin Books, 1966), p. 31.

26. See J.T. Reinaud, *Fragments arabes et persans inédits relatifs a l'Inde, antérieurement au XIe siècle* (Arab text and original French translation by M. Reinaud, Paris: 1845), collected and compiled by Joseph-Toussaint Reinaud (Frankfurt am Main: Institute for the History of Arabic-Islamic Science at the Johann Wolfgang Goethe University, 1993), pp. 17–29.

27. Carl W. Ernst, 'Muslim Studies of Hinduism? A Reconstruction of Arabic and Persian Translations from Indian Languages,' *Iranian Studies*, vol. 36, no. 2, June 2003, p. 182.

28. Ibid., p. 183.

29. H. Blochmann (ed.), *A'in-I Akbari Part II* (Calcutta, 1867–77), p. 236. One of Akbar's sayings is recorded: 'In India no one has even claimed to be a prophet. The reason is that claims to divinity are customary.' Quoted in Shireen Moosvi, 'The Mughal Encounter with Vedanta: Recovering the Biography of 'Jadrup',' *Social Scientist*, vol. 30, no. 7/8, July–Aug. 2002, p. 21, fn. 3.

30. G. Meredith-Owens and R.H. Pinder-Wilson, 'A Persian Translation of the "Mahābhārata", with a Note on the Miniatures,' *British Museum Quarterly*, vol. 20, no. 3, March 1956, p. 62.

31. W.N. Lees and Ahmad Ali (eds), *Muntakhabi't Tawarikh Badauni* (Calcutta, 1856–69), Part II, pp. 413–14.

32. IFS Officer no. 13.

33. IFS Officer no. 11.

34. 'MF Husain's paintings take the US flight,' *Hindustan Times*, 11 September 2006. http://www.hindustantimes.com/MF-Husain-s-paintings-take-the-US-flight/Article1–148597.aspx

35. M.F. Husain quoted in Sotheby's Online Catalogue. http://www.sothebys.com/app/live/lot/LotDetail.jsp?lot_id=159619220

36. Shashi Tharoor, *The Great Indian Novel* (New York: Arcade Publishing, 1993).

37. Shashi Tharoor, 'Our Stories,' *The Hindu Magazine*, 26 November 2006. http://www.hindu.com/mag/2006/11/26/stories/2006112600090300.htm

38. Jawaharlal Nehru, *The Discovery of India* (Centenary edition) (New Delhi: Oxford University Press, 1985), p. 108.

39. K.P.S. Menon, *Changing Patterns of Diplomacy*, Saiyidain Memorial Lectures (Bombay: Bharatiya Vidya Bhavan, 1977), pp. 4–5.

40. John Dunham, 'Manuscripts used in the Critical Edition of the Mahabharata: A Survey and Discussion' in Arvind Sharma (ed.), *Essays on the Mahabharata* (Leiden: E.J. Brill, 1991).

41. James L. Fitzgerald, 'India's Fifth Veda: The Mahabharata's Presentation of Itself', in Arvind Sharma (ed.), *Essays on the Mahabharata* (Leiden: E.J. Brill, 1991), p. 151.

42. See Joseph Dahlman, *Das Mahabharata als Epos und Rechtsbuch* (Berlin, 1895), p. 142. He saw the Mb as *'die Erzieherin des Volkes zu höheren religiösen und sittlichen Ideen, Lehrerin*

des Volkes' ('the tutor of the people for higher religious and moral ideas, the schoolmistress of the people, Genesis …').

43. Arvind Sharma, *Classical Hindu Thought* (New Delhi: Oxford University Press, 2000).

44. Daud Ali and Anand Pandian, 'Introduction' in Ali and Pandian (eds), *Ethical Life in South Asia* (Bloomington, IN: Indiana University Press, 2010), p. 7.

45. Benjamin Nelson, 'Communities, Societies, Civilizations-Postmillennial Views on the Faces and Masks of Time' in Manfred Stanley (ed.), *Social Development* (New York: Basic Books, 1972), pp. 105–33.

46. Benjamin Nelson, 'Civilizational Complexes and Intercivilizational Encounters,' *Sociological Analysis*, vol. 34, no. 2, 1973.

47. Ibid., pp. 87–8.

48. See Rama Mantena, 'The Question of History in Precolonial India,' in *History and Theory*, vol. 46, 2007.

49. IFS Officer no. 22.

50. Even in the Western tradition, the question of genre was in flux until the 19th century when the discipline of history was born. This genre claimed to monopolize the past as historicized truth.

51. Velcheru Narayana Rao, David Shulman and Sanjay Subrahmanyam, 'Forum: Textures of Time, A Pragmatic Response,' *History and Theory*, vol. 46, October 2007, pp. 412–13.

52. Mantena, 2007, p. 408.

53. Paul Veyne, *Did the Greeks Believe in Their Myths? An Essay on Constitutive Imagination* trans. Paula Wissing, Chicago University Press, 1988), pp. 65–9.

54. Paul Veyne (1988), pp. 30–31, 33. On the rise of 'professional investigators' see Samuel J. Preus, *Explaining Religion: Criticism and Theory from Bodin to Freud* (New Haven: Yale University Press, 1987), pp. 40–55.

55. Lévi-Strauss's response to myth was to reconstruct mythic consciousness in contradistinction to the historical consciousness of the West (something that Vico attempted in the seventeenth century; Cassirer, inspired by Vico, also tried to provide a logic to myth). See Claude Lévi-Strauss, *The Savage Mind* (Chicago University Press, 1966); Giambattista Vico, *The New Science of Giambattista Vico*, unabridged translation of the third edition (1744) with the addition of 'Practic of the New Science', trans. Thomas Goddard Bergin and Max Harold Fisch (Ithaca, NY: Cornell University Press, 1984); E. Cassirer, *Language and Myth*, trans. S.K. Langer (New York: Dover, 1946).

56. Paul Veyne (1988), p. 11.

57. Ibid., p. 21–2.

58. Ibid., p. 98.

59. Ibid., p. 113.

60. Jonardon Ganeri, 2008, pp. 551–62.

61. Philip Pomper, 'World History and its Critics,' *History and Theory*, vol. 34, no. 2, May 1995, p. 4. The failure is not due to the striving amongst historians, which peaked in a science of source criticism grading the value of information to be controlled; it was because that value was judged on the basis of what was most sensible to the historian. See Edwin Jones, *John Lingard and the Pursuit of Historical Truth* (Brighton: Sussex Academic Press, 2001).

62. Ashis Nandy, 'History's Forgotten Doubles,' *History and Theory*, vol. 34, no. 2, 1995, pp. 53–4.

63. Ibid., pp. 64–5.

64. Defined as 'principled forgetfulness'. Ibid., pp. 47–51.

65. It traps the individual into evolutionary sequencing. Ibid., p. 48.

66. Ibid., p. 51. George Orwell, *Nineteen Eighty-Four* (London: Secker and Warburg, 1949), Part I, Chapter 3, pp. 32.

67. For instance Vivekananda. See Ashis Nandy (1995).

68. Roger Smith, 'Reflections on the Historical Imagination,' *History of the Human Sciences*, vol. 13, no. 4, November 2000, p. 103 and Nandy (1995), p. 65.

69. Nandy (1995), p. 64.

70. Freud wrote that 'psychoanalysis is my creation; for ten years I was the only one occupied with it ....' Sigmund Freud, *The History of the Psychoanalytic Movement*, trans. A.A. Brill (New York: Nervous and Mental Disease Pub. Co., 1917). Furthermore, psychoanalysis' roots are entrenched in the intersection of Enlightenment and Romanticist culture in Europe. M.S. Bergmann, 'Reflections on the History of Psychoanalysis,' *Journal of the American Psychoanalytic Association*, vol. 41, no. 4, 1993, pp. 929–55. Psychoanalysis was also a product of a crisis in Austrian liberal culture and internalized liberalism, 'psychologized' liberalism. See W. McGrath, 'Freud and the Force of History' in T. Gelfand and J. Kerr (eds), *Freud and the History of Psychoanalysis* (Hillside, NJ: The Analytic Press, 1992). In following Bose, Ashis Nandy keeps to these alien analytical systems. Ashis Nandy (1995), p. 64.

71. Similar to Maurice Bloch (1998).

72. Nandy (1995), p. 60–61.

73. Janine R. Wedel, Cris Shore, Gregory Feldman and Stacy Lathrop, 'Toward an Anthropology of Public Policy,' *Annals of the American Academy of Political and Social Science*, vol. 600, no. 1, 2005, p. 43. See also Don Kalb, 'Localizing Flows: Power, Paths, Institutions, and Networks' in Don Kalb, Marco van der Land, Richard Staring, Bart van Steenbergen and Nico Wilterdink (eds), *The Ends of Globalization: Bringing Society back in* (New York: Rowman & Littlefield Publishers, 2000), p. 8.

74. See Introduction.

75. Jonardon Ganeri, 2008, p. 558.

76. See Alf Hiltebeitel, *Rethinking the Mahabharata: A Reader's Guide to the Education of the Dharma King* (Chicago University Press, 2001), p. 1.

77. IFS Officer no. 31.

78. Vishnu S. Sukthankar, *On the Meaning of the Mahabharata* (Bombay: The Asiatic Society, 1957), p. 32.

79. Edward C. Dimock, Jr *et al.*, The Literature of India: An Introduction (Chicago University Press, 1974).

80. The *Mb* also refers to itself as a 'conversation', which emphasizes its constructedness. Wendy Doniger, *The Hindus: An Alternative History* (New York: Penguin, 2009), p. 302.

81. It is possible to translate *itihasa* by dividing the compound thus: *iti-hasa*, which can be rendered 'So? Derision!' i.e. So it could never have been! This is nearer in sense to the 'Once upon a time' used in speech.

82. See Vishnu S. Sukthankar, Prolegomena, in Vishnu S. Sukthankar et al., eds, *The Ādiparvan*, being the first book of the *Mahābhārata, the Great Epic of India* (Poona: Bhandarkar Oriental Research Institute, 1933), pp. xxxiv, liv-v, lxxxviii-xci. The amount of unity that exists particularly between geographically remote traditions which often have discrepant traditions intervening between them, such as Kashmir and Kerala, can be explained only on the assumption of a fixed text antecedent to those manuscripts, an archetype. For the variations which exist can be explained as later, particular innovations resulting from various dynamic factors in the tradition, while the unity cannot be explained, generally, as parallel independent invention.

83. Hayden White, 'The Value of Narrativity in the Representation of Reality,' *Critical Enquiry*, vol. 7, no. 1, Autumn 1980, p. 5; see also J.L. Mehta, *Philosophy and Religion: Essays in Interpretation* (New Delhi: Indian Council of Philosophical Research and Munshiram Manoharlal, 1990), p. 262.

84. A 'theory of moral behaviour'. See Bimal Krishna Matilal (2002), p. 50.
85. James L. Fitzgerald (trans., ed. & annotated), *Book of Peace, Part One* (Chicago University Press, 2004), p. 295; Alf Hiltebeitel (2001). *Mb* 12.56.2, 12.161.48, 12.353.8.
86. Alf Hiltebeitel (2001), p. 208.
87. Bimal Krishna Matilal (2002), p. 23.
88. Wendy Doniger O'Flaherty and J. Duncan M. Derrett, 'Introduction' in Doniger and Derrett, eds, *The Concept of Duty in South Asia* (New Delhi, 1978), p. vii. Emphasis added.
89. As I discovered during innumerable conversations with diplomats.
90. Seen in Jaswant Singh's parliamentary office, 30 May 2007.
91. The central story of the *Mb* is a succession story. It does however also have a 'fuzzy' beginning of men and gods, and there are at least three beginnings but no mention of anything remotely approaching 'anarchy'. All are individuals with their own pasts and the characters might be located in families or clans or as illegitimate offspring. Johannes Adrianus van Buitenen (trans.), *The Mahabharata, Volume 1, Book 1: The Book of the Beginning* (Chicago University Press, 1973), pp. xvi-xvii, 5–6.
92. James L. Fitzgerald (trans., ed., & annotated), *Book of Peace, Part One* (Chicago University Press, 2004), pp. 304–312. *Mb* 12.59.
93. James L. Fitzgerald (2004), pp. 534–41. *Mb* 12.139.
94. The point was made by Simon Brodbeck, email communication, 16 May 2010.
95. James L. Fitzgerald (2004), pp. 304–312. *Mb* 12.59.
96. James L. Fitzgerald (2004), p. 367. *Mb* 12.79.31.
97. Ibid., pp. 523–9. *Mb* 12.137.
98. Johannes Adrianus van Buitenen (trans.), *The Mahabharata: The Book of the Effort* (Chicago University Press, 1978), pp. 445–50.
99. Chaturvedi Badrinath, *The Mahābhārata: An Enquiry into the Human Condition* (New Delhi: Orient Longman, 2006), p. 443; *Mb* 12.109.28; James L. Fitzgerald (2004), p. 443. Mb. 12.109.28.
100. James L. Fitzgerald (2004), pp. 541–542. Mb. 12.140.3.
101. *Mb* 1.101; cf. 1.57.78–71; O'Flaherty (1990), pp. 51–3.
102. James L. Fitzgerald (2004), p. 212. Mb. 12.21.7–10.
103. Imanuel Kant quoted in Bimal Krishna Matilal, 2002, p. 25.
104. Ibid., pp. 31–2.
105. Thais E. Morgan, 'Is There an Intertext in this Text?: Literary and Interdisciplinary Approaches to Intertextuality,' *American Journal of Semiotics*, vol. 3, 1985, p. 1; J. Kristeva, 'Word, Dialogue and Novel' in Toril Moi (ed.), *The Kristeva Reader*, trans. Leon S. Roudiez (New York: Columbia University Press, 1986), p. 35–6.
106. Roland Barthes, 'The Death of the Author' in Stephen Heath (ed. and trans.), *Image, Music, Text*, (New York: Hill and Wang, 1977.
107. Wendy Doniger, 'Many Gods, Many Paths: Hinduism and Religious Diversity' in Religion and Culture Web Forum, February 2006. http://divinity.uchicago.edu/martycenter/publications/webforum/022006/commentary.shtml
108. Plato, *The Republic of Plato*, trans., Francis MacDonald Cornford (Oxford University Press, 1941).
109. The use of reason is the greatest good, but it is not reason if used capriciously, argues Jonardon Ganeri, 2001, pp. 7–8. See also Bimal Krishna Matilal (2002), pp. 49–71.
110. To the surrounding characters, that is, the protagonists, Krsna appears as a man, though there are suspicions that he is a god. See James W. Laine, *Visions of God: Narratives of Theophany in the Mahabharata* (New Delhi: Motilal Banarsidass, 1990). Alf Hiltebeitel, *The Ritual of Battle: Krisna in the Mahābhārata* (Ithaca, NY: Cornell University Press, 1976), pp. 126–7.

111. Johannes Adrianus van Buitenen (trans.), *The Mahabharata: The Book of the Forest* (Chicago University Press, 1978), p. 374.

112. Ibid., p. 379. *Mb.* 5.93.3–4.

113. For a useful overview about military thinking in the *Mb*, see Rajendra Nath, *Military Leadership in India: Vedic Period to Indo-Pakistan War* (New Delhi: Lancer Books, 1990).

114. Johannes Adrianus van Buitenen (trans.) (1978), pp. 365–6. *Mb.* 5.86.1.

115. Ibid., p. 366. *Mb.* 5.86.1.

116. This is based on interview evidence and from the essays set in class.

117. R. Shamasastry, Kautilya's Arthaśāstra, 8th edition, (Mysore: Mysore Printing and Publishing House, 1967), pp. vi.

118. Johannes Adrianus van Buitenen (trans.), (1978), pp. 134–8.

119. Ibid., pp. 460–61. *Mb* 5.148.

120. Ibid., pp. 415–16. *Mb* 5.122.

121. Ibid., p. 421. *Mb* 5.126.

122. Ibid., p. 422. *Mb* 5.126.30.

123. Ibid., pp. 460–61. *Mb* 5.148.

124. Subversion of a potential enemy's allies is acceptable. Ibid., pp. 135,445–450. *Mb* 5.139.1—5.141.45

125. Ibid., p. 461. *Mb* 5.148.15.

126. D. Mackenzie Brown, 'The Premises of Indian Political Thought,' *The Western Political Quarterly*, vol. 6, no. 2, June 1953, pp. 243–9.

127. Email communication from Simon Brodbeck, to whom I am indebted for making me aware of this frame.

128. *Mb* 5.91.4–18. Verses 16–17. Email from Simon Brodbeck.

129. See Chapter 2, 'Structure-of-structures' section.

130. Simon Brodbeck, 'Calling Krsna's Bluff: Non-Attached Action in the Bhagavadgītā,' *Journal of Indian Philosophy*, vol. 32, no. 1, 2004, p. 84.

131. Simon Brodbeck, 'Krsna's Action as the Paradigm of *asakta karman* in the Bhagavadgītā,' in Renata Czekalska and Halina Marlewicz (eds), 2nd international Conference on Indian Studies Proceedingsm (Kraków: Jagiellonian University), p. 85. *Mb* 3.22, 4.14.

132. Historically there was a challenge from the Buddhist ideal of asceticism at the time. Wendy Doniger, *The Hindus: An Alternative History* (New York: Penguin, 2009), pp. 283–4.

133. Johannes Adrianus van Buitenen (1978), pp. 428–9. *Mb* 5.129.

134. Simon Brodbeck, 'Introduction' in *The Bhagavad Gita* (London: Penguin Books, 2003), p. xlviii.

135. S.S. More, *Krsna: The Man and his Mission. An Enquiry into the Rationale of Inter-relationship between Krsna's Life, Mission and Philosophy* (Pune: Gaaj Krakashan, 1995).

136. Brodbeck, 2004, p. 97.

137. Brodbeck, 2004, p. 89.

138. Michael Smith, *The Moral Problem* (Oxford: Blackwell, 1994), p. 93.

139. David Hume, *An Enquiry concerning Human Understanding* (Oxford University Press, 1999), p. 95.

140. Brodbeck (2004), p. 93.

141. Alf Hiltebeitel (2001), p. 270.

142. Jonardon Ganeri, 2001, p. 4.

143. Amartya Sen, *The Argumentative India: Writings on Indian History, Culture and Identity* (London: Allen Lane, 2005), pp. 23–5.

144. Swami Nikhilananda, 'The Realistic Aspect of Indian Spirituality,' *Philosophy East and West*, vol. 9, 1959, p. 66.

4. INVERTED 'HISTORY'

1. Nirupama Rao, Keynote address by Foreign Secretary Smt. Nirupama Rao at the symposium on 'The Future of India-Pakistan relations', Jamia Millia Islamia University, 19 October 2010, http://mea.gov.in/mystart.php?id=550316574

2. Hedley Bull (1977), pp. 316–17. For updated Western triumphalism see Barry Buzan, 'From International System to International Society: Structural Realism and Regime Theory Meet the English School,' *International Organization*, vol. 47, no. 3, Summer 1993, pp. 348–9.

3. Muzaffar Alam, *The Languages of Political Islam in India: c. 1200–1800* (Chicago University Press, 2004), p. 184.

4. Shankar Bajpai, conversation, his residence, New Delhi, 22 April 2008. Bajpai is the son of Girija Shankar Bajpai and was a career diplomat. After retirement he was Chairman of the National Security Advisory Board.

5. Hence the reverse of the theory of system transforming into society. See Adam Watson, *The Evolution of International Society* (London: Routledge, 1992), p. 51.

6. Marshall Sahlins, *Historical Metaphors and Mythical Realities: Structure in the Early History of the Sandwich Islands Kingdom* (Ann Arbor: University of Michigan Press, 1981), p. 8. The indigenization of the Mughals in India is explored in the next chapter. For now, the focus is on the coming of diplomatic modernity to Mughal India.

7. The insertion was physical. In the 1780s one-third of British men were leaving all their possessions to local women, but the figures rapidly fell as notions of race took hold. See William Dalrymple, *The White Mughal: Love and Betrayal in Eighteenth-Century India* (New Delhi: Penguin, 2004).

8. Adam Watson, 'Hedley Bull, State Systems and International Studies,' *Review of International Studies*, vol. 13, no. 2, 1987; James Der Derian (1987).

9. Benjamin Nelson (1981), pp. 203–05.

10. Benno Teschke, 'Theorising the Westphalian System of States: International Relations from Absolutism to Capitalism,' European Journal of International Relations, vol. 8, no. 1, 2002, p. 8.

11. Akbar made an unsuccessful attempt to communicate with the Spanish King Philip II in 1582 to create an alliance against the Ottomans. See Abu'l Fazl, *Abul Mukatabat-i-Alalmi (Cartas del emperador Akbar)* (New Delhi, 1998), pp. 37–9. The letter is dated Rabiul evvel, 900 A.H./March–April 1582. Also see E. Rehatsek, 'A Letter of the Emperor Akbar Asking for the Christian Scriptures,' *The Indian Antiquary*, April 1887, pp. 135–9. For another interpretation of the purpose of this embassy see M.S. Renick, 'Akbar's First Embassy to Goa: Its Diplomatic and Religious. Aspects,' *Indica*, vol. 1, 1970, pp. 46–7.

12. See Abul Fazl Allámi, *Aín i Akbari*, Vol. I, II, II, trans. H. Blochman and H.S. Jarrett (Calcutta: Asiatic Society of Bengal, 1873–1907). See http://persian.packhum.org/persian/main?url=pf%3Ffile%3D00702051%26ct%3D0

13. H. Blochman, 'Preface' in Abul Fazl Allámi, *Ā'in-i Akbari*, Vol. I (Calcutta: Asiatic Society of Bengal, 1873).

14. Akbar's minister and friend, the *mir munshi*, lived between 1551 and 1602.

15. Abul Fazl Allámi, 'Abul Fazl's Preface' in Abu'l Fazl Allámi, *Ā'in-i Akbari*, vol. I (Calcutta: Asiatic Society of Bengal, 1873), pp. 1–10. See also S.K. Das, Public Office, *Private Interest: Bureaucracy and Corruption in India* (Oxford University Press, 2001), pp. 48–9.

16. Harbans Mukhia, 'Time in Abu'l Fazl's Historiography,' *Studies in History*, vol. 35, no. 1, January 2009, p. 3.

17. Harbans Mukhia, 2009, p. 5.

18. Gerhard Böwering, 'The Concept of Time in Islam,' *Proceedings of the American Philosophical Society*, vol. 141, no. 1, 1997, p. 62.

19. Ibid., pp. 57–8.

20. Ibid., p. 60.

21. For Akbar's intellectual differentiation from Islam see Iqtidar Alam Khan, 'Akbar's Personality Traits and World Outlook—a Critical Reappraisal' in Irfan Habib (ed.), *Akbar and his India* (New Delhi: Oxford University Press, 1997), pp. 82–92; S.A.A. Rizvi, 'Dimensions of Sulh-I Kul (Universal Peace) in Akbar's Reign and the Sufi Theory of Perfect Man' in Iqtidar Alam Khan (ed.), *Akbar and his Age* (New Delhi: Northern Book Centre, 1999), pp. 2–22. For a political explanation see Iqtidar Alam Khan, 'The Nobility under Akbar and the Development of his Religious Policy, 1560–80,' *Journal of the Royal Asiatic Society*, vol. 1, no. 2, 1968, pp. 29–36.

22. Munis D. Faruqui, 'The Forgotten Prince: Mirza Hakim and the Formation of the Mughal Empire in India,' *Journal of the Economic and Social History of the Orient*, vol. 48, no. 4, 2005, p. 488.

23. Munis Faruqui (2005), p. 490.

24. The percentage of Turanis fell from 52.9% in 1555 (the last year of Humayun's reign) to 24.26% in 1580. The ones who gained were Indian Muslims and Rajputs whose numbers rose from almost nothing to 16.17% and 15.83% respectively. See Iqtidar Alam Khan, 1968, p. 36.

25. Munis Faruqui (2005), p. 507. See also Hamid Algar, 'A Brief History of the Naqshbandi Order' in Marc Gaborieau, Alexandre Popovic and Thierry Zarcone (eds), *Naqshbandis: Cheminements et situation actuelle d'un ordre mystique musulman, Actes de la Table Ronde de Sèvres, 2–4 May 1985* (Istanbul: Institut Français d'Études Anatoliennes: Éditions Isis, 1990), pp. 3–44.

26. Munis Faruqui (2005), p. 511. See also Glenn D. Lowry, 'Humayun's Tomb: Form, Function, and Meaning in Early Mughal Architecture,' *Muqarnas* vol. 4, 1988, pp. 133–48; D. Fairchild Ruggles, 'Humayun's Tomb and Garden: Typologies and Visual Order' in Attilio Petruccioli (ed.), *Gardens in the Time of the Great Muslim Empires* (Leiden: E.J. Brill, 1997), pp. 173–86.

27. Munis Faruqui (2005), p. 518. See also M. Athar Ali, 'Akbar and Islam (1581–1605)' in N. Wagle and M. Israel (eds), *Islamic Society and Culture* (New Delhi: Manohar, 1983), p. 124.

28. Munis Faruqui (2005), p. 520.

29. Quoted by Khaliq Ahmad Nizami, *Some Aspects of Religion and Politics in India during the Thirteenth Century* (Delhi: Idarah-i-Adabiyat-i-Delli, 1961), p. 174.

30. Jahangir, *Tūzuk-i-Jahāngīrī or Memoirs of Jahāngīr, From the First to the Twelfth Year of his Reign*, trans. Alexander Rogers, ed. Henry Beveridge (London, 1909), p. 15.

31. Abdul Aziz, *The Mansabdari System and the Mughal Army* (New Delhi: Idarah-i-Adabiyat-i-Delli, 1952), p. 2.

32. Weber emphasized impersonality amongst other qualities. Max Weber, *Economy and Society: An Outline of Interpretive Sociology* ed. Guenther Roth and Claus Wittich (Berkeley: University of California Press, 1978). See also Peter M. Blau, 'Critical Remarks on Weber's Theory of Authority,' *American Political Science Review*, vol. 57, no. 2, 1963.

33. N.K. Singh and A. Samiuddin, *Encyclopaedia Historiography of the Muslim World* (New Delhi: Global Vision Publishing House, 2004), p. 72.

34. Chetan Singh, 'Centre and Periphery in the Mughal State: The Case of the 17th Century Panjab,' *Modern Asian Studies*, vol. 22, no. 12, 1988, p. 306.

35. B.B. Misra, *The Bureaucracy in India—A Historical Analysis of Development Up to 1947* (New Delhi: Oxford University Press, 1977), pp. 55, 184.

36. U.N. Day, *The Mughal Government: A.D. 1556–1707* (New Delhi: Munshiram Manoharlal, 1970), pp. 30, 35, 39.

37. Khaliq Ahmad Nizami, *Some Aspects of Religion and Politics in India during the Thirteenth Century* (Delhi: Asia Publishing House, 1961), pp. 327–8.

38. Sidi Ali Reïs, *The Travels and Adventures of the Turkish Admiral Sidi Ali Reïs in India, Afghanistan, Central Asia, and Persia during the Years 1553–1556*, trans. A. Vambéry (London, 1899), Chapter VIII, 'My experiences in Hindustan,' http://www.columbia.edu/itc/mealac/pritchett/00generallinks/sidialireis/txt_023_hindustan.html

39. Naimur Rahman Farooqi, *Mughal-Ottoman Relations: A Study of the Political & Diplomatic Relations between Mughal India and the Ottoman Empire, 1556–1748* (Delhi: Idarah-I Adabiyat-I Delli, 2009), pp. 16–17.

40. Ibid., p. 19.

41. Abu-l-Fazl, *The Akbarnama*, Vol. III, trans. H. Beveridge (Calcutta: Asiatic Society, 1939), Chapter XXVII, LXVII.

42. Basvekalet Arsivi, *Divani-i-Humayun Muhimme Defterleri*, vol. 39, pp. 160, Farman number 349, 13 February 1580.

43. Ibid., vol. 39, p. 238, Farman number 471, 6 March 1580.

44. Naimur Rahman Farooqi, *Mughal-Ottoman Relations* (2009), p. 20.

45. Father Monserrate, *The Commentary of Father Monserrate, S.J. on his Journey to the Court of Akbar*, trans. J.S. Hoyland and S.N. Banerjee (London: Oxford University Press, 1922), pp. 159, 163, 172.

46. Basvekalet Arsivi, *Divani-i-Humayun Muhimme Defterleri*, vol. 62, p. 205, Farman number 457, 1 December 1587.

47. Father Monserrate (1922), p. 205.

48. Abu-l-Fazl, *The Akbarnama*, Vol. III, trans. H. Beveridge (Calcutta: Asiatic Society, 1939), Chapter XC.

49. Hedley Bull (1977), pp. 33–9.

50. According to the articles of agreement. See G.C.M. Birdwood and W. Foster, The Register of Letters etc. of the Governour and Company of Merchants of London trading into the East Indies, 1600–1619 (London: B. Quaritch, 1893), p. 446.

51. Sir Thomas Roe, *The Embassy of Sir Thomas Roe to India 1615–19*, ed. William Foster, 2 vols. (Oxford University Press, 1926), p. 54.

52. Ibid., p. 53.

53. 'The King,' wrote Roe, 'never used any Ambassador with so much respect.' Ibid., p. 112.

54. William Foster, England's Quest of Eastern Trade (London: A & C Black, 1933), p. 283.

55. Quoted in N.R. Farooqi, 'Diplomacy and Diplomatic Procedure under the Mughals,' *The Medieval History Journal*, vol. 7, no. 1, 2004, p. 71.

56. Sir Thomas Roe (1926), p. 470.

57. C.R. Wilson, 'Introduction' in C.R. Wilson (ed.), *The Early Annals of the English in Bengal: The Bengal Public Consultations for the First Half of the Eighteenth Century, Vol II, Part II: The Surman Embassy* (Calcutta: The Bengal Secretariat Book Depot, 1911), p. vi.

58. Niccolao Manucci, Storia do Mogor (Mogul India, 1653–1708) trans. and ed. William Irvine (Calcutta: Editions Indian, 1965), p. 59.

59. Ibid., p. 69.

60. Ibid., p. 70.

61. Ibid., Chapter xix, pp. 84–5.

62. William Wilson Hunter, *A History of British India*, vol. 2, (London: Longmans, 1901), pp. 355–7.

63. Ibid., pp. 154–5.

64. C.R. Wilson, 'Introduction' (1911), p. x.

65. Walter Kelly Firminger (ed.), *The Fifth Report on East India Company Affairs—1812* (Calcutta: R. Cambray. 1917–1918), p. vi.

66. C.R. Wilson, 'Introduction' (1911), p. vi.

67. John Surman and Edward Stephenson, '12. Consultation' in *Diary of Messrs. Surman and Stephenson, during their Embassy to the Great Mogul, 15 Aug. 1714 to 14 Dec. 1717'* in C.R. Wilson (1911), p. 18. Henceforth *Diary*.

68. Niccolao Manucci, Storia do Mogor (Mogul India, 1653–1708), trans. and ed. William Irvine (1965), p. 87.

69. Surman and Stephenson, '9. Consultation' in *Diary* (1911), p. 11.

70. Surman and Stephenson, '5. Consultation' in *Diary* (1911), p. 8.

71. Surman and Stephenson, '5. Consultation' in *Diary* (1911), pp. 7–8; 'Appendix, 9; Bengal Instructions' in ibid., p. 275.

72. Surman and Stephenson, '10. Consultation' in *Diary* (1911), p. 13; '31. Consultation,' ibid., p. 29. And see '47. Consultation,' ibid., p. 45; '48. Diary', ibid., pp. 46, 49; 'Letter I,' ibid., pp. 46–7; & '50. Consultation,' ibid., pp. 48–9.

73. Surman and Stephenson, '54. Letter II' in *Diary* (1911), p. 50; Surman and Stephenson, '106. Diary,' ibid., p. 101; '58. Consultation,' ibid., p. 54.

74. Surman and Stephenson, '64. Consultation' in *Diary* (1911), p. 59; 'Letter VIII,' ibid., pp. 77–8; '87. Letter IX,' ibid., pp. 79–80.

75. Surman and Stephenson, '66. Consultation: A translate off a general petition, to the King, in order to our obtaining a phirmaund' in *Diary* (1911), p. 60.

76. Surman and Stephenson, '88. The first petition examined' in *Diary* (1911), p. 81.

77. Surman and Stephenson, '90. Consultation' in *Diary* (1911), p. 83; Surman & Stephenson, '91. Consultation,' ibid., p. 84.

78. Surman and Stephenson, '99. Letter XI' in *Diary* (1911), p. 91.

79. Surman and Stephenson, '105. Letter XIII' in *Diary* (1911), p. 100.

80. Ibid.

81. Surman and Stephenson, '104. Consultation' in *Diary* (1911), pp. 98–9; Surman and Stephenson, '119. Consultation,' ibid.,p. 111.

82. Surman and Stephenson, '115. Consultation' in *Diary* (1911), p. 110; '117 Consultation,' ibid., p. 110; '118. Diary,' ibid., p. 110; '123. Letter XVI,' ibid., p. 116.

83. Surman and Stephenson, '122. Diary' in *Diary* (1911), p. 114; '133. Diary,' ibid.,p. 124.

84. Hugh Barker and Thomas Phillips, 'Letter XXIV' in *Diary* (1911), p. 152.

85. Surman and Stephenson, '139. Diary' in *Diary* (1911), p. 131.

86. Surman and Stephenson, '147. Diary' in *Diary* (1911), p. 140.

87. Ibid.

88. Surman, '149. Letter XXII' in *Diary* (1911), p. 141.

89. Surman and Stephenson, '152. Consultation' in *Diary* (1911), p. 143.

90. Surman and Stephenson, '190. Diary', '191. Consultation', '192. Diary' in *Diary* (1911), pp. 198–201.

5. DEATH OF DIPLOMACY

1. C.R. Wilson, 'Introduction' (1911), p. lvii.

2. In 1700, the majority of the world's population lived in Asia (60%) and this proportion had

only slightly decreased to 56% in the year 2000 (Asia does not include the Commonwealth of Independent States or the Middle East which had 5% and 4% respectively). Europe accounted for 14% of the world total, approximately the same as in Africa at that time. Latin America accounted for less than 2% and Oceania and North America were virtually uninhabited with 0.2%. The India region's population density was around 32 inh/km² in 1700, second was Europe with 12 inh/km². Kees Klein Goldewijk, 'Three Centuries of Global Population Growth: A Spatial Referenced Population (Density) Database for 1700–2000,' *Population and Environment*, vol. 26, no. 4, March, 2005, pp. 356, 359.

3. Of course race is just another fiction of modernity. See Kathleen Wilson, 'Introduction' and 'Chapter I' in *The Island Race: Englishness, Empire and Gender in the Eighteenth Century* (London: Routledge, 2003), p. 11. On the subjectivity of science in India see Bernard S. Cohn, *An Anthropologist among the Historians and Other Essays* (New Delhi: Oxford University Press, 1990), pp. 224–54.

4. M. Athar Ali, 'The Passing of Empire: The Mughal Case,' *Modern Asian Studies*, vol. 9, no. 3, 1975, p. 396.

5. Charles Tilly, 'Reflections on the History of European State Making' in Charles Telly (ed.), *The Formation of National States in Europe* (Princeton University Press, 1975), p. 31; W.H. McNeill, *The Pursuit of Power: Technology, Armed Force, and Society since A.D. 1000* (Chicago University Press, 1982).

6. Unmentioned are separate extractions to other regions of the British Empire, for instance the Rs. 6 million extracted from Oudh to Iraq. See Meir Litvak, 'Money, Religion, and Politics: The Oudh Bequest in Najaf and Karbala, 1850–1903,' *International Journal of Middle East Studies*, vol. 33, no. 1, February 2001.

7. Romesh Chander Dutt, *Economic History of India* (London: Kegan Paul, Trübner Trench, 1908).

8. Ranajit Guha, *A Rule of Property for Bengal: An Essay on the Idea of Permanent Settlement* (Durham, NC.: Duke University Press, 1996), pp. 137–9.

9. Harry Verelst, *A View of the Rise, Progress and Present State of the English Governemt in Bengal: including a Reply to the Misrepresentations of Mr. Bolts, and Other Writers* (London: J. Nourse [etc.], 1772), Appendix, p. 59.

10. Irfan Habib, *Essays in Indian History: Towards a Marxist Perception* (New Delhi: Tulika Books, 1995), p. 304.

11. Javier Cuenca Esteban, 'The British Balance of Payments, 1772–1820: India Transfers and War Finance,' *The Economic History Review New Series*, vol. 54, no. 1, 2001, p. 69.

12. In actual fact there was continuity. See P.J. Marshall, *Bengal: The British Bridgehead: Eastern India 1740–1828* (Cambridge University Press, 1987), p. 172.

13. Dina Rizk Khoury and Dane Keith Kennedy, 'Comparing Empires: The Ottoman Empires and the British Raj in the Long Nineteenth Century,' *Comparative Studies of South Asia, Africa and the Middle East*, vol. 27, no. 2, 2007, p. 214.

14. Ibid., p. 237.

15. Mike Davis, *Late Victorian Holocausts: El Niño Famines and the Making of the Third World* (London: Verso, 2001).

16. Christopher Alan Bayly, *Indian Society and the Making of the British Empire* (Cambridge University Press, 1988), p. 116.

17. P.J. Marshall (1987), pp. 140–44; Rajat Datta, *Society, Economy, and the Market: Commercialization in Rural Bengal, 1760–1800* (New Delhi: Manohar, 2000), pp. 333–8.

18. Douglas M. Peers, 'Gunpowder Empires and the Garrison State: Modernity, Hybridity, and the Political Economy of Colonial India, circa 1750–1860,' *Comparative Studies of South Asia, Africa and the Middle East*, vol. 27, no. 2, 2007, pp. 245–258

19. Appendix to *Report from the Select Committee on Indian Territories, Parliamentary Papers* 10 (1852), pp. 276–9.

20. Henry Lawrence, 'The Indian Army,' *Calcutta Review*, vol. 26 (1856), p. 185.

21. See chapter 1.

22. Douglas M. Peers, *Between Mars and Mammon: Colonial Armies and the Garrison State in Early 19th Century India* (London: I.B. Tauris, 1995), p. 9.

23. John Malcolm, *The Political History of India from 1784 to 1823, vol. II* (London: John Murray, 1826), p. 52.

24. [Anon.], 'The Indian Army,' *United Services Journal*, vol. 19, 1835, p. 311.

25. 'Munro to Canning, 14 Oct 1820' in G.R. Glieg, *The Life of Major General Sir Thomas Munro, vol. II* (London: Colburn and Bentley, 1830), p. 52.

26. 'Metcalfe's memo, nd. (1815/16?)', in J.W. Kaye, *Life and Correspondence of Lord Metcalfe* (London: Smith, Elder and Co., 1858), vol. I, p. 442 n.

27. [W.W], 'Consideration on the Native Army and General Defence of India,' *United Services Journal*, no. 7, 1831, p. 1.

28. Ochterlony to Court, 1825 in David Ochterlony, *Selections from the Ochterlony Papers (1818–1825) in the National Archives of India* (Calcutta: University of Calcutta, 1964), p. 435.

29. Christopher Alan Bayly (1988), p. 5.

30. Douglas M. Peers (2007) p. 246.

31. P.J. Marshall, *East Indian Fortunes* (Oxford University Press, 1992), p. 182.

32. Philip Harling and Peter Mandler, 'From 'Fiscal-Military State to Laissez-Faire State, 1760–1850,' *Journal of British Studies*, vol. 32, 1993.

33. Douglas M. Peers (1995), p. 244.

34. Chapman, 'India and its Finances,' *Westminster Review*, vol. 4, 1853, p. 192.

35. Douglas M. Peers (1995), p. 8.

36. James Fitzjames Stephen, 'Foundations of the Government of India,' *Nineteenth Century*, vol. 80, 1883. See also Uday Singh Mehta, *Liberalism and Empire: A Study in Nineteenth-Century British Liberal Thought* (Chicago University Press, 2000).

37. Michael H. Fisher, 'The Resident in Court Ritual, 1764–1858,' *Modern Asian Studies*, vol. 24, no. 3, 1990, p. 430.

38. Ibid.

39. Ibid.

40. Quoted in Nicholas B. Dirks, *The Scandal of Empire: India and the Creation of Imperial Britain* (Cambridge, MA.: Harvard University Press, 2006), p. 4.

41. The Bengal Presidency covered approximately 221,000 square miles or 570,000 sq/km, which exceeds the size of France. See 'India: Its Extent and Population,' *Journal of the American Geographical and Statistical Society*, vol. 1, no. 1, January 1859, pp. 22–3. And https://www.cia.gov/library/publications/the-world-factbook/geos/fr.html

42. G.J. Bryant, 'Asymmetric Warfare: The British Experience in Eighteenth-Century India,' *The Journal of Military History*, vol. 68 no. 2, 2004, p. 448.

43. Ibid., p. 465. See Madras to Colonel Campbell, 14 April 1765, P/251/52, p. 291, Oriental and India Office Collections, British Library, London. Colonel Muir to Hastings, 28 April 1781: 'spirited Resolves and brisk Actions Generally serve better [in this country] than Slow Counsels and too Circumspect a Conduct', f. 81, Add. MSS 29119, British Library, London. And see J. Luvaas (ed.), *Frederick the Great on the Art of War* (New York: The Free Press, 1966), pp. 139–41.

44. The treaty between the EIC and Siraj-ud-daula of February 1757 permitted fortification

of Calcutta. The treaty with Mir Jafar on 15 July 1757 made Bengal responsible for financing British wars and the treaty with Mir Kasim of 27 September 1760 made the EIC partners. Mir Jafar on 10 July 1763 specified Bengal's military contributions to the EIC. The treaty of February 1765 with Najm-ud-daula stated, 'I [Najm-ud-daula] will only maintain such (troops) as are absolutely necessary for the dignity of my own person and government, and the business of my collections throughout the provinces.' Quoted in Walter Kelly Firminger (ed.), *The Fifth Report on East India Company Affairs—1812* (Calcutta: R. Cambray, 1917–1918), pp. vi, viii-ix. See also C.U. Aitchison (ed.), *A Collection of Treaties, Engagements and Sanads*, vol. I, Calcutta: Superintendent Government Printing.

45. R. Gopal, *How the British Occupied Bengal: A Corrected Account of 1756—1765 Events* (Bombay: Asia Publishing House, 1963).

46. Robert Orme, *A History of the Military Transactions of the British Nation in Indostan …*, 4th ed., 2 vols. (London: John Nourse, 1803), p. 282. Another ex-EIC man suggested that the Indians were already beaten in their minds when faced by a successful general, such as Clive, because they believed that God was behind him: Luke Scrafton, *Reflections on the Government of Indostan with A Short Sketch Of The History Of Bengal from 1739 to 1756* (London: W. Richardson and S. Clark, 1770), pp. 115–16.

47. Clive to Colonel Caillaud, 17 November 1765, pp. 25–7, Clive MSS, 222, Nat. Lib. of Wales, Aberystwyth, Ceredigion, Wales; see Bengal to Court, 20 March 1776: 'The Influence of the British Empire in India is founded in some degree on our effective Power but more perhaps on the Credit of former Successes and the Reputation of our Arms': pp. 87–8, E/4/35, Oriental and India Office Collections, British Library.

48. For a Mughal perspective on this period in Bengal see Abdul Majed Khan, *The Transition in Bengal, 1756–1775: a Study of Muhammad Reza Khan* (Cambridge University Press, 1969). Reza Khan was the minister who ran Bengal for the British in the 1760s, and 'his constant aim … was to persuade his English masters to accept Mughal ideas as their own.' Majed Khan (1969), p. 16.

49. Bernard S. Cohn, 'Law and the Colonial State in India' in June Starr and Jane F. Collier (eds), *History and Power in the Study of Law: New Directions in Legal Anthropology* (Ithaca, NY: Cornell University Press (1989), p. 133.

50. Warren Hastings quoted in Nicholas Dirks (2006), p. 185.

51. Ibid., p. 187.

52. Michael H. Fisher, *Indirect Rule in India: Residents and the Residency System, 1764–1858* (New Delhi: Oxford University Press, 1991), p. 442.

53. Political Letter from Governor-General to Court of Directors 15 August 1815, quoted in Michael H. Fisher (1991), p. 444.

54. Quoted in James W. Massie, *Continental India: Travelling Sketches and Historical Recollections, Illustrating the Antiquity, Religion, and Manners of the Hindoos, the Extent of British Conquests, and the Progress of Missionary Operations, Vol. I* (London: Thomas Ward & Co. Paternoster Row, 1840), pp. 309–310.

55. Michael H. Fisher (1991), p. 444. For example, Governor-General Dalhousie accepted the sovereignty of Indian Rulers even as he annexed their states in violation of explicit treaty rights. Governor-General's Minute of 18 June 1855, Foreign Political Consultations, India Office Library, 28 December 1855, No. 319.

56. Michael H. Fisher (1991), p. 49.

57. Michael H. Fisher, 'Indirect Rule in the British Empire: The Foundations of the Residency System in India (1764–1858),' *Modern Asian Studies*, vol. 18, no. 3, 1984, p. 399; Ernest Satow, *A Guide to Diplomatic Practise*, ed. Nevile Bland (London, 1961), p. 165.

58. Michael H. Fisher (1984), p. 393.

59. For example: *Jahangir, Tūzuk-i-Jahāngīrī or Memoirs of Jahāngir, From the First to the Twelfth Year of his Reign*, trans. Alexander Rogers, ed. Henry Beveridge (London, 1909).

60. Michael H. Fisher (1984), pp. 399–400.

61. Riazul Islam, *Indo-Persian Relations: A Study of the Political and Diplomatic Relations between the Mughal Empire and Iran*, 'Sources of the History and Geography of Iran' no. 32 (Teheran: Iranian Culture Foundation, 1970), p. 226.

62. Michael H. Fisher (1984), p. 401.

63. Ibid., pp. 401–02.

64. Early bureaucracies were staffed by military men: Michael Mann, *The Sources of Social Power: The Rise of Classes and Nation-States, 1760–1914, vol. II* (Cambridge University Press, 1993).

65. '"Political" meant diplomatic in the old East Indian Company lexicon, and a "political" was a Resident, Political or Assistant Political Officer employed in that line.' See Hogben W. Murray, 'An Imperial Dilemma: The Reluctant Indianization of the Indian Political Service,' *Modern Asian Studies*, vol. 15, no. 4, 1981, p. 752.

66. Michael H. Fisher (1984), p. 407.

67. Bernard S. Cohn, 'Recruitment and Training of British Civil Servants in India, 1600–1860' in Ralph Braibanti (ed.), *Asian Bureaucratic Systems Emergent from the British Imperial Tradition* (Durham, NC: Duke University Press, 1966), p. 103.

68. Michael H. Fisher (1984), p. 408.

69. Quoted in ibid., p. 409.

70. Ibid., p. 409. Even though the total number of military in the service actually declined during his administration, Ellenborough regarded this as the major factor in his quarrel with the Directors: Ellenborough to Wellington, 9 June 1842, cited in W. Broadfoot, *The Career of Major Broadfoot in Afghanistan and the Punjab* (London: John Murray, 1888), p. 195.

71. Michael H. Fisher (1984), p. 411.

72. Men such as Warren Hastings found them altogether indispensable. See Muzaffar Alam and Seema Alavi, *A European Experience of the Mughal Orient: The I jazi Arsalami-Persian Letters, 1773–79 of Antoine Polier* (New Delhi: Oxford University Press, 2001), pp. 13–14.

73. In the reign of Aurangzeb there was the *Nigarnamah-'I Munshī* (*Munshī*'s Letterbook), concerned with how to train a *munshi* and what he ought to know. See S. Nurul Hasan, 'Nigar Nama-i-Munshi: A Valuable Collection of Documents of Aurangzeb's Reign,' *Proceedings of the Indian History Congress 15ᵗʰ Session* (Gwalior: Indian History Congress, 1952). During Jahangir's period there was the *Insha'-I Harkaran*, a book which was translated into English by the EIC and printed as a model text for its own early administrators. See Francis Balfour (ed., and trans.), *Insha'-i Harkaran* (Calcutta: Charles Wilson, 1781).

74. Muzaffar Alam and Sanjay Subrahmanyam, 'The Making of a Munshi,' *Comparative Studies of South Asia, Africa and the Middle East*, vol. 24, no. 2, 2004, p. 61. For a standard issue 'secular' reading of Emperor Akbar's policies see B.N. Goswamy and J.S. Grewal, *The Mughal and the Jogis of Jakhbar* (Shimla: Indian Institute of Advanced Studies, 1967); for a similar treatment of Jahangir see Sajida S. Alvi, 'Religion and State during the Reign of Mughal Emperor Jahāngīr (1605–27): Nonjuristical Perspectives,' *Studia Islamica*, vol. 69, 1989.

75. Quoted in Muzaffar Alam and Sanjay Subrahmanyam, 2004, p. 64.

76. Ibid., pp. 71, 67.

77. Michael H. Fisher, 'The Office of Akhbār Nawīs: The Transition from Mughal to British Forms,' *Modern Asian Studies*, vol. 27, no. 1, 1993, pp. 46, 82.

78. F. Steingass, *A Comprehensive Persian-English Dictionary* (New Delhi: Asian Educational Services, 1973), p. 446a.

79. Michael H. Fisher (1993), p. 46.

80. This process largely reflected how the Mughals worked in general: building a distinctive patrimonial-bureaucratic empire by synthesizing elements from pan-Islamic institutions, imperial Persian models (especially from the Safawid court, established in 1501), their own dynastic traditions from Central Asia, and the administrative forms they found in India. See Stephen P. Blake, 'The Patrimonial Bureaucratic Empire of the Mughals,' *Journal of Asian Studies*, vol. 39, no. 1, 1979.

81. See Abu'l Fazl, Ain-I Akbari (trans. H. Blochmann), vol. I (Calcutta, 1927).

82. Jahangir, *Tūzuk-i-Jahāngīrī or Memoirs of Jahāngīr, From the First to the Twelfth Year of his Reign*, trans. Alexander Rogers, ed. Henry Beveridge (London, 1909), pp. 247–8. Yusuf Husain Khan says Akbar established a *wāqi 'a nawīs* in each province from 1586: 'Seventeenth Century Waqai' in the Central Records Office, Hyderabad,' *Islamic Culture*, vol. 28, no. 3, July 1954, p. 460. For an excellent survey of the Mughal information systems see Jagdish Narayan Sarkar, 'Newswriters of Mughal India' in S.P. Sen (ed.), *The Indian Press* (*A Collection of Papers Presented at the 4th Annual Conference of the Institute*) (Calcutta: Institute of Historical Studies, 1967), pp. 110–45. Quoted in Fisher H. Michael (1993), p. 50.

83. Muhammad Zameeruddin Siddiqi, 'The Intelligence Services under the Mughals' in *Medieval India: A Miscellany, vol. 2* (London, 1972), p. 54.

84. Ali Muhammad Khan, *Mirat-i-Ahmedi*, Supplement, trans. Syed Nawab Ali and Charles Norman Siddon (Baroda, 1924), p. 171.

85. Michael H. Fisher (1993), p. 53.

86. Jadunath Sarkar (ed. and trans.), *Persian Records of Maratha History, vol. I Delhi Affairs* (1761–1788) (Newsletters from Parasnis Collection) (Bombay, 1953), p. 88.

87. Sewak Ram's letter from Calcutta, 26 March 1779, quoted in Jadunath Sarkar (1953), pp. 96–8.

88. 5 February 1787, ibid., p. 154.

89. Persian Correspondence, Translation of Persian Letters Received and Issued I770, no. 48, pp. 15–16, National Archives of India.

90. Ibid., no. 52, pp. 184–5, National Archives of India.

91. This was his second 'petition' to the Governor-general, the first having elicited no response. From Ghulam Muhammad Khan, 24 May 1782, Persian Correspondence, Translation of Persian Letters Received, vol. 19, no. 25, pp. 55–7, National Archives of India.

92. Resident Poona to Gov. Gen. 21 February 1795, Foreign Political Consultations 23 March I795, no. II, India Office Library.

93. E.g. To Vizier, 27 February 1767, Persian Correspondence, Copy of Letters Issued 1766–67, no. 70, p. 30, National Archives of India.

94. Humble Petition of Motee Loll, 4 January 1833, Foreign Political Consultations 12 March 1833, no. 12, India Office Library.

95. Rsdt Delhi to Secy to Govt, 9 July 1815, Foreign Political Consultations 26 July 1815, no. 62, India Office Library.

96. Envoy to King of Oude to Secy to Govt of India, Foreign Department, 31 August 1844, Foreign Political Consultations 5 October 1844, no. 155, India Office Library.

97. John M. Roberts, *The Triumph of the West* (London: BBC Books, 1985), p. 28.

98. Quoted in Natasha Eaton, 'Between Mimesis and Alterity: Art, Gift and Diplomacy in Colonial India, 1770–1800,' *Comparative Studies in Society and Art*, vol. 5, no. 4, 2008, p. 819. See F. Buckler, 'The Oriental Despot' in M. Pearson (ed.), *Legitimacy and Symbols* (Ann Arbor, MI: Center for South and Southeast Asian Studies, University of Michigan, 1992); Stewart Gordon and G. Hambly (eds), *Robes of Honour: The Medieval World of Investiture* (New York: St. Martin's Press, 2000).

99. Quoted in Eaton, 2008, p. 819. See Michael Brand, *The Vision of Kings: Art and Experience in India* (Canberra: National Gallery of Australia, 1997).

100. John McLane, *Land and Local Kingship in 18th Century Bengal* (Cambridge University Press, 1993), p. 43.

101. Eaton (2008), p. 819.

102. Nicholas B. Dirks, 'From Little King to Landlord' in N. Dirks (ed.), *Colonialism and Culture* (Ann Arbor: University of Michigan Press, 1992), p. 200.

103. See Louise Lippincott, 'Expanding on Portraiture: The Market, the Public and the Hierarchy of Genres in 18th-Century Britain' in Ann Bermingham and John Brewer (eds), *The Consumption of Culture: Image, Object, Text* (London: Routledge, 1995).

104. Eaton (2008), p. 820.

105. P.J. Marshall, 'The Making of an Imperial Icon: The Case of Warren Hastings,' *Journal of Imperial and Commonwealth History*, vol. 27, no. 3, September 1999, p. 6.

106. Abu'l Fazl, *Ain-I Akbari*, trans. H. Blochmann, vol. I (Calcutta, 1927), p. 115.

107. Asaf wanted Resident Bristow to be recalled; if Hastings did not comply, he also threatened to write to the British Prime Minister. See Eaton (2008), p. 827.

108. It seems to have been Zoffany's normal practice to take five or six sittings for a portrait, which was also continued at the court of Lucknow. See Hastings, *Diary*, Hastings Papers British Library: Add Ms.39,879.

109. Hastings Papers British Library: Add Ms. 29,121, 3 May 1784.

110. Mir Muhammad Taqi 'Mir', *Zikr-i Mir: The Autobiography of the 18th Century Mughal Poet: Mir*, trans. C.M. Naim (Delhi: Oxford University Press, 1999), p. 124.

111. Eaton (2008), p. 830.

112. E.g. From the Nawāb of Arcot 28 September 1775, Persian Correspondence, Copies of Letters Received, vol. 4, no. 16, pp. 21–3, National Archives of India. In sending such news reports to Calcutta, the Nawāb may have been trying to ingratiate himself with the Governor-General so as to overrule the Governor of Madras, an overt opponent of the Nawāb.

113. From the Nawab of Arcot, 3 September 1777, Persian Correspondence, Copies of Letters Received, vol. 9, no. 2I, pp. 30–2.

114. Soon after Richard Sulivan wrote this, he himself began a brief and controversial career as a Resident at Arcot and then Hyderabad: Richard Joseph Sulivan, *An Analysis of the Political History of India: In which is Considered The Present Situation of the East And The Connections of its Several Powers with The Empire of Great Britain* (London: T. Becket, 1784), p. 31.

115. Michael H. Fisher, 'Indian Political Representations in Britain during the Transition to Colonialism,' *Modern Asian Studies*, vol. 38, no. 3, 2004.

116. Ibid., p. 651. See for example Rungo Bapojee, whose publications included *Vindex, Dethroned Rajah of Sattarah* (London, 1843). Bapojee was the representative of the Maharaja of Satara and though he barely spoke English, went to London as the Maharajah's envoy. See Michael H. Fisher (2004), p. 664.

117. In this too Bapojee was quite sucessful. See Michael H. Fisher (2004), p. 668. Bapojee's efforts led to debate in Parliament and the revelation of secret papers. See Court Minutes 27 July 1842 and 29 July 1842, B/204, ff. 379–80, 410–11, British Library. 'Rajah of Sattara: The Debate on the Motion of Joseph Hume, Esq., M.P. in the House of Commons, Tuesday, July 22nd, 1845' (London, 1845).

118. Homi K. Bhabha, *The Location of Culture* (London, 1994), Homi K. Bhabha (1994), p. 330.

119. Eyre Coote to Governor-general in Council 16 January 1781, Foreign Secret Consultations, 23 February 1782, no. 7, India Office Library.

120. Richard Joseph Sulivan (1784), pp. 307–08. Rsdt Delhi to Secy to Govt, 13 October 1813, Foreign Political Consultations, 1 June 1816, no. 13, India Office Library. These views are repeated in Minute of Sir C.T. Metcalfe, 14 December 1829, Foreign Political Consultations 14 December 1829, no. 22, India Office Library.

121. Resident Hyderabad to Secretary to Government, 5/9/1816, Foreign Political Consultations, 28 September 1816, no. 15, India Office Library.

122. Lt James Davidson to Department Persian Translation, 16 Aug. 1791, Foreign Miscellaneous Series, Vol. 52, Nagpore Residency, 19 April 1792, India Office Library.

123. William Lee-Warner, *The Native States of India* (London: Macmillan, 1910), p. 220.

124. C.U. Aitchison, *A Collection of Treaties, Engagements, and Sanads Relating to India and Neighbouring Countries*, 14 vols. (Calcutta, 1909).

125. See Sardar Ganda Singh, 'Akhbarat-i-Lahaur-o-Multan,' *Proceedings of the Indian Historical Records Commission* 21 (Dec. 1944), pp. 43–6. Singh surmises from internal evidence that these *akhbarat*s from Aug. 1848 to Jan. 1849 for Ahmadpur, Bahawalpur, Lahore, Multan, and elsewhere were written for the Maharaja of Patiala. They were found among other discarded papers from a collection in Multan. Their language is sympathetic to the English and hostile to the Sikhs opposing the English.

126. Secy to Govt to Acting Rsdt Nagpur, 15 Oct. 1813, Foreign Political Consultations, 15 Oct. 1813, nos 3, 4, India Office Library; C.U. Aitchison (1909), vol. 2, pp. 519–27.

127. See: Bulan Lahiri, 'In conversation: Speaking to Spivak,' *The Hindu*, 5 February 2011. http://www.thehindu.com/arts/books/article1159208.ece See also Dinitia Smith, 'Creating a stir wherever she goes,' *New York Times* (Arts), 9 February 2002. http://www.nytimes.com/2002/02/09/arts/creating-a-stir-wherever-she-goes.html?pagewanted=all&src=pm

128. Little is known of B.L. Gupta outside his family. My information is from his granddaughter, my grandmother. See Richard Symonds, *The British and their Successors* (London: Faber and Faber, 1966), p. 79.

129. Memo. D 233, 'Admission of a Native of India to the Political Dept', and undated 1918 note by H.W. Garrett, India Office Library, in L/P&S/18; for a fuller account of the topic see R. Satakopan, 'The Indian Political Services,' *New Review*, vol. 13, 1941.

130. Quoted in W. Murray Hogben (1981), p. 753.

131. Quoted in ibid., pp. 760–61.

132. W. Murray Hogben (1981), p. 767.

133. B.N. Puri, *History of Indian Administration, Medieval Period, vol. II* (Bombay: Bhartiya Vidya Bhavan, 1975), p. iv.

134. Sanjay Subrahmanyam, 'Connected Histories: Notes toward a Reconfiguation of Early Modern Eurasia,' *Modern Asian Studies*, vol. 31, no. 3, July 1997, p. 737.

135. Benjamin Nelson (1981), pp. 184, 178.

136. Donald A. Nielsen, September 2001, p. 409.

6. DIPLOMACY REBORN

1. M.K. Gandhi, 'Message to Shanti Sena Dal,' *The Hindustan Standard*, 5 September 1947 (original in Bengali), in CWMG-EB, vol. 96, p. 342.

2. Ft. Nt. Reference: R.K. Karanjia, The Mind of Mr. Nehru: An Interview with R.K. Karanjia (London: George Allen & Unwin, 1961), pp. 24.

3. James Der Derian (1987), p. 23.

4. Partha Chatterjee, *The Nation and its Fragments* (Princeton University Press, 1993), pp. 17, 168, 169.

5. Thomas Hobbes, *Leviathan*, Revised Student Edition (Cambridge University Press, 1996), pp. 88, 140.

6. Sunil Khilnani and Ramachandra Guha, 'Series Editors Preface' in Srinath Raghavan, *War and Peace in Modern India: A Strategic History of the Nehru Years* (Ranikhet: Permanent Black, 2010), p. vii.

7. The word 'politics' is retained in describing what Gandhi creates despite its having a very different meaning from politics as conceptualized by modernity and postmodernity. Violence unifies their understandings. The 'realist' notion that politics is amoral masks the assumption that all men are 'evil' and hence politics is about controlling people violently. More recently, postmodernists speak of 'governmentality', which replaces 'realist' violence (enacted as oppressive legislation) with surveillance an expression of the inescapable network of oppressive power. Similar are ecosystems but they remove the need for politics altogether. Resolutely political, Gandhi devises something quite different but it is still politics, because it deals with the complex of relations between people living in society but integrated in a school of thought alternate. The very integrated nature of Gandhi's thought and practice is also why terms such as 'ethics' and 'morality' do not suffice because they are a step away from the actual practice of conducting oneself in society or what is termed politics. In short, Gandhi's politics is ethics and morals. For realist politics see Niccolò Machiavelli, *The Prince*, trans. Luigi Ricci (New York: The New American Library, 1959); for postmodern politics see Michel Foucault, 'Governmentality' in Graham Burchell, Colin Gordon and Peter Miller (eds), *The Foucault Effect: Studies in Governmentality* (University of Chicago Press, 1991). On Gandhi himself defining politics as 'all human relations' see M.K. Gandhi, 'Discussion with B.G. Kher and others,' *Harijan*, 15 August 1940, in CWMG-EB, vol. 79, p. 121.

8. Faisal Devji makes a similar point, except that he talks of 'customs and rituals' which had rarely if ever assumed a political character. The argument here is that these customs and rituals ideate a rationality, made political by Gandhi, in a way not seen before. See Faisal Devji, *The Impossible Indian: Gandhi and the Temptations of Non-violence* (London: C. Hurst & Co., 2012), p. 10.

9. Chapter III. Balaka's transportation to heaven despite destroying a beast intent on destruction is an example of how the *Mb* rewards those who destroy to preserve.

10. Faisal Devji (2012) 'Conclusion'.

11. M. K. Gandhi, 'FAITH v. REASON', *Harijan*, 23 December 1939, in CWMG-EB, vol. 77, pp. 155–6.

12. Manfred Steger, 'Searching for Satya through Ahimsa: Mahatma Gandhi's Challenge to Western Discourses of Power', *Constellations: An International Journal of Critical and Democratic Theory*, vol. 13, no. 3, September 2006, p. 345. See M.K. Gandhi, 'Statement to disorders inquiry committee,' Sabarmati, 5 January 1920, CWMG-EB, vol. 19, pp. 206–07. Gandhi's evidence shows Steger's argument of Gandhi being perspectival as misguided. However, the argument is not new. See Joan Bondurant, *Conquest of Violence: The Gandhian Philosophy of Conflict* (Princeton University Press, 1958).

13. Manfred Steger, *Gandhi's Dilemma: Nonviolent Principles and Nationalist Power* (New York: St. Martin's Press, 2000), pp. 104–06.

14. Lloyd I. Rudolph and Susanne Hoeber Rudolph, *Postmodern Gandhi and Other Essays: Gandhi in the World and at Home* (Chicago University Press, 2006).

15. Peter Van der Veer (2001), pp. 3–8.

16. See Chapter 3 for how this issue never arises in the intellectual stream generated by the Mb.

17. See Sasheej Hegde's review of 'Postmodern Gandhi,' *Contributions to Indian Sociology*, vol. 41, no. 2, 2007, p. 261.
18. Rudolph and Rudolph (2006), p. 159.
19. Sublime as an adjective.
20. Akeel Bilgrami, 'Gandhi's Integrity: The Philosophy Behind the Politics,' *Postcolonial Studies*, vol. 5, no. 1, 2002, p. 82.
21. Bilgrami (2002), p. 89.
22. M.K. Gandhi, 'Discussion with Basil Mathews and others,' *Harijan*, 5 December 1936, CWMG-EB, Vol. 70, p. 117.
23. G. Bühler, *The Laws of Manu, Sacred Books of the East*, vol. XXV (Delhi: Motilal Banarsidass, 1964), p. 30.
24. Bilgrami (2002), p. 83.
25. Akeel Bilgrami, 'Occidentalism, the Very Idea: An Essay on Enlightenment and Enchantment,' *Critical Enquiry*, vol. 32, Spring 2006, p. 25.
26. A more standard 'historical' context is provided by Devji (2012), Chapter I, p. 11.
27. Claude Markovits, *Ungandhian Gandhi: The Life and After Life of the Mahatma* (New Delhi: Permanent Black, 2006), p. 62.
28. Javed Majeed, 'Gandhi, "Truth" and Translatability,' *Modern Asian Studies*, vol. 40, no. 2, 2006, p. 307.
29. M.K. Gandhi, 'Sikhism', *Young India*, 1 October 1925, in CWMG-EB, vol. 33, p. 32.
30. M.K. Gandhi, 'Oriental Ideal of Truth', *Indian Opinion*, 1 April 1905, in CWMG-EB, vol. 4, p. 227.
31. M.K. Gandhi, 'Conundrums,' *Harijan*, 30 September, 1939, in CWMG-EB, vol. 76, p. 356.
32. Akeel Bilgrami (2002), pp. 87–8.
33. M.K. Gandhi, 'What is One's Dharma,' *Navjivan*, 21 July 1929, in CWMG-EB, vol. 46. p. 296.
34. M.K. Gandhi, 'Some Reminiscences of Raychandbhai,' Preface to 'Shrimad Rajchandra', 5 November 1926, in CWMG-EB, vol. 36, p. 475.
35. Piers Vitebsky, 'Is Death the Same Everywhere? Contexts of Knowing and Doubting' in Mark Hobart (ed.), *An Anthropological Critique of Development: the Growth of Ignorance* (London: Routledge, 1993), p. 106.
36. M.K. Gandhi, 'Teaching of Hinduism,' *Harijan*, 3 October 1936, in CWMG-EB, vol. 69, p. 420.
37. The former being the modern notion.
38. M.K. Gandhi, 'Letter to Sumangal Prakash,' 5 April 1933, in CWMG-EB, vol. 60, p. 275.
39. M.K. Gandhi, 'Discussion with a Jain "Muni" at Palitana,' *Navjivan*, 12 April 1925, in CWMG-EB vol. 31, p. 113.
40. Quoted in P. Jain, 'Mahatma Gandhi's Notion of Dharma: An Explication' in Ashok Vohra, Arvind Sharma and Mrinal Miri (eds), *Dharma: The Categorical Imperative* (New Delhi: D.K. Printworld, 2005), pp. 109–111.
41. James L. Fitzgerald (2004), pp. 304–312.
42. M.K. Gandhi, 'Teaching of Hinduism,' *Harijan*, 3 October 1936, in CWMG-EB, vol. 69, p. 420.
43. Michel Foucault (1977).
44. Faisal Devji (2012), p. 40.
45. Gandhi translated the text and presented it at the Satyāgraha Ashram at Ahmedabad from 24 February to 27 November 1926. See M.K. Gandhi, 'Discourses on the Gita', in CWMG-EB, vol. 37, pp. 75–354.

46. In keeping with Ganeri's notion of rationality. See Jonardon Ganeri (2001), p. 4.
47. Johan Galtung, 'Violence, Peace, and Peace Research,' *Journal of Peace Research*, vol. 6, no. 3, 1969, p. 168.
48. M.K. Gandhi, 'Problem of Non-violence,' *Navjivan*, 6 June 1926, in CWMG-EB, vol. 35, pp. 323–4.
49. M.K. Gandhi, 'Letter to Ambalal Sarabhai,' 11 July 1926, in CWMG-EB, vol. 36, p. 30. See also: M.K. Gandhi, 'Letter to Premabehn Kantak,' 17 June 1932, vol. 56, p. 267. And he specifically talks about how a non-violent polity ought to deal with invasion:M.K. Gandhi, 'Triumph of Non-violence,' *Navajivan*, 21 November 1920, vol. 21, p. 515.
50. M.K. Gandhi, 'Interview to Capt. Strunk,' *Harijan*, 3 July 1937, CWMG-EB, vol. 71, p. 405.
51. M.K. Gandhi, 'Requisite qualifications,' *Harijan*, 25 March 1939, in CWMG-EB, vol. 75, p. 196.
52. M.K. Gandhi, 'Khilafat,' *Young India*, 17 March 1920, in CWMG-EB, vol. 19, p. 466.
53. See Chapter 3.
54. Robert E. Klitgaard, 'Gandhi's Non-Violence as a Tactic,' *Journal of Peace Research*, vol. 8, no. 2, 1971, p. 148.
55. M.K. Gandhi, 'Letter to George Joseph,' 12 April 1924, in CWMG-EB, vol. 27, p. 225.
56. Faisal Devji, 2012, p. 113.
57. M.K. Gandhi, 'What is One's Dharma?' *Navajivan*, 21 July 1929, in CWMG-EB, vol. 46, p. 296.
58. Dennis Dalton, *Gandhi, Nonviolent Power in Action* (New York: Columbia University Press, 2012).
59. Akeel Bilgrami, *Self-Knowledge and Resentment* (Cambridge, MA.: Harvard University Press, 2006), p. 88.
60. Robert E. Klitgaard (1971).
61. Parshotam Mehra, *A Dictionary of Modern Indian History, 1707–1947* (New Delhi: Oxford University Press, 1985), p. 497; William Napier (ed.), *The Life and Opinions of General Sir Charles James Napier*, vol. 4, 2nd ed. (London, 1857).
62. M.K. Gandhi, 'Hind Swaraj,' Chapter XVI: 'Brute force' in CWMG-EB, vol. 10, p. 287.
63. M.K. Gandhi, 'What is one's dharma?' *Navajivan*, 21 July 1929, in CWMG-EB, vol. 46, p. 298.
64. M.K. Gandhi, 'Talk to inmates of Satyagraha Ashram, Vykom,' *Young India*, 19 March 1925, in CWMG-EB, vol. 30, p. 382.
65. Richard Rorty, 'Objectivity or Solidarity?' in *Objectivity, Relativism, and Truth: Philosophical Papers vol. 1* (New York: Cambridge University Press, 1991), p. 21.
66. M.K. Gandhi, 'Speech at Exhibition Ground, Faizpur,' *Harijan*, 2 January 1937, in CWMG-EB, vol. 70, p. 232.
67. M.K. Gandhi, 'Independence,' *Harijan*, 5 May 1946, in CWMG-EB, vol. 90, p. 327.
68. See Chapter 1.
69. M.K. Gandhi, 'Discussion with B.G. Kher and others,' *Harijan*, 25 August 1940, in CWMG-EB, vol. 79, p. 122.
70. M.K. Gandhi, 'Hind Swaraj,' Chapter IV: 'What is Swaraj?' in CWMG-EB, vol. 10, p. 255.
71. M.K. Gandhi, 'War or peace,' *Young India*, 20 May 1926, in CWMG-EB, vol. 35, pp. 245–6.
72. The Nazis' unopposed occupation of Czechoslovakia outraged *The Times* which moved from supporting appeasement to condemning it. See *The Times*, 16, 17 and 20 March 1939. For a useful summary of Britain's press coverage of Nazi Germany see Franklin Reid Gannon, *The British Press and Germany 1936–1939* (Oxford University Press, 1971).

73. Ajay Skaria, 'Relinquishing Republican Democracy: Gandhi's Ramarajya,' *Postcolonial Studies*, vol. 14, no. 2, p. 205.

74. M.K. Gandhi, 'Discussion with B.G. Kher and others,' *Harijan*, 25 August 1940, in CWMG-EB, vol. 79, pp. 121–2.

75. Tapan Raychaudhuri (1988), pp. ix, 345.

76. Jawaharlal Nehru, *The Discovery of India* (Centenary edition) (New Delhi: Oxford University Press, 1985).

77. Jawaharlal Nehru, *Toward Freedom: The Autobiography of Jawaharlal Nehru* (New York: The John Day Company, 1941), p. 72.

78. M.K. Gandhi, 'Speech at AICC meeting,' *Harijan*, 25 January 1942, CWMG-EB, vol. 81, pp. 432–3.

79. Ibid.

80. Loy Henderson quoted in Andrew J. Rotter, *Comrades at Odds: the United States and India, 1947–1964* (Ithaca: Cornell University Press, 2000), p. 168.

81. Quoted in Loy Henderson to the State Department. Telegram 3031 from New Delhi to the Department of State, 30 April 1951, File 891.03/4–3051, 1950–54 Central Decimal File, RG 59, National Archives, Washington.

82. Robert J. McMahon, 'Food as a Diplomatic Weapon: the India Wheat Loan of 1951,' *Pacific Historical Review*, vol. 56, no. 3, 1987, p. 374.

83. The debate swings between accusations of Nehru being an idealist and a realist. On the former see Shashi Tharoor, *Reasons of State: Political Development and India's Foreign Policy under Indira Gandhi, 1966–1977* (New Delhi: Vikas, 1982), p. 26. On the latter see Benjamin Zachariah, *Nehru* (London: Routledge, 2004); T.T. Poulose, 'Viewpoint: India's Deterrence Doctrine: A Nehruvian Critique,' *Nonproliferation Review*, vol. 6, Fall 1998. Srinath Raghavan (2010) attempts to craft a mix of these two modernist doctrines, thereby continuing to encage Nehru in the modern as opposed to his own notions.

84. Srinath Raghavan (2010), pp. 8, 19.

85. For a critique from within the bounds of modernity of combining these two discordant sub-categories see Priya Chacko, 'Srinath Raghavan, War and Peace in Modern India: A Strategic History of Nehru Years,' *Indian Economic & Social History Review*, vol. 48, no. 2, April 2011. This is to say nothing about the fact that realism and liberalism are reliant on violence, something Nehru sought to eschew.

86. The problem with liberalism is that it—like realism—is violence, and hence incapable of capturing either Gandhi or Nehru. The violence of liberalism is best explained in terms of Barthes. He simply multiplied the sources for conflict, because in his intellectual stream 'authority' is fundamentally alienated and needs to be established by readers to become authors. Locke presaged Barthes and though he famously modified Hobbes' state of nature by positing a Law behind it, made God the source of that Law, also called 'reason'! It is well known that he wrote: 'The State of Nature has a Law of Nature to govern it, which obliges every one: And Reason, which is that Law, teaches all Mankind, who will but consult it, that being all *equal and independent*, no one ought to harm another in his Life, Health, Liberty, or Possessions.' What is less quoted is that immediately after these lines Locke writes, 'for men being all the workmanship of one omnipotent, and infinitely wise maker', and says this is why the source of reason, and reason itself, must always lie elsewhere. It means that we are all, curiously, unified in only our alienation from reason, and this opens the door to individualistic competition and hence violence in the search for reason (which has variously been understood by moderns as God or utopia). Hence, it is wrong to say liberalism condemns violence, for it is liberalism. None of this is the case in Gandhi's intellectual stream which, in denying the falsehood of alienation, makes for a completely differ-

ent ontological subject for it is founded on the unity that is the cosmos. See John Locke, *Two Treatises of Government*, Book II, Chapter II, Section VI, http://www.ilt.columbia.edu/publications/projects/digitexts/locke/second/locke2nd.txt

87. Jawaharlal Nehru (1985), pp. 107–08.

88. Sunil Khilnani, Ramachandra Guha, 'Series Editors Preface', in Raghavan (2010), p. x.

89. Jawaharlal Nehru (1941), p. 313.

90. For an example of Nehru grappling with Gandhi's language see Jawaharlal Nehru (1941), pp. 243 and 72.

91. Ibid., p. 72.

92. Jawaharlal Nehru (1985), pp. 442–9, esp. p. 447.

93. Jawaharlal Nehru, 'Meeting Ground of East and West. Speech in the Constituent Assembly (Legislative), New Delhi, 8 March 1949,' in *Jawaharlal Nehru's Speeches*, vol. 1. September 1946–MAY 1949 (Publications Division, Ministry of Information and Broadcasting, Government of India, 2nd ed., 1963), p. 237.

94. R.K. Karanjia, *The Mind of Mr. Nehru: An Interview with R.K. Karanjia* (London: George Allen & Unwin, 1961), pp. 22–4, 25.

95. Manmohan Singh, conversation, 7 Racecourse Road, New Delhi, 24 August 2010.

96. Fred Dallmayr, *Peace Talks—Who will Listen?* (Notre Dame, Ind.: University of Notre Dame Press, 2004), pp. 188–9.

97. For Nehru's explanation of this see A. Appadoria, 'Non alignment: Some important issues' in K.P. Mishra (ed.), *Non-Alignment: Frontier Dynamics* (New Delhi: Vikas, 1982). The following speeches are especially relevant for the Gandhian influence on Nehru: the Prime Minister's Statement on Foreign Policy, 7 September 1946; the Prime Minister on the Ideal of One World, 22 January 1947; the Prime Minister on the Implications of Non-alignment, 4 December 1947; the Prime Minister's Statement that Non-alignment 'can only be a policy of acting in accordance to our best judgement,' 9 December 1958; the Prime Minister on Racial Equality, 22 March 1949; the Prime Minister on means and ends, 20 December 1956.

98. K.P.S. Menon, *Many Worlds. An Autobiography* (London: Oxford University Press. 1965), p. 272. Menon writes: 'if India had no precedents of her own to guide her in the international, she at least had a tradition, of which Mahatma Gandhi was the embodiment.' J.N. Dixit, *Makers of India's Foreign Policy: Raja Ram Mohun Roy to Yashwant Sinha* (New Delhi: HarperCollins, 2004), p. 34. On p. 50 Dixit writes: 'Mahatma Gandhi imparted impulses against realpolitik as a factor in foreign policy decisions. All this was underpinned by his conviction that ends did not justify means, and that world peace and stability could only be achieved on the basis of the moral terms of reference of justice, fair play, abjuring the use of force, mutual respect and mutual cooperation. In a manner, he provided a conceptual framework on the basis of which the five principles of peaceful coexistence and the ideology of nonalignment emerged in later years.'

99. K.M. Panikkar, *Indian States and the Government of India* (London: Martin Hopkinson, 1927), pp. 90–122. See also Sunanda K Datta-Ray (2009), pp. 7–8, 30–32.

100. A.P. Saxena, *Nehru on Administration* (New Delhi: Uppal Publishing House, 1990), p. 4.

101. Jawaharlal Nehru, *An Autobiography* (1962), p. 445.

102. *The Indian Annual Register*, July–Sept. 1946. pp. 289–90.

103. Jawaharlal Nehru quoted in S.R. Maheshwari, 'Nehru's Thoughts on Public Administration' in P.L. Sanjeev and R.K. Tiwari (eds), *Jawaharlal Nehru and Public Administration* (New Delhi: Indian Institute of Public Administration, 2004), p. 174.

104. Jawaharlal Nehru, *Letters to Chief Ministers: 1947–1949*, vol. I ed. G. Parthasarathi (New Delhi: Oxford University Press, 1985), p. 493

105. M.O. Mathai, *My Days with Nehru* (New Delhi: Vikas, 1979), p. 133.

106. M.K. Gandhi, Letter to additional secretary, Home Department, Government of India, 4 March 1944, in CWMG-EB, vol. 84, p. 24; M.K. Gandhi, A letter, 21 April 1947, in CWMG-EB, vol. 94, p. 351.

107. Bajpai to Sapru [3 May 1921], Sapru Mss. Vol. III, B8. National Library, Calcutta Quoted Low, Feb. 1966, pp. 241–59 (p. 249).

108. Vishnu Sahay, 'Nehru as first Prime Minister and his Impact on Public Administration' in P.L. Sanjeev and R.K. Tiwari (eds), *Jawaharlal Nehru and Public Administration* (New Delhi: Indian Institute of Public Administration, 2004), p. 154. In fact Gandhi made the very same recommendation on the same grounds in 1947. See M.K. Gandhi, A Letter, 21 April 1947, in CWMG-EB, vol. 94, p. 351; M.K. Gandhi, Talk with Dr. Syed Mahmud, 26 July 1947, vol. 96, pp. 147–8.

109. Jawaharlal Nehru, 'Jawaharlal Nehru to Asaf Ali,' 7 April 1947, in *Selected Works of Jawaharlal Nehru*, 2nd series. vol. 2 (New Delhi: Oxford University Press, 1984), p. 516–17.

110. Subimal Dutt, *With Nehru in the Foreign Office* (Calcutta: Minerva Associates, 1977), pp. 23–4.

111. Walter Crocker quoted in Neville Maxwell, *India's China War* (New York: Pantheon Books, 1970), p. 91.

112. Ramachandra Guha, An Uncommon Diplomacy: Walter Crocker's 'Nehru: A Contemporary's Estimate'. http://www.themonthly.com.au/books-ramachandra-guha-uncommon-diplomacy-walter-crocker-s-nehru-contemporary-s-estimate-310

113. S. Kesava Iyengar, 'Indian Democracy and Socialist Planning,' *Annals of Public and Cooperative Economics*, vol. 38, no. 2, 1967, pp. 38–41.

114. N.V. Gadgil, *Government from Inside* (Meerut: Meenakshi Prakashan, 1968), pp. 83–4 & 182.

115. Vishnu Sahay (2004), pp. 157–8.

116. Senior cabinet minister no. 1, conversation, his residence, New Delhi, 2 December 2008.

117. Rajeshwar Dayal, *A Life of our Times* (New Delhi: Orient Longman, 1998), p. 593.

118. IFS Officer no. 15, 27, 38 stated this.

119. IFS Officer no. 26. Other officers agreed, in particular, IFS Officers no. 17, 24, 35.

120. Nuri Vittachi, *The Brown Sahib Revisited* (New Delhi: Penguin Books, 1987), pp. 22–3.

121. P.C. Hota, *Constitutional Status of the UPSC and its Impact on the Public Services, Platinum Jubilee Souvenir 1926–2001* (New Delhi: UPSC, 2001). pp. 5

122. Jawaharlal Nehru quoted in R.L.M. Patil, 'National Security and Foreign Policy' in Amal Ray, N. Bhaskara Rao and Vinod Vyasulu (eds), *The Nehru Legacy: An Appraisal* (New Delhi, Oxford and IBH Publishing Company, Private Ltd, 1991), p. 307.

123. Ibid.

124. Jawaharlal Nehru, 'Speech made at the conference of information ministers of the states,' 25 October, in Sarvepalli Gopal, *Jawaharlal Nehru: A Biography*, vol. 3 (Cambridge, MA: Harvard University Press, 1984), p. 223.

125. George Perkovich, *India's Nuclear Bomb: the Impact on Global Proliferation* (Berkeley: University of California Press, 2001), p. 46.

126. This continues to this day with writers like Perkovich (2001), ignoring the context for this statement, which is quoted next.

127. Jawaharlal Nehru quoted in R.L.M. Patil (1991), p. 307.

128. M.K. Gandhi, 'Speech at prayer meeting' in CWMG-EB, 11 November 1947, vol. 97, p. 286.

129. M.K. Gandhi, 'Speech at prayer meeting,' 4 January 1948, in CWMG-EB, vol. 98, p. 170.

130. M.K. Gandhi, 'Speech at prayer meeting,' 2 January 1948, in CWMG-EB, vol. 98, p. 161.

131. M.K. Gandhi, 'Speech at prayer meeting,' 20 January 1948, in CWMG-EB, vol. 98, p. 275.

132. M.K. Gandhi, 'Speech at prayer meeting,' New Delhi, 20 December 1947, in CWMG-EB, vol. 98, p. 85.

133. M.K. Gandhi, 'Speech at prayer meeting, 25 December 1947, in CWMG-EB, vol. 98, p. 113.

134. Pyarelal Nayyar, *Mahatma Gandhi: The Last Phase, vol. 1* (Ahmedabad: Navjivan Publishing House, 1968), p. 502.

135. Jonardon Ganeri, *Ethics and Epics: Philosophy, Culture, and Religion* (New Delhi, 2002), pp. 235–6.

136. Alastair Lamb, *The China-India Border: The Origins of the Disputed Boundaries* (London: Oxford University Press, 1964); Lamb, *The McMahon Line*, 2 vols. (London: Routledge, 1966); Lamb, *The Sino-Indian Boundary in Ladakh* (Columbia: University of South Carolina Press, 1975); Lamb, *Tibet, China and India* (Hertingfordbury, Hertfordshire: Roxford Books, 1989); Neville Maxwell (1970). For the confluence of Lamb and Maxwell see Alastair Lamb, 'War in the Himalayas,' *Modern Asian Studies*, vol. 5, no. 4, 1971.

137. Most of these works are unwilling to take cognizance of local imperatives, instead foisting their own ideological lenses. For works approaching Indian international relations from a Cold War perspective see John A. Rowland, *A History of Sino-Indian Relations: Hostile Co-Existence* (Princeton, NJ: D. Van Nostrand, 1967); Lorne J. Kavic, *India's Quest for Security:* Defence Policies, 1947–1965 (Berkeley: University of California Press, 1967).

138. Note by K.M. Panikkar, 9 June 1948, FO 371/70042, Records of the Foreign Office, The National Archives, London.

139. Statement, 20 November 1950, *Selected Works of Jawaharlal Nehru*, Second Series, ed. Sarvepalli Gopal, Ravinder Kumar, H.Y. Sharada Prasad, A.K. Damodaran and Mushirul Hasan (New Delhi: Jawaharlal Nehru Memorial Fund, 1984–), vol. 15, pt. ii, p. 348. (Henceforth SWJN-SS)

140. Note, 18 November 1950, SWJN-SS, vol. 15, pt. II, pp. 342–7.

141. Note by K.P.S. Menon, 11 April 1952, Subject File No. 24, Vijayalakshmi Pandit Papers, 2nd Instalment, Nehru Memorial Museum & Library (henceforth NMML).

142. Letter to Chief Ministers, 2 August 1952, in Sarvepalli Gopal (ed.), *Selected Works of Jawaharlal Nehru*, First Series, vol. 19, p. 695. Henceforth SWJN. Note to Secretary General, Foreign Secretary & Joint Secretary T.N. Kaul, 25 October 1953, SWJN, vol. 24, pp. 596–98.

143. R.K. Nehru, Oral History Transcript, pp. 17–18 & p. 31, NMML. Also see Karunakar Gupta, *Sino-Indian Relations, 1948–52: Role of K. M. Panikkar (*Calcutta: Minerva Associates), 1987, pp. 64–5.

144. B.N. Mullik, *My Years with Nehru: The Chinese Betrayal* (New Delhi: Allied Publishers, 1971), p. 122; Karunakar Gupta, *The Hidden History of the Sino-Indian Frontier* (Calcutta, 1974), p. 9; Lorne J. Kavic (1967), p. 46.

145. Note to Secretary General, 3 December 1953, SWJN, vol. 24, pp. 598–9.

146. Neville Maxwell (1970), p. 76; Gopal, *Jawaharlal Nehru*, vol. 2, Cambridge, MA: Harvard University Press, p. 179.

147. Telegram 825 from New Delhi to the Department of State, 7 June 1950, File 691.00/6-750, 1950–54 Central Decimal File, RG 59, National Archives, Washington. Quoted in K.V. Kesavan, 'Nehru, Henderson and the Japanese Peace Treaty,' *International Studies*, vol. 40, no. 3, August 2003, p. 250.

148. Raghavan, 2010, p. 238.

149. IFS Probationer no. 3.

150. Note to Secretary General & Foreign Secretary, 1 July 1954, SWJN, vol. 25, pp. 481–4.

151. Neville Maxwell (1970), p. 80.

152. See Mira Sinha, 'China: Making and Unmaking of Nehru's Foreign Policy,' *China Report*, vol. 15, no. 2, March–April 1979, pp. 61–2.

153. Minutes of talk with Zhou En-Lai, Beijing, 20 October 1954, SWJN, vol. 27, pp. 17–20.

154. B.N. Mullik (1971), pp. 196–9.

155. Note to Krishna Menon, 6 May 1956, SWJN-SS, vol. 33, pp. 475–7. Also see Note, 12 May 1956, SWJN-SS, vol. 33, pp. 477–9.

156. Record of conversation between Nehru and Zhou 31 December 1956/1 January 1957, SWJN-SS, vol. 36, pp. 600–01; Subimol Dutt (1977), pp. 116–17.

157. R.K. Nehru, the Ambassador in Beijing, also recalled that 'the experts were doubtful whether a protest should be lodged at all'. Confidential Note, 'Our China Policy: A Personal Assessment,' 30 July 1958, R.K. Nehru Papers, Writings by him, serial no. 5, Nehru Memorial Library. Note to Foreign Secretary, 4 February 1958, cited in Sarvepalli Gopal (ed.), SWJN, vol. 3, p. 79.

158. Zhou to Nehru, 23 January 1959, White Paper I, pp. 52–4.

159. Sarvepalli Gopal, *Jawaharlal Nehru: A Biography*, vol. 3 (Cambridge, MA: Harvard University Press, 1984), p. 89.

160. Chen Jian, 'The Tibetan Rebellion of 1959 and China's Changing Relations with India and the Soviet Union,' *Journal of Cold War Studies*, vol. 8, no. 3, Summer 2006, pp. 80–89.

161. Jagat S. Mehta, 'S. Gopal and the Boundary Question,' *China Report*, vol. 39, no. 1, February 2003, p. 72.

162. Ibid., p. 73.

163. Nehru to Harold Macmillan, 30 September 1959, FO 371/141271, Records of the Foreign Office, The National Archives, London.

164. Indian note, 12 February 1960, White Paper III, p. 86.

165. Subimal Dutt (1977), p. 131; Steven A. Hoffmann, *India and the China Crisis* (Berkeley: University of California Press, 1990), p. 87.

166. Nehru's reported comments at a meeting at the 'turn of 1959–60', cited in Neville Maxwell (1970), p. 161.

167. Report of conversation with Secretary General N.R. Pillai, 17 March 1960; Report of conversation with Finance Minister Morarji Desai, 5 April 1960, UK HC India to CRO, DO 35/8822, Records of the Dominion Office and Commonwealth Relations Office, The National Archives, London.

168. Report of conversation with Finance Minister, Morarji Desai, 5 April 1960, UK HC India to CRO, DO 35/8822, Records of the Dominion Office and Commonwealth Relations Office, The National Archives, London; Subimal Dutt (1977), p. 131; Sarvepalli Gopal's views in Steven A. Hoffmann (1990), p. 87.

169. Record of talks with Nehru by Mountbatten, 13–15 May 1960, DO 35/8822, Records of the Dominion Office and Commonwealth Office, The National Archives, London.

170. Report of conversation with N.R. Pillai, 25 April 1960, UK HC India to CRO, FO 371/150440, Records of the Foreign Office, The National Archives.

171. Subimal Dutt, 1977, p. 128. 'Nehru's statement in Lok Sabha, 26 April 1960', Prime Minister on Sino-Indian Relations (New Delhi: Ministry of External Affairs, Government of India, 1961–62), vol. I, pt. I, pp. 333–4.

7. VIOLENCE OF IGNORANCE

1. Jawaharlal Nehru, 'Defence policy and national development', 3 February 1947, *SWJN-SS*, vol. 2 (New Delhi: Jawaharlal Nehru Memorial Fund, 1984), p. 364.

2. C. Raja Mohan, *Crossing the Rubicon: the Shaping of India's New Foreign Policy* (New Delhi: Penguin, 2003), p. xxii. There appears to be consensus on Gandhian thought being on the wane. See Kanti Bajpai, 'Indian Conceptions of Order and Justice: Nehruvian, Gandhian, Hindutva and Neo-Liberal' in Rosemary Foot *et al.*, *Order and Justice in International Relations* (New York: Oxford University Press, 2003). On 'ad hocism' see P.R. Kumaraswamy, 'National Security: A Critique' in P. R. Kumaraswamy (ed.), *Security Beyond Survival: Essays for K. Subrahmanyam* (New Delhi: Sage, 2004).

3. T.V. Paul, 'Integrating International Relations Studies in India to Global Scholarship,' *International Studies*, vol. 46 no. 1–2, 2010.

4. Mark Hobart, 'Introduction: the Growth of Ignorance?' in Mark Hobart (ed.), *An Anthropological Critique of Development* (London: Routledge, 1993), p. 1.

5. For instance see Itty Abraham, *The Making of the Indian Atom Bomb: Science, Secrecy and the Post-Colonial State* (London: Zed Books, 1998), pp. 4–5.

6. Srirupa Roy, 'The Politics of Death: the Antinuclear Imaginary in India' in Itty Abraham (ed.), *South Asian Cultures of the Bomb: Atomic Publics and the State in India and Pakistan* (Bloomington: Indiana University Press, 2009), p. 114.

7. Itty Abraham (1998), pp. 18–19.

8. M.V. Ramana & C. Rammanohar Reddy, 'Introduction' in M.V. Ramana and C. Rammanohar Reddy (eds), *Prisoners of the Nuclear Dream* (Hyderabad: Orient Longman, 2003), p. 23.

9. Raminder Kaur, 'Gods, Bombs and the Social Imaginary', in Itty Abraham (ed.) (2009), pp. 150–72.

10. M.V. Ramana, 'India's Nuclear Enclave and the Practice of Secrecy' in Itty Abraham (ed.) (2009), pp. 41–67.

11. Sunanda K. Datta-Ray, *Waiting for America: India And The US In The New Millennium* (New Delhi: HarperCollins, 2002), pp. viii–ix.

12. Anon, 'PM: To aid research, may consider declassification,' *Indian Express*, 18 April 2006. http://www.indianexpress.com/news/pm-to-aid-research-may-consider-declassification/2732/

13. Manmohan Singh, conversation, 7 Racecourse Road, New Delhi, 12 October 2009.

14. Email from FS to author, 27 July 2007.

15. In particular under Article 309. IFS Probationer no. 16.

16. IFS Probationer no. 23.

17. Max Weber, 'Bureaucracy' in H.Gerth and C. Wright Mills (eds), *Essays in Sociology*, 1958.

18. Karsten Frey, *India's Nuclear Bomb and National Security* (Abingdon: Oxon: Routledge, 2006), pp. 197, 200.

19. Karsten Frey, 'Guardians of the Nuclear Myth: Politics, Ideology, and India's Strategic Community' in Itty Abraham (ed.) (2009), pp. 195–212.

20. Ibid., p. 196.

21. See Itty Abraham (1998), pp. 11–14; Itty Abraham, 'Introduction: Nuclear Power and Atomic Publics' in Itty Abraham (ed.), *South Asian Cultures of the Bomb: Atomic Publics and the State in India and Pakistan* (Bloomington: Indiana University Press, 2009), pp. 8, 9; M. V. Ramana, 'India's Nuclear Enclave and the Practice of Secrecy' in Itty Abraham (ed.), (2009).

22. Karsten Frey (2006), p. 202.

23. Itty Abraham (1998), pp. 11–13.

24. See Chapter 2.

25. Akeel Bilgrami, 'Occidentalism, the Very Idea: An Essay on Enlightenment and Enchantment,' *Critical Enquiry*, vol. 32, no. 3, Spring 2006.

26. Itty Abraham, 'The Ambivalence of Nuclear Histories,' *Osiris*, vol. 21, 2006, p. 62.

27. For example, the US 'Atom for Peace' initiative. President Dwight Eisenhower in 1953 considered that if applied peacefully, atoms could be 'developed into a great boon, for the benefit of all mankind.' US Department of State, *Documents on Disarmament, 1945–1959* (Washington, DC: Department of State Publication, 1960), p. 399.

28. Nehru's statement at inauguration of Aspara, India's first nuclear reactor, at Trombay on 20 January 1957, quoted in David Cortright and Amitabh Mattoo, 'Elite Public Opinion and Nuclear Weapons Policy in India,' *Asian Survey*, vol. 36, no. 6, June 1996, p. 549.

29. John Wilson Lewis and Xue Litai, *China Builds the Bomb* (Stanford University Press, 1991), pp. 35–72.

30. Jawaharlal Nehru, *India's Foreign Policy: Selected Speeches, September 1946—April 1961* (New Delhi: Ministry of Information and Broadcasting, 1961), p. 235.

31. Lorne J. Kavic, *India's Quest for Security: Defense Policies: 1947–1965* (Berkeley: University of California Press, 1967), p. 214.

32. *Lok Sabha Debates*, vol. 15, 3rd Series (New Delhi: Lok Sabha Secretariat, 23 March 1963), col. 5780–5783.

33. Nehru wrote this in the margin of a memo in 1964. Ashok Kapur, *India's Nuclear Option: Atomic Diplomacy and Decision Making* (New York: Praeger, 1976), p. 194.

34. IFS Officer no. 1. The point was also made by IFS Officers no. 3, 5, 6, 10, 34, 38, 40, 41 and 42.

35. Quoted in G.G. Mirchandani, *India's Nuclear Dilemma* (New Delhi: Popular Book Services, 1968), p. 242.

36. See Chapter 6.

37. Karsten Frey (2006), p. 196.

38. A.G. Noorani, 'India's Quest for a Nuclear Guarantee,' *Asian Survey*, vol. 7, no. 7, July 1967, pp. 490–502. He discusses both PM Shastri's and FM Swaran Singh's thinking and requests for a nuclear shield.

39. K. Subrahmanyam, 'Indian Nuclear Policy—1964–98 (A Personal Recollection)' in Jasjit Singh (ed.), *Nuclear India* (New Delhi: Knowledge World, 1998), pp. 6–53.

40. 'Time for A-bomb—say 100 M.P.'s,' *Indian Express*, 23 September 1965.

41. Faisal Devji (2012), p. 113.

42. Resolution 2028 (XX) presented by India and seven other nations and adopted by 20th session of the United Nations General Assembly, in *Disarmament: India's Initiatives* (External Publicity Division: MEA: Government of India, 1988), pp. 29–34.

43. K. Subrahmanyam, conversation, his residence, Noida, 27 April 2008.

44. M.K. Rasgotra, 'Brown Man's Burden,' *The Outlook*, 10 May 1999. http://www.outlookindia.com/article.aspx?207434

45. K. Subrahmanyam, *Nuclear Myths and Realities: India's Dilemma* (New Delhi: ABC Publishing House, 1981), pp. i-iv.

46. Hugh Gusterson, *People of the Bomb: Portraits of America's Nuclear Complex* (Minnesota, University of Minneapolis Press, 2004), p. 24.

47. Hugh Gusterson, 'A Double Standard on Nuclear Weapons', MIT Center for International Studies, April 2006. http://web.mit.edu/cis/pdf/gusterson_audit.pdf

48. Gayatri Chakravorty Spivak (2006), p. 28.

49. Gayatri Chakravorty Spivak, quoted in Leon de Kock, 'Interview With Gayatri Chakravorty Spivak: New Nation Writers Conference in South Africa,' *ARIEL: A Review of International English Literature*, vol. 23, no. 3, July 1992, p. 44–7.

50. Itty Abraham, 'Contra-Proliferation: Interpreting the Meanings of India's Nuclear Tests

in 1974 and 1998' in Scott Sagan (ed.), *Inside Nuclear South Asia* (Stanford University Press, 2009), pp. 106–133 & 124–5.

51. This was despite the fact that the IAEA had held four technical conferences on PNE technology. The United States too supported PNE at the UN. See *Year Book of the United Nations* (New York: Office of Public Information United Nations, 1971), p. 78. Even the claim of a key scientist that a bomb was tested does not negate the PNE hypothesis. A nuclear explosion, is after all, an explosion and therefore similar to a bomb. See Adirupa Sengupta, 'Scientist says bomb was tested in '74,' *India Abroad*, 17 October 1997, p. 14.

52. Gayatri Chakravorty Spivak (2006), p. 28.

53. Charles H. Murphy, 'Mainland China's Evolving Nuclear Deterrent,' *Bulletin of the Atomic Scientists*, January 1972, p. 30.

54. Declassified US cable. http://www.gwu.edu/~nsarchiv/nukevault/ebb253/doc07.pdf

55. See Surjit Mansingh, *India's Search for Power: Indira Gandhi's Foreign Policy 1966–1982* (New Delhi: Sage, 1984); Bhabani Sen Gupta, *Nuclear Weapons: Policy Options for India* (Center for Policy Research, New Delhi: Sage, 1983).

56. Ashok Kapur (1976), p. 21.

57. Jeffrey G. Snodgrass, 'Imitation Is Far More than the Sincerest of Flattery: The Mimetic Power of Spirit Possession in Rajasthan, India,' *Cultural Anthropology*, vol. 17, no. 1, February 2002, p. 51.

58. Jaswant Singh, conversation, Parliament Chamber, Parliament, New Delhi, 30 May 2007.

59. A.G. Noorani, 'India's Quest for a Nuclear Guarantee,' *Asian Survey*, vol. 7, no. 7, 1967.

60. Rajeshwar Dayal, *A Life of our Times* (New Delhi: Orient Longman, 1998), pp. 588–9.

61. Jacques E.C. Hymans, *The Psychology of Nuclear Proliferation: Identity, Emotions and Foreign Policy* (Cambridge University Press, 2006), p. 7.

62. Declassified US cable http://www.gwu.edu/~nsarchiv/nukevault/ebb367/docs/1–19–74.pdf

63. P.R. Kumaraswamy, 'National Security: A Critique in P.R. Kumaraswamy (ed.), *Security Beyond Survival: Essays for K. Subrahmanyam*, (New Delhi: Sage, 2004), p. 22; Karsten Frey (2006), p. 49.

64. B.N. Pande, *Indira Gandhi* (New Delhi: Publications Division: Ministry of Information and Broadcasting, 1989), p. 363.

65. Sumit Ganguly, 'India's Pathway to Pokhran II: The Prospects and Sources of New Delhi's Nuclear Weapons Program,' *International Security*, vol. 23, no. 4, Spring 1999, pp. 171–2.

66. This is Frey's explanation for the tests of 1998 that confirmed India's weapons status. Karsten Frey (2006), pp. 195, 197, 201.

67. K. Subrahmanyam, 'Indian Nuclear Policy—1964–98 (A Personal Recollection)' in Jasjit Singh (ed.), *Nuclear India* (New Delhi: Knowledge World, 1998), p. 44.

68. Raj Chengappa, *Weapons of Peace: The Secret Story of India's Quest to Be a Nuclear Power* (New Delhi: HarperCollins, 2000), p. 304.

69. Rajesh Basrur, *South Asia's Cold War: Nuclear Weapons and Conflict in Comparative Perspective* (Abingdon, Oxon.: Routledge, 2008), pp. 191.

70. Ibid., p. 194.

71. M.K. Rasgotra, *Rajiv Gandhi* (New Delhi: Vikas Publishing House), 1991.

72. K. Subrahmanyam, in Jasjit Singh (ed.) (1998), p. 44. The decision was taken in 1988. Weaponization was achieved between 1992 and 1994. See *From Surprise to Reckoning: The Kargil Review Committee Report* (New Delhi: Sage Publications, 2000), p. 205.

73. *From Surprise to Reckoning: The Kargil Review Committee Report* (2000), p. 205.

74. M.K. Gandhi, Speech at prayer meeting, 20 December 1947, in CWMG-EB vol. 98, p. 85.

75. Sunanda K. Datta-Ray, (2009), p. 41.

76. 'NUCLEAR ANXIETY; Indian's letter to Clinton on the nuclear testing,' *New York Times*, 13 May 1998. See: http://www.nytimes.com/1998/05/13/world/nuclear-anxiety-indian-s-letter-to-clinton-on-the-nuclear-testing.html?scp=3&sq=vajpayee%20overt%20 nuclear%20state&st=cse.

77. Sisir Gupta, 'The Indian Dilemma' in Alastair Buchan (ed.), *A World of Nuclear Powers* (Englewood Cliffs, NJ: Prentice Hall, 1966), p. 62.

78. Zachary S. Davis, 'China's Nonproliferation and Export Control Policies: Boom or Bust for the NPT Regime?' *Asian Survey*, vol. 35, no. 6, June 1995, pp. 589–90 & 595.

79. Retired FS from the 1980s no. 1, his residence, New Delhi, 10 July 2007.

80. Alastair Iain Johnston, 'China's New "Old Thinking": The Concept of Limited Deterrence,' *International Security*, vol. 20, no. 3, 1995, p. 21.

81. Guan Jixian, *Gao jishu jubu zhanzheng zhanyi* (Campaigns in high tech limited wars) (Beijing: National Defence University Press, 1993), pp. 112–13. Quoted in Johnston (1995), pp. 22–3.

82. See Zhang Jing and Yao Yanjin, *Jiji fangyu zhanlue qianshuo* (An introduction to the active defence strategy), (Beijing: Liberation Army Publishing House, 1985), p. 137. Quoted in Johnston (1995), p. 23.

83. Guan Jixian, *Gao jishu jubu zhanzheng* (Campaigns in high tech limited wars) (Beijing: National Defence University Press, 1993), p. 141. Quoted in Johnston, 1995, p. 23.

84. Faisal Devji (2012), p. 113.

85. John W. Garver, 'The Restoration of Sino-Indian Comity following India's Nuclear Tests,' *The China Quarterly*, No. 168, December 2001, pp. 867–8.

86. For the connection between truth and practice see M.K. Gandhi, 'Hind Swaraj,' Chapter XVII: Passive resistance, in CWMG-EB, vol. 10, pp. 297–8.

87. In 1995 Prime Minister Narasimha Rao ordered a series of tests that were cancelled following internal disagreements and US pressure. Of his two successors, Atal Behari Vajpayee also ordered tests, but his government fell in thirteen days, while H.D Deve Gowda felt that other matters were more pressing than nuclear tests, even though the test site was ready and explosives were in place. See Raj Chengappa, 2000, pp. 390–95. See also George Perkovich (2001).

88. Stephen P. Cohen, *India: Emerging Power* (Washington: Brookings Institution Press, 2001), p. 304.

89. George Perkovich (2001), p. 505.

90. For a recent discussion between NFU scholars see Morton H. Halperin, Bruno Tertrais, Keith B. Payne, K. Subrahmanyam and Scott D. Sagan, 'The Case for No First Use: An Exchange,' *Survival*, vol. 51, no. 5, October–November 2009.

91. Sanjay Subrahmanyam, 'A Rather Personal Biography' in P.R. Kumaraswamy (ed.), *Security beyond Survival: Essays for K. Subrahmanyam* (New Delhi: Sage, 2004), pp. 244–5. Also conversation with K. Subrahmanyam, his residence, 27 April 2008.

92. K. Subrahmanyam, conversation, his residence, Noida, 27 April 2008. This section draws upon the interview.

93. Noted grudgingly even by his son, Sanjay Subrahmanyam. See Sanjay Subrahmanyam, 'A Rather Personal Biography' in P.R. Kumaraswamy (ed.) (2004).

94. K. Subrahmanyam, *Security in a Changing World* (New Delhi: B.R. Pub. Corp., 1990), p. 85.

95. K. Subrahmanyam, 'Dharma was killed in Gujarat,' *Times of India*, 4 April 2002. http://timesofindia.indiatimes.com/home/opinion/edit-page/SPEAKING-TREEbrDharma-was-Killed-In-Gujarat/articleshow/5707330.cms. Though unnamed, the piece is confirmed

as his by his son. See Sanjay Subrahmanyam in P.R. Kumaraswamy (ed.) (2004), p. 257, fn. 10.

96. K. Subrahmanyam, 'Alternative Security Doctrines,' *Security Dialogue*, vol. 21, no. 1, 1990, pp. 84–5.

97. George Perkovich (2001), p. 505.

98. L.K. Advani, conversation, his residence, 6 June 2007. Jaswant Singh, conversation, Parliament Chamber, Parliament, New Delhi, 30 May 2007.

99. See Chapter 2, Menon's comments.

100. IFS officer no. 1. The vast majority of officers and probationers mentioned this.

101. Manmohan Singh, conversation, 7 Raccourse Road, New Delhi, 24 August 2010.

102. IFS Officer no. 21.

103. Sunanda K. Datta-Ray (2002), p. 97.

104. 'Soviet Acquisition of Militarily Significant Western Technology: An Update, September 1985.' This document updates the April 1982 version, which was Exhibit No. 1, Hearings Before the Permanent Subcommittee on Investigations of the Committee on Governmental Affairs, US Senate, 4, 5, 6, 11 and 12 May 1982.

105. Sunanda K. Datta-Ray (2002), p. 124.

106. K.N. Hari Kumar, 'Trading Non-Alignment for High Tech? Rajiv's Second US Visit,' *Economic and Political Weekly*, 23 April 1988.

107. Brajesh Mishra, 'Statement made the Principal Secretary to the Prime Minister Brajesh Mishra on nuclear tests on 11 May 1998' in K.R. Gupta (ed.), *Select Documents on Nuclear Disarmament* (New Delhi: Atlantic Publishers), 2000, pp. 228–9 (emphasis added).

108. Government of India, 'Press Statements on India's Nuclear Tests, issued on May 11 & 13, 1998,' *India News* (Washington: Embassy of India, 16 May–15 June 1998), p. 8.

109. Atal Bihari Vajpayee, 'Prime Minister's reply to the discussion in Lok Sabha on nuclear tests on May 29, 1998,' *India News* (16 May–15 June 1998), pp. 9, 11.

110. This was also attested to by L.K. Advani, conversation, his residence, 6 June 2007.

111. L.K. Advani, conversation, his residence, 6 June 2007; Jaswant Singh, conversation, Parliament Chamber, Parliament, New Delhi, 30 May 2007.

112. Alastair Iain Johnston, *Cultural Realism: Strategic Culture and Grand Strategy in Chinese History* (Princeton University Press), 1995.

CONCLUSIONS

1. Manmohan Singh, 'Keynote address by Prime Minister Dr. Manmohan Singh at the India Today Conclave,' 23 March 2007, in Avtar Singh Bhasin (ed.) (2008), 23 March 2007, p. 196.

2. Partha Chatterjee, 'Democracy and the Violence of the State: a Political Negotiation of Death,' *Inter-Asia Cultural Studies*, vol. 2, no. 1, 2001, p. 20.

3. Max Weber, *The Theory of Social and Economic Organization*, A.M. Henderson and Talcott Parsons, (New York: Oxford University Press, 1947), p. 339.

4. Vinay Lal, 'Coming out from Gandhi's shadow: With its nuclear tests, India may have gained a short-term show of might but at the cost of its defeat as a civilization', in *Los Angeles Times*, 19 May 1998, (http://articles.latimes.com/1998/may/19/local/me-51284).

5. IFS Officer no. 44, public conversation, 15 June 2012.

6. See Sunanda K Datta-Ray, 'Pomp and circumstance,' *Business Standard*, 28 July 2012, http://www.business-standard.com/india/news/sunanda-k-datta-ray-pompcircumstance/481624/

7. Prem Budhwar, *A Diplomat Reveals* (New Delhi: Dorling Kinderlay, 2007).

8. Salman Haider in Amar Nath Ram (ed.), 2012. See too Sunanda K. Datta-Ray, 'Twenty

Years of Looking East,' *Business Standard*, 14 July 2012, http://www.business-standard.com/india/news/sunanda-k-datta-ray-twenty-yearslooking-east/480356/

9. Interview, Imperial Hotel, New Delhi, May 2011.

10. The first example of this was seen in November 1988 in the Bhoopal household in Mandeville Gardens in Calcutta. The idea, according to a resident in that house, came from a similarly adorned house in nearby Rowland Road.

11. With apologies to M.K. Gandhi, who famously described Katherine Mayo's book as a 'drain inspector's report.'

12. See http://allaboutbelgaum.com/lifestyle/young-guns/indian-foreign-service-the-belgaum-connection/

13. For instance: select readings in political concepts and constitution of India; select readings in public administration, 81st foundation course, Lal Bahadur Shastri National Academy of Administration Mussoorie (India); select readings in management and behavioural sciences, 81st foundation course, Lal Bahadur Shastri National Academy of Administration; select readings in Indian history and culture, 81st foundation course, Lal Bahadur Shastri National Academy of Administration.

14. Gandhiji's talisman: I will give you a talisman. Whenever you are in doubt, or when the self becomes too much with you, apply the following test. Recall the face of the poorest and the weakest man whom you may have seen, and ask yourself, if the step you contemplate is going to be of any use to him. Will he gain anything by it? Will it restore him to a control over his own life and destiny? In other words, will it lead to *swaraj* for the hungry and spiritually starving millions? Then you will find your doubts and your self melt away. Mahatma Gandhi, quoted in Course Manual, 81st foundation course (19 August—30 November, 2007). Also in M.K. Gandhi, 'A note,' vol. 96, p. 311.

15. Julien Benda, *The Great Betrayal (La trahison des clercs)*, trans. Richard Aldington, (London: Routledge, 1928).

16. Robert J. Niess, `Evolution of an idea: Julien Benda's La Trahison Des Clercs,' *The French Review*, vol. 20, no. 5, March 1947.

17. Jeremy Jennings and Anthony Kemp-Welch (eds.), *Intellectuals in Politics: From the Dreyfus Affair to Salman Rushdie* (London: Routledge, 1997), p. 13.

18. David Milne, `America's `Intellectual' Diplomacy,' *International Affairs*, vol. 86, no. 1, 2010, p. 68.

19. Bruce Kuklick, Blind Oracles: *Intellectuals and War from Kennan to Kissinger* (Princeton: Princeton University Press, 2006), pp. 229–30.

20. Martin Wight, *Power Politics*, ed. Hedley Bull and Carsten Holbraad (London: Leicester University Press, 1978), p. 58.

21. IAS Probationer no. 5.

22. Justin Rosenberg, `Why is there no International Historical Sociology?' *European Journal of International Relations*, vol. 12, no. 3, 2006, pp. 308, 313, 320.

23. Ibid., p. 325.

24. William Brown, `Reconsidering the Aid Relationship: International Relations and Social Development,' *The Round Table*, vol. 98, no. 402, 2009, p. 5.

25. Kamran Matin, `Redeeming the Universal: Postcolonialism and the Inner Life of Eurocentrism,' *European Journal of International Relations*, 24 January 2012.

26. Francis Fukuyama, *The End of History and the Last Man* (New York: Free Press, 2006).

27. John P. Carse, *Finite and Infinite Games* (New York: Free Press, 1986).

BIBLIOGRAPHY

Primary Sources

1. *Oral Testimony (politicians, civil servants [named] and others)*

Advani, L.K. 6 June 2007, conversation, his residence, New Delhi.
Aiyar, Mani Shankar. 3 February 2008, interview, his residence, New Delhi.
Bajpai, Shankar. 22 April 2008, conversation, his residence, New Delhi.
BCG Consultant. 10 February 2010, interview, his residence, London.
DPS R.K. Puram teacher, 1 February 2008, conversation, her residence, New Delhi,.
Economist at Research and Information System for Developing Countries. 10 August 2011, conversation, India Habitat Centre, New Delhi.
Ghosh, Arundhati. 6 May 2008, conversation, India International Centre, New Delhi.
Jaishankar, S. 5 January 2008, conversation, High Commissioner's residence, Singapore.
Mishra, Brajesh. 8 June 2007, conversation, his residence, New Delhi.
S.R. Nathan. 22 May 2012, conversation, his office, Institute of South East Asian Studies, Singapore.
Retired FS from the 1980s. 10 July 2007, his residence, New Delhi.
Senior Congress cabinet minister no. 1. 12 July 2007, conversation, his residence, New Delhi.
Senior Congress cabinet minister no. 1. 2 December 2008, conversation, his residence, New Delhi.
Senior Congress cabinet minister no. 2. 8 December 2008, conversation, his office, New Delhi.
Senior Congress cabinet minister no. 3. 30 May 2008, conversation, his office, New Delhi.
Senior Singaporean official. 12 April 2011, interview, Oberoi Hotel, New Delhi.
Shourie, Arun. 1 June 2007, conversation, his residence, New Delhi.
Singh, Jaswant. 30 May 2007, conversation, Parliament Chamber, Parliament, New Delhi.
Singh, Natwar. 4 June 2007, conversation, his residence, New Delhi.
Singh, Manmohan. 13 June 2007, conversation, 7 Racecourse Road, New Delhi.
Singh, Manmohan. 21 May 2008, conversation, 7 Racecourse Road, New Delhi.
Singh, Manmohan. 25 May 2008, conversation, 7 Racecourse Road, New Delhi.
Singh, Manmohan. 12 October 2009, conversation, 7 Racecourse Road, New Delhi.
Singh, Manmohan. 24 August 2010, conversation, 7 Racecourse Road, New Delhi.
Subrahmanyam, K. 27 April 2008, conversation, his residence, Noida.

Thadani, Jivat. 20 March 2011, conversation, India International Centre, New Delhi.
Western High Commissioner. May 2011, interview, Imperial Hotel, New Delhi.

Note on oral testimony

The sections in the introduction and Chapter 2 on the fieldwork—particularly conversations and interviews—would be incomplete without a supplementary note on how the data were collected. This does not necessitate a detailed framing of the setting and people in Kathinka Frøystadt's mould, for this exegesis is no conventional ethnography. However, there is an overlap with Hugh Gusterson's work because it deals with 'subjects both more urgently in need of anonymity and more legitimate objects of the naming gaze than traditional ethnographies' (Hugh Gusterson, *Nuclear Rites: A Weapons Laboratory at the End of the Cold War* [Berkeley: University of California Press, 1998, p. xvii]). Anonymity is required because it sustains moderns and the Ministry of External Affairs is constantly confronting them, but also because several diplomats made disclosures or behaved in manners that would compromise them—as was evident from their reflecting on that behaviour. Misbehaviour is significant for diplomats are accountable to the citizens who employ them. And yet, this is a study of diplomacy, not how well service rules are adhered to. That is why diplomats' privacy is upheld, to protect individual diplomats from themselves. The means include presenting a person with a number, but at other times under his real name. This is done to maximize documentary verisimilitude and not to honour some privacy contract (for that was not mentioned with the vast majority of people I engaged, though all were well aware of my purpose in following and speaking to them). If information publicly attributable to an individual is used, then he is named. Additionally, many characters have been restructured at my discretion, for given who they are, they are all too easily recognizable.

As for the questions, they arose from my purpose but I was intent on answering them via contextualized participant observation. This is why the interviews are by and large an extension of my general encounter with diplomats in a multitude of settings and manners. Such a means of operating meant that while some questions were general and repeated (at the simplest level, why they chose to do what they did and how it was done), every interview very quickly became unique in its detail because of the subject's biography. There was however consistency in what made for their accessibility. It was axiomatic that I was not 'white' and did not behave in a 'white' manner, for instance speak with a distinguishably European or North American accent. At its simplest, if I were a foreigner, I would never have been allowed in. More complex was that colour made for subtle differences in the manner in which bureaucrats behaved. Time and again, for instance, I noticed that diplomats clammed up when faced with Westerners, changing their very manner of behaving. No one disagreed with my observing this, but most were unable to explain why they became artificial (most commonly by becoming reserved or exceedingly polite). How this occurred in practice may be gauged by the reaction of three diplomats whom I had introduced to a Russian. He told me that none of the diplomats—nor for that matter any Indian of position—would respond to him at a personal level. The Indian officers I had introduced the Russian to claimed in private that he was an intelligence officer. But this was unverifiable and, along with other unquotable evidence, leads me to conclude that the notion of the 'foreign hand' really masked something else: the kind of people who become Indian diplomats today are somewhat apprehensive about 'whites', but this reaction is well cloaked when forced to engage whites socially (not officially). While the reasons for this Indian response lie beyond the scope of this exegesis, it meant that though my biography was unknown to most new diplomats, there was a familiarity that would have been impossible if I was of a different hue.

As for the much smaller set of conversations with politicians and the most senior bureaucrats, the interlocutor was my father and he gave these interactions a particular flavour. The tenor and tone may be apprehended by an example. Not having met Kamal Nath, then a Minister, for 20 years, my father found his number on the internet and phoned his office for an appointment at my behest. Walking into the minister's office the first thing he did was to rise with arms outstretched and exclaim: 'Sunanda, I've written a book. You never thought I could write did you?!' It was only after he had thrust a signed copy to my father, and then indulged in reminiscing that he turned to ask me, 'and what can I do for you?'

2. *Unpublished written sources*

Nehru Memorial Museum and Library, New Delhi

R.K. Nehru papers
Vijaylakshmi Pandit papers

The National Archives, London

DO 35: Records of the Dominions Office and Commonwealth Relations Office
FO 371: Records of the Foreign Office

India Office Library, London

Foreign Miscellaneous Series
Foreign Political Consultations (FPC)
Foreign Secret Consultations
Political and Secret

Collected Correspondence of East India Company Officials:

Hastings, Warren: Eur. MSS Addl., 29,121, 39,879

National Archives of India, New Delhi

Persian Correspondence (PC), Copies of Letters Received, vol. 4, no. 16.

BIBLIOGRAPHY

PC, Copies of Letters Received, vol. 9, no. 21.
PC, Translation of Persian Letters Received, vol. 19, no. 25.
PC, Copy of Letters Issued 1766–67, no. 70.
PC, Translation of Persian Letters Received and Issued 1770, no. 48.
PC, Translation of Persian Letters Received and Issued 1770, no. 52.

National Archives, Washington

Record Group 59: General Records of the Department of State.

Foreign Service Institute, New Delhi

Aiyar, Mani Shankar. 27 August 2007, 'India of my dreams', Lecture at Foreign Service Institute, New Delhi.
Menon, Shiv Shankar. 17 August 2007, [Untitled], Lecture at Foreign Service Institute, New Delhi.
Yadav, Lalu Prasad. 28 June 2007, 'India of my Dreams', Lecture at Foreign Service Institute, New Delhi.

Assorted documents

Note from Foreign Secretary's office: No. 9475/FS/2007, 27 July 2007.
Slide on Evolution supplied by MEA. The slide is from a database used every year by the Undersecretary (Foreign Service Personnel) to induct probationers.

Archives of the Prime Minister's Office, Turkey

Başvekâlet Arşivi, *Divani-i-Humayun Mühimme Defterleri*, vol. 39, 1955, Ankara.
Başvekâlet Arşivi, *Divani-i-Humayun Mühimme Defterleri*, vol. 62, 1955, Ankara.

3. *Published*

Personal papers

Dass, Durga (ed.), 1973. *Sardar Patel's Correspondence*, vol. VIII, Ahmedabad: Navjivan Publishing House.
Gandhi, M.K. 1999. *The Collected Works of Mahatma Gandhi (Electronic Book)*, 98 vols, New Delhi: Publications Division Government of India.
Glieg, G.R. 1830. *The Life of Major General Sir Thomas Munro*, vol. II. London: Colburn and Bentley.
Gopal, Sarvepalli (ed.), 1972–82. *Selected Works of Jawaharlal Nehru, First Series*, 15 vols, New Delhi: Orient Longman.
Gopal, Sarvepalli, Ravinder Kumar, H.Y. Sharada Prasad, A.K. Damodaran and Mushirul Hasan (eds), 1984–. *Selected Works of Jawaharlal Nehru, Second Series*, 37 vols, New Delhi: Jawaharlal Nehru Memorial Fund.
Jahangir, 1909. *Tūzuk-i-Jahāngīrī or Memoirs of Jahāngīr, From the First to the Twelfth Year of his Reign*, trans. Alexander Rogers, ed. Henry Beveridge, London.
Kaye, J.W. 1858. *Life and Correspondence of Lord Metcalfe*, vol. I., London: Smith, Elder and Co.

Ochterlony, David. 1964. *Selections from the Ochterlony Papers (1818–1825) in the National Archives of India*, ed. Narendra Krishna Sinha and Arun Kumar Dasgupta, University of Calcutta.

Nehru, Jawaharlal, 1985. *Letters to Chief Ministers: 1947–1949*, vol. I, ed. G. Parthasarathi, New Delhi: Oxford University Press.

Official works, publications, statements and collections

Abu-l-Fazl, 1897–1939. *The Akbarnama*, 3 vols, trans. H. Beveridge. Calcutta: Asiatic Society. http://persian.packhum.org/persian/main?url=pf%3Ffile%3D00701020%26c t%3D0

Anon., 2011. *2011 World Development Indicators*. Washington: The World Bank. http://issuu.com/world.bank.publications/docs/9780821387092/52?mode=a_p

Anon., 29 June 1852. *Appendix to Report from the Select Committee on Indian Territories, Parliamentary Papers 10*. London: House of Commons.

Anon., 1988. *Disarmament: India's Initiatives*. New Delhi: External Publicity Division, MEA, Government of India.

Aitchison, C.U. 1909. *A Collection of Treaties, Engagements, and Sanads Relating to India and Neighbouring Countries*, 14 vols. Calcutta.

Allámi, Abul Fazl, 1873–1907. *Aín i Akbari, vol. I, II, III*, trans. H. Blochman and H.S. Jarrett. Calcutta: Asiatic Society of Bengal. (http://persian.packhum.org/persian/main?url=pf%3Ffile%3D00702051%26ct%3D0).

Balfour, Francis (ed. and trans.), 1781. *Insha'-i Harkaran*. Calcutta: Charles Wilson.

Bhasin, Avtar Singh (ed.) 2006. *India's Foreign Relations—2005*. New Delhi: Geetika Publishers.

——— 2007. *India's Foreign Relations—2006*. New Delhi: Geetika Publishers.

——— 2008. *India's Foreign Relations—2007*. New Delhi: Geetika Publishers.

——— 2009. *India's Foreign Relations—2008*. New Delhi: Geetika Publishers.

Birdwood, G.C.M. and W. Foster, 1893. *The Register of Letters etc. of the Governor and Company of Merchants of London Trading into the East Indies, 1600–1619*. London: B. Quaritch.

Bowles, *Canadians warn GOI on NPT*, 12 December 1967. New Delhi: American Embassy. http://www.gwu.edu/~nsarchiv/nukevault/ebb253/doc07.pdf

Coleman-Jensen, Alisha, Mark Nord, Margaret Andrews and Steven Carlson, September 2011. *Household Food Security in the United States in 2010*, ERR-125. U.S. Dept. of Agriculture, Econ. Res. Serv. http://www.ers.usda.gov/Publications/ERR125/ERR125.pdf)

Communication dated 25 July 2008 Received from the Permanent Mission of India Concerning a Document Entitled "Implementation of the India-United States Joint Statement of July 18, 2005: India's Separation Plan", INFCIRC/731. 25 July 2008. (http://www.iaea.org/Publications/Documents/Infcircs/2008/infcirc731.pdf).

Fendrick, Reed J., 2004. 'Diplomacy as an Instrument of National Power' in J. Boone Bartholomees, Jr.(ed.). U.S. Army War College *Guide to National Security Policy and Strategy*, July 2004.

Firminger, Walter K. (ed.), 1917–1918. *The Fifth Report on East India Company Affairs—1812*. Calcutta: R. Cambray.

Gupta, K.R. (ed.), 2000. *Select Documents on Nuclear Disarmament*. Atlantic Publishers: New Delhi.

Hota, P.C., 2001. *Constitutional Status of the UPSC and its Impact on the Public Services, Platinum Jubilee Souvenir 1926–2001*. New Delhi: UPSC.

Husain, M.F. in Sotheby's Online Catalogue, (http://www.sothebys.com/app/live/lot/LotDetail.jsp?lot_id=159619220).

India Kargil Review Committee, 2000. *From Surprise to Reckoning: The Kargil Review Committee Report*. New Delhi: Sage Publications.

India News, 16 May—15 June 1998. Washington: Embassy of India.

Indian Foreign Service, A Backgrounder. http://meaindia.nic.in/mystart.php?id=5002

Indo-US 123 Agreement, 1 August 2007. http://www.hindu.com/nic/123agreement.pdf

Karanjia, R.K. 1961. *The Mind of Mr. Nehru: An Interview with R. K. Karanjia*, London: George Allen & Unwin.

Kaur, Preneet. 19 February 2014. *Lok Sabha Unstarred Question No. 4201*. http://www.mea.gov.in/lok-sabha.htm?dtl/22943/Q+NO+4201+SC+ST+AND+OBCs+IN+FOREIGN+SERVICES

Kaur, Preneet, 10 August 2011. *Lok Sabha Unstarred Question No. 1648*. http://meaindia.nic.in/mystart.php?id=500418071

Khan, Ali Muhammad, 1924. *The Supplement to the Mirat-i-Ahmadi*, trans. Syed Nawab and Charles Norman Seddon. Baroda: Education Department.

Lok Sabha Debates, 3rd Series, vol. 15, 23 March 1963. New Delhi: Lok Sabha Secretariat.

Macartney, Suzanne. *Child Poverty in the United States 2009 and 2010: Selected Race Groups and Hispanic Origin, US Census Data (November 2011)*. http://www.census.gov/prod/2011pubs/acsbr10–05.pdf

Menon, Shivshankar. 1 April 2010. 'Keynote address by National Security Advisor at ICWA & ICS seminar on 'India and China: Public diplomacy, building understanding'. http://mea.gov.in/mystart.php?id=550315693

Ministry of External Affairs Annual Report 2008–2009, 2009, New Delhi: Policy Planning and Research Division, MEA. http://meaindia.nic.in/meaxpsite/annualreport/12ar012009.pdf

Ministry of External Affairs Annual Report 2011–2012, 2012, New Delhi: Policy Planning and Research Division, MEA.

Moynihan [Daniel], 'India's Nuclear Intentions,' 19 January 1974. New Delhi: American Embassy. http://www.gwu.edu/~nsarchiv/nukevault/ebb367/docs/1–19–74.pdf.

Mukherjee, Pranab, 29 November 2006. 'Appointment of High Commissioners/Ambassadors,' Lok Sabha Unstarred Question No. 1209. http://meaindia.nic.in/mystart.php?id=220212069

Narayanan, M.K. 18 February 2010. '*Observations of Shri M.K. Narayan Governor of West Bengal at the release of the book Looking East to Look West: Lee Kuan Yew's Mission India authored by Shri Sunanda K. Datta-Ray*'. http://rajbhavankolkata.gov.in/WriteReadData/Speeches/BOOK%20RELEASE%20LOOKING%20EAST%20TO%20LOOK%20WEST.pdf

Nehru, Jawaharlal, July–December 1946. *The Indian Annual Register, vol. II*. Calcutta: The Annual Register Officer.

——— 1961. *India's Foreign Policy: Selected Speeches, September 1946—April 1961*, New Delhi: Ministry of Information and Broadcasting.

——— 1963. *Jawaharlal Nehru's Speeches, vol. I, September 1946–May 1949*, New Delhi: Publications Division, Ministry of Information and Broadcasting, Government of India.

BIBLIOGRAPHY

Pande, B.N., 1989. *Indira Gandhi*. New Delhi: Publications Division, Ministry of Information and Broadcasting, Government of India.

Prime Minister on Sino-Indian Relations, vol. I., 1961. New Delhi: Ministry of External Affairs, Government of India.

Rajah of Sattara: The Debate on the Motion of Joseph Hume, Esq., M.P. in the House of Commons, Tuesday, July 22nd, 1845. London: G. Woodfall and Son.

Reinaud, Joseph Toussaint, 1993. *Fragments arabes et persans inédits relatifs à l'Inde, antérieurement au XIe siècle* (Arabic text and original French translation by M. Reinaud, Paris, 1845), Frankfurt am Main: Institute for the History of Arabic-Islamic Science at the Johann Wolfgang Goethe University.

Sarkar, Jadunath (trans.), P.M. Joshi (ed.), 1953. *Persian Records of Maratha History, vol. I, Delhi Affairs, 1761–1788, Newsletters from Parasnis Collection*. Bombay.

Standing Committee on External Affairs, 2006–07, 14th Lok Sabha, Fifteenth Report, Ministry of External Affairs Demands For Grants, 2007–08, April 2007. New Delhi: Lok Sabha Secretariat.

US Department of Defence, September 1985. '*Soviet Acquisition of Militarily Significant Western Technology: An Update (Intelligence Community White Paper)*'. Washington.

US Department of State, 1960. *Documents on Disarmament, 1945–1959*. Washington: Department of State Publication.

Verma, K.G. *Clarifications Regarding Creamy Layer amongst OBCs, Document No. 36033/5/2004-Estt.(Res.)*, 14 October 2004. Government of India, Ministry of Personnel, Public Grievances & Pensions, Department of Personnel & Training. http://circulars.nic.in/WriteReadData/CircularPortal/D2/D02adm/36033_5_2004_01April 2005.htm

'Wikileaks cables,' *The Hindu* http://www.thehindu.com/news/the-india-cables/the-cables/

White Paper I to VIII, 1959–1963. New Delhi: Ministry of External Affairs.

Year Book of the United Nations, 1971. New York: Office of Public Information, United Nations.

Newspapers, periodicals and broadcast media

BBC (UK)
Financial Times (UK)
Hindustan Times (India)
Los Angeles Times
South China Morning Post
The Asian Age (India)
The Economic Times (India)
The Hindu (India)
The Indian Express
The New York Times
The Outlook (India)
The Pioneer (India)
The Straits Times (Singapore)
The Times (UK)
The Times of India

United Services Journal (India)
Westminster Review (UK)

Memoirs, autobiographies, diaries and literature by officials and politicians

Ali Reïs, Sidi, 1899. *The Travels and Adventures of the Turkish Admiral Sidi Ali Reïs in India, Afghanistan, Central Asia, and Persia during the Years 1553–1556*, trans. A. Vambéry. London. http://www.columbia.edu/itc/mealac/pritchett/00generallinks/sidialireis

Bapojee, Rungo, 1843. *Vindex, Dethroned Rajah of Sattarah*. London: Munro and Congreve.

Broadfoot, W., 1888. *The Career of Major Broadfoot in Afghanistan and the Punjab*, London: John Murray.

Budhwar, Prem, 2007. *A Diplomat Reveals*. New Delhi: Dorling Kindersley.

Das, S.K., 2001. *Public Office, Private Interest: Bureaucracy and Corruption in India*. Oxford University Press.

Dayal, Rajeshwar, 1988. *A Life of our Times*. New Delhi: Orient Longman.

Dixit, J.N., 2004. *Makers of India's Foreign Policy: Raja Ram Mohun Roy to Yashwant Sinha*. New Delhi: HarperCollins.

Dutt, Subimal, 1977. *With Nehru in the Foreign Office*. Calcutta: Minerva Associates.

Gadgil, N.V., 1968. *Government from Inside*. Meerut: Meenakshi Prakashan.

Manucci, Niccolao, 1907. *Storia do Mogor, Mogul India, 1653–1708*, 3 vols., trans. and ed. William Irvine, London: John Murray.

Mathai, M.O., 1979. *My Days with Nehru*. New Delhi: Vikas.

Mehta, Jagat S., February 2003. 'S. Gopal and the Boundary Question,' *China Report*, vol. 39, no. 1.

Menon, K.P.S., 1965. *Many Worlds. An Autobiography*. London: Oxford University Press.

——— 1977. *Changing Patterns of Diplomacy, Saiyidain Memorial Lectures*. Bombay: Bharatiya Vidya Bhavan.

Menon, V.P., 1956. *The Story of the Integration of Indian States*. London: Longmans, Green.

Mirchandani, G.G., 1968. *India's Nuclear Dilemma*. New Delhi: Popular Book Services.

Mishra, Brajesh, 2006. '"Mao's Smile" Revisited: Sino-Indian Relations during an Important Period,' *Indian Foreign Affairs Journal*, vol. 1, no. 4.

Monserrate, S.J., 1922. *The Commentary of Father Monserrate, S.J. on his Journey to the Court of Akbar*, trans. J.S. Hoyland and S.N. Banerjee. London: Oxford University Press.

Mullik, B.N., 1971. *My Years with Nehru: The Chinese Betrayal*. New Delhi: Allied Publishers.

Napier, Sir William (ed.), 1857. *The Life and Opinions of General Sir Charles James Napier, vol. 4*. London: John Murray.

Nehru, Jawaharlal, 1941. *Toward Freedom: The Autobiography of Jawaharlal Nehru*. New York: The John Day Company.

——— 1962. *An Autobiography: With Musings on Recent Events in India*. Bombay: Allied Publishers.

——— 1985. *The Discovery of India (Centenary edition)*. New Delhi: Oxford University Press.

Orme, Robert, 1803. *A History of the Military Transactions of the British Nation in Indostan…*, 2 vols. London: John Nourse.

Panikkar, K.M., 1927. *Indian States and the Government of India*. London: Martin Hopkinson.

Sahay, Vishnu, 2004. 'Nehru as first Prime Minister and his Impact on Public Administration' in L. Sanjeev and R.K. Tiwari (eds), *Jawaharlal Nehru and Public Administration*. New Delhi: Indian Institute of Public Administration.

Polier, Antoine, 2001. *A European Experience of the Mughal Orient: The I jazi Arsalami-Persian Letters, 1773–79 of Antoine Polier*, trans. and ed. Muzaffar Alam and Seema Alavi. New Delhi: Oxford University Press.

Rasgotra, M.K., 1991. *Rajiv Gandhi*. New Delhi: Vikas Publishing House.

Roe, Sir Thomas, 1899. *The Embassy of Sir Thomas Roe to India 1615–19*, 2 vols., ed. William Foster. London: The Hakluyt Society.

Saxena, A.P., 1990. *Nehru on Administration*. New Delhi: Uppal Publishing House.

Scrafton, Luke, 1770. *Reflections on the Government of Indostan with A Short Sketch of the History of Bengal from 1739 to 1756*. London: W. Richardson and S. Clark.

Sikri, Rajiv, 25 September 2007. 'India's Foreign Policy Priorities in the Coming Decade,' *ISAS Working Paper, no. 25*. Singapore.

——— 2009. *Challenge and Strategy: Rethinking India's Foreign Policy*. New Delhi: Sage.

Subrahmanyam, K., 1981. *Nuclear Myths and Realities: India's Dilemma*. New Delhi: ABC Publishing House.

——— 1990. *Security in a Changing World*. New Delhi: B.R. Pub. Corp.

Sulivan, Richard Joseph, 1784. *An Analysis of the Political History of India: In which is Considered The Present Situation of the East And The Connections of its Several Powers with The Empire of Great Britain*. London: T. Becket.

Surman, John and Edward Stephenson, 1911. 'Diary of Messrs. [John] Surman and [Edward] Stephenson, during their Embassy to the Great Mogul, 15 Aug. 1714 to 14 Dec. 1717', in C.R. Wilson (ed.), *The Early Annals of the English in Bengal: The Bengal Public Consultations for the First Half of the Eighteenth Century, vol II, part II: The Surman Embassy*. Calcutta: The Bengal Secretariat Book Depot.

Verelst, Harry, 1772. *A View of the Rise, Progress and Present State of the English Government in Bengal: Including a Reply to the Misrepresentations of Mr. Bolts, and Other Writers*. London: J. Nourse [etc.].

Secondary sources

1. Books

Abraham, Itty, 1998. *The Making of the Indian Atom Bomb: Science, Secrecy and the Post-colonial State*, London: Zed Books.

Alam, Muzaffar, 2004. *The Languages of Political Islam in India: c. 1200–1800*, Chicago University Press.

Alcorn, Lauren, 2006. *Indigenous Education at Crossroads: James Bay Cree and the Tribal People of Orissa*, Bhubhaneshwar: Sikshasandhan.

Aloysius, G., 1997. *Nationalism without a Nation in India*, Oxford University Press.

Anderson, Benedict, 1983. *Imagined Communities: Reflections on the Origin and Spread of Nationalism*, London: Verso.

——— 1998. *The Spectre of Comparison: Nationalism, Southeast Asia and the World*, London: Verso.

Appiah, Kwame A., 1992. *In my Father's House: Africa in the Philosophy of Culture*, New York: Oxford University Press.

BIBLIOGRAPHY

Arnason, Johann P., 2003. *Civilizations in Dispute: Historical Questions and Theoretical Traditions*, Leiden: E.J. Brill.

Arnold, David and Stuart Blackburn, 2004. *Telling Lives in India: Biography, Autobiography, and Life History*, Bloomington: Indiana University Press.

Aron, Raymond, 1966. *Peace and War: A Theory of International Relations*, trans. Richard Howard and Annette Baker Fox, Garden City, NY: Doubleday.

Aziz, Abdul, 1952. *The Mansabdari System and the Mughal Army*, New Delhi: Idarah-i-Adabiyat-i-Delli.

Bajpai, Kanti P., P.R. Chari, Pervaiz Iqbal Cheema, Stephen P. Cohen and Sumit Ganguly, 1995. *Brasstacks and Beyond: Perception and Management of Crisis in South Asia*, New Delhi: Manohar.

Barlow, Connie, 1991. *From Gaia to Selfish Genes: Selected Writings on the Life Sciences*, Cambridge, MA: MIT Press.

Barnes, Barry, 2000. *Understanding Agency: Social Theory and Responsible Action*, London: Sage Publications.

Basrur, Rajesh, 2008. *South Asia's Cold War: Nuclear Weapons and Conflict in Comparative Perspective*, Oxford: Routledge.

Bayly, Christopher Alan, 1988. *Indian Society and the Making of the British Empire*, Cambridge University Press.

Benda, Julien, 1928. *The Great Betrayal (La trahison des clercs)*, trans. Richard Aldington, London: Routledge.

Bernstein, Richard, 1992. *The New Constellation: The Ethical-political Horizons of Modernity/Postmodernity*, Cambridge, MA: MIT Press.

Bernstein, Richard and Ross H. Munro, 1997. *The Coming Conflict with China*, New York: Alfred Knopf.

Berridge, G.R., ed. Alan James, 2001. *A Dictionary of Diplomacy*, New York: Palgrave.

Berridge, G.R., Maurice Keens-Soper and T.G. Otte, 2001. *Diplomatic Theory from Machiavelli to Kissinger*, New York: Palgrave.

Bhabha, Homi K., 1994. *The Location of Culture*, London: Routledge.

Bilgrami, Akeel, 2006. *Self-knowledge and Resentment*, Cambridge, MA: Harvard University Press.

Billig, Michael, 1995. *Banal Nationalism*, London: Sage.

Bloch, Maurice, 1992. *Prey into Hunter: The Politics of Religious Experience*, Cambridge University Press.

Bloch, Maurice, 1998. *How we Think they Think: Anthropological Approaches to Cognition, Memory and Literacy*, Boulder, CO: Westview Press.

Bondurant, Joan, 1958. *Conquest of Violence: The Gandhian Philosophy of Conflict*, Princeton University Press.

Bourdieu, Pierre, 1989. *La noblesse d'Etat: grandes écoles et esprit de corps*, Paris: Les Editions de Minuit.

Brand, Michael, 1997. *The Vision of Kings: Art and Experience in India*, Canberra: National Gallery of Australia.

Breton, Albert, Gianluigi Galeotti, Pierre Salmon and Ronald Winterobe (eds), 1995. *Nationalism and Rationalists*, New York: Cambridge University Press.

Brown, S. 1980. *Political Subjectivity: Applications of Q Methodology in Political Science*, New Haven, CT: Yale University Press.

Bühler, G., 1964. *The Laws of Manu, Sacred Books of the East, vol. XXV*, Delhi: Motilal Banarsidass.

Bull, Hedley, 1977. *The Anarchical Society*, New York: Columbia University Press.

Burke, Kenneth, 1966. *Language as Symbolic Action: Essays on Life, Literature and Method*, Berkeley, CA: University of California Press.

Buzan, Barry and Lene Hansen, 2009. *The Evolution of International Security Studies*, Cambridge University Press.

Candau, Joël, 1998. *Mémoire et identité*, Paris: Presses Universitaires de France.

Carse, John P., 1986. *Finite and Infinite Games*, New York: Free Press.

Carsten, Janet, 2004. *After Kinship*, Cambridge University Press.

Casey, Catherine, 1995. *Work, Self and Society: After Industrialism*, London: Routledge.

Cassirer, E., 1946. *Language and Myth*, trans. S.K. Langer, New York: Dover.

Chakrabarty, Dipesh, 2000. *Provincializing Europe: Postcolonial Thought and Historical Difference*, Princeton University Press.

———— 2002. *Habitations of Modernity: Essays in the Wake of Subaltern Studies*, University of Chicago Press.

Chakravorty Spivak, Gayatri, 1990. *Post Colonial Critic: Interviews, Strategies and Dialogues*, ed. Sarah Harasym, London: Routledge.

Chatterjee, Indrani (ed.), 2004. *Unfamiliar Relations: Family and History in South Asia*, New Delhi: Permanent Black.

Chatterjee, Partha, 1986. *Nationalist Thought and the Colonial World: A Derivative Discourse*, Tokyo: United Nations University, London: Zed Books.

———— 1993. *The Nation and its Fragments*, Princeton University Press.

———— 2004. *The Politics of the Governed: Reflections on Popular Politics in Most of the World*, New York: Columbia University Press.

Chengappa, Raj, 2000. *Weapons of Peace: The Secret Story of India's Quest to be a Nuclear Power*, New Delhi: HarperCollins.

Cohen, Stephen P., 2001. *India: Emerging Power*, Washington: Brookings Institution Press.

Cohn, Bernard S., 1990. *An Anthropologist among the Historians and Other Essays*, New Delhi: Oxford University Press.

Conner, Paul W., 1966. *Poor Richard's Politicks: Benjamin Franklin and the New American Order*, New York: Oxford University Press.

Connolly, William E., 1999. *Why I am not a Secularist*. Minneapolis: University of Minnesota Press.

———— 2002. *Identity/Difference: Democratic Negotiations of Political Paradox*, Minneapolis: University of Minnesota Press.

Constantinou, C.M. 1996. *On the Way to Diplomacy*, Minneapolis: Minnesota University Press.

Constas, Helen, 1954. *Bureaucratic Collectivism: an Analysis of the Historical Examples of Pharaonic Egypt and Soviet Russia*, New York: New School for Social Research.

Cullen, Jim, 2003. *The American Dream: A Short History of an Idea that Shaped a Nation*, New York: Oxford University Press.

Dahlman, Joseph, 1895. *Das Mahabharata als Epos und Rechtsbuch*, Berlin.

Dallmayr, Fred, 2004. *Peace Talks—Who will Listen?* Notre Dame, Ind.: University of Notre Dame Press.

Dalrymple, William, 2004. *The White Mughal: Love and Betrayal in Eighteenth-century India*, New Delhi: Penguin.

Dalton, Dennis, 2012. *Gandhi, Nonviolent Power in Action*, New York: Columbia University Press.

BIBLIOGRAPHY

Datta, Rajat, 2000. *Society, Economy, and the Market: Commercialization in Rural Bengal, 1760–1800*, New Delhi: Manohar.

Datta-Ray, Sunanda K., 2002. *Waiting for America: India and the US in the New Millennium*, New Delhi: HarperCollins.

——— 2009. *Looking East to Look West: Lee Kuan Yew's Mission India*, Singapore: ISEAS Press.

Davis, Mike, 2001. *Late Victorian Holocausts: El Niño Famines and the Making of the Third World*, London: Verso.

Day, U.N., 1970. *The Mughal Government: A.D. 1556–1707*, New Delhi: Munshiram Manoharlal.

de Boton, Alain, 2004. *Status Anxiety*, New York: Pantheon.

de Certeau, Michel, 1988. *The Writing of History*, trans. Tom Conley, New York: Columbia University Press.

——— 1998. *The Practice of Everyday Life*, trans. Steven Rendall, Berkeley: University of California Press.

de Gaulejac, Vincent, 1999. *La névrose de classe: Trajectoire sociale et conflits d'identité*, Paris: Hommes et Groupes Editeurs.

de Sousa Santos, Boaventura, 1995. *Towards a New Common Sense: Law, Science and Politics in the Paradigmatic Transition*, New York: Routledge.

de Tocqueville, Alexis, 1978. *The Old Régime and the French Revolution*, trans. Stuart Gilbert, Gloucester: Peter Smith.

Delanty, Gerard, 1995. *Inventing Europe: Idea, Identity, Reality*, Basingstoke: Macmillan Press.

Der Derian, James, 1987. *On Diplomacy: A Genealogy of Western Estrangement*, Oxford University Press.

——— 2001. *Virtuous War: Mapping the Military-industrial-media-entertainment Network*, Boulder, CO: Westview Press.

Derrida, Jacques, 1976. *Of Grammatology*, trans. Gayatri Chakravorty Spivak, Baltimore: Johns Hopkins University Press.

Devji, Faisal, 2012. *The Impossible Indian: Gandhi and the Temptations of Non-violence*, London: C. Hurst & Co.

Dewes, C.L., C.L. Barney and Carolyn Leste Law (eds), 1995. *This Fine Place so Far from Home: Voices of Academics from the Working Class*, Philadelphia: Temple University Press.

Dikötter, Frank, 2003. *"Patient zero": China and the myth of the 'opium plague',* Inaugural lecture, London: School of Oriental and African Studies.

Dimock, Jr, Edward C. *et al.*, 1974. *The Literatures of India: An Introduction*, Chicago University Press.

Dirks, Nicholas B., 2006. *The Scandal of Empire: India and the Creation of Imperial Britain*, Cambridge, MA: Harvard University Press.

Doniger, Wendy, 2009. *The Hindus: An Alternative History*, New York: Penguin.

Dunne, Timothy and Nicholas J. Wheeler (eds), 1999. *Human Rights in Global Politics*, Cambridge University Press. Durkheim, Emile, 1949. *The Division of Labor in Society*, trans. George Simpson, New York: Free Press.

——— 1968. *Suicide: A Study in Sociology*, ed. George Dimpson, trans. John A. Spaulding and George Simpson, New York: Free Press.

Dutt, Romesh Chander, 1908. *Economic History of India*, London: Kegan Paul, Trübner Trench.

Eisenstadt, Shmuel N., 1978. *Revolutions and the Transformation of Societies*, New York: Free Press.

Farooqi, Naimur Rahman, 1989. *Mughal-Ottoman Relations: A Study of the Political & Diplomatic Relations between Mughal India and the Ottoman Empire, 1556–1748*, Delhi: Idarah-I Adabiyat-I Delli.

Faubion, James D., 1993. *Modern Greek Lessons: A Primer in Historical Constructivism*, Princeton University Press.

Ferguson, James, 1999. *Expectations of Modernity: Myth and Meanings of Urban Life on the Zambian Copperbelt*, Berkeley: University of California Press.

Feuerstein, G., S. Kak and D. Frawley, 1995. *In Search of the Cradle of Civilization*, Wheaton: Quest Books.

Fisher, Michael H., 1991. *Indirect Rule in India: Residents and the Residency System, 1764–1858*, New Delhi: Oxford University Press.

Fitzgerald, James L. (trans. and ed.), 2004. *The Mahābhārata, Volume 7*, University of Chicago Press.

Foster, William, 1933. *England's Quest of Eastern Trade*, London: A & C Black.

Foucault, Michel, 1972. *The Archaeology of Knowledge*, trans. A.M. Sheridan-Smith, London: Routledge.

——— 1977. *Discipline and Punish: The Birth of the Prison*, trans. A.M. Sheridan-Smith, Harmondsworth: Penguin.

——— 2006. *History of Madness*, trans. J. Murphy and J. Khalfa, London: Routledge.

Freud, Sigmund, 1917. *The History of the Psychoanalytic Movement*, trans. A.A. Brill, New York: Nervous and Mental Disease Pub. Co.

——— 1961. *Civilization and its Discontents*, trans. and ed. James Strachey, New York: W.W. Norton.

Frey, Karsten, 2006. *India's Nuclear Bomb and National Security*, Abingdon, Oxon.: Routledge.

Friedman, Jonathan, 1994. *Cultural Identity and Global Process*, London: Sage.

Frøystad, Kathinka, 2005. *Blended Boundaries: Caste, Class and Shifting Faces of 'Hinduness' in a North Indian City*, New Delhi: Oxford University Press.

Fukuyama, Francis, 2006. *The End of History and the Last Man*, Free Press: New York.

Ganeri, Jonardon, 2001. *Philosophy in Classical India: The Proper Work of Reason*, London: Routledge.

Ganguly, Sumit, 2001. *Conflict Unending: India-Pakistan Tensions since 1947*, New York: Columbia University Press.

Gasché, Rodolphe, 1986. *Tain of the Mirror: Derrida and the Philosophy of Reflection*, Cambridge, MA: Harvard University Press.

Ghosh, Aurobindo, 1919. *The Ideal of Human Unity*, Madras.

Ghosh, Nagendranath, 1919. *Comparative Administrative Law*, Calcutta: Butterworth.

Goody, Jack, 1986. *The Logic of Writing and the Organization of Society*, Cambridge University Press.

Gopal, Sarvepalli, 1975–84. *Jawaharlal Nehru: A Biography*, 3 vols, Cambridge, MA: Harvard University Press.

Gopal, R., 1963. *How the British Occupied Bengal: A Corrected Account of 1756—1765 Events*, Bombay: Asia Publishing House.

Gordon, Milton M., 1958. *Social Class in American Sociology*, Durham, NC: Duke University Press.

Gordon, Stewart and G. Hambly (eds), 2000. *Robes of Honour: The Medieval World of Investiture*, New York: St. Martin's Press.

Gore-Booth, Lord, 1979. *Satow's Guide to Diplomatic Practice*, London: Longman.

Goswami, Manu, 2004. *Producing India: From Colonial Economy to National Space*, Chicago University Press.

Goswamy, B.N. and J.S. Grewal, 1967. *The Mughal and the Jogis of Jakhbar*, Shimla: Indian Institute of Advanced Studies.

Guan, Jixian, 1993. *Gao jishu jubu zhanzheng*, Beijing: National Defence University Press.

Guha, Ranajit, 1996. *A Rule of Property for Bengal: An Essay on the Idea of Permanent Settlement*, Durham, NC: Duke University Press.

Gupta, Dipankar, 2000. *Interrogating Caste: Understanding Hierarchy and Difference in Indian Society*, New Delhi: Penguin.

Gupta, J.N., 1911. *Life and Work of Romesh Chunder Dutt C.I.E.*, London: J.M. Dent & Sons.

Gupta, Karunakar, 1974. *The Hidden History of the Sino-Indian Frontier*, Calcutta: Minerva Associates.

——— 1987. *Sino-Indian Relations, 1948–52: Role of K. M. Panikkar*, Calcutta: Minerva Associates.

Gusterson, Hugh, 2004. *People of the Bomb: Portraits of America's Nuclear Complex*, Minneapolis: University of Minnesota Press.

Haas, Ernst B., 1997. *Nationalism, Liberalism, and Progress: The Rise and Decline of Nationalism*, Ithaca, NY: Cornell University Press.

Habermas, Jürgen, 1972. *Knowledge and Human Interests*, trans. Jeremy Shapiro, London: Heinemann.

——— 2001. *The Inclusion of the Other: Studies in Political Theory*, Cambridge, MA: MIT Press.

Habib, Irfan, 1995. *Essays in Indian History: Towards a Marxist Perception*, New Delhi: Tulika Books.

Halbfass, Wilhelm, 1988. *India and Europe: An Essay in Understanding*, Albany, NY: SUNY.

Hegel, Georg W.F., 1956. *The Philosophy of History*, trans. J. Sibree, New York: Dover Publications.

——— 1977. *The Static & the Dynamic Philosophy of History & the Metaphysics of Reason: George Wilhelm Friedrich Hegel*, Albuquerque, NM: American Classical College Press.

Heidenheimer, Arnold J. (ed.), 1978. *Political Corruption: Readings in Comparative Analysis*, New Brunswick, NJ: Transaction Books.

Hiltebeitel, Alf, 1976. *The Ritual of Battle: Krsna in the Mahābhārata*, Ithaca, NY: Cornell University Press.

——— 2001. *Rethinking the Mahābhārata: A Reader's Guide to the Education of the Dharma King*, Chicago University Press.

Hobbes, Thomas, 1996. *Leviathan: Revised Student Edition*, Cambridge University Press.

Hoffman, Martin L., 2000. *Empathy and Moral Development: Implications for Caring and Justice*, Cambridge University Press.

Hoffmann, Steven A., 1990. *India and the China Crisis*, Berkeley: University of California Press.

Hoggart, Richard, 1957. *The Uses of Literacy: Aspects of Working-class Life, with Special References to Publications and Entertainments*, London: Chatto and Windus.

Hopper, Earl, 1981. *Social Mobility: A Study of Social Control and Insatiability*, Oxford: Basil Blackwell Publishers.

BIBLIOGRAPHY

Hume, David, 1999. *An Enquiry Concerning Human Understanding*, Oxford University Press.

Hunter, William Wilson, 1901. *A History of British India, vol. 2*, London: Longmans.

Huntington, Samuel, 1991. *The Third Wave: Democratization in the Late Twentieth Century*, Norman: University of Oklahoma Press.

Hymans, Jacques E.C., 2006. *The Psychology of Nuclear Proliferation: Identity, Emotions and Foreign Policy*, Cambridge University Press.

Iedema, Rick, 2003. *The Discourses of Post-bureaucratic Organization*, Amsterdam: John Benjamins Publishing Company.

Inayatullah, Naeem and David L. Blaney, 2004. *International Relations and the Problem of Difference*, New York: Routledge.

Inden, Ronald B., 1990. *Imagining India*, Oxford: Basil Blackwell.

Irving, Robert G., 1981. *Indian Summer: Lutyens, Baker, and Imperial Delhi*, New Haven: Yale University Press.

Islam, Riazul, 1970. *Indo-Persian Relations: A Study of the Political and Diplomatic Relations between the Mughal Empire and Iran, Sources of the History and Geography of Iran, no. 32*, Teheran: Iranian Culture Foundation.

Jaffrelot, Christophe, 2003. *India's Silent Revolution: Rise of Lower Castes in North India*, London: C. Hurst & Co.

Jennings, Jeremy and Anthony Kemp-Welch (eds), 1997. *Intellectuals in Politics: From the Dreyfus Affair to Salman Rushdie*, London: Routledge.

Johnston, Alastair Iain, 1995. *Cultural Realism: Strategic Culture and Grand Strategy in Chinese History*, Princeton University Press.

Jones, Edwin, 2001. *John Lingard and the Pursuit of Historical Truth*, Brighton: Sussex Academic Press.

Kant, Immanuel, 1991. *The Metaphysics of Morals*, trans. Mary J. Gregor, Cambridge University Press.

Kapur, Ashok, 1976. *India's Nuclear Option: Atomic Diplomacy and Decision Making*, New York: Praeger.

Kavic, Lorne J., 1967. *India's Quest for Security: Defence Policies: 1947–1965*, Berkeley: University of California Press.

Khilnani, Sunil, 1997. *The Idea of India*, London: Hamish Hamilton.

Kissinger, Henry, 2001. *Does America Need a Foreign Policy? Towards a Diplomacy for the 21st Century*, New York: Free Press.

Koselleck, Reinhart, 2002. *The Practice of Conceptual History: Timing History, Spacing Concepts*, trans. Todd Samuel Presner *et al.*, Stanford University Press.

Kuklick, Bruce, 2006. *Blind Oracles: Intellectuals and War from Kennan to Kissinger*, Princeton University Press.

Laine, James W., 1990. *Visions of God: Narratives of Theophany in the Mahābhārata*, New Delhi: Motilal Banarsidass.

Lall, Arthur, 1968. *How Communist China Negotiates*, New York: Columbia University Press.

Lamb, Alastair, 1964. *The China-India Border: The Origins of the Disputed Boundaries*, London: Oxford University Press.

Lamb, Alastair, 1966. *The McMahon Line*, 2 vols, London: Routledge.

——— 1975. *The Sino-Indian Boundary in Ladakh*, Columbia: University of South Carolina Press.

——— 1989. *Tibet, China and India*, Hertingfordbury, Hertfordshire: Roxford Books.

Lebow, R.N., 2008. *A Cultural Theory of International Relations*, Cambridge University Press.

Lee-Warner, William, 1910. *The Native States of India*, London: Macmillan.

Lees, W.N. and Ahmad Ali (eds), 1856. *Muntakhabi't Tawarikh Badauni*, Calcutta.

Lévi-Strauss, Claude, 1966. *The Savage Mind*, Chicago University Press.

Lewis, John Wilson and Xue Litai, 1991, *China Builds the Bomb*, Stanford University Press.

Lipschutz, Ronie D. and Judith Mayer, 1996. *Global Civil Society and Global Environmental Governance*, Albany, NY: State University of New York Press.

Luhmann, Niklas, 1997. *Die Gesellschaft der Gesellschaft, Erster und zweiter Teilband*, Frankfurt am Main: Suhrkamp.

Luvaas, J. (ed.), 1966. *Frederick the Great on the Art of War*, New York: The Free Press.

Lyotard, Jean-François, 1984. *The Postmodern Condition: A Report on Knowledge*, trans. Geoff Bennington and Brian Massumi, Minneapolis: University of Minnesota Press.

———— 1988, *The Differend: Phrases in Dispute*, trans. Georges Van Den Abbeele, Minneapolis: University of Minnesota Press.

Machiavelli, Niccolò, 1959. *The Prince*, trans. Luigi Ricci, New York: The New American Library.

Majed Khan, Abdul, 1969. *The Transition in Bengal, 1756–1775: a Study of Muhammad Reza Khan*, Cambridge University Press.

Malcolm, John, 1826. *The Political History of India from 1784 to 1823, vol. II*, London: John Murray.

Mann, Michael, 1993. *The Sources of Social Power: The Rise of Classes and Nation-states, 1760–1914, vol. II*, Cambridge University Press.

Mansingh, Surjit, 1984. *India's Search for Power: Indira Gandhi's Foreign Policy 1966–1982*, New Delhi: Sage.

Markovits, Claude, 2006. *Ungandhian Gandhi: The Life and After Life of the Mahatma*, New Delhi: Permanent Black.

Marshall, P.J., 1987. *Bengal: The British Bridgehead: Eastern India 1740–1828*, Cambridge University Press.

———— 1992. *East Indian Fortunes*, Oxford University Press.

Massie, James W., 1840. *Continental India: Travelling Sketches and Historical Recollections, Illustrating the Antiquity, Religion, and Manners of the Hindoos, the Extent of British Conquests, and the Progress of Missionary Operations, vol. I*, London: Thomas Ward & Co. Paternoster Row.

Matilal, Bimal Krishna, 2002. *Mind, Language, and World: the Collected Essays of Bimal Krishna Matilal, vol. I*, ed. Jonardon Ganeri, Oxford University Press.

———— 2002. *Ethics and Epics: Philosophy, Culture, and Religion*, ed. Jonardon Ganeri, New Delhi: Oxford University Press.

Maxwell, Neville, 1970. *India's China War*, New York: Pantheon Books.

McLane, John, 1993. *Land and Local Kingship in 18th Century Bengal*, Cambridge University Press.

McNeill, W.H., 1982. *The Pursuit of Power: Technology, Armed Force, and Society since A.D. 1000*, Chicago University Press.

Mehra, Parshotam, 1985. *A Dictionary of Modern Indian History, 1707–1947*, New Delhi: Oxford University Press.

BIBLIOGRAPHY

Mehta, J.L., 1990. *Philosophy and Religion: Essays in Interpretation*, New Delhi: Indian Council of Philosophical Research, Munshiram Manoharlal.

Mehta, Uday Singh, 1999. *Liberalism and Empire: A Study in the 19th Century British Liberal Thought*, Chicago University Press.

Miller, David, 1994. *Modernity: An Ethnographic Approach*, Oxford University Press.

'Mir', Mir Muhammad Taqi, 1999. *Zikr-i Mir: The Autobiography of the 18th Century Mughal Poet: Mir*, trans. C.M. Naim, Delhi: Oxford University Press.

Misra, B.B., 1961. *The Indian Middle Class: Their Growth in Modern Times*, Bombay: Oxford University Press.

———— 1977. *The Bureaucracy in India—A Historical Analysis of Development up to 1947*, New Delhi: Oxford University Press.

Mohanty, Ranjita and Rajesh Tandon (eds), 2006. *Participatory Citizenship: Identity, Exclusion, Inclusion*, New Delhi: Sage.

More, S.S., 1995. *Krsna: The Man and his Mission. An Enquiry into the Rationale of Inter-relationship between Krsna's Life, Mission and Philosophy*, Pune: Gaaj Krakashan.

Morgenthau, Hans J., 1967. *Politics among Nations: The Struggle for Power and Peace*, New York: Alfred A. Knopf.

Nandy, Ashis, 1983. *The Intimate Enemy: Loss and Recovery of Self under Colonialism*, New Delhi: Oxford University Press.

Nath, Rajendra, 1990. *Military Leadership in India: Vedic Period to Indo-Pakistan War*, New Delhi: Lancer Books.

Nayyar, Pyarelal, 1968. *Mahatma Gandhi: The Last Phase, vol. I*, Ahmedabad: Navjivan Publishing House.

Neumann, Iver B., 1996. *Russia and the Idea of Europe: a Study in Identity and International Relations*, London: Routledge.

Nicolson, Harold, 1955. *Good Behaviour: Being a Study of Certain Types of Civility*, London: Constable.

———— 1964. *Diplomacy*, New York: Oxford University Press.

Nielsen, Donald A., 1999. *Three Faces of God: Society, Religion and the Categories of Totality in the Philosophy of Émile Durkheim*, Albany, NY: State University of New York Press.

Nietzsche, Friederich W., 1968. *The Will to Power*, trans. W. Kaufmann and R.J. Hollingdale, New York: Vintage Books.

Nizami, Khaliq Ahmad, 1961. *Some Aspects of Religion and Politics in India during the Thirteenth Century*, Delhi: Idarah-i-Adabiyat-i-Delli.

O'Hagan, Jacinta, 2002. *Conceptions of the West in International Relations: From Spengler to Said*, Basingstoke: Palgrave.

Ortner, Sherry B., 1996. *Making Gender: The Politics and Erotics of Culture*, Boston: Beacon Press.

Orwell, George, 1949. *Nineteen Eighty-four*, London: Secker and Warburg.

Osella, Filippo and Caroline, 2000. *Social Mobility in Kerala: Modernity and Identity in Conflict*, London: Pluto Press.

Oye, Keneth A. (ed.), 1986. *Cooperation under Anarchy*, Princeton University Press.

Paolini, Albert, 1999. *Navigating Modernity: Post-colonialism, Identity and International Relations*, Boulder, CO: Lynne Rienner.

Parsons, Talcott, 1966. *Societies: Evolutionary and Comparative Perspectives*, Englewood Cliffs, NJ: Prentice-Hall.

———— 1971. *The System of Modern Societies*, Englewood Cliffs, NJ: Prentice-Hall.

Peers, Douglas M., 1995. *Between Mars and Mammon: Colonial armies and the Garrison State in Early 19th Century India*, London: I.B. Tauris.

Perkovich, George, 2001. *India's Nuclear Bomb: The Impact on Global Proliferation*, Berkeley: University of California Press.

Perrow, Charles, 1986. *Complex Organizations: A Critical Essay*, New York: Random House.

Plato, 1941. *The Republic of Plato*, trans. Francis MacDonald Cornford, Oxford University Press.

Prasad, Bishwanath, 1968. *The Indian Administrative Service*, New Delhi: S. Chand.

Preus, Samuel J., 1987. *Explaining Religion: Criticism and Theory from Bodin to Freud*, New Haven: Yale University Press.

Puri, B.N., 1975. *History of Indian Administration, Medieval Period, vol. II*, Bombay: Bhartiya Vidya Bhavan.

Raghavan, Srinath, 2010. *War and Peace in Modern India: A Strategic History of the Nehru Years*, Ranikhet: Permanent Black.

Raja Mohan, C., 2003. *Crossing the Rubicon: The Shaping of India's New Foreign Policy*, New Delhi: Penguin.

Ramusack, Barbara N., 1978. *The Princes of India in the Twilight of Empire: Dissolution of a Patron-client system, 1914–1939*, Columbus: Ohio State University Press.

Raychaudhuri, Tapan, 1988. *Europe Reconsidered: Perceptions of the West in Nineteenth Century Bengal*, New York: Oxford University Press.

Reid Gannon, Franklin, 1971. *The British Press and Germany 1936–1939*, Oxford University Press.

Richardson, C. James, 1977. *Contemporary Social Mobility*, London: Francis Pinter Publishers.

Roberts, John M., 1985. *The Triumph of the West*, London: BBC Books.

Rorty, Richard, 1991. *Objectivity, Relativism, and Truth: Philosophical Papers vol. I*, New York: Cambridge University Press.

Rotter, Andrew J., 2000. *Comrades at Odds: the United States and India, 1947–1964*, Ithaca, NY: Cornell University Press.

Rowland, John A., 1967, *A History of Sino-Indian Relations: Hostile Co-existence*, Princeton, NJ: D. Van Nostrand.

Rudolph, Lloyd I. and Susanne Hoeber Rudolph, 2006. *Postmodern Gandhi and other Essays: Gandhi in the World and at Home*, Chicago University Press.

Rumbold, Horace, 1944. *The War Crisis in Berlin July—August 1914*, London: Constable.

Russell, Bertrand, 2004. *A History of Western Philosophy*, London: Routledge.

Ryan, Jake and Charles Sackrey. 1984. *Strangers in Paradise: Academics from the Working Class*, Boston: South End Press.

Sahlins, Marshall, 1981. *Historical Metaphors and Mythical Realities: Structure in the Early History of the Sandwich Islands Kingdom*, Ann Arbor: University of Michigan Press.

Scott, James C., 1998. *Seeing Like a State: How Certain Schemes to Improve the Human Condition have Failed*, New Haven: Yale University Press.

Seligman, Adam, 1989. *Order and Transcendence: The Role of Utopias and the Dynamics of Civilizations*, Leiden: E.J. Brill.

Sen, Amartya, 1999. *Development as Freedom*, New York: Alfred A. Knopf.

Sen Gupta, Bhabani, 1983. *Nuclear Weapons: Policy Options for India*, Center for Policy Research, New Delhi: Sage.

BIBLIOGRAPHY

Shamasastry, R. 1967. *Kautilya's Arthaśāstra*, 8th edition, Mysore: Mysore Printing and Publishing House.

Sharma, Arvind, 2000. *Classical Hindu Thought*, New Delhi: Oxford University Press.

Sherif, Muzafer and Carolyn W. Sherif, 1953. *Groups in Harmony and Tension: An Integration of Studies on Intergroup Relations*, New York: Harper.

Sherwin-White, Adrian. 1973. *The Roman Citizenship*, Oxford University Press.

Shklar, Judith N., 1984. *Ordinary Vices*, Cambridge, MA: Belknap Press of Harvard University Press.

Singh, N.K. and A. Samiuddin. 2004. *Encyclopaedia Historiography of the Muslim World*, New Delhi: Global Vision Publishing House.

Slater, Philip, 2008. *The Chrysalis Effect: The Metamorphosis of Global Culture*, Brighton: Sussex Academic Press.

Smith, Anthony D., 1986. *The Ethnic Origins of Nations*, Oxford: Basil Blackwell.

Smith, Gaddis, 1986. *Morality, Reason and Power: American Diplomacy in the Carter Years*, New York: Hill and Wang.

Smith, Michael, 1994. *The Moral Problem*, Oxford: Blackwell.

Sparke, Matthew, 2005. *In the Space of Theory: Postfoundational Geographies of the Nation-state*, Minneapolis: University of Minnesota Press.

Steger, Manfred, 2000. *Gandhi's Dilemma: Nonviolent Principles and Nationalist Power*, New York: St. Martin's Press.

Steingass, F., 1973. *A Comprehensive Persian-English Dictionary*, New Delhi: Asian Educational Services.

Sukthankar, Vishnu S., 1957. *On the Meaning of the Mahābhārata*, Bombay: The Asiatic Society.

Taylor, Charles, 2007. *A Secular age*, Cambridge, MA: The Belknap Press of Harvard University Press.

Thapar, Romilla, 1966. *A History of India, vol. I*, Baltimore: Penguin Books.

Tharoor, Shashi, 1982. *Reasons of State: Political Development and India's Foreign Policy under Indira Gandhi, 1966–1977*, New Delhi: Vikas.

———— 1993. *The Great Indian Novel*, New York: Arcade Publishing.

Tharu, Susie and K. Lalita (eds), 1991. *Women Writing in India: 600 BC to the Present, vol. I*. New York: Feminist Press.

Thompson, Leigh L., 2001. *The Mind and Heart of the Negotiator*, Upper Saddle River, NJ: Prentice Hall.

Torpey, John C., 2000. *The Invention of the Passport. Surveillance, Citizenship and the State*, Cambridge University Press.

Traweek, Sharon, 1988. *Beamtimes and Lifetimes: The World of High Energy Physicists*, Cambridge, MA: Harvard University Press.

Uberoi, J.P. Singh, 2002. *The European Modernity: Science, Truth and Method*, New Delhi: Oxford University Press.

van Buitenen, Johannes Adrianus (trans.), 1973. *The Mahābhārata: I. The Book of the Beginning*. Chicago University Press.

van der Veer, Peter, 2001. *Imperial Encounters: Religion and Modernity in India and Britain*, Princeton University Press.

Veblen, Thorstein, 1918. *The Higher Learning in America: A Memorandum on the Conduct of Universities by Business Men*, New York: BW Heubsch.

Veyne, Paul, 1988. *Did the Greeks Believe in their Myths? An Essay on Constitutive Imagination*, trans. Paula Wissing, Chicago University Press.

Vico, Giambattista, 1984. *The New Science of Giambattista Vico. Unabridged Translation of the Third Edition* (1744) with the addition of *Practic of the New Science*, trans. Thomas Goddard Bergin and Max Harold Fisch, Ithaca, NY: Cornell University Press.

Vincent, J.D.B. and R.J. Vincent (eds), 1990. *Order and Violence: Hedley Bull and International Relations*, Oxford University Press.

Virilio, Paul, 1986. *Speed and Politics: An Essay on Dromology*, trans. Mark Polizzotti, New York: Semiotext(e).

Vittachi, Nuri, 1987. *The Brown Sahib Revisited*, New Delhi: Penguin Books.

Vogelin, Eric, 1975. *From Enlightenment to Revolution*, ed. John H. Hallowell, Durham, NC: Duke University Press.

von Glasenapp, Helmuth, 1960. *Das Indienbild deutscher Denker*, Stuttgart: Koehler.

von Laue, Theodore H., 1987. *The World Revolution: The Twentieth Century in Global Perspective*, New York: Oxford University Press.

Wainwright, Martin, 2008. '*The Better Class' of Indians: Social Rank, Imperial Identity, and South Asians in Britain, 1858–1914*, Manchester University Press.

Waltz, Kenneth N., 1979. *Theory of International Politics*, Reading, MA: Addison-Wesley.

Watson, Adam, 1982. *Diplomacy: The Dialogue between States*, London: Methuen.

——— 1992. *The Evolution of International Society*, London: Routledge.

Weber, Max, 1946. *From Max Weber: Essays in Sociology*, trans. and ed. H.H. Gerth and C. Wright Mills, New York: Oxford University Press.

——— 1958. *The Protestant Ethic and the Spirit of Capitalism*, trans. Talcott Parson, New York: Scribner.

——— 1978. *Economy and Society: An Outline of Interpretive Sociology*, ed. Guenther Roth and Claus Wittich, Berkeley: University of California Press.

Wendt, Alexander, 1999. *Social Theory of International Politics*, New York: Cambridge University Press.

Wight, Martin, 1977. *Systems of States*, ed. Hedley Bull, Leicester University Press.

——— 1978. *Power Politics*, ed. Hedley Bull and Carsten Holbraad, London: Leicester University Press.

Wilson, Kathleen, 2003. *The Island Race: Englishness, Empire and Gender in the Eighteenth Century*, London: Routledge.

Yack, Bernard, 1998. *The Fetishism of Modernities: Epochal Self-consciousness in Contemporary Social and Political Thought*, Notre Dame, Ind.: University of Notre Dame Press.

Young, Crawford, 1976. *The Politics of Cultural Pluralism*, Madison: University of Wisconsin Press.

Young, Kenneth T., 1968. *Negotiating with the Chinese Communists: The United States Experience, 1953–1967*, New York: McGraw Hill.

Zachariah, Benjamin, 2004. *Nehru*, London: Routledge.

Zhang, Jing and Yao Yanjin, 1985. *Jiji fangyu zhanlue qianshuo*, Beijing: Liberation Army Publishing House.

2. Articles and book chapters

Abraham, Itty, 2006. 'The Ambivalence of Nuclear Histories,' *Osiris*, vol. 21.

——— 2009. 'Contra-Proliferation: Interpreting the Meanings of India's Nuclear Tests in 1974 and 1998' in Scott Sagan (ed.), *Inside Nuclear South Asia*, Stanford University Press.

———— 2009. 'Introduction: Nuclear Power and Atomic Publics' in Itty Abraham (ed.), *South Asian Cultures of the Bomb: Atomic Publics and the State in India and Pakistan*, Bloomington: Indiana University Press.

Acharya, Amitav, Winter 2003/04. 'Will Asia's Past be its Future?' *International Security*, vol. 28, no. 3.

Adas, Michael, 1991. 'South Asian Resistance in Comparative Perspective' in Douglas Haynes and Gyan Prakash (eds), *Contesting Power: Resistance and Everyday Social Relations in South Asia*, New Delhi: Oxford University Press.

Alam, Javed, 1999. 'The Composite Culture and its Historiography,' *South Asia*, vol. 22, Special Issue.

Algar, Hamid, 1990. 'A Brief History of the Naqshbandi Order' in Marc Gaborieau, Alexandre Popovic and Thierry Zarcone (eds), *Naqshbandis: Cheminements et situation actuelle d'un ordre mystique musulman, Actes de la Table Ronde de Sèvres, 2–4 May 1985*, Istanbul: Institut Français d'Études Anatoliennes: Éditions Isis.

Alam, Muzaffar and Sanjay Subrahmanyam, 2004. 'The Making of a Munshi,' *Comparative Studies of South Asia, Africa and the Middle East*, vol. 24, no. 2.

Ali, Daud and Anand Pandian, 2010. 'Introduction' in Daud Ali and Anand Pandian (eds), *Ethical Life in South Asia*, Bloomington: Indiana University Press.

Alvi, Sajida S., 1989. 'Religion and State during the Reign of Mughal Emperor Jahăngĭr (1605–27): Nonjuristical Perspectives,' *Studia Islamica*, vol. 69.

Anon., January 1859. 'India: Its Extent and Population,' *Journal of the American Geographical and Statistical Society*, vol. 1, no. 1.

Appadoria, A., 1982. 'Non Alignment: Some Important Issues' in K.P. Mishra (ed.), *Non-Alignment: Frontier Dynamics*, New Delhi: Vikas.

Athar Ali, M., 1975. 'The Passing of Empire: The Mughal Case,' *Modern Asian Studies*, vol. 9, no. 3.

———— 1983. 'Akbar and Islam (1581–1605)' in N. Wagle and M. Israel (eds), *Islamic Society and Culture*, New Delhi: Manohar.

Bajpai, Kanti, 2003. 'Indian Conceptions of Order and Justice: Nehruvian, Gandhian, Hindutva and Neo-Liberal' in Rosemary Foot *et al.* (eds), *Order and Justice in International Relations*, Oxford University Press.

Balagangadhara, S.N., 1990, 'Understanding and Imagination, A Critical Notice of Halbfass and Inden,' *Cultural Dynamics*, vol. 3.

Banerjee, Swapna M., 2006. 'Subverting the Moral Universe: 'Narratives of Transgression' in the Construction of Middle-class Identity in Colonial Bengal' in Crispin Bates (ed.), *Beyond Representation: Colonial and Postcolonial Constructions of Indian Identity*, New Delhi: Oxford University Press.

Barkawi, Tarak and Mark Laffey, 2006. 'The Post-Colonial Moment in Security Studies,' *Review of International Studies*, vol. 32, no. 2.

Barthes, Roland, 1977. 'The Death of the Author' in Stephen Heath (ed. and trans.), *Image, Music, Text/Roland Barthes*, London: Fontana Press.

Behera, Navnita Chadha, 2007. 'Re-imagining IR in India,' *International Relations of the Asia Pacific*, vol. 7, no. 3.

Bergmann, M.S., 1993. 'Reflections on the History of Psychoanalysis,' *Journal of the American Psychoanalytic Association*, vol. 41, no. 4.

Bhabha, Homi K., 1983. 'Difference, Discrimination and the Discourse of Colonialism' in F. Barker, P. Hulme, M. Iversen and D. Loxley (eds), *The Politics of Theory*, Colchester: University of Essex.

Bhattacharya, Tithi, 2006. 'A World of Learning: the Material Culture of Education and Class in Nineteenth-century Bengal' in Crispin Bates (ed.), *Beyond Representation: Colonial and Postcolonial Constructions of Indian Identity*, New Delhi: Oxford University Press.

Bilgrami, Akeel, 2002. 'Gandhi's Integrity: The Philosophy Behind the Politics,' in *Postcolonial Studies*, vol. 5, no. 1.

—— Spring 2006, 'Occidentalism, the Very Idea: An Essay on Enlightenment and Enchantment,' *Critical Enquiry*, vol. 32.

Blake, Stephen P., 1979. 'The Patrimonial Bureaucratic Empire of the Mughals,' *The Journal of Asian Studies*, vol. 39, no. 1.

Blaker, Michael, January 1978. 'Japan in 1977: An Emerging Consensus,' *Asian Survey*, vol. 18, no. 1.

Blau, Peter Michael, 1956. 'Social Mobility and Interpersonal Relations,' *American Sociological Review*, vol. 21, no. 3.

Blau, Peter M., 1963. 'Critical Remarks on Weber's Theory of Authority,' *American Political Science Review*, vol. 57, no. 2.

Blochman, H., 1873. 'Preface' in Abul Fazl Allámi, *Ā'īn-i Akbarī, vol. I*, Calcutta: Asiatic Society of Bengal.

Blondel, Eric, 1994. 'The Question of Genealogy' in Richard Schacht (ed.), *Nietzsche, Genealogy, Morality: Essays on Nietzsche's Genealogy of Morals*, Berkeley, CA: University of California Press.

Booth, Ken, 1991. 'Security in Anarchy: Utopian Realism in Theory and Practice,' *International Affairs*, vol. 67, no. 3.

Böwering, Gerhard, 1997. 'The Concept of Time in Islam,' *Proceedings of the American Philosophical Society*, vol. 141, no. 1.

Brass, Paul R., 20–26 July 2002. 'India, Myron Weiner and the Political Science of Development,' *Economic and Political Weekly*, vol. 37, no. 29.

Braudel, Fernand, 1958. 'Histoire et sciences sociales. La longue durée,' *Annales E.S.C.*, vol. 13.

Brodbeck, Simon, 2003. 'Introduction,' *The Bhagavad Gita*, London: Penguin Books.

—— 2004. 'Calling Krsna's Bluff: Non-Attached Action in the Bhagavadgītā,' *Journal of Indian Philosophy*, vol. 32, no. 1.

Brown, William, 2009. 'Reconsidering the Aid Relationship: International Relations and Social Development,' *The Round Table*, vol. 98, no. 402.

Bryant, G.J., 2004. 'Asymmetric Warfare: The British Experience in Eighteenth-Century India,' *The Journal of Military History*, vol. 68, no. 2.

Buckler, F., 1992. 'The Oriental Despot' in M. Pearson (ed.), *Legitimacy and Symbols*, Ann Arbor, MI: Center for South and Southeast Asian Studies, University of Michigan.

Bull, Hedley, 1966. 'Society and Anarchy in International Relations' in Martin Wight and Herbert Butterfield (eds), *Diplomatic Investigations, Essays in the Theory of International Politics*, London: Allen & Unwin.

—— Winter 1981. 'Hobbes and International Anarchy,' *Social Research*, vol. 48, no. 4.

—— 1984. 'The Emergence of a Universal International Society' in Hedley Bull and Adam Watson (eds), *The Expansion of International Society*, Oxford: Clarendon Press.

Buzan, Barry, Summer 1993. 'From International System to International Society:

Structural Realism and Regime Theory Meet the English School,' *International Organization*, vol. 47, no. 3.

Chacko, Priya, April 2011. 'Srinath Raghavan, *War and Peace in Modern India: A Strategic History of Nehru Years*', *Indian Economic & Social History Review*, vol. 48, no. 2.

Chakrabarty, Dipesh, February 2008. 'In Defense of Provincializing Europe: A Response to Carola Dietze,' *History and Theory*, vol. 47, no. 1.

Chakravorty Spivak, Gayatri, 1988. 'Can the Subaltern Speak?' in Cary Nelson and Lawrence Grossberg (eds), *Marxism and the Interpretation of Culture*, Urbana: University of Illinois Press.

——— 2006. 'Can the Subaltern Speak? (Abbreviated by the author)' in Bill Ashcroft, Gareth Griffiths and Helen Tiffin (eds), *The Post-colonial Studies Reader*, Oxford: Routledge.

Chandhoke, Neera, 12–18 March 2005. '"Seeing" the State in India,' *Economic and Political Weekly*, vol. 40, no. 11.

Chatterjee, Partha, 2001. 'The Nation in Heterogeneous Time,' *The Indian Economic and Social History Review*, vol. 38, no. 4.

Chauhan, D.S., 1976. 'India's Underprivileged Classes and the Higher Public Service: Towards Developing a Representative Bureaucracy,' *Review of Administrative Sciences*, vol. 42.

Chen, Jian, Summer 2006. 'The Tibetan Rebellion of 1959 and China's Changing Relations with India and the Soviet Union,' *Journal of Cold War Studies*, vol. 8, no. 3.

Chomsky, Noam and Michel Foucault, 1974. 'Human Nature: Justice versus Power' in Fons Elders (ed.), *Reflexive Water: The Basic Concerns of Mankind*, London: Souvenir Press.

Clémençon, Raymond, 1995. 'Global Climate Change and the Trade System: Bridging the Culture Gap,' *Journal for Environmental Development*, vol. 4.

Cohen, Raymond, 4 May 1998. 'Putting Diplomatic Studies on the Map,' *Diplomatic Studies Programme Newsletter*.

Cohn, Bernard S., 1966. 'Recruitment and Training of British Civil Servants in India, 1600–1860' in Ralph Braibanti (ed.), *Asian Bureaucratic Systems Emergent from the British Imperial Tradition*, Durham, NC: Duke University Press.

——— 1989. 'Law and the Colonial State in India' in June Starr and Jane F. Collier (eds), *History and Power in the Study of Law: New Directions in Legal Anthropology*, Ithaca, NY: Cornell University Press.

Coleman, James, 1988. 'Social Capital in the Creation of Human Capital,' *American Journal of Sociology*, vol. 94, Supplement.

Comaroff, John L., October 1991. 'Humanity, Ethnicity, Nationality: Conceptual and Comparative Perspectives on the USSR,' *Theory and Society*, vol. 20, no. 5.

Connolly, William E., October 2000. 'Speed, Concentric Cultures, and Cosmopolitanism,' *Political Theory*, vol. 28, no. 5.

Cortright, David and Amitabh Mattoo, June 1996. 'Elite Public Opinion and Nuclear Weapons Policy in India,' *Asian Survey*, vol. 36, no. 6.

Cox, Robert, December 2000. 'Thinking about Civilizations,' *Review of International Studies*, vol. 26, no. 2.

Crandall, Christian S., 1994. 'Prejudice against Fat People: Ideology and Self-interest,' *Journal of Personality and Social Psychology*, vol. 66, no. 5.

——— 2000. 'Ideology and Lay Theories of Stigma: The Justification of Stigmatization' in Todd F. Heatherton, Robert E. Kleck, Michelle R. Hebl and Jay G. Hull (eds), *The Social Psychology of Stigma*, New York: Guildford Press.

Curry, G.N., 2003. 'Moving beyond Post-development: Facilitating Indigenous Alternatives for 'Development',' *Economic Geography*, vol. 79, no. 4.

Dandekar, R.N., 1954. 'The Mahabharata: Origins and Growth,' *University of Ceylon Review*, vol. 12, no. 2.

Datta, Pradip, 2005. 'Historic Trauma and the Politics of the Present in India,' *Interventions*, vol. 7, no. 3.

Datta-Ray, Sunanda K., 2005. 'The Last Ingabanga' in *First Proof: The Penguin Book of New Writing from India*, New Delhi: Penguin.

Davis, Zachary S., June 1995. 'China's Nonproliferation and Export Control Policies: Boom or Bust for the NPT Regime?' *Asian Survey*, vol. 35, no. 6.

de Certeau, Michel, Autumn 1980. 'On the Oppositional Practices of Everyday Life,' trans. Fredric Jameson and Carl Lovitt, *Social Text*, vol. 3.

de Kock, Leon, July 1992. 'Interview With Gayatri Chakravorty Spivak: New Nation Writers Conference in South Africa,' *ARIEL: A Review of International English Literature*, vol. 23, no. 3.

de Neve, Geert, 2003. 'Expectations and Rewards of Modernity: Commitment and Mobility among Rural Migrants in Tirupur, Tamil Nadu' in *Contributions to Indian Sociology*, vol. 37, no. 1, 2.

Deleuze, Gilles, 1992. 'What is a dispositif?' in Timothy J. Armstrong (ed. and trans.), *Michel Foucault: Philosopher*, New York: Routledge.

Der Derian, James, April 1987. 'Mediating Estrangement: A Theory for Diplomacy,' *Review of International Studies*, vol. 13, no. 2.

―――― 1999. 'The Conceptual Cosmology of Paul Virilio,' *Theory Culture Society*, vol. 16, no. 5–6.

Deweese-Boyd, Ian, Spring 2012 Edition. 'Self-deception' in Edward N. Zalta (ed.), *The Stanford Encyclopedia of Philosophy*, http://plato.stanford.edu/entries/self-deception/.

Dietze, Carola, February 2008. 'Toward a History on Equal Terms: A Discussion of Provincializing Europe,' *History and Theory*, vol. 47, no. 1.

Dirks, Nicholas B., 1992. 'From Little King to Landlord' in Nicholas Dirks (ed.) *Colonialism and Culture*, Ann Arbor: University of Michigan Press.

Doniger, Wendy, February 2006. 'Many Gods, Many Paths: Hinduism and Religious Diversity,' Religion and Culture Web Forum. (http://divinity.uchicago.edu/martycenter/publications/webforum/022006/commentary.shtml).

Doniger O'Flaherty, Wendy and J. Duncan M. Derrett, 1978. 'Introduction' in Wendy Doniger O'Flaherty and J. Duncan M. Derrett (eds), *The Concept of Duty in South Asia*, New Delhi: Vikas.

Duara, Prasenjit, April 1998. 'Why is History Antitheoreatical?' *Modern China*, vol. 24, no. 2.

Duggal, Ravi, Sunil Nandraj and Asha Vadair, 15 April 1995. 'Health Expenditure across States—Part I,' *Economic and Political Weekly*, vol. 30, no. 15.

―――― 22 April 1995. 'Health Expenditure across States—Part II,' *Economic and Political Weekly*, vol. 30, no. 16.

Dunham, John, 1991. 'Manuscripts Used in the Critical Edition of the Mahābhārata: A Survey and Discussion' in Arvind Sharma (ed.), *Essays on the Mahābhārata*, Leiden: E. J. Brill.

BIBLIOGRAPHY

Durkheim, Émile and Marcel Mauss, 1971. 'Note on the Notion of Civilization,' trans. Benjamin Nelson, *Social Research*, vol. 38, no. 4.

Duvernay-Bolens, J., 1993. 'Un trickster chez les naturalistes: la notion d'hybride,' *Ethnologie Française*, vol. 23, no. 1.

Eaton, Natasha, 2008. 'Between Mimesis and Alterity: Art, Gift and Diplomacy in Colonial India, 1770–1800,' *Comparative Studies in Society and Art*, vol. 5, no. 4.

Eisenstadt, Shmuel N., June 1981. 'Cultural Traditions and Political Dynamics, The Origin and Mode of Ideological Politics,' *British Journal of Sociology*, vol. 32, no. 2.

——— 1985. 'Comparative Liminality: Liminality and Dynamics of Civilizations,' *Religion*, vol. 15, no. 3.

——— Winter 2000. 'Multiple Modernities,' *Daedalus*, vol. 129, no. 1.

Engeström, Yrjö, 1999. 'How We Think They Think: Anthropological Approaches to Cognition, Memory, and Literacy,' *American Ethnologist*, vol. 26, no. 3.

Ernst, Carl W., June 2003. 'Muslim Studies of Hinduism? A Reconstruction of Arabic and Persian Translations from Indian Languages,' in *Iranian Studies*, vol. 36, no. 2.

Errington, Frederick and Deborah Gewertz, 1996. 'The Individuation of Tradition in a Papua New Guinea Modernity,' *American Anthropologist*, vol. 98, no. 1.

Esteban, Javier Cuenca, 2001. 'The British Balance of Payments, 1772–1820: India Transfers and War Finance,' *The Economic History Review*, vol. 54, no. 1.

Farooqi, Naimur Rahman, 2004. 'Diplomacy and Diplomatic Procedure under the Mughals,' *The Medieval History Journal*, vol. 7, no. 1.

Faruqui, Munis D., 2004. 'The Forgotten Prince: Mirza Hakim and the Formation of the Mughal Empire in India,' *Journal of the Economic and Social History of the Orient*, vol. 48, no. 4.

Feldman, Gregory, September 2005. 'Estranged States: Diplomacy and the Containment of National Minorities in Europe,' *Anthropological Theory*, vol. 5, no. 3.

Fine, Gary Alan, 1984. 'Negotiated Orders and Organizational Cultures,' *Annual Review of Sociology*, vol. 10.

Fisher, Michael H., 1984. 'Indirect Rule in the British Empire: The Foundations of the Residency System in India (1764–1858),' *Modern Asian Studies*, vol. 18, no. 3.

——— 1990. 'The Resident in Court Ritual, 1764–1858,' *Modern Asian Studies*, vol. 24, no. 3.

——— 1993. 'The Office of Akhbār Nawīs: The Transition from Mughal to British Forms,' *Modern Asian Studies*, vol. 27, no. 1.

——— 2004. 'Indian Political Representations in Britain during the Transition to Colonialism,' *Modern Asian Studies*, vol. 38, no. 3.

Fitzgerald, James L., 1991. 'India's Fifth Veda: The Mahābhārata's Presentation of Itself' in Anand Sharma (ed.), *Essays on the Mahābhārata*, Leiden: E. J. Brill.

Fleming, Peter, Graham Sewell, 2002. 'Looking For "The Good Soldier, Švejk": Alternative Modalities of Resistance in the Contemporary Workplace,' *Sociology*, vol. 36, no. 4.

Foucault, Michel, 1991. 'Governmentality' in Graham Burchell, Colin Gordon and Peter Miller (eds), *The Foucault Effect: Studies in Governmentality*, University of Chicago Press.

Frey, Karsten, 2009. 'Guardians of the Nuclear Myth: Politics, Ideology, and India's Strategic Community' in Itty Abraham (ed.), *South Asian Cultures of the Bomb: Atomic Publics and the State in India and Pakistan*, Bloomington: Indiana University Press.

Fuller, Christopher and Harpriya Narasimhan, 2007. 'Information Technology Professionals and the New-rich Middle Class in Chennai (Madras),' *Modern Asian Studies*, vol. 41, no. 1.

Galtung, Johan, 1969. 'Violence, Peace, and Peace Research,' *Journal of Peace Research*, vol. 6, no. 3.

Ganeri, Jonardon, 2008. 'Contextualism in the Study of Indian Intellectual Cultures,' *Journal of Indian Philosophy*, vol. 36.

——— 2009. 'Intellectual India: Reason, Identity, Dissent: Amartya Sen and the Reach of Reason,' *New Literary History*, vol. 40, no. 2.

Ganguly, Sumit, Spring 1999. 'India's Pathway to Pokhran II: The Prospects and Sources of New Delhi's Nuclear Weapons Program,' *International Security*, vol. 23, no. 4.

Gaonkar, Dilip P., 2001. 'On Alternative Modernities' in Dilip P. Gaonkar (ed.), *Alternative Modernities*, Durham, NC: Duke University Press.

Garver, John W., December 2001. 'The Restoration of Sino-Indian Comity following India's Nuclear Tests,' *The China Quarterly*, no. 168.

Gillespie, Kate and Gwenn Okruhlik, October 1991. 'The Political Dimensions of Corruption Cleanups: A Framework for Analysis,' *Comparative Politics*, vol. 24, no. 1.

Godin, Christian, 2000. 'The Notion of Totality in Indian Thought,' trans. Richard Stamp, *Diogenes*, no. 189 (vol. 48, no. 1).

Goldewijk, Kees Klein, March 2005. 'Three Centuries of Global Population Growth: A Spatial Referenced Population (Density) Database for 1700–2000,' *Population and Environment*, vol. 26, no. 4.

Gould, Harold A., 1988. 'Lucknow Rickshawallas: The Social Organization of an Occupational Category' in Harold A. Gould (ed.), *Caste Adaptation in Modernizing Indian Society*, New Delhi: Chanakya Publications.

Guha, Ramachandra, November 2006. 'An Uncommon Diplomacy: Walter Crocker's 'Nehru: A Contemporary's Estimate',' *The Monthly*. http://www.themonthly.com.au/books-ramachandra-guha-uncommon-diplomacy-walter-crocker-s-nehru-contempo-rary-s-estimate-310

Gupta, Akhil, Autumn 1992. 'The Reincarnation of Souls and the Rebirth of Commodities: Representations of Time in East and West,' *Cultural Critique*, No. 22.

——— 2005. 'Narrating the State of Corruption', in Dieter Haller and Cris Shore (eds), *Corruption: Anthropological Perspectives*, London: Pluto Press.

Gupta, Sisir, 1966. 'The Indian Dilemma' in Alastair Buchan (ed.), *A World of Nuclear Powers*, Englewood Cliffs, NJ: Prentice Hall.

Gusterson, Hugh, April 2006. 'A Double Standard on Nuclear Weapons,' MIT Center for International Studies. (http://web.mit.edu/cis/pdf/gusterson_audit.pdf).

Habermas, Jürgen. 1997. 'Kant's Idea of Perpetual Peace, with the Benefit of Two Hundred Years Hindsight' in James Bohman and Matthias Lutz-Bachman (eds), *Perpetual Peace: Essays on Kant's Cosmopolitan Ideal*, Cambridge, MA: MIT Press.

Halliburton, Murphy, 2004. 'Social Thought & Commentary: Gandhi or Gramsci? The Use of Authoritative Sources in Anthropology,' in *Anthropological Quarterly*, vol. 77, no. 4.

Halperin, Morton H., Bruno Tertrais, Keith B. Payne, K. Subrahmanyam and Scott D. Sagan, October–November 2009. 'The Case for No First Use: An Exchange,' *Survival*, vol. 51, no. 5.

Hannerz, Ulf, 1990. 'Cosmopolitans and Locals in World Culture,' *Theory, Culture and Society*, vol. 7, no. 2–3.

BIBLIOGRAPHY

Hari Kumar, K.N., 23 April 1988. 'Trading Non-Alignment for High Tech? Rajiv's Second US Visit,' *The Economic and Political Weekly.*

Harling, Philip and Peter Mandler, 1993. 'From 'Fiscal-Military State to Laissez-Faire State, 1760–1850,' *Journal of British Studies*, vol. 32.

Harris, Martin, 2006. 'Technology, Innovation and Post-bureaucracy: The Case of the British Library,' *Journal of Organization Change Management*, vol. 19, no. 1.

Hatcher, Brian A., January 1994. '"The Cosmos is One Family" (Vasudhaiva Kutumbakam): Problematic Mantra of Hindu Humanism,' *Contributions to Indian Sociology*, vol. 28, no. 1.

Haynes, Douglas, 1991. 'From Avoidance to Confrontation? A Contestory History of Merchant-state Relations in Surat, 1600–1924' in Douglas Haynes and Gyan Prakash (eds), *Contesting Power: Resistance and Everyday Social Relations in South Asia*, New Delhi: Oxford University Press.

Hegde, Sasheej, 2007. 'Review of 'Postmodern Gandhi',' *Contributions to Indian Sociology*, vol. 41, no. 2.

Hobart, Mark, 1993. 'Introduction: the Growth of Ignorance?' in Mark Hobart (ed.), *An Anthropological Critique of Development*, London: Routledge.

Hoffmann, Stanley, 1977. 'An American Social Science: International Relations,' *Daedalus*, vol. 106, no. 3.

Höpfl, H.M., 2006. 'Post-bureaucracy and Weber's "Modern" Bureaucrat,' *Journal of Organization Change Management*, vol. 19, no. 1.

Hopgood, Stephen, Fall 2003. 'Socialising IR,' *GSC Quarterly 10.*

Inden, Ronald, 1986. 'Orientalist Constructions of India,' *Modern Asian Studies*, vol. 20, no. 3.

Irwin, Katz and R. Glen Haas, 1988. 'Racial Ambivalence and American Value Conflict: Correlational and Priming Studies of Dual Cognitive Structures,' *Journal of Personality and Social Psychology*, vol. 55, no. 6.

Iyengar, S. Kesava, 1967. 'Indian Democracy and Socialist Planning,' *Annals of Public and Cooperative Economics*, vol. 38, no. 2.

Jain, P., 2005. 'Mahatma Gandhi's Notion of Dharma: An Explication' in Ashok Vohra, Arvind Sharma and Mrinal Miri (eds), *Dharma: The Categorical Imperative*, New Delhi: D.K. Printworld.

Jayaramu, P.S., April–July 2010. 'Critiquing Indian Foreign Policy,' *International Studies*, vol. 47, no. 2–4.

Johnston, Alastair Iain, 1995. 'China's New "Old Thinking": The Concept of Limited Deterrence,' *International Security*, vol. 20, no. 3.

Kalb, Don, 2000. 'Localizing Flows: Power, Paths, Institutions, and Networks' in Don Kalb, Marco van der Land, Richard Staring, Bart van Steenbergen and Nico Wilterdink (eds), *The Ends of Globalization: Bringing Society Back*, New York: Rowman & Littlefield Publishers.

Kang, David C., Spring 2003. 'Getting Asia Wrong: The Need for New Analytical Frameworks,' *International Security*, vol. 27, no. 4.

Kant, Immanuel, 1991. 'Toward Perpetual Peace' in H.S. Reiss (ed.), *Kant: Political Writings*, Cambridge University Press.

Kapchan, Deborah A. and Pauline Turner Strong (eds), 1999. 'Theorizing the Hybrid,' *The Journal of American Folklore*, vol. 112, no. 445.

Kärreman, Dan and Mats Alvesson, January 2004. 'Cages in Tandem: Management

Control, Social Identity, and Identification in a Knowledge-intensive Firm,' *Organisation*, vol. 11, no. 1.

Kassim, Hussein and Anand Menon, February 2003. 'The Principalagent Approach and the Study of the European Union: Promise Unfulfilled?' *Journal of European Public Policy*, vol. 10, no. 1.

Kaur, Raminder, 2009. 'Gods, Bombs and the Social Imaginary' in Itty Abraham (ed.), *South Asian Cultures of the Bomb: Atomic Publics and the State in India and Pakistan*, Bloomington: Indiana University Press.

Kaviraj, Sudipta, 1997. 'The Modern State in India' in Sudipta Kaviraj and Martin Doornbos (eds), *Dynamics of State Formation: India and Europe Compared*, New Delhi: Sage.

——— Winter 2000. 'Modernity and Politics in India,' *Daedalus*, vol. 129, no. 1.

——— 2001. 'In Search of Civil Society' in Sudipta Kaviraj and Sunil Khilnani (eds), *Civil Society: History and Possibilities*, Cambridge University Press.

Keohane, Robert O. and Lisa L. Martin, Summer 1995. 'The Promise of Institutionalist Theory,' *International Security*, vol. 20, no. 1.

Kesavan, K.V., August 2003. 'Nehru, Henderson and the Japanese Peace Treaty,' *International Studies*, vol. 40, no. 3.

Khan, Iqtidar Alam, 1968. 'The Nobility under Akbar and the Development of his Religious Policy, 1560–80,' *Journal of the Royal Asiatic Society*, vol. 1, no. 2.

——— 1997. 'Akbar's Personality Traits and World Outlook—a Critical Reappraisal' in Irfan Habib (ed.), *Akbar and his India*, New Delhi: Oxford University Press.

Khan, Yusuf Husain, July 1954. 'Seventeenth Century Waqai' in the Central Records Office, Hyderabad,' *Islamic Culture*, vol. 28, no. 3.

Khoury, Dina Rizk and Dane Keith Kennedy, 2007. 'Comparing Empires: The Ottoman Empires and the British Raj in the Long Nineteenth Century,' *Comparative Studies of South Asia, Africa and the Middle East*, vol. 27, no. 2.

Kimberly, James C., 1967. 'Status Inconsistency: A Reformulation of a Theoretical Problem,' *Human Relations*, vol. 20, no. 2.

Kleiner, R.J. and S. Parker, 1963. 'Goal-striving and Psychosomatic Symptoms in a Migrant and Nonmigrant Population' in M.B. Kantor (ed.), *Mobility and Mental Health*, Springfield, IL: Charles C. Thomas.

Klitgaard, Robert E., 1971. 'Gandhi's Non-Violence as a Tactic,' *Journal of Peace Research*, vol. 8, no. 2.

Kraynak, Robert P., 2005. 'Hobbes, Thomas (1588–1679)' in Adam Kuper and Jessica Kuper (eds), *The Social Science Encyclopaedia*, London: Routledge.

Kristeva, Julia, 1986. 'Word, Dialogue and Novel' in Toril Moi (ed.), Leon S. Roudiez (trans.), *The Kristeva Reader*, New York: Columbia University Press.

Kumar, Rajesh and Verner Worm, 2004. 'Institutional Dynamics and the Negotiation Process: Comparing India and China,' *International Journal of Conflict Management*, vol. 15, no. 3.

Kumaraswamy, P.R., 2004. 'National Security: A Critique', in P.R. Kumaraswamy (ed.), *Security Beyond Survival: Essays for K. Subrahmanyam*, New Delhi: Sage.

Lake, David A., Summer 2007. 'Escape From the State of Nature: Authority and Hierarchy in World Politics,' *International Security*, vol. 32, no. 1.

Lamb, Alastair, 1971. 'War in the Himalayas,' *Modern Asian Studies*, vol. 5, no. 4.

Lawrence, Henry, 1856. 'The Indian Army,' *Calcutta Review*, vol. 26.

Levy, Sheri R., Antonio L. Freitas and Peter Salovey, 2002. 'Construing Action Abstractly and Blurring Social Distinctions: Implications for Perceiving Homogeneity among, but also Empathizing with and Helping, Others,' *Journal of Personality and Social Psychology*, vol. 83, no. 5.

Lippincott, Louise, 1995. 'Expanding on Portraiture: The Market, the Public and the Hierarchy of Genres in 18th-Century Britain' in Ann Bermingham and John Brewer (eds), *The Consumption of Culture: Image, Object, Text, The Consumption of Culture: Image, Object, Text*, London: Routledge.

Litvak, Meir, February 2001. 'Money, Religion, and Politics: The Oudh Bequest in Najaf and Karbala, 1850–1903,' *International Journal of Middle East Studies*, vol. 33, no. 1.

Löfgren, Orvar, 1989. 'The Nationalization of Culture,' *Ethnologia Europaea*, vol. 19.

Low, Choo Ming, 2005. 'Reflections of 33 Years in Diplomacy' in Tommy Koh and Chan Li Lin (eds), *The Little Red Dot: Reflections by Singapore's Diplomats*, Singapore: World Scientific Publishing.

Lowry, Glenn D., 1988. 'Humayun's Tomb: Form, Function, and Meaning in Early Mughal Architecture,' *Muqarnas*, vol. 4.

MacIntyre, Alasdair, November

1983. 'Books in Review,' *Political Theory*, vol. 11, no. 4.

Mackenzie Brown, D., June 1953. 'The Premises of Indian Political Thought,' *The Western Political Quarterly*, vol. 6, no. 2.

Maheshwari, S.R., 2004. 'Nehru's Thoughts on Public Administration' in P.L. Sanjeev and R.K. Tiwari (eds), *Jawaharlal Nehru and Public Administration*, New Delhi: Indian Institute of Public Administration.

Majeed, Javed, 2006. 'Gandhi, "Truth" and Translatability,' *Modern Asian Studies*, vol. 40, no. 2.

Makeig, Douglas C., Summer 1987. 'War, No-War, and the India Pakistan Negotiating Process,' *Pacific Affairs*, vol. 6, no. 2.

Mantena, Rama, 2007. 'The Question of History in Precolonial India,' *History and Theory*, vol. 46.

Marshall, P.J., September 1999. 'The Making of an Imperial Icon: The Case of Warren Hastings,' *Journal of Imperial and Commonwealth History*, vol. 27, no. 3.

Matin, Kamran, 2012. 'Redeeming the Universal: Postcolonialism and the Inner Life of Eurocentrism,' *European Journal of International Relations*, 24 January 2012. published online DOI: 10.1177/1354066111425263.

Mayer, Judith, 2002. 'Chapter 6: Environmental Organising in Indonesia: The Search for a Newer Order' in Ronnie D. Lipschutz and Judith Mayer (eds), *Global Civil Society & Global Environmental Governance: The Politics of Nature from Place to Planet*, Albany, NY: SUNY.

McCarthy, John F., April 2008. 'Short Stories at Work: Storytelling as an Indicator of Organizational Commitment,' *Group and Organization Management*, vol. 33, no. 2.

McGrath, W., 1992. 'Freud and the Force of History' in T. Gelfand and J. Kerr (eds), *Freud and the History of Psychoanalysis*, Hillside, NJ: The Analytic Press.

McMahon, Robert J., 1987. 'Food as a Diplomatic Weapon: the India Wheat Loan of 1951,' *Pacific Historical Review*, vol. 56, no. 3.

Meredith-Owens, G. and R.H. Pinder-Wilson, March 1956. 'A Persian Translation of the "Mahābhārata", with a Note on the Miniatures,' *The British Museum Quarterly*, vol. 20, no. 3.

Merton, Robert K., 1938. 'Social Structure as Anomie,' *American Sociological Review*, vol. 3, no. 5.

———— 1964. 'Anomie, Anomia, and Social Interaction: Contexts of Deviant Behaviour' in Marshall B. Clinard (ed.), *Anomie and Deviant Behaviour: A Discussion and Critique*, New York: Free Press of Glencoe.

Miller, Raegen T., Richard J. Murnane and John B., Willet, June 2008. 'Do Teacher Absences Impact Student Achievement? Longitudinal Evidence from one Urban School District,' *Educational Evaluation and Policy Analysis*, vol. 30, no. 2.

Miller, S.M., 1960. 'Comparative Social Mobility: A Trend Report,' *Current Sociology*, vol. 9, no. 1.

Milne, David, 2010. 'America's 'Intellectual' Diplomacy,' *International Affairs*, vol. 86, no. 1.

Milner, Helen, January 1991. 'The Assumption of Anarchy in International Relations Theory: A Critique,' *Review of International Studies*, vol. 17, no. 1.

Mitchell, Katharyne, 1997. 'Different Diasporas and the Hype of Hybridity,' *Environment and Planning D: Society and Space*, vol. 15, no. 5, 1997.

Moosvi, Shireen, Aug.–Jul. 2002. 'The Mughal Encounter with Vedanta: Recovering the Biography of 'Jadrup',' *Social Scientist*, vol. 30, no. 7–8.

Morgan, Thais E., 1985. 'Is There an Intertext in this Text?: Literary and Interdisciplinary Approaches to Intertextuality,' *American Journal of Semiotics*, vol. 3, no. 1–2.

Morrill, Calvin, 2008. 'Culture and Organization Theory,' *The Annals of the American Academy of Political and Social Science*, vol. 619, no. 1.

Mukhia, Harbans, January 2009. 'Time in Abu'l Fazl's Historiography,' *Studies in History*, vol. 35, no. 1.

Murphy, Charles H., January 1972. 'Mainland China's Evolving Nuclear Deterrent,' *Bulletin of the Atomic Scientists*.

Murray, Hogben W., 1981. 'An Imperial Dilemma: The Reluctant Indianization of the Indian Political Service,' *Modern Asian Studies*, vol. 15, no. 4.

Nanda, Nitya, 2009. 'The Indian Growth Story: Myths and Tealities,' *Journal of Asian and African Studies*, vol. 44, no. 6.

Nandy, Ashis, 1995. 'History's Forgotten Doubles,' *History and Theory*, vol. 34, no. 2.

———— 1998. 'The Politics of Secularism and the Recovery of Religious Tolerance,' *Alternatives*, vol. 13, no. 2.

———— January 2004. 'The Beautiful, Expanding Future of Poverty: Popular Economics as a Psychological Defence,' *Economic and Political Weekly*, vol. 39, no. 1, 3–9.

Narayana Rao, Velcheru, David Shulman and Sanjay Subrahmanyam, October 2007. 'Forum: Textures of Time, A Pragmatic Response,' *History and Theory*, vol. 46, no. 3.

Naudet, Jules, 2008. '"Paying-Back to Society": Upward Social Mobility among Dalits,' *Contributions to Indian Sociology*, vol. 42, no. 3.

Nelson, Benjamin, 1972. 'Communities, Societies, Civilizations—Postmillennial Views on the Faces and Masks of Time' in Manfred Stanley (ed.), *Social Development*, New York: Basic Books.

———— 1981. 'Civilizational Complexes and Intercivilizational encounters' in Toby E. Huff (ed.), *On the Roads to Modernity: Conscience, Science and Civilizations, Selected Writings by Benjamin Nelson*, Totowa, NJ: Rowman and Littlefield.

Neumann, Iver B., 2005. 'To be a Diplomat,' *International Studies Perspective*, vol. 6, no. 1.

Nielsen, Donald A., September 2001. 'Rationalization, Transformations of Consciousness and Intercivilizational Encounters: Reflections on Benjamin Nelson's Sociology of Civilizations,' *International Sociology*, vol. 16, no. 3.

Niess, Robert J., March 1947. 'Evolution of an idea: Julien Benda's La Trahison Des Clercs,' *The French Review*, vol. 20, no. 5.

Nikhilananda, Swami, 1959. 'The Realistic Aspect of Indian Spirituality,' *Philosophy East and West*, vol. 9, no. 1–2.

Noorani, A.G., 1967. 'India's Quest for a Nuclear Guarantee,' *Asian Survey*, vol. 7, no. 7.

Nurul Hasan, S., 1952. 'Nigar Nama-i-Munshi: A Valuable Collection of Documents of Aurangzeb's Reign' in *Proceedings of the Indian History Congress 15th Session*, Gwalior: Indian History Congress.

O'Brien, Rourke L. and David S. Pedulla, Fall 2010. 'Beyond the Poverty Line,' *Stanford Social Innovation Review*. http://www.ssireview.org/articles/entry/beyond_the_poverty_line

O'Hanlon, Rosalind and David Washbrook, 2000. 'After Orientalism: Culture, Criticism and Politics in the Third World' in Vinayak Chaturvedi (ed.), *Mapping Subaltern Studies and the Postcolonial*, London: Verso.

Ortiz, Renato, Winter 2000. 'From Incomplete Modernity to World Modernity,' *Daedalus*, vol. 129, no. 1.

Ortner, Sherry B., January 1995. 'Resistance and The Problem of Ethnographic Refusal,' *Comparative Studies in Society and History*, vol. 37, no. 1.

Osella, Filippo and Katy Gardner. 2003, 'Migration, Modernity and Social Transformation in South Asia: an Overview,' *Contributions to Indian Sociology*, vol. 37, no. 1–2.

Parker, Kunal M., Fall 2005. 'The Historiography of Difference,' *Law and History Review*, vol. 23, no. 3.

Patil, R.L.M., 1991. 'National Security and Foreign Policy' in Amal Ray, N. Bhaskara Rao and Vinod Vyasulu (eds), *The Nehru Legacy: An Appraisal*, New Delhi: Oxford and IBH Publishing Company.

Paul, T.V., 2010. 'Integrating International Relations Studies in India to Global Scholarship,' *International Studies*, vol. 46, no. 1–2.

Peers, Douglas M., 2007. 'Gunpowder Empires and the Garrison State: Modernity, Hybridity, and the Political Economy of Colonial India, circa 1750–1860,' *Comparative Studies of South Asia, Africa and the Middle East*, vol. 27, no. 2.

Pomper, Philip, May 1995. 'World History and its Critics,' *History and Theory*, vol. 34, no. 2.

Poulose, T.T., Fall 1998. 'Viewpoint: India's Deterrence Doctrine; A Nehruvian Critique,' *Nonproliferation Review*, vol. 6, no. 1.

Prakash, Gyan, 2000. 'A'. 'Writing Post-Orientalist Histories of the Third World: Perspectives from Indian Historiography' in Vinayak Chaturvedi (ed.), *Mapping Subaltern Studies and the Postcolonial*, London: Verso.

———— 2000. 'B'. 'Can the 'Subaltern' Ride? A Reply to O'Hanlon and Washbrook' in Vinayak Chaturvedi (ed.), *Mapping Subaltern Studies and the Postcolonial*, London: Verso.

Pratto, Felicia, James Sidanius, Lisa M. Stallworth and Bertram F. Malle, 1994. 'Social Dominance Orientation: A Personality Variable Predicting Social and Political Attitudes,' *Journal of Personality and Social Psychology*, vol. 67, no. 4.

Quinn, Diane M. and Jennifer Crocker, August 1999. 'When Ideology Hurts: Effects of Feeling Fat and the Protestant Ethic on the Psychological Well-being of Women,' *Journal of Personality and Social Psychology*, vol. 77, no. 2.

Rahnema, Majid, Spring 1991. 'Global Poverty: A Pauperising Myth,' *Intercultural*, vol. 14, no. 2.

Ramana, M.V., 2009. 'India's Nuclear Enclave and the Practice of Secrecy' in Itty Abraham (ed.), *South Asian Cultures of the Bomb: Atomic Publics and the State in India and Pakistan*, Bloomington: Indiana University Press.

Ramana, M.V. and C. Rammanohar Reddy, 2003. 'Introduction' in M.V. Ramana and C. Rammanohar Reddy (eds), *Prisoners of the Nuclear Dream*, Hyderabad: Orient Longman.

Rapport, Nigel, 1999. 'Context as an Act of Personal Externalisation, Gregory Bateson and the Harvey Family in the English Village of Wanet' in Roy Dilley (ed.), *The Problem of Context*, New York: Berghahn Books.

Rehatsek, E., April 1887. 'A Letter of the Emperor Akbar Asking for the Christian Scriptures,' *The Indian Antiquary*.

Renick, M.S., 1970. 'Akbar's First Embassy to Goa: Its Diplomatic and Religious Aspects,' *Indica*, vol. 1.

Rizvi, S.A.A., 1999. 'Dimensions of Sulh-I Kul (Universal Peace) in Akbar's Reign and the Sufi Theory of Perfect Man' in Iqtidar Alam Khan (ed.), *Akbar and his Age*, New Delhi: Northern Book Centre.

Rosenberg, Justin, 2006. 'Why is there no International Historical Sociology?' *European Journal of International Relations*, vol. 12, no. 3.

——— 2007. 'International Relations—The 'Higher Bullshit': A Reply to the Globalization Theory Debate,' *International Politics*, vol. 44, no. 4.

Roy, Srirupa, 2009. 'The Politics of Death: the Antinuclear Imaginary in India' in Itty Abraham (ed.), *South Asian Cultures of the Bomb: Atomic Publics and the State in India and Pakistan*, Bloomington: Indiana University Press.

Ruggles, D. Fairchild, 1997. 'Humayun's Tomb and Garden: Typologies and Visual Order' in Attilio Petruccioli (ed.), *Gardens in the Time of the Great Muslim Empires*, Leiden: E.J. Brill.

Salzman, Philip Carl, September 2002. 'On Reflexivity,' *American Anthropologist*, vol. 104, no. 3.

Satakopan, R., 1941. 'The Indian Political Services,' *The New Review*, vol. 13.

Saurette, Paul, March 1996. 'I Mistrust All Systematizers and Avoid Them: Nietzsche, Arendt and the Will to Order in International Relations Theory,' *Millennium Journal of International Relations*, vol. 25, no. 1.

Schütz, Alfred, 1944. 'The Stranger: An Essay in Social Psychology,' *American Journal of Sociology*, vol. 49, no. 6.

Sen, Amartya, Spring 1997. 'Indian Traditions and the Western Imagination,' *Daedalus*, vol. 126, no. 2.

Sen, Geeti, 2003. 'Preface: National Culture and Cultural Nationalism' in Geeti Sen (ed.), *India: A National Culture?*, Thousand Oaks, CA: Sage.

Sengupta, Adirupa, 1997 'Scientist says bomb was tested in '74,' *India Abroad*, 17 October 1997.

Seshadri-Crooks, K., 2000. 'Surviving Theory: A Conversation with Homi K. Bhabha' in F. Afzal-Khan and K. Seshadri-Crooks (eds), *The Pre-occupation of Postcolonial Studies*, F. Afzal-Khan and K. Seshadri-Crooks (eds), Durham, NC: Duke University Press.

Sewell, Graham, 1998. 'The Discipline of Teams: The Control of Team-based Industrial Work through Electronic and Peer Surveillance,' *Administrative Science Quarterly*, vol. 43, no. 2.

Sewell, Graham and James R, Barker. 2006. 'Coercion versus Care: Using Irony to Make Sense of Organizational Surveillance,' *Academy of Management Review*, vol. 31, no. 4.

Sharp, Paul, 1999. 'For Diplomacy: Representation and the Study of International Relations,' *International Studies Review*, vol. 1, no. 1.

——— 2005. 'Revolutionary States, Outlaw Regimes and the Techniques of Public Diplomacy' in Jan Melissen (ed.), *The New Public Diplomacy: Soft Power in International Relations*, Basingstoke: Palgrave.

Simpson, Barbara, December 2009. 'Pragmatism, Mead and the Practice Turn,' *Organisation Studies*, vol. 30, no. 12.

Simpson, Smith, 1995. 'Of Diplomats and Their Chroniclers, Review of Craig and Loewenheim,' *Virginia Quarterly Review*, vol. 71, no. 4.

Singer, Milton, 1972. 'Industrial Leadership, the Hindu Ethic and the Spirit of Socialism' in Milton Singer (ed.), *When a Great Tradition Modernizes: An Anthropological Approach to Indian Civilization*, New York: Praeger.

Singh, Chetan, 1988. 'Centre and Periphery in the Mughal State: The Case of the 17th Century Panjab,' *Modern Asian Studies*, vol. 22, no. 12.

Singh, Sardar Ganda, December 1944. 'Akhbarat-i-Lahaur-o-Multan,' *Proceedings of the Indian Historical Records Commission 21*.

Sinha, Mira, March–April 1979. 'China: Making and Unmaking of Nehru's Foreign Policy,' *China Report*, vol. 15, no. 2.

Skaria, Ajay, 2011. 'Relinquishing Republican Democracy: Gandhi's Ramarajya,' *Postcolonial Studies*, vol. 14, no. 2.

Smith, Roger, November 2000. 'Reflections on the Historical Imagination,' *History of the Human Sciences*, vol. 13, no. 4.

Snodgrass, Jeffrey G., February 2002. 'Imitation is Far More than the Sincerest of Flattery: The Mimetic Power of Spirit Possession in Rajasthan, India,' *Cultural Anthropology*, vol. 17, no. 1.

Soares, Benjamin and Filippo Osella, May 2009. 'Islam, Politics, Anthropology,' *Journal of the Royal Anthropological Institute*, vol. 15, no. 1.

Steger, Manfred, September 2006. 'Searching for Satya through Ahimsa: Mahatma Gandhi's Challenge to Western Discourses of Power,' *Constellations: An International Journal of Critical and Democratic Theory*, vol. 13, no. 3.

Stephen, James Fitzjames, 1883. 'Foundations of the Government of India,' *Nineteenth Century*, vol. 80.

Strand, Eric, Winter 2005. 'Gandhian Communalism and the Midnight Children's Conference,' *ELH*, vol. 72, no. 4.

Subrahmanyam, K., 1990. 'Alternative Security Doctrines,' *Security Dialogue*, vol. 21, no. 1.

——— 1998. 'Indian Nuclear Policy—1964–98 (A Personal Recollection)' in Jasjit Singh (ed.), *Nuclear India*, New Delhi: Knowledge World.

Subrahmanyam, Sanjay, July 1997. 'Connected Histories: Notes toward a Reconfiguration of Early Modern Eurasia,' *Modern Asian Studies*, vol. 31, no. 3.

——— 2004. 'A Rather Personal Biography' in P.R. Kumaraswamy (ed.), *Security beyond Survival: Essays for K. Subrahmanyam*, New Delhi: Sage.

Suganami, Hidemi, 1984. 'Japan's Entry into International Society' in Hedley Bull and Adam Watson (eds), *The Expansion of International Society*, Hedley Bull and Adam Watson (eds), Oxford: Clarendon.

Suhrud, Tridip, 20 November 2004. '"Re-editing" Gandhi's Collected Works,' *Economic and Political Weekly*, vol. 39, no. 46, 47.

BIBLIOGRAPHY

Sukthankar, Vishnu S., 1933. '"Prolegomena" to the Critical Edition of the *Mahābhārata*' in Vishnu S. Sukthankar (ed.), *Ādiparvan, vol. 1 of The Mahābhārata*, Poona: Bhandarkar Oriental Research Institute.

Taylor, Charles, 1999. 'Two Theories of Modernity,' *Public Culture*, vol. 11, no. 1.

Teschke, Benno, 2002. 'Theorising the Westphalian System of States: International Relations from Absolutism to Capitalism,' *European Journal of International Relations*, vol. 8, no. 1.

Tickner, Arlene B., 2003. 'Seeing IR Differently: Notes from the Third World,' *Millennium: Journal of International Studies*, vol. 32, no. 2.

Tilly, Charles, 1975. 'Reflections on the History of European State Making' in Charles Tilly (ed.), *The Formation of National States in Europe*, Princeton University Press.

Turner, Bryan, 2007. 'Enclave Society: Towards a Sociology of Immobility,' *European Journal of Social Theory*, vol. 10, no. 2.

van Maanen, J. and S. Barley, 1985. 'Cultural Organizations: Fragments of a Theory' in P.J. Frost, L.F. Moore, M.R. Louis, C.C. Lundberg and J. Martin (eds), *Organizational Culture*, Beverley Hills, CA: Sage Publications.

Vijayalakshmi, K.P., 2008. 'American Worldview and its Implications for India,' *South Asian Survey*, vol. 15, no. 2.

Vitebsky, Piers, 1993. 'Is Death the Same Everywhere? Contexts of Knowing and Doubting' in Mark Hobart (ed.), *An Anthropological Critique of Development: the Growth of Ignorance*, London: Routledge.

Watson, Adam, 1987. 'Hedley Bull, State Systems and International Studies,' *Review of International Studies*, vol. 13, no. 2.

Wedel, Janine R., Cris Shore, Gregory Feldman and Stacy Lathrop, 2005. 'Toward an Anthropology of Public Policy,' *Annals of the American Academy of Political and Social Science*, vol. 600, no. 1.

White, Hayden, Autumn 1980. 'The Value of Narrativity in the Representation of Reality,' *Critical Enquiry*, vol. 7, no. 1.

Wight, Martin, 1966. 'Why is There no International Theory?' in Martin Wight and Herbert Butterfield (eds), *Diplomatic Investigations, Essays in the Theory of International Politics*, London: Allen & Unwin.

Wilkening, Kenneth E., 1999. 'Culture and Japanese Citizen Influence on the Transboundary Air Pollution Issue in Northeast Asia,' *Political Psychology*, vol. 20, no. 4.

Xia, Y., 2006. 'Cultural Values, Communications Styles, and Use of Mobile Communications in China,' *China Media Research*, vol. 2, no. 2.

Zameeruddin, Siddiqi Muhammad, 1972. 'The Intelligence Services under the Mughals' in *Medieval India: A Miscellany, vol. 2*, Aligarh.

Zhao, Ruohui and Liqun Cao, March 2010. 'Social Change and Anomie: A Cross-national Study,' *Social Forces*, vol. 88, no. 3.

INDEX

INDEX

INDEX